THE FIRST-YEAR EXPERIENCE® MONOGRAPH SERIES   NO.45

The Role of the Library in the First College Year

LARRY L. HARDESTY, EDITOR

Association of College & Research Libraries, Division of the American Library Association

National Resource Center for The First-Year Experience® & Students in Transition

University of South Carolina, 2007

Cite as:

Hardesty, L. (Ed.). (2007). *The role of the library in the first college year* (Monograph No. 45). Columbia, SC: University of South Carolina, National Resource Center for The First-Year Experience and Students in Transition.

Sample chapter citation:

Kuh, G. D., Boruff-Jones, P. D., & Mark, A. E. (2007). Engaging students in the first college year: Why academic librarians matter. In L. Hardesty (Ed.), *The role of the library in the first college year* (Monograph No. 45, pp. 17-24). Columbia, SC: University of South Carolina, National Resource Center for The First-Year Experience and Students in Transition.

Additional copies pf this monograph may be obtained from the National Resource Center for The First-Year Experience and Students in Transition, University of South Carolina, 1728 College Street, Columbia, SC 29208. Telephone (803) 777-6229. Fax (803) 777-4699.

Library of Congress Cataloging-in-Print Data

The role of the library in the first college year / Larry Hardesty, editor.
    p. cm. -- (The first-year experience monograph series ; no. 45)
Includes bibliographical references.
ISBN 978-1-889271-54-5
1. Library orientation for college students--United States. 2. Information literacy--Study and teaching (Higher)--United States. 3. Academic libraries--United States--Case studies. 4. Academic achievement--United States--Case studies. 5. College freshmen--United States. I. Hardesty, Larry L. II. National Resource Center for the First-Year Experience & Students in Transition (University of South Carolina)
Z711.25.C65R65 2007
025.5'677--dc22

2006100837

Dedication

This monograph is dedicated to the memory of Ilene Rockman, manager of the information competence initiative for the Office of the Chancellor of the California State University (CSU) system.

Ilene worked tirelessly to promote information literacy; and while her list of accomplishments is lengthy, her dedication to this area cannot be given justice in this short space. She served as a consultant to the Educational Testing Service on the development and implementation of the Information and Communications Technology (ICT) Literacy assessment instrument. In 2004, she served as editor and contributing author to *Integrating Information Literacy Into the Higher Education Curriculum*. In 2005, she received the Instruction Librarian of the Year award from the Instruction Section of Association of College and Research Libraries (ACRL) for her numerous activities promoting information literacy. In further recognition of her numerous professional contributions to academic librarianship in the area of information literacy, the Instruction Section of ACRL recently renamed its publication award the Ilene F. Rockman Instruction Publication of the Year Award.

It is difficult to describe adequately the devotion she had to library-user education. Even in her last days in fall 2005, as she struggled with what proved to be a terminal malignancy, she continued to edit drafts of her chapter and respond to my queries and suggestions. Although never one to complain or to offer excuses, I could tell by the tone of her e-mails that she was fighting a losing battle. Determined as she was, Ilene did not quite make it to the final version of her chapter, but she tried mightily. For this reason, I dedicate this book to her. May the reader find this monograph useful and be inspired to carry on the cause that Ilene believed in so much but had to leave before it could be completely realized. She will be greatly missed by all who knew her.

Acknowledgments

Many individuals helped to make this monograph a reality. First, I want to thank John Gardner for his challenge that served as its impetus. However, its origins go further back when Ilene Rockman, as co-chair of the invited speakers committee, first recommended that John speak at the 11th National ACRL conference, which I chaired. Yet, Ilene's contribution goes far beyond the recommendation that set the machinery in motion for its publication. She also contributed a significant chapter to this work.

There is a temptation here to list each author by name, and they are certainly worthy of acknowledgment and my gratitude and appreciation. However, their names are elsewhere, and I hope the reader will come to appreciate their hard work, as I do.

Two individuals whose names do not appear elsewhere in this monograph are my longtime Eckerd College colleagues and friends, Jamie Gill and David Henderson. They read and commented on the drafts of almost every chapter. I appreciate their careful review. I would also like to thank, Tracy Skipper, editorial projects coordinator at the National Resource Center for The First-Year Experience and Students in Transition. Tracy is both diligent and patient—a rare combination. Without her tactful nudging, I acknowledge I would have never finished this book. Without her careful editing, I also acknowledge it would not have the quality it has. Any errors, omissions, and other shortcomings of the monograph are my responsibility. She did this all while having a very busy and event-filled life, including having a baby.

Finally, I want to thank my wife of 36 years, Carol Hardesty, who has continued to provide unconditional support when I once again sequestered myself away for another writing project. For the past three years, she patiently accepted, although probably not always believing me, the excuse, "I need to work on the book" when I headed to my home office instead of doing my numerous chores. Well, the usefulness of that excuse has ended for me, as it has for all the contributors of this book, perhaps to the universal relief of their spouses, friends, and colleagues.

This book truly has been the result of a lot of hard work by a lot of people. I do not know all the hours of work and effort that went into writing each chapter, but I do know it was considerable. For this, I thank each of the contributors. I hope their efforts are rewarded by readers who act upon their contributions by furthering the cooperation and collaboration between the librarians and those committed to learning and success in the first college year.

Contents

Section 3   *Connections*

Section 4   *Campus Case Studies*

Foreword

This monograph reviews the present state of practice in integrating library instruction and first-year college programs in order to more effectively educate students and prepare them for the realities of the 21st century. In doing so, it provides literature reviews of key issues, explorations of current strategies, and case studies of best practices.

While this is a monograph for practitioners—both librarians and faculty members—it is explicitly and implicitly much more. This monograph really indicates the evolution of what will prove to be the most critical and central learning environment of undergraduate education in the United States—the library.

Beginning as far back as the late 1800s, some academic librarians have taught bibliography sessions and provided library tours and orientation sessions for students. However, the growing complexity of libraries and information resources made such efforts insufficient. Reflecting this growing complexity, librarians in the early 1970s began with new levels of sophistication to teach students research skills so students could successfully seek out their own answers rather than depend primarily on reference librarians for help. Using bibliographic instructional guides in a host of disciplines and encouraging faculty to ask them into their introductory courses, librarians often worked by themselves with very limited institutional and classroom faculty support. Because of their commitment to serving students and their perseverance, library instruction in courses has become more commonplace over the last three decades.

During this time, this emphasis on teaching students how to access library and information resources has joined with the incredible advances in information technology and databases and evolved into a widespread emphasis in higher education on information literacy. In this process, libraries are moving from a static center of the campus (basically a passive receptacle for books, information, and student questions where students learn mostly by trial and error how to access resources, if they learn at all) to a dynamic, ever-changing, critical center of student learning within our colleges and universities. The growing discussion and conversion of libraries to information commons testifies to this change—a transformation that is still in its early stages.

While these powerful changes were evolving, colleges and universities were also being challenged by student failure in the first year of college. Long ignored by classroom faculty and academic administrators, who viewed this failure as the students' problem, attrition became more serious as accountability pressures from state and federal sources mounted, significant tuition increases heightened parental concerns and student and media interest, and institutional revenue remained unchanged or declined. How does one explain losing 25% to 30% of your entering class in the first year? Given increased competition for students in the 1980s and 1990s, how can one justify the need to continually replenish these losses and the expenses involved in doing so? And, how can one justify such systemic attrition given society's need for an educated and productive citizenry?

The "wasteland" of the first year of college as evidenced by these attrition statistics (and the inability to really justify them) led many to seek out the pioneering efforts of John Gardner and his colleagues who advocated transforming the first year of college into a positive experience for students. The amazing growth of the first-year programs over the last 25 years reflects the growing concern (often externally induced) among colleges and university leaders and faculty about the failure of students and the financial and educational costs of their failure.

These two significant movements—the transformation of libraries into dynamic, teaching/learning institutions and of the first year of college—have gained considerable energy from the financial struggles of colleges and universities in the 1990s and into the present. Librarians have to do more with less, and institutions have to retain more students.

For me, the most interesting—even exciting—part of this monograph is the implicit and explicit focus on student learning in both the transformation of the library and the creation of the first-year programs. The underlying educational philosophy of these two movements is that students can be successful if given the right tools and learning environments and that colleges and universities need to focus on student learning rather than solely on what faculty teach in the classroom. By focusing on student learning, these two movements seek to continually transform the structure and processes of what they do to enable students to learn and succeed. In effect, this commitment to student learning and success means adjusting to the changing nature of students entering college—whether they be the next generation of young students or the adult learners returning to fulfill their educational aspirations and/or needs.

In really believing in and practicing this commitment to student learning (and success), librarians and first-year (and now second-year, as well) program advocates have much to teach the rest of higher education. The oft-discussed but rarely implemented paradigm shift from teaching to learning must be taken seriously to ensure the future success of undergraduate education at our colleges and universities.

Both librarians and first-year program advocates have also taught higher education institutions the need and importance of moving beyond special academic interests and breaking down the walls of academic and administrative silos. Boundary spanning, as some call it, *is* the future, because the compartmentalized structures of higher education institutions—in both academic and administrative areas—do not reflect the best way to educate students. Academic silos are inefficient and very costly in a time of limited resources.

While this monograph focuses on best practices as of 2006, I would be remiss in this foreword—at least I think so—if I did not follow some of the implications for the future of the philosophy underlying the practices of these two movements.

Libraries are being transformed in ways that will lead them to look, sound, and feel very different from their traditional, monumental forebears. From quiet, large, and sometimes ornate reading areas surrounded by books, they are becoming noisy, active, learning environments that contain numerous areas—open and enclosed—for group interaction surrounded by the latest technology. They are also places where students can study alone and where books are still visible. Increasingly, they are becoming centralized learning support units integrating technology and writing centers as well as places to eat, talk, and interact socially. In many ways, the library is becoming, and will be, a campus community center focused on student learning.

It will be interesting to see how the next generation of students, who grow up with the Internet and Google and are involved in elaborate virtual networks based on high-intensity technology use, influences our colleges and universities. How will first-year programs be impacted by the recent advent of technologically simulated environments where people interact virtually with others using likenesses of themselves? How will the joining together of high-quality academic content and simulated environments (the latter being common in computer games) in the hands (and heads) of this new generation change how we conceive of viable learning environments and learning communities? How might it force us to revisit or redefine our belief that learning should/does only occur in classrooms and labs?

Adapting the first year of college and our notions of information literacy to this new generation and these new developments will be a great challenge, especially for faculty and our academic and administrative structures. I expect that the advocates for and practitioners of first-year programs and their focus on student learning will be important in helping faculty and academic administrators make this adjustment. These advocates and practitioners will likely be among the first to deal with these new developments. But, I would guess that the leaders in dealing with these incredible changes will be the librarians who have traveled the farthest and changed the most in transforming their staid academic units into the most exciting, dynamic, and central learning environments of our colleges and universities.

Alan E. Guskin
Distinguished University Professor, Ph.D. Program in Leadership and Change
University President Emeritus, Antioch University
October 4, 2006
Edmonds, Washington

Preface

Drawing on the Past, in the Present, to Shape the Future of the First-Year Experience in American Higher Education

John N. Gardner & Andrew K. Koch

If you were to ask us (which you have not) to identify the most important task that new students must accomplish to succeed in college, and beyond, we would argue it is developing purpose. In other words, students must answer the question, why am I in college, this college in particular, at this time in my life, and in this particular period of history? Many components of the college experience may and can provide answers and directions to this essential question, including information literacy—or what we would prefer to be known as "information fluency." We believe information fluency to be the set of requisite 21st century skills needed to succeed in the information economy. In that spirit, we welcome you and introduce you to this monograph, which was designed to provide information and promote reflection, inspiration, and, ultimately and most importantly, action. As educators, we share the conviction that the role of the library and academic librarians must be more central to the design and execution of the beginning college experience and to the dynamic ongoing reform conversation in American higher education about how to achieve a more effective beginning for our students.

Further, we believe that human purpose is informed and inspired by achieving a greater understanding of historical context. The context for both the first-year reform movement and the role of libraries as we have known them is changing rapidly. Thus, we set out to provide the historical origins of this monograph, both very immediately as the literal context that moved it from conception to publication, and the larger context of the historical factors that are responsible for shaping the first year of college as we know it today.

Quite simply, this monograph resulted from the original vision of the publication's editor, Larry Hardesty, who was the chair of the 2003 meeting for the Association of College and Research Libraries (ACRL) in Charlotte, North Carolina. Hardesty's original vision was that a major plenary session be dedicated to delivering a strong message to academic librarians on the need to increase their level of involvement in and leadership for efforts transforming how we introduce new students to higher education. Hardesty turned to me to deliver this message because of my more-than-a-quarter-century advocacy for first-year students.[1]

At the 2003 ACRL meeting, I used the words of the former president of the Urban League, Vernon Jordan, "If you ain't in the room, you ain't part of the action!" to lay out a strong call for action. I noted that in all my years working with hundreds of colleges and universities to support their efforts to improve the first year, I had observed that librarians were dramatically underrepresented in the power groups that convened on campuses to develop new visions for improving the first year. Moreover, I expressed in unambiguous terms my unhappiness with that underrepresentation and issued a challenge, a charge, and a call to arms to the assembled ACRL members to become more active, assertive, involved, and invested in supporting and shaping this reform movement.

In response to that call, ACRL convened a working group led by Larry Hardesty and ACRL Executive Director, Mary Ellen Davis, to discuss further how ACRL and academic librarians might become more influential players in this reform work. This response led to discussions with these ACRL leaders, me, and my colleagues at the University of South Carolina's National Resource Center for The First-Year Experience and Students in Transition about what steps could be taken in such a partnership. The foundational step was the production of this monograph. We all believed that we had to lay out a compelling rationale for a greater level of initiative on the part of librarians. Further, we believed that we could and should provide examples of best practices.

However, before librarians can fully address their role in the so-called "first-year experience" movement, they must understand the historical context associated with it. Just where did the movement come from and what have been its influences on the academy? To answer these questions, we begin by examining events that transpired during the early part of the 20th century—an era when the first-year experience was far from being considered a "movement." Nonetheless, through hindsight, we can see the early vestiges of first-year, student-focused reform efforts in the initial decades of the 20th century—specifically the advent of first-year orientation seminars.

The initial first-year orientation seminar for academic credit was launched at Reed College (in Oregon) in 1911 (where men and women were taught in gender-segregated versions of the course). Slowly gaining momentum, four other American postsecondary institutions followed Reed's example and offered credit-bearing first-year orientation seminars of their own by the 1915-1916 academic year. By 1925-1926, 82 American universities did so (Brubacher & Rudy, 1956)—including Princeton, Indiana, Stanford, Northwestern, Johns Hopkins, and Ohio State (Gordon, 1989). By 1938, 9 out of 10 first-year students in American universities were required to take an orientation course (Gordon). However, this would be the apex of first-year seminar offerings during the first half of the 20th century. Following the middle part of the 1930s, the courses began to wane in both number and, where they still existed, scope. The first-year experience scholar/practitioner Virginia Gordon shares that the number of courses decreased "because of faculty objections to offering credit for their 'life adjustment' content" (p. 188). In other words, in the minds of those who objected to them, the first-year seminars were too remedial and non-academic to be tolerated. By the early 1960s, the first-year orientation seminar was practically nonexistent on American university campuses (Gordon). It took campus unrest and student violence in the early 1970s to change this.

The events that occurred at Kent State University during spring 1970 attracted the national media's and American public's attention more than any other student protest of that era. In May 1970, National Guardsmen were summoned to the Ohio institution to confront a campus demonstration, and, in the ensuing confusion, they killed four students—two of them merely walking to class—and injured nine more. A study from the Urban Institute soon after the event concluded that the Kent State shootings were the single factor causing the only nationwide college student strike in U.S. history (Katsiaficas, 1987). Over four million students at more than 900 American colleges and universities took part in the ensuing protests—both violent and non-violent. The University of South Carolina (USC) may have experienced one of the more contentious protests during this period. Witnesses might have wondered what was accomplished by students' storming the administration building on the campus' historical Horseshoe and burning records and by the South Carolina National Guard's tear gas response to the angry participants. However, as time would show, the Kent State-related riot at USC did more than serve as a vehicle for protest—it served as the catalyst for what would become a national first-year student reform movement.

In response to the protest that shook his campus, Thomas F. Jones, the president at the University of South Carolina, revived the first-year seminar, University 101, at his institution. Unlike its early 20th century antecessor, this seminar was focused much more on "humanizing" the learning experience. In his words, Jones wanted the University to offer the course to "teach students not to riot" (Watts, 1999, p. 246). In its early days in the 1970s, the course was not without its opponents. Faculty critics decried the course's lack of "structure" and pointed out that it was missing any credible evaluation results that could convince them of its educational value. When Jones announced his intention to resign following the end of the 1974 academic year, it came as little surprise that the future existence of University 101 was in doubt. Jones and his administrative colleagues did what they could to preserve the course and shore it up for the future. One such action was finding a person to serve as the course's director. Of the three names considered for the search, the first two persons to whom the job was offered declined the position. I was one of the original faculty members who had been trained to teach the course and was the third person offered the job. At the time, I was an untenured faculty member recognized for my teaching effectiveness.

Over the next few years, I set out to add more traditional structure and academic content to University 101, boost student enrollment in the course, and provide credible research data to prove that students and the University benefited from offering the course. I worked with Paul Fidler, a faculty member and administrator at USC who focused his research efforts on student outcomes, to conduct an assessment of University 101. By the end of January 1975, Fidler and his associates provided results showing that University 101 students were significantly more likely to be retained than students who did not take the course. Specifically, students who started at USC during the fall of one academic year were more likely to return for the start of the next academic year if they had enrolled in the University 101 first-year seminar. The outcomes also showed that students who took the course were better informed about the University, made more frequent use of the University's resources and services, and participated in extracurricular activities to a greater extent than non-participants. With these outcomes presented to him, the University's new president decided that the course would continue as long as student interest and need continued to exist (Watts, 1999).

By the late 1970s, concern over retaining students—and with them the tuition they generated—was beginning to mount. With the end of the Vietnam War and the tapering off of the baby boom generation, the double-digit annual enrollment increases that were common in the 1960s shrank to a more typical 2% to 4% increase. In addition, many higher education enrollment analysts predicted that by the 1980s, American universities would experience declines in enrollment (Centra, 1980). Consequently, as a means of preserving themselves and avoiding drastic financial cutbacks, universities focused more attention on efforts that would help them retain the students they already had. Proven retention-enhancing programs were sought out and, when found, quickly imitated. Because outcomes associated with University 101 had been shared widely at regional and national conferences, the first-year seminar was one of the most frequently copied retention-enhancing initiatives. Presently, first-year seminars are offered by "80 percent of all four-year and 62 percent of all two-year institutions," making them "the most commonly implemented curricular intervention designed specifically for first-year students" in American higher education today (Barefoot, 2005, p 56).

In 1981, after making numerous presentations about USC's first-year seminar at an array of professional meetings over the previous five year period, assisting a host of other postsecondary institutions launch equivalent courses, and finding no literature or higher education professional association focused on first-year students, I decided to host a national conference on the first-year orientation course in Columbia, South Carolina. I anticipated having approximately 50 colleagues in attendance. To my surprise, nearly 175 higher educators from the United States and Canada made the trek to Columbia to take part in and listen to more than 30 descriptions of first-year orientation courses. The conference exceeded our expectations, prompting my colleagues at USC and me to offer the meeting on a recurring basis under the title "The Freshman Year Experience." The change in title expanded the scope of the effort to include first-year student curricular and cocurricular innovations beyond first-year seminars. Watts (1999) suggests that the conference provided an annual meeting point for members of the first-year experience movement, an expanded focus, and a name flexible enough to accommodate the growth and increased scope of the movement in the decades to follow.

Two factors fueled the interest in and growing importance of the first-year experience movement in the United States during the 1980s. First, reports such as *A Nation at Risk: The Imperative for Educational Reform* released in 1983 by the Presidential Commission on Excellence in Education (Zeller, 1984) brought increased public attention to educational performance and the quality of undergraduate education. Second, there was a decrease in direct federal funding for higher education. In particular, changes in federal financial aid funding policies made retaining the individual student of increasingly greater significance.

As a result of the steadily increasing interest in the first-year experience, I began actively advancing a plan to create a research and "resource" center for the first-year experience at the University of South Carolina. After nearly two years of planning, the National Center for the Study of The Freshman Year Experience opened in July 1987.[2] Soon thereafter, the Center launched its *Freshman Year Experience Newsletter*. During the same year, it also began the scholarly, blind refereed *Journal of The Freshman Year Experience*. Hitting desks and library shelves in fall 1988, the journal, like the newsletter, found a ready and eager readership. In an effort to provide extended research reports and examples of good practice, the Center also initiated a monograph series. To date, the monograph series includes more than 40 titles—several of which have multiple editions. Through its conference series and publications, the Center has helped highlight and promote other first-year focused initiatives that frequently had parallel histories to and intersected with the first-year seminar. Two such innovations are learning communities and Supplemental Instruction.

Learning communities are academic programs, largely for first-year students, which allow a single cohort of students to enroll in two or more linked courses. All learning community programs can trace their roots back to the University of Wisconsin at Madison's Experimental College in the 1920s and 1930s (Gabelnick, MacGregor, Matthews, & Smith, 1990). In the 1960s and 1970s, a handful of institutions tried similar experiments, but the growth of learning communities, like first-year seminars can be attributed to changing attitudes toward teaching and learning and concerns about retention (Goodsell Love, 1999). According to the National Survey of First-Year Practices, learning communities "are now found at 37 percent of four-year and 23 percent of two-year institutions" (Barefoot, 2005, p. 56). Moreover, 77% of all research institutions offer learning communities for their first-year students (Barefoot). The rapid adoption and application of the learning-community concept can be explained as an intentional effort to "make the large environment seem smaller by creating defined, manageable academic structures"—structures that build community among the student, faculty, and staff participants and create cohesion in the curriculum (Barefoot).

Like first-year seminars and learning communities, Supplemental Instruction—also called SI—arose as a direct result of the desire to retain students. In the early 1970s, Deanna C. Martin created SI at the University of Missouri-Kansas City (UMKC) in response to declining student success rates in the institution's rapidly diversifying schools of medicine, pharmacy, and dentistry. After initially offering SI to students in UMKC's health science professional schools, the program was extended to high-risk courses across the university. Today, SI is typically defined as an academic assistance program based on peer-led study sessions that target historically difficult, entry-level courses—typically 100- or 200-level courses in which 30% or more of the students generally earn a D, F, or withdraw. These are the courses in which first-year students are most likely to enroll.

Because SI is targeted at high-risk courses, not high-risk students, there is no remedial stigma attached to it—and, thus, students are more likely to take part. Specifically, SI uses students who previously completed a given course with distinction to conduct informal review meetings during which they facilitate the comparison of notes, discussion of readings, development of content organizational tools, and problem solving for students currently enrolled in the same course. Through this approach, participants learn how to integrate course content with study skills. According to the outcomes of the National Survey of First-Year Practices, at the start of the 21st century, 36% of America's colleges and universities offered a formal SI program "linked to one or more of the 'killer' courses taken by first-year students" (Barefoot, 2005, p. 57).

The proliferation of first-year seminars, learning communities, SI, and other comparable initiatives during the last decade of the 20th century must be viewed in context with the era's changing demographic composition and the rise of a culture of accountability. The unprecedented growth in first-year programs came in response to criticism of America's educational system found in a series of books, notably Allan Bloom's 1987 bestseller, *The Closing of the American Mind*, and reports, such as *An American Imperative: Higher Expectations for Higher Education* issued by the Wingspread Group in 1993, and *The Student Learning Imperative*, published by the American College Personnel Association in 1994. These publications prompted educators to concentrate on showing measurable improvement within the core functions of the educational enterprise—student learning and development. This quality movement—in part, an extension of the quality movement in American industry—was endorsed with vigor by the major postsecondary professional associations in the United States, especially the American Association for Higher Education and the Association of American Colleges and Universities. The emphasis on quality came at the same time as a wave of new immigration, principally from Latin America and Asia, and increased racial diversity in higher education brought less prepared, but nonetheless eager, students to American campuses.

Prompted by increasingly vigorous calls for accountability and the growing influence of accrediting agencies, I worked with Betsy Barefoot (who had been a codirector of the National Resource Center) to launch the Policy Center on the First Year of College located in Brevard, North Carolina, in 1999. With funding provided by three American philanthropic organizations—The Pew Charitable Trusts, The Atlantic Philanthropies, and later Lumina Foundation for Education—the Policy Center expanded on and complemented the work of the National Resource Center by focusing squarely on shaping higher-education policy at the campus level through the improvement of overall assessment of the first college year. The Policy Center's current project, the Foundations of Excellence in the First Year of College, is an effort that helps American colleges and universities develop a research-based, comprehensive, aspirational model of the first year that is attainable and immediately usable to increase student learning, success, and retention and a method to measure and evaluate their level of achievement of the model.

Thus, from its humble beginnings with the University 101 course at the University of South Carolina in 1971, to its current state in which two national resource centers help shape the success of first-year students across the nation, the first-year experience movement has been a story of innovation and adaptation, successfully meeting the postsecondary educational needs of a steadily diversifying and increasingly accountability-oriented society. Since 1971, the scope of the movement has grown in both depth and breadth—from one seminar at the University of South Carolina to an array of initiatives such as learning communities, SI, orientation programming, summer reading experiences, service-learning efforts, and living-learning programs. In the process of doing so, the first-year experience-related centers and the initiatives with which they are associated have become part of the fabric of higher education in the United States today.

When we look at the history of the first-year experience movement in the United States, we are reminded, contrary to what our Puritan forbearers would have us believe, that not everything in history is predetermined. Our will and our choices have direct bearing on our world. Little did the originators and early leaders in first-year seminars, learning communities, and SI envision the far-reaching impact of their work when they started. Their early efforts were designed to address local issues and concerns. Later, they realized they had the opportunity to act *in* history to *make* history, to enhance learning and success for all first-year students. And like these first-year experience innovators, librarians have an essential role to play in helping our students succeed, particularly in today's high-tech, information-saturated world.

It is our belief that this monograph will serve as a tool that helps today's librarians draw on the history of the first-year experience in American higher education to shape its future. In so doing, academic librarians will become more central to the conversation about and design and execution of an intentional, student learning-focused beginning for college students in the United States and beyond.

Notes

[1] First-person references in the essay refer to the first author John Gardner.

[2] Early in the Center's history, the name was changed to the National Resource Center for The Freshman Year Experience. In 1995, the phrase "Students in Transition" was added to reflect an expanding mission to support strategies to improve success among transfer students, sophomores, and seniors. In 1998, in recognition of the growing sentiment among American higher education practitioners that the word "freshman" was sexist and politically incorrect, the Center removed the term from the organization's name, replacing it with the gender-neutral phrase "first-year." The Center's name became the "National Resource Center for The First-Year Experience and Students in Transition," the designation it still holds today and which has been adopted by its publications and conference series.

References

American College Personnel Association. (1994). *The student learning imperative: Implications for student affairs.* Alexandria, VA: Author.

Barefoot, B. O. (2005). Current institutional practices in the first college year. In M. L. Upcraft, J. N. Gardner, & Barefoot, B. O. (Eds.), *Challenging and supporting the first-year student: A handbook for improving the first year of college* (pp. 47-63). San Francisco: Jossey-Bass.

Bloom, A. (1987). *The closing of the American mind.* New York: Simon and Schuster.

Brubacher, J. S. & Rudy, W. (1956). *Higher education in transition: An American history, 1636-1956.* New York: Harper and Brothers.

Centra, J. A. (1980, January-February). College enrollment in the 1980s: Projections and possibilities. *The Journal of Higher Education, 51,* 18-39.

Gabelnick, F., MacGregor, J., Matthews, R. S., & Smith, B. L. (1990). *Learning communities: Creating connections among students, faculty and disciplines* (New Directions for Teaching and Learning Monograph Series, 41). San Francisco: Jossey-Bass.

Goodsell Love, A. (1999). What are learning communities? In J. H. Levine (Ed.), *Learning communities: New structures, new partnerships for learning* (Monograph No. 26, pp. 1-8). Columbia, SC: University of South Carolina, National Resource Center for The First-Year Experience & Students in Transition.

Gordon, V. (1989). Origins and purposes of the freshman seminar. In M. L. Upcraft, & J. N. Gardner (Eds.), *The freshman year experience: Helping students survive and succeed in college* (pp. 183-197). San Francisco: Jossey-Bass.

Katsiaficas, G. (1987). *The imagination of the New Left: A global analysis of 1968.* Boston, MA: South End Press.

Watts, E. I. (1999). *The freshman year experience, 1962-1990: An experiment in humanistic higher education.* Unpublished doctoral dissertation, Queens University.

Wingspread Group on Higher Education. (1993). *An American imperative: Higher expectations for higher education.* Racine, WI: Author.

Zeller, T. (1984, July). "A nation at risk:" Mandate for change in arts education. *Art Education, 37, 6-9.*

Introduction

Larry L. Hardesty

Almost a decade ago, I mused in print about whether academic library-user education had made any progress in the past 25 years (Hardesty, 1999). As I wrote then, my career has spanned most of the modern era of library-user instruction, which I date from a presentation by Evan Farber, then College Librarian at Earlham College, at the 1969 American Library Association Conference (see Kennedy, 1970). Library-user education (an umbrella term for one of the various rubrics used over the years, e.g. library orientation, bibliographic instruction, library instruction, information literacy, information fluency) has had a long history dating back to the 19th century (Hardesty, Schmidt, & Tucker, 1986). In the mid-1970s, the Instruction Section of the Association of College and Research Libraries (ACRL) formed (originally as the Bibliographic Instruction Section) and soon became the second largest section in ACRL, and arguably the most active. As a result, academic librarians began discussing elements of library-user instruction with increasingly sophisticated understanding of the challenges involved and how to address them. Yet, its progress has been uncertain (Hardesty & Tucker, 1989), and many of the challenges for library-user education that existed in the past continued to exist in the late 1990s (Rockman, 1999). Thus, I had good reasons for my hesitancy about declaring library-user instruction an unqualified success.

Still, library instruction has evolved from library orientation tours and a focus on explaining reference works to students over the past three decades. Since the late 1990s, the academic library profession has engaged in increasingly sophisticated thinking regarding information literacy, as Tom Kirk notes in chapter 1. Academic librarians also have become more intentional in developing their teaching skills, largely through programs, such as the National Information Literacy Institute championed by Cerise Oberman, Dean of Library and Information Services at SUNY Plattsburgh, in the late 1990s (Oberman, Gratch Lindauer, & Wilson, 1998). Other librarians initiated numerous efforts about the same time that moved library-user education forward in the profession (Grassian & Clark, 1999). In fact, librarians involved in library-user education remain among the most creative, dynamic, and energetic members of the profession.

Yet, most of the progress in library-user education during the past three decades, including the past 10 years, has been made on the library side. I have found that with few exceptions (e.g., Boyer, 1987), the higher education literature gives little attention to library-user education, in particular—or even the role of the academic library in undergraduate education, in general. Academic administrators too often support the library as a "good thing" in the abstract; but as I found in my study of chief academic officers at liberal arts colleges, few had given much thought as to how they might actively support it in reality—beyond a line in the budget (Hardesty, 1991b). Most important, certain aspects of faculty culture have historically impeded library-instruction efforts (Hardesty, 1995). In addition to the traditional emphasis on research and graduate education, many classroom faculty members have never had occasion to think about the library as a major educational resource for undergraduate students. I discovered through my doctoral dissertation study, which involved interviews of dozens of classroom faculty members at numerous institutions and a survey of several hundred classroom faculty members at four institutions, relatively few of them could convincingly articulate (with evidence of application) how they supported the educational role of the library in undergraduate education. Certainly, a small number of individual faculty members could point to their integration of the library into their courses, but very seldom did I find evidence that classroom faculty members had discussed the role of the library in undergraduate education with their colleagues (Hardesty, 1991a).

This lack of progress in engaging a significant portion of other members of higher education, particularly classroom faculty and academic administrators, in actualizing the educational potential of the academic library in undergraduate education continues to concern me. Until more substantial progress occurs, many classroom faculty members and academic administrators also will not understand the need for the time and effort involved in guiding students in the use of the library, and the future of library-user education will remain fragile and uncertain.

Nevertheless, I am optimistic about the future library-user education, in large part because of this publication and the circumstances that led to its creation and publication. My aspiration is that this monograph will add a much-needed dimension to library-user education by going beyond the academic library community. Most of the chapters are co-authored by classroom faculty members and librarians, and numerous other nonlibrarians have made significant contributions to this work, including John Gardner and Randy Swing (both from the Policy Center on the First Year of College), George Kuh (director of the National Survey of Student Engagement), and Leticia Oseguera (reporting on research from the Higher Education Research Institute at UCLA).

In fact, the monograph had its origins when John Gardner spoke at the Association of College and Research Libraries National Conference in April 2003 and challenged the librarians to become more active in the first-year movement. Gardner promised that if someone would step forward and write a book about the role of the academic library in the first-year experience that he would get it onto the desk of higher education administrators in this country. No doubt, many in the room thought librarians had been quite active in promoting library-user instruction in all areas of higher education, including the first year. Nevertheless, after many years of academic librarians trying to involve classroom faculty members, academic administrators, members of higher education associations, accreditation agencies, and others in library education with some, but often modest, success, I found myself hearing a major leader of an educational reform movement (i.e., the first-year experience) reach out with enthusiasm and challenge academic librarians to join him in his efforts to promote library-user education in the first college year. Here was someone representing a group with very similar interests (the academic success of students) to academic librarians who, for a change, was knocking on our door. Gardner presented an opportunity (and a challenge) to which I knew I (and my librarian colleagues) had to respond. The rest, as they say, is history, but, as usual, is more complicated than appearances might suggest.

For example, from the beginning, I realized that to do justice to the topic that numerous perspectives, particularly from nonlibrarians, must be well represented. The result is this monograph with most of the chapters written through the collaborations of both librarians and nonlibrarians, including classroom faculty members, administrators, and researchers. As further evidence of the collaborative nature of this work, while published by the National Resource

Center for The First-Year Experience and Students in Transition, it is jointly distributed by the Center and the Association of College and Research Libraries.

The work is a deliberate effort to provide the reader with a description of the philosophical and the pragmatic, the state-of-the-present and a history of how we got here, the successes we have achieved, and the challenges that remain. Most important, it is a combination of numerous perspectives of the role of the library in the first-year experience offered by not only librarians in the trenches, but also classroom faculty members and leaders in higher education.

Organization of the Monograph

The monograph opens with a foreword by Guskin, which is followed by a preface by Gardner and Koch that provides a brief history of the first-year experience movement and a rationale for closer work between librarians and the first-year educators in furthering information literacy efforts. The first section of the monograph offers a series of foundational chapters that describe information literacy and offer a glimpse at today's entering student population. In the opening chapter, Kirk provides a librarian's perspective with the recent history of information literacy standards and puts forth a call for action to position information literacy for a more assured future. Kuh, Boruff-Jones, and Mark follow with a discussion of the library's role in promoting student engagement and establishing a solid foundation for academic success. In chapter 3, Oseguera draws upon the data from the CIRP Freshman Survey and Your First College Year survey to give the reader an understanding of the nature of today's first-year college students and how these characteristics impact their use and experience of the library.

The next section provides a broad overview of current efforts to involve the library in the first-year experience. Malone and Videon (chapter 4) report on a national survey that identified model programs throughout the first year, while Boff and Johnson (chapter 5) provide an in-depth analysis of the results of their 2001 survey of library instruction in first-year seminars. In chapter 6, the late Ilene Rockman describes a system-wide effort to improve information-competency skills in the first college year in the California State University system, the largest system of higher education in North America. Boff, Albrecht, and Armstrong offer an introductory glance at first-year librarian positions in chapter 7. The final two chapters in the section highlight specific strategies for providing information literacy instruction in the first year. In chapter 8, I describe characteristics of effective library assignments while Cahoy and Snavely (chapter 9) examine library-related cocurricular activities in the first year.

The third section provides research frameworks through which to examine the results of the library involvement in the first-year experience and looks to the future. In chapter 10, Fitzpatrick and Swing discuss the importance of assessing library instruction in the first-year experience and provide examples of evaluation techniques directly relevant to the library. Since much of the first-year experience focuses on increasing student retention (and, more generally, student success), Pierard and Graves in chapter 11 provide a review of the research on student retention theory and discuss its implications regarding the library involvement in the first-year experience. In the final chapter, I look at where the library instruction movement needs to go in the future.

The final section of the monograph provides the pragmatic perspective through a series of 13 case studies from a range of different colleges and universities. The authors report on long-standing and relatively new initiatives, describing processes of innovation, adaptation, and institutionalization. Highlighted in the case studies are strategies for collaboration, faculty involvement, and innovative use of technology in library instruction.

Through these contributions, this monograph brings together two innovative movements in higher education, both of which have their roots in the last quarter of the 20th century—the first-year experience and the information literacy movements. As an academic librarian involved in library-user education for more than 30 years, I feel more qualified to assess its status than that of the first-year experience movement. As I note here (and elaborate elsewhere in this monograph), this volume is not intended as a record of the success of library-user education. While librarians involved in library-user education have accomplished much, there is still much to do, and it cannot be accomplished by librarians working alone. Hopefully, this work will provide the information and the impetus for librarians and those involved in the first-year experience (e.g., classroom faculty, administrators, student affairs personnel, and others) to better understand each other's perspectives of how our goals overlap and how, by working together and sharing our perspectives and expertise, we can more effectively contribute to the success of our students. While the reader will see that the challenges are considerable and remain incompletely addressed after 30 years, I also hope the reader will conclude the purpose of the two movements, enhanced success of our students, is too important and too overlapping for us not to join forces and work together.

References

Boyer, E. L. (1987). *College: The undergraduate experience in America.* New York: Harper & Row.

Grassian, E., & Clark, S. E. (1999). Information literacy sites: Background and ideas for program planning and development. *College & Research Libraries News, 60*(2), 78-81, 92.

Hardesty, L. L. (1991a). *Faculty and the library: The undergraduate experience.* Norwood, NJ: Ablex.

Hardesty, L. L. (1991b). The bottomless pit revisited. *College & Research Libraries News, 52,* 219-229.

Hardesty, L. L. (1995). Bibliographic instruction and faculty culture. *Library Trends, 44*(2), 339-367.

Hardesty, L. L. (1999). Reflections on 25 years of library instruction: Have we made progress? *Reference Services Review, 27*(3), 242-246.

Hardesty, L. L., Schmidt, J. P., & Tucker, J. M. (Eds.). (1986). *User instruction in academic libraries: A century of selected readings.* Metuchen, NJ: Scarecrow Press.

Hardesty, L. L., & Tucker. J. M. (1989). An uncertain crusade: The history of library use instruction in a changing educational environment. In J. V. Richardson & J. Y. Davis (Eds.), *Academic librarianship: Past, present, and future* (pp. 97-111). Littleton, CO: Libraries Unlimited.

Kennedy, J. R. (1970). Integrated library instruction. *Library Journal, 95,* 1450-1453.

Oberman, C., Gratch Lindauer, B., & Wilson, B. (1998). Integrating information literacy into the curriculum: How is your library measuring up? *College & Research Libraries News, 59*(5), 347-352

Rockman, I. F. (1999). End-use services in academic libraries: A 1999 perspective. *Reference Services Review, 27*(3), 254-258.

SECTION 1

Chapter 1

Recent History and Definition of Information Literacy and Future Directions

Thomas G. Kirk, Jr.

Information literacy refers to a concept through which the library plays an important role in the individual's educational development. The term encompasses a body of skills, behaviors, and attitudes that people use to recognize when information is needed and to locate, evaluate, and effectively use the needed information (American Library Association, 1989). First used in 1974, the term has become endemic in the academic library and higher education literature. Nevertheless, despite the increased interest in the concept, differences in terminology (e.g., bibliographic instruction, information competency, and information fluency) abound. In addition, over the past 30 years, a variety of definitions have emerged, perhaps because of the interdisciplinary nature of the concept. As a result, a great deal of confusion about information literacy continues to exist. A clarification of the concept and an understanding of its evolution are important for those members of the academic community seeking to integrate the skills and attitudes related to information literacy into the first-year experience.

Therefore, my goals for this chapter are to lay out the intellectual territory occupied by the concept of information literacy, provide some perspective on where we are in the evolving definition, and convey the significance of the concept to readers, especially those involved in first-year experience initiatives. The two ideas—information literacy and the first-year experience—have in common a focus on developmental processes that seek to enhance students' capacity to function effectively in their academic work. The focus of the introductory part of this chapter is a brief history of the development of the concept, while other sections examine recent explorations of the concept and its increasing level of sophistication. Finally, in this chapter, I suggest where proponents should go to advance the effectiveness of information literacy programs, which, in turn, will have an impact on how information literacy is implemented in first-year experience programs.

Early History of the Concept

Zurkowski probably first used the term "information literates" in a paper entitled "The Information Service Environment: Relations and Priorities," presented to the National Commission on Libraries and Information Science in November 1974. In the paper, Zurkowski wrote about the challenges presented by the increasing quantity and complexity of information people encounter, which are further compounded by the rising use of technology to manage this information. According to Zurkowski, "People trained in the application of information resources to their work can be called information literates" (p. 6). While the Zurkowski paper is often cited as the first articulation of information literacy (e.g., Johnston & Webber, 2003; Owusu-Ansah, 2003; Ridgeway, 1990), Bruce (1997) rightly pointed out that the origins of the concept, if not the terminology, go back much further. Information literacy is rooted in the library-focused service of library instruction and the emergence of bibliographic instruction in the 1970s and 1980s (Kirk, 1999).

The appearance of the terms "bibliographic instruction" and "information literacy" in the ERIC database illustrates the early evolution of the information literacy concept. As Figure 1 shows, writers first used the term "bibliographic instruction" in the late 1960s, and its use grew significantly until it reached a peak in the 1990s. "Information literacy" made its appearance during the late 1980s, and the dramatic increase of its use suggests that it rapidly eclipsed "bibliographic instruction," largely replacing it and all other terminology related to the concept by the mid-1990s. Obviously, individuals not closely involved with this change in language and the increasing sophistication of the concept may well be confused by the variety of terms.

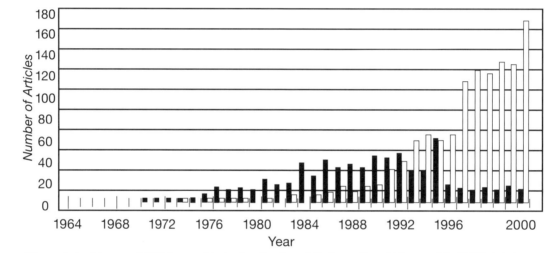

Figure 1. Incidence of "Bibliographic Instruction" and "Informational Literacy" in ERIC database, 1964-2002. Bibliographic Instruction (Black) and Information Literacy (White).

Why are the differences between the two terms significant to the reader? Rader and Coons helped make a distinction between the earlier concepts, such as bibliographic instruction, and the more recent concept of information literacy: "Bibliographic instruction is more often a situation-specific response, whereas information literacy contributes towards life-long learning by educating individuals to effectively utilize and evaluate information" (as cited in Snavely & Cooper, 1997, p. 10). Furthermore, while Snavely and Cooper distinguished between bibliographic instruction and information literacy, they acknowledged the origins of information literacy in the expanding definition of bibliographic instruction. Tucker (1984), writing earlier and from a longer historical perspective, also recognized the evolution of the concept from its antecedents. He suggested that the concept we now label "information literacy" evolved from librarians' and other academics' professional interest in improving students' use of the bibliographic tools and resources of the academic world. No doubt, users of such terms as "bibliographic instruction" and "library instruction" had similar interests while not necessarily sharing an understanding of the more fully developed concept of "information literacy."

"The teaching library" is also part of the history of information literacy. Williamson (1971) originally coined the term to describe a new role for the Swarthmore College library. Guskin, Stoffle, and Boisse (1978; Stoffle, Guskin, & Boisse, 1984) and others (Breivik, 1978;

Gorman, 1981) explored the definition of the concept in greater detail and expanded the use of the term. The teaching library, broadly defined, encompasses the role of the library in serving the total educational mission of the parent institution. It influenced librarians' thinking about bibliographic instruction and eventually about information literacy. Further, its use provides clear evidence of the teaching role of academic libraries that became fundamental to the concept of information literacy. This teaching role has been thoroughly absorbed into the philosophy of academic librarianship.

The Association of College and Research Libraries' (ACRL, 1987) *Model Statement of Objectives for Academic Bibliographic Instruction* and the American Library Association's (1989) *Presidential Committee on Information Literacy Report* represent the widely held perceptions of bibliographic instruction and information literacy in the late 1980s. Despite differences in terminology in the titles—bibliographic instruction, information literacy—the concepts represented in these documents provide further evidence of the convergence of the two ideas, with information literacy replacing bibliographic instruction. The differences in terminology can be explained by understanding that the broader concept of information literacy incorporated all aspects of bibliographic instruction (Kirk, 1999). That is, information literacy expands the earlier concept by adding three ideas: (a) the importance of effective use of technology; (b) the notion of information as a commodity that has legal, social, and economic qualities; and (c) the deep relationship between the skills of information seeking, information use, and critical thinking.

The concept of information literacy has also been labeled "information fluency" and "information competency." Often, individuals use these alternate names for two distinct reasons. For some practitioners, the term "literacy" has political and social overtones because, in their minds, proponents of a number of skill areas have used the "literacy" label as a way of establishing creditability and authority (Arp, 1990). For others, the term "literacy" implies a basic or functional skill level needed "to act autonomously and communicate within information domains and public spheres" (Reffell & Whitworth, 2002, p. 433). Such a basic skill set is assumed to have a threshold below which one is not literate. Proponents hold that "information fluency" refers to more sophisticated cognitive skills, which they prefer. This reaction to the term "literacy" persists despite the view by many observers that literacy may be viewed as a continuum ranging from basic to highly sophisticated skills (Behrens, 1994; Owusu-Ansah, 2003). These alternatives seem to be more a reaction against certain highly nuanced connotations of the terminology rather than differences in the substance of the definitions. Such differences should not hinder the development of effective programs in which first-year students can develop needed library-related skills. For first-year students, the focus of discussion should be on the level of sophistication of information literacy they need and how best to achieve that level.

Differences in the concept are more noteworthy when the word "computer" precedes literacy, competency, or fluency, because that addition places emphasis on the use of technology (Ayersman, Ackermann, & Zisman, 1996) and gives little or no attention to print information resources and their physical organization in libraries. Proponents of the term "computer literacy," like those using the term "information literacy," are focused on the meta-issues of critical thinking and a broad understanding of how technology influences the access to and use of information.

In some cases, the definition of information literacy shifts to focus on the role of technology in information searching and use (e.g., Lyman, 2001). Within this framework, "information literacy' is not only about *reading* digital representations, it is also about designing new genres for *writing* digital documents" (Lyman, p. 30). In any case, I contend that the debate about the language (e.g., information literacy, information competency, information fluency, computer literacy, computer competency, computer fluency) is now largely resolved because of the emergence of the *Information Literacy Competency Standards for Higher Education*

(ACRL, 2000). While the conversation about terminology may not be critical currently, the scope of information literacy and the methods of program implementation, such as in first-year experience programs, continue to be points of ongoing discussion.

This overview should provide a sufficient understanding of the evolution of the concept and the current status of the definition for those seeking to integrate information literacy into the first-year experience. Students of information literacy who wish to follow the nuances of the definition's evolution should consult articles by Arp (1990), Behrens (1994), Bruce (1997), Owusu-Ansah (2003), Shapiro and Hughes (1996), Snavely and Cooper (1997), and Tucker (1984).

Assessing Information Literacy

In 2000, the Association of College and Research Libraries developed the *Information Literacy Competency Standards for Higher Education (Standards)* which several other higher education organizations (ACRL, 2000; Council of Independent Colleges, 2004; Ratteray, 2002) subsequently adopted. In practice, these *Standards* have become the most influential definition of information literacy and play a defining role within the United States higher education community. A multidisciplinary group of higher education professionals including librarians, a library educator, a classroom faculty member, an academic administrator, and a representative of a higher education organization composed the *Standards*, which comprise three levels: (a) five standards, (b) 22 performance indicators, and (c) 87 outcomes. The five standards (skills) categories define the broad scope of information literacy. See Appendix A for the *Standards* in their entirety.

Each skills category is divided into "performance indicators," broad statements outlining categories of *behavior* that give evidence of information literacy. These general behaviors can be demonstrated in a number of specific ways. Two examples will illustrate the nature of the performance indicators. Under Standard 4, one of the performance indicators states, "The information literate student applies new and prior information to the planning and creation of a particular product or performance." Under Standard 2, Access, a performance indicator states, "The information literate student retrieves information online or in person using a variety of methods." Evidence of these behaviors indicates "the information literate student."

Performance indicators are further elaborated through the articulation of "outcomes" or specific behaviors provided as examples of each indicator. Again, examples illustrate the nature of the outcomes. Standard 2 has four outcomes, the first of which is "Uses various search systems to retrieve information in a variety of formats." The fourth is "Uses surveys, letters, interviews, and other forms of inquiry to retrieve primary information." The document's authors considered these outcomes as specific behaviors that can be measured to determine information literacy achievement. In these examples, approaches to assessment would seek ways to determine how many search systems students used; the variety of formats used; and the number of surveys, letters, and other direct methods used as information-gathering strategies. Together, the 87 outcomes represent the set of behaviors that demonstrate information literacy.

A review of the U.S. literature on academic library services suggests that since the publication of the *Standards* in 2000, librarians have made a major effort to use them for assessment purposes (e.g., ACRL, 2003b; Avery, 2003; Lindauer, 1998; Lindauer, Arp, & Woodward, 2004). Four assessment efforts are illustrative of recent developments. The first is the influence of the *Standards* on the accreditation process of the Middle States Commission on Higher Education (Ratteray, 2002, 2004). As a result of the synergy between the Middle States Commission's own process for developing new standards and the development of the *Standards,* the Middle States Commission has placed information literacy programming and outcomes assessment squarely within the accreditation process.

While the Middle States' accreditation guidelines do not require use of the *Standards* as a basis for program assessment, clearly they are a strong presence in how Middle States views information literacy.

Project SAILS (Standardized Assessment of Information Literacy Skills), created by Kent State University libraries, with the co-sponsorship of the Association of Research Libraries and funding from the Institute for Museum and Library Services, is the second development in assessment. Project SAILS is an objective test that measures students' level of information literacy by testing the 87 outcomes from the *Standards* (Project SAILS, 2005).

A third project, still in its infancy, grew out of the synergy that developed when George Kuh delivered a paper at the ACRL 2003 National Conference in Charlotte, North Carolina. The paper was subsequently published (Kuh & Gonyea, 2003). Kuh used the results from many years of the College Student Experiences Questionnaire (CSEQ) to examine the role of libraries and information resources in promoting student learning. In the discussions among conference attendees, Kuh and Gonyea's paper generated considerable interest in the "engagement" approach to assessing information literacy. This approach is based on a well-understood relationship between student involvement in significant academic activities and overall quality of the academic experience (Kuh, 2004).

While attendees at Kuh's presentation expressed considerable interest in this approach to information literacy assessment, some also expressed dissatisfaction with the items that were drawn from the CSEQ. They contended the activities Kuh used did not adequately represent information literacy and were not well linked to the *Standards* (e.g., used the library as a quiet place to read or study materials you brought with you). Those librarians understood the need to better represent the concept of information literacy through a survey instrument that aligned information literacy activities with engagement more carefully. They called for the redesign or addition of survey items to better represent the concept of information literacy.

Their concerns led to the formation of the Information Literacy College Student Surveys Project within ACRL's Institute for Information Literacy. Chaired by Bonnie Gratch Lindauer, the project launched an effort to explore how information literacy might more effectively be represented in such national surveys as the CSEQ and, more particularly, the National Survey of Student Engagement (NSSE). The committee is currently developing survey items for incorporation into the NSSE on an experimental basis. The proposed items will reflect the level of student engagement in activities that represent information literacy. Those involved in the project completed this phase of the work in fall 2005 and submitted a list of survey items to Kuh, Project Director of NSSE.

Although there is an inherent weakness in the *post facto* identification of information literacy-related items in the CSEQ, two studies suggest that mapping items to the *Standards* has been a useful exercise (Bordonaro, 2004; Mark & Boruff-Jones, 2004). The mapping exercise identifies items on the CSEQ instrument that relate to information literacy skills as well as the gaps in the coverage. Similarly, the careful linking of elements of the *Standards* to items on the NSSE should result in the survey being used with more confidence to indicate the quality of specific aspects of an information literacy program and, therefore, make the results more useful as a diagnostic tool. At the same time, the identification of gaps in coverage of the *Standards* points to the inadequacy of the CSEQ unless items are added to the survey.

The Educational Testing Service (ETS) has started a fourth assessment effort, in cooperation with college officials from, among others, the California Community College System and California State University System. The Information and Communication Technology Literacy Assessment is an online test that attempts to measure computer proficiency as well as information-processing skills (Young, 2004). The scenario-based instrument asks test-takers to solve problems that demonstrate both technical and cognitive skills (Educational Testing Service, 2005). ETS intends to have baseline data collected by 2006.

Refining Our Approach to Information Literacy

The definition of information literacy as encompassed in the *Standards* has become the conventional definition of the profession. The most recent explorations of the concept (Johnston & Webber, 2003; Marcum, 2002; Owusu-Ansah, 2003; Pawley, 2003) recognize the *Standards* as an important, perhaps watershed, document in defining information literacy. Nevertheless, some observers remain concerned that the current definition and its implementation have problems that need to be addressed.

Information Literacy Competency Standards for Higher Education Overreach

Owusu-Ansah (2003) raised a number of concerns in a recent paper; among them is what he calls the overreach of the *Standards*. He criticized the *Standards* for trying to create a comprehensive standard for all higher education, contending that they try to be "all-inclusive and complete" (p. 226) and, in so doing, go beyond librarians to establish responsibilities for classroom faculty and other academic staff. These responsibilities, Owusu-Ansah wrote, are often out of step with the realities of the structure and traditional roles within institutions of higher education and the librarians and faculty members who populate them. However, Owusu-Anash's criticism seems to overlook the intended role of the *Standards*. The document is not intended to defend the status quo but rather to call for change—a change that will improve the quality of education by disseminating responsibility for information literacy throughout the institution. While this change may not be easily achieved, evidence exists of its possibility (e.g., Baker & Kirk, case 9 in this monograph; Hutchins, Fister, & MacPherson, 2002; Klavano & Kulleseid, 1995).

Furthermore, Owusu-Ansah (2003) viewed the scope of the *Standards'* definition of information literacy as too broad. Critical thinking, writing skills, and self-analysis are all included as part of the *Standards* and, thus, blur the distinction between information literacy and skills widely recognized as part of general education (Owusu-Ansah)—a criticism shared by several other students of information literacy (e.g., Snavely & Cooper, 1997). Yet, information literacy is a concept deeply embedded in and related to a wide variety of education concepts, such as learning and information processing, critical thinking, presentation and writing skills, and computer literacy. Advocates of information literacy should acknowledge this embeddedness and not try to appropriate all related fields to create a grand, all-encompassing definition of information literacy. Instead, they should explore these relationships and plan for developing those skills and attitudes in students in collaboration with a variety of institutional stakeholders. Put another way, exploration of the definition of information literacy should not be a surrogate for the territorial battle over responsibility for teaching information literacy. The development of the definition should be an exercise of articulating educational goals in the broad context of general education.

To be fair, the authors of the *Standards,* in their introductory comments, do recognize that different disciplines may place greater emphasis on some aspects of the competencies than others. Missing from the *Standards* is a manual on how to use them to implement institutional programs. ACRL members intimately involved with the Association's work on this topic recognized this limitation and developed a web site entitled "Standards Toolkit" (ACRL, 2003b). The toolkit provides numerous suggestions on how to use the *Standards*. However, these suggestions are always within the *Standards'* construct of information literacy and provide little guidance on the need to define the concept at the campus level. In spite of this, practitioners have created different definitions for information literacy that they believe are appropriate to their institutions (e.g., Academic Senate for California Community Colleges, 1998; Hutchins et al., 2002).

This deep relationship among information literacy, critical thinking, learning theory, information processing, and computer literacy and the need for cooperative planning, brings to the fore the essential ingredient in the development of an effective information literacy program—classroom faculty-librarian collaboration. Since the early days of bibliographic instruction, the importance of collaboration with classroom faculty has been central to a library's program (Farber, 1999), and the essential nature of this collaboration is further emphasized by the case studies in this monograph. That collaboration has become even more important because the definition of information literacy, as presented in the *Standards,* anticipates the varying ways classroom faculty, librarians, and information technologists contribute to the development of the program. Librarians and others involved in first-year experience programs should keep the importance of collaboration in the forefront of their minds.

Characteristics of Programs of Information Literacy That Illustrate Best Practices: A Guideline

The *Standards* provide a comprehensive definition of information literacy that lead to the development of assessment focused on student learning outcomes. However, the *Standards* do not provide guidance in assessing the characteristics of an information literacy program. Nor do they provide answers to the overarching question, "Is an institution's information literacy program operating effectively?" They also do not answer many related questions about staffing, budgeting, administrative support, and management of the program. As a response to the perceived need for guidance in the development of an effective information literacy program, a committee, the Best Practices Project Team, was created within ACRL's Institute for Information Literacy. This committee intended to fill a gap in the tools available to those responsible for information literacy programs. Using the concepts of best practices and benchmarking as program assessment tools, the Project Team developed a document entitled *Characteristics of Programs of Information Literacy That Illustrate Best Practices: A Guideline* (ACRL, 2003a).

The Project Team used a Delphi method to gain input from the higher education community on those characteristics of information literacy programming that exemplify a quality program. The Delphi method is a recursive process of gaining input from a broad group of knowledgeable and/or interested people to define the scope and content of a concept or practice (ACRL, 2004; Doyle, 1993). Over a period of 18 months, the Project Team refined a statement of characteristics describing a quality information literacy program and then used the statement to develop application criteria for an invitational conference. Through the work of conference participants, a final draft of the *Characteristics* was developed and ultimately approved by the ACRL Board of Directors in June 2003 (ACRL, 2002, 2003a, 2004).

Several characteristics of quality programs are particularly relevant to first-year programs. They include adequate library staff, institutional support and planning, and attention to teaching styles for first-year students. The Project Team deliberately avoided ranking these various characteristics since no research evidence exists to suggest which characteristics (e.g., number of librarians, size of budget) are most critical to the quality of an information literacy program. In conference discussions, however, the universal response was that the number one predictor of success in information literacy programs is the quality of classroom faculty-librarian collaboration (Kirk, 2002). This collaboration is essential in first-year programs. As staff involved in programs develop their educational goals, librarians and classroom teachers need to work together to ensure that program activities will adequately address those goals and all participating staff understand the respective roles classroom faculty and librarians will play in implementing the program. As part of this understanding, classroom faculty need to know what research processes and resources students should be able to successfully carry out to complete course activities. This critical factor is reinforced throughout the case studies in this monograph.

Using Models of Information-Knowledge Transformation and Learning With Information Literacy

The definition of information literacy must be consistent with models of information seeking, learning, and information-knowledge transformation since they are each integral to the concept. Two papers (Marcum, 2002; Webber & Johnston, 2000) raise questions about the current definition of information literacy because, in their views, the definition does not adequately accommodate advances in the understanding of these related models. In exploring these concepts, Webber and Johnston probably have identified the most critical problem: "a lack of information on how students experience and define information literacy" (p. 391). This lack of empirical data on students' experiences means that much of the scholarly view of information literacy is based on theoretical models coming from a variety of research domains in learning theory, information processing, decision making, and other areas.

Kuhlthau's work on high school and college students' research experiences (Kuhlthau, 1985; Kuhlthau, Turock, George, & Belvin, 1990) exemplifies the importance of empirical data to understanding the nature of information literacy. Her work revealed that students' attitudes toward their research changes during the research process. This changing emotional state influences student behavior and the way they approach the research process. Therefore, the definition of information literacy should also take into account this shifting emotional status. Within the framework of the current *Standards,* a statement should be included acknowledging that information literate people understand a changing emotional status as a normal part of the research process and can develop mechanisms for preventing emotional status from inhibiting progress.

The work of Marcum (2002) and Webber and Johnston (2000) suggests the need for an even more extensive revision of the definition of information literacy. The traditional information-processing paradigm examined by Marcum suggests that humans receive information largely as noise that must be organized into structures as data and then fitted into a construct, i.e., knowledge. This paradigm suggests that information literacy must incorporate strategies for acquiring data and converting it into useful knowledge. Further, the traditional paradigm assumes that converting data into useful knowledge depends on expertise. In terms of information literacy, this implies a process that requires the development of increasing expertise in order to absorb more complex data. Marcum, in contrast to this traditional view, suggests that new paradigms of information processing do not require the prior development of expertise to absorb new data. Instead, new models provide for an interactive process through which a person, without prior knowledge, creates a knowledge structure and incorporates new information as it is acquired. In short, the researcher may recursively create and recreate meaning and structure (i.e., knowledge) as information is absorbed. A good overview of learning styles and learning theory is provided by Grassian and Kaplowitz (2001). Further, Macpherson (2004) introduces a new concept of information processing from her analysis of undergraduates' use of electronic databases. Practitioners working with first-year students may find this research, and others like it, helpful in developing students' information literacy skills.

In more practical terms, Webber and Johnston (2000) describe the unique nature of information processing. They believe an information literacy program should emphasize the development of reflective thinking rather than a prescription of certain behaviors. Extending King's (1993) concept of a teacher as a "guide on the side," information literacy instructors should coach students in the use of critical thinking and other general intellectual skills to process information found. For Johnston and Webber (2003), Bruce's (2000) relational approach is a more appropriate way to define information literacy than the behaviorist approach of the currently accepted definition. The relational approach grows out of an understanding of the actual experience of information literacy rather than from a prescribed set of behaviors.

The shifting perspectives within the information literacy community are similar to changes that occurred in the 1980s when bibliographic instruction shifted from teaching bibliographic research as a fixed sequential process to a dynamic problem-solving process (Kirk, 1999). The two shifts suggest that, in the initial stages of defining a new concept, the definition be as detailed and comprehensive as possible. In the current outcomes assessment climate, the definition should be stated in behavioral terms in order to make its outcomes measurable. Subsequently, as we learn more about the nature of the concept, it becomes more open-ended, incorporating an increasing number of contingencies and recognition of individual differences.

Contradiction Within the Information Literacy Paradigm

Pawley (2003) sees a basic contradiction in the current definition of information literacy between its purpose of providing students with the skills needed to be an effective participant in a free society (i.e., providing greater access) and its approach of using analysis of resource quality as a way of moderating the amount of information selected (i.e., limit the amount of material used). Pawley goes on to explore the origins of this contradiction, suggesting that those who are information literate should understand the ways in which the construction of information packages (e.g., encyclopedias and dictionaries) and scholarly discourse can control information-seeking or information-processing activities. In order to overcome this controlling phenomenon and remain consistent with the purpose of information literacy, Pawley suggests that, at its heart, information literacy education should be about helping students engage effectively in an "open communication system" (p. 440). For Pawley, information literacy is more than a set of tools and skills. It is also understanding the context and process by which information is shaped and how that shape is a reflection of one's view of the world. Pawley calls for a definition of information literacy that retains the tension between the use of conventions to evaluate the quality of information sources and the promise of freedom that comes with greater access as a result of better search skills. The highest level of information literacy is the ability to steer an effective path through the contradiction. This issue should be of particular concern to those teaching in a first-year program because it is so central to the challenge of helping students understand how to evaluate information resources.

Conclusion and a Call for Action

The discussion of a definition of information literacy, despite the high level of arcane academic hair-splitting and some authors' call for a discussion moratorium (e.g., Owusu-Ansah, 2003), is an important exercise and one that must be continued in order to better understand the nature of the enterprise in which we are engaged. For those involved in first-year programs, the responses can vary considerably. Some may respond with total confusion to what they perceive as mystifying jargon. Others may continue to oversimplify the skills involved in making sophisticated use of library resources. Despite the long evolution leading to the current concept of "information literacy," some first-year instructors still schedule "a visit to the library" where their students can walk through the building. These visits offer an orientation to the facility but do not have the goal of helping students take the developmentally appropriate next steps in strengthening their information literacy skills. Frequently, there is no library assignment integral to the goals of the course to provide practice in developing these skills. Hopefully, the discussion in this chapter will help faculty, administrators, and librarians define better information literacy programs for first-year students. The academic exercise of defining information literacy, however, is not the same as implementing a program of information literacy. In fact, defining information literacy is not necessarily the first step in developing a program, although an institutional definition of information literacy should emerge as part of program development (ACRL, 2004). In concluding his history of the concept and the recent elaborations on it, Owusu-Ansah (2003) expressed this sentiment when he called on:

> Academic librarians to develop some consensus on the desired structure and content of a program that is comprehensive enough to ensure the information literacy training of every college and university student, and to convince the entire college/university community of the viability and effectiveness of that program. (p. 226)

The academic library profession has developed mechanisms for reaching this consensus in the *Characteristics of Programs of Information Literacy That Illustrate Best Practices: A Guideline* (ACRL, 2003a). This document acknowledges that no single structure or body of content exists for an effective information literacy program. Instead, the *Characteristics* assume that important environmental factors will dictate the appropriate type of program. In first-year programs, these environmental factors, among others, will include the diversity of research experiences of new students, their ability to present an effective written or oral synthesis based on diverse information resources and their knowledge of information resources, and how to evaluate them. Practitioners in the field of information literacy programming are challenged to use all we know about the nature of the information seeking and usage behaviors to develop a program that helps students become more proficient researchers and users of information. The use of the *Characteristics* described by Hunt and Birks (2004) and the call for further research on student attitudes toward information literacy (Webber & Johnston, 2000) exemplify the kind of efforts that practitioners should undertake to meet this challenge. Developing a body of such studies will shed new light on the most effective ways of carrying out information literacy programs.

While individual institutions' faculty and academic professionals, including librarians, need to develop their information literacy programs, the larger professional community needs to advance the concept of information literacy by addressing the issues identified in this chapter. I propose the formation of a joint working group with representatives from ACRL and other education organizations, such as the National Resource Center for The First-Year Experience and Students in Transition, American Educational Research Association (AREA), Association for Library and Information Science Education (ALISE), Council of Independent Colleges (CIC), National Association of Independent Colleges and Universities (NAICU), National Association of State Universities and Land-Grant Colleges (NASULGC), National Council of Teachers of English (NCTE), and American Society for Information Science and Technology (ASIS&T). This broadly representative group will provide a mechanism for addressing a wide range of information literacy issues. Furthermore, such a body should generate credible results.

The working group should be charged to review the latest advances in research on learning, information access and information-knowledge processing, and critical thinking. Based on that review, the *Information Literacy Competency Standards for Higher Education* should be revised. Furthermore, the working group should combine the *Standards* with the *Best Practices and Assessment of Information Literacy Programs* document to create a comprehensive guide for information literacy program development. Such a guide should include practical approaches to program and outcomes assessment. This joint effort will help infuse the field of information literacy with concepts from the underlying research fields and help develop a broader base of support for information literacy planning from all parts of the higher education community. By bringing the two existing documents on information literacy in higher education into a new complementary relationship, the higher education community will create tools that aid individual institutions in assessing both the outcomes of information literacy programs and their programs' efficacy.

Acknowledgment

The author gratefully acknowledges the contributions of Elizabeth McMahon and the volume editors in my preparation of this chapter.

References

Academic Senate for California Community Colleges. (1998). *Information competency in the California community colleges.* Sacramento, CA: Author. (ERIC Document Reproduction Service No. ED 421 191)

American Library Association. (1989). *Presidential committee on information literacy: Final report.* Retrieved May 11, 2005, from http://www.ala.org/ala/acrl/acrlpubs/whitepapers/presidential.htm

Arp, L. (1990). Information literacy or bibliographic instruction: Semantics or philosophy? *RQ, 30*(1), 46-49

Association of College and Research Libraries (ACRL). (1987). Model statement of objectives for academic bibliographic instruction: Draft revision. *College & Research Libraries News, 48*(5), 256-261.

Association of College and Research Libraries (ACRL). (2000). *Information literacy comptency standards for higher education.* Chicago, IL: Author. Retrieved December 8, 2005, from http://www.ala.org/ala/acrl/acrlstandards/informationliteracycompetency.htm

Association of College and Research Libraries (ACRL). (2002). *ACRL best practices in information literacy invitational conference.* Chicago, IL: Author. Retrieved June 20, 2005 from http://www.earlham.edu/~libr/iil/conference.pdf

Association of College and Research Libraries (ACRL). (2003a). *Characteristics of programs of information literacy that illustrate best practices: A guideline.* Chicago, IL: Author. Retrieved June 20, 2005, from http://www.ala.org/ala/acrl/acrlstandards/characteristics.htm

Association of College and Research Libraries (ACRL). (2003b). *Using standards – Assessment.* Chicago, IL: Author. Retrieved July 15, 2005, from http://www.ala.org/ala/acrl/acrlissues/acrlinfolit/infolitstandards/using/assessment.htm

Association of College and Research Libraries (ACRL). (2004). *Best practices and assessment of information literacy programs.* Retrieved July 30, 2005, from http://www.ala.org/acrl/acrlissues/acrlinfolit/professactivity/iil/bestpractices/bestpracticesdescription.htm

Avery, E. F. (2003). *Assessing student learning outcomes for information literacy instruction in academic institutions.* Chicago, IL: Association of College and Research Libraries.

Ayersman, D. J., Ackermann, E. C., & Zisman, P. M. (1996). Creating a computer competency requirement for Mary Washington College students. *Association of Small Computer Users in Education (ASCUE) Summer Conference Proceedings (29th)*, North Myrtle Beach, SC. (ERIC Document Reproduction Service No. ED 405 810)

Behrens, S. J. (1994). A conceptual analysis and historical overview of information literacy. *College & Research Libraries, 55*(4), 309-322.

Bordonaro, K. (2004) *National survey of student engagement / assessing information literacy outcomes.* Buffalo: Canisius College. Retrieved December 21, 2004, from http://www2.canisius.edu/canhp/canlib/NSSE.pdf

Breivik, P. S. (1978). Leadership, management, and the teaching library. *Library Journal, 103*(18), 2045-48.

Bruce, C. S. (1997). *The seven faces of information literacy.* Adelaide, Australia: Auslib Press.

Bruce, C. S. (2000). Information literacy research: Dimensions of the emerging collective consciousness. *Australian Academic and Research Libraries, 31*(2), 91-109.

Council of Independent Colleges. (2004, Winter/Spring). *CIC endorses ACRL literacy standards.* Retrieved June 20, 2005, from http://www.cic.org/publications/independent/online/winterspring2004/cic_endorses.htm

Doyle, C. S. (1993). The Delphi method as a qualitative assessment tool for development of outcome measures for information literacy. *School Library Media Annual, 11,* 132-144.

Educational Testing Service. (2005). *ICT literacy assessment overview.* Retrieved October 16, 2005, from http://www.ets.org/portal/site/ets/menuitem.1488512ecfd5b8849a77b13bc3921509?vgnextoid=fde9af5e44df4010VgnVCM10000022f95190RCRD&vgnextchannel=69d246f1674f4010VgnVCM10000022f95190RCRD

Farber, E. I. (1999). College libraries and the teaching/learning process: A 25-year reflection. *Journal of Academic Librarianship, 25*(3), 171-177.

Gorman, M. (1981). The new "teaching library." *American Libraries, 12*(11), 670-671.

Grassian, E. S., & Kaplowitz, J. R. (2001). *Information literacy instruction: Theory and practice.* New York: Neal-Schuman.

Guskin, A. E., Stoffle, C. J., & Boisse, J. A. (1979). The academic library as a teaching library: A role for the 1980s. *Library Trends, 28,* 281-296.

Hunt, F., & Birks, J. (2004). Best practices in information literacy. *portal: Libraries and the Academy, 4*(1), 27-39.

Hutchins E. O., Fister, B., & MacPherson, K. (2002). Changing landscapes, enduring values: making the transition from bibliographic instruction to information literacy. *Journal of Library Administration, 36*(1/2), 3-19.

Johnston, B., & Webber, S. (2003). Information literacy in higher education: A review and case study. *Studies in Higher Education, 28*(3), 335-352.

King, A. (1993). From sage on the stage to guide on the side. *College Teaching, 41*(1), 30-35.

Kirk, T. G. (1999). Course-related bibliographic instruction in the '90s. *Reference Services Review, 27*(3), 235-241.

Kirk, T. G. (2002, June 11-13). Unpublished notes from ACRL Institute for Information Literacy's Best Practices Project Conference, Atlanta, GA.

Klavano, A. M., & Kulleseid, E. R. (1995). Bibliographic instruction: Renewal and transformation in one academic library. *Reference Librarian, 51/52,* 359-383.

Kuh, G. D. (2004). *The national survey of student engagement: Conceptual framework and overview of psychometric properties.* Retrieved December 21, 2004, from http://nsse.iub.edu/2003_annual_report/pdf/NSSE_2003_Framework.pdf

Kuh, G. D., & Gonyea, R. M. (2003). The role of the academic library in promoting student engagement in learning. *College & Research Libraries, 64*(4), 256-83. Retrieved June 20, 2005, from http://www.ala.org/ala/acrl/acrlpubs/crljournal/backissues2003b/july-month/candrljuly2003.htm

Kuhlthau, C. C. (1985). A process approach to library skills instruction: An investigation into the design of the library search process. *School Library Media Quarterly, 13*(1), 35-40.

Kuhlthau, C. C., Turock, B. J., George, M. W., & Belvin, R .J. (1990). Validating a model of the search process: A comparison of academic, public, and school library users. *Library and Information Science Research, 12*(1), 5-31.

Lindauer, B. G. (1998). Defining and measuring the library's impact on campuswide outcomes. *College & Research Libraries, 59*(6), 546-570.

Lindauer, B. G., Arp, L., & Woodard, B. S. (2004). The three arenas of information literacy assessment. *Reference & User Services Quarterly, 44*(2), 122-130.

Lyman, P. (2001). Information literacy. *Liberal Education, 87*(1), 28- 37.

Macpherson, K. (2004). An information processing model of undergraduate electronic database information retrieval. *Journal of the American Society for Information Science and Technology, 55*(4), 333-347.

Marcum, J. W. (2002). Rethinking information literacy. *The Library Quarterly, 72*(1), 1-26.

Mark, A. E., & Boruff-Jones, P. D. (2004). Information literacy and student engagement: What the national survey of student engagement reveals about your campus. *College & Research Libraries, 64*(6), 480-494. Retrieved December 8, 2005, from http://www.ala.org/ala/acrl/acrlpubs/crljournal/backissues2003b/nov03/mark.pdf

Owusu-Ansah, E. K. (2003). Information literacy and the academic library: A critical look at a concept and the controversies surrounding it. *Journal of Academic Librarianship 29*(4), 219-230.

Pawley, C. (2003). Information literacy: A contradictory coupling. *Library Quarterly, 73*(4), 422-450.

Project SAILS (2005). *Project SAILS: Overview.* Retrieved December 6, 2005, from http://www.projectsails.org/sails/overview.php?page=aboutSAILS

Ratteray, O. M. T. (2002). Information literacy in self-study and accreditation. *The Journal of Academic Librarianship, 28*(6), 368-375.

Ratteray, O. M. T. (2004). The strategic triad supporting information literacy assessment. In P. Hernon & R. E. Dugan (Eds.), *Outcomes assessment in higher education: Views and perspectives* (pp. 135-148). Westport, CT: Libraries Unlimited.

Reffell, P., & Whitworth, A. (2002). Information fluency: Critically examining IT education. *New Library World 103*(11/12), 427-435.

Ridgeway, T. (1990). Information literacy: An introductory reading list. *College & Research Libraries News, 51*(7), 645-648.

Shapiro, J. J., & Hughes, S. K. (1996). Information literacy as a liberal art: Enlightenment proposals for a new curriculum. *Educom Review, 31*(2), 31-35. Retrieved on May 11, 2005, from http://www.educause.edu/pub/er/review/reviewarticles/31231.html

Snavely, L., & Cooper, N. (1997). The information literacy debate. *The Journal of Academic Librarianship, 23*(1), 9-14.

Stoffle, C. J., Guskin, A. E., & Boisse, J. A. (1984). Teaching, research, and service: The academic library's role. In T. G. Kirk (Ed.), *Increasing the teaching role of academic libraries* (pp. 3-14). San Francisco: Jossey-Bass.

Tucker, J. M. (1984). Emerson's library legacy: Concepts of bibliographic instruction. In T. G. Kirk (Ed.), *Increasing the teaching role of academic libraries* (pp. 15-24). San Francisco: Jossey-Bass.

Webber, S., & Johnston B. (2000). Conceptions of information literacy: New perspectives and implications. *Journal of Information Science, 26*(6), 381-397.

Williamson, J. G. (1971). Swarthmore College's "teaching library" proposals. *Drexel Library Quarterly, 7*(3/4), 203-215.

Young, J. R. (2004, November 12). Testing service to unveil an assessment of computer and information literacy. *Chronicle of Higher Education,* p. A33.

Zurkowski, P. (1974). *The information service environment : Relations and priorities.* Washington, DC: National Commission on Libraries and Information Science. (ERIC Document Reproduction Service No. ED 100 391)

Chapter 2

Engaging Students in the First College Year: Why Academic Librarians Matter

George D. Kuh, Polly D. Boruff-Jones, & Amy E. Mark

> Because individual effort and involvement are the critical determinants of college impact, institutions should focus on the ways they can shape their academic, interpersonal, and extracurricular offerings to encourage student engagement. (Pascarella & Terenzini, 2005, p. 602)

There is a lot of buzz these days about student success. It is an umbrella term for a host of desirable college outcomes including achievement, satisfaction, a variety of learning and personal development results, and degree attainment. As college costs rise and participation in postsecondary education becomes ever more important, the federal government, parents, and prospective and current students, among others, are asking tough questions about what they can reasonably expect an institution of higher education to contribute to student success. As Pascarella and Terenzini (2005) concluded from their most recent synthesis of the student development research, one of the more promising approaches to improving undergraduate education is for institutions to more consistently engage students in educational activities with demonstrated effectiveness.

It is especially important that students be exposed to effective educational practices at the beginning of college in order to develop a solid foundation for success (Kuh, 2001b, 2005; Upcraft, Gardner, & Barefoot, 2005). For various reasons, many first-year students are ill-prepared to succeed academically. Among them are some who are the first in their families to go to college and who lack tacit knowledge about what college will be like. Other traditional-age students are not developmentally "ready" to do serious academic work. For these and a host of other reasons—most of which they cannot control—students struggle academically and socially. Indeed, some sizeable fraction is figuratively lost at sea. They see few markers on their daily horizons that direct them toward familiar activities, allow them to build on their strengths, give them confidence to try new things, and motivate them to invest the necessary time and energy to meet academic challenges. These are among the behaviors associated with success in college. But for many reasons, large numbers of students do not engage in them often or well enough, though they are capable of doing so. The result? They leave college. Many never return to try again. It does not have to be this way. Along with their faculty and student affairs colleagues, academic librarians can play a key role in changing the culture of college campuses to enhance student and institutional performance.

In this chapter, we address this challenge by discussing how librarians can help establish the conditions that enhance student engagement and success in the first year of college. The chapter is divided into three parts. The first part is devoted to the student engagement construct—what it is, where it came from, and the empirical basis for its importance to student learning and success. Next, we offer examples of how librarians at strong performing institutions use their informed perspectives and expertise to promote student engagement and success. Finally, we review some ways that librarians can collaborate with faculty and staff to use engaging pedagogies in their quest to teach information literacy competencies to first-year students.

Student Engagement: The Right Idea at the Right Time

Where do first-year students get their first impression of the university library and librarians? On some campuses, it may be during student orientation. On others, it may be in the classroom when the students encounter their first library instruction session or perhaps not until the students' first visit to the library to do research. All of these interactions provide the opportunity for librarians to develop a relationship with first-year students that can last throughout the students' academic careers. Equally important, librarians can collaborate with classroom faculty to teach students how to take advantage of their institution's resources for learning and personal development. A key first step is to encourage students to engage in educationally productive activities.

The Engagement Construct

The student engagement premise is deceptively simple, even self-evident: The more students do something, the more proficient they become (Kuh, 2003). That is, the more students study a particular subject, the more they learn about it. The more students practice a particular skill such as reading, writing, and problem solving, the more adept they become at those activities. We have been aware of the importance of student engagement for many years (Astin, 1977, 1984; Chickering, 1969, 1974; Feldman & Newcomb, 1969; Kuh, 1981; Pace, 1982). The link between student engagement and learning, personal development, and other indicators of success has been corroborated countless times (Banta & Associates, 1993; Ewell & Jones, 1996). Moreover, engaging in effective educational practices seems to benefit all students to about the same degree (Kuh, 2003; National Survey of Student Engagement, 2002). Thus, in the absence of direct evidence of student learning, student engagement data are "process indicators" or proxies for learning. Among the better-known process indicators are the seven "good practices" in undergraduate educations, such as setting high expectations and providing prompt feedback (Chickering & Gamson, 1987).

The conceptual underpinning for the current use of the student engagement construct is Pace's (1982) "quality of effort" concept, which Astin (1984) subsequently extended with his "theory of involvement." Kuh, Schuh, Whitt, and Associates (1991) illustrated how selected colleges and universities were able to leverage student engagement outside the classroom with their "involving colleges" study. The widely used National Survey of Student Engagement (NSSE) has popularized student engagement (Kuh, 2001a, 2003). Even so, many colleges and universities have not yet created the conditions that research shows to be effective educational practice.

Student engagement has two critical features. The first is student-driven—the amount of time and effort students put into their studies and other educationally purposeful activities. The second is institution-driven—how a school deploys its resources and organizes the curriculum, other learning opportunities, and support services to induce students to participate in activities that lead to the experiences and outcomes that constitute student success (i.e., persistence, satisfaction, learning, and graduation).

When used appropriately, active and collaborative learning pedagogies are especially powerful for engaging students. Collaborative learning strategies set the stage for substantive peer interactions that, in turn, can stimulate individual and group learning as students work together to seek answers and solve problems. Students are often motivated to work harder and tend to learn more in the company of peers.

Another key to student success is the *nature* and *frequency* of contact with agents of socialization, including librarians and faculty members. For some forms of interaction, "occasional" contact with faculty members and librarians may be enough to assist students in understanding what they need to do to succeed. As an example, four of the six behaviors contributing to NSSE's student-faculty interaction cluster of effective educational practices are of this kind: (a) discussing grades and assignments, (b) discussing career plans, (c) working with a faculty member outside of class on a committee or project, and (d) doing research with a faculty member. For most students, doing the first three of these once or twice a semester is probably good enough. That is, "occasionally" discussing career plans with a faculty member is enough for students to see the relevance of their studies to a self-sufficient, satisfying life after college. Collaborating with a faculty member or librarian on a research project just once during college could be a life-altering experience as could working side-by-side with librarians as a work-study employee. The other two activities included in the student-faculty interaction cluster are getting prompt feedback and discussing ideas presented in readings or class discussions. Here, it is plausible that the more frequent the behavior, the better.

Finally, student engagement is both a means and an end. That is, it serves as a proxy for collegiate quality by reflecting the degree to which students take advantage of their institutions' learning opportunities. The very act of being engaged is also an important outcome of college. Taking part in educationally purposeful activities builds the foundation for acquiring and integrating other essential skills, such as learning how to learn, being able to identify problems independently, developing and testing potential solutions, and synthesizing and applying information. More to the point, being able to evaluate critically and discern the quality of information is, for example, a vitally important skill that all students must master. Thus, during college, students should participate meaningfully in a variety of educationally purposeful activities that enables them to develop the habits of the mind that increase their capacity for continuous learning.

Promoting Student Engagement: What Librarians Can Do

Some colleges and universities have organized their educational resources to foster high levels of student success, as we learned in the Documenting Effective Educational Practices (DEEP) project, a two-year study of 20 four-year institutions that had higher than predicted graduation rates and higher than predicted scores on the National Survey of Student Engagement (Kuh, Kinzie, Schuh, Whitt, & Associates, 2005). During this project, we observed a variety of ways that librarians can collaborate with their colleagues to make important contributions to their institutions' environments for learning and educational effectiveness. To put this discussion in context, it is necessary to understand some of the key factors and conditions these institutions have in common.

Creating Pathways to Engagement

One noteworthy characteristic of Project DEEP institutions is that they create clear pathways to engagement to help students more easily find their way to educational resources and become involved in educationally purposeful activities. In this regard, these institutions do two things very well to channel student time and energy toward effective educational activities. First, they teach students early on how to take advantage of institutional resources for their learning. Second, they make available to students *what* they need *when* they need it.

With regard to the former, these institutions combine intentionally crafted policies and practices to teach students, long before they arrive on campus, what they can expect from librarians, faculty, staff, and other students and what they themselves need to do to thrive. They arrange for students to participate in events and activities upon matriculation to help them effectively navigate their new environment and make meaning of their experiences. And they monitor student performance in the crucial first weeks and months of college, giving students plenty of early feedback about the nature and quality of their work.

Minimizing Library Anxiety

To ensure students take advantage of these resources, these colleges sometimes *require* certain students to participate in activities, such as summer advising and orientation, as well as substantive fall welcome week events. Faculty and staff members identify at-risk students and assiduously follow up with proactive advising and other mechanisms, enabling students to mark their progress over the course of the first year.

College and university libraries can be intimidating structures for many first-year students (Mellon, 1986). Bostick (1993) reported "a tendency for students to view library staff, particularly librarians, as intimidating and aloof" (p. 6). To overcome and counteract these preconceptions, it is important for librarians to reach out to put students at ease. Involvement in classroom instruction gives librarians visibility and helps them connect to students. Many librarians know a good deal about how students spend their research time, yet they are an underused educational resource. DEEP colleges take advantage of librarians' expertise by sewing them into redundant safety nets that help enrich the student experience and promote student success. Academic librarians, along with student affairs staff, support staff, and classroom faculty work together to limit the number of students who might fall through the cracks.

For example, the senior capstone project at California State University (CSU) Monterey Bay is, according to some classroom faculty members, comparable to master's degree level work. One alumna characterized the project as both a "challenge and nightmare." Another called it her "defining academic experience as an undergraduate." How do undergraduate students get through it? The university begins preparing students in the first-year seminar by acquainting them with the variety of resources that are available to assist with the senior capstone. Especially important is for first-year students to come to know librarians as both sources of academic support and information they can draw on during the course of their studies. In the junior year, librarians help instruct the required ProSeminar, helping students develop research questions to be pursued in their senior-year capstone project. The capstone project itself is divided into two semesters of work. Many students use the first semester to brainstorm with their peers, faculty members, and librarians to further flesh out the topic and approach. The second semester is dedicated to completing the project. Writing tutors are on hand to help.

The scaffolding provided by librarians at CSU Monterey Bay helps allay some of the fears associated with a major project, but exploring new purposes and physical structures for the library may also reduce anxiety. The library, as a physical space, continues to be important to student learning and development. For example, when Wofford College relocated its Writing Center to the second floor of the library, use of the center "jumped dramatically" as students had ready access to library resources and computers for research and word processing.

The University of Michigan has made extensive efforts to connect life in campus residences to academics and the intellectual life of the campus. Along with a library in every hall, students also have access to an academic advisor, minority peer advisors, and technology assistance dedicated to their residence.

The Evergreen State College introduced a novel initiative that has now become an annual tradition—classroom faculty member and librarian exchanging roles. Each year, a classroom faculty member rotates into the library staff and performs many regular library-related tasks, such as working the reference desk, helping build and maintain the library collection in their areas of expertise, as well as other areas, and conducting workshops for various groups on campus. By knowing more about the librarian's work, faculty members can become important ambassadors to students and others. In turn, a librarian assumes the role of a classroom instructor in order to better understand the challenges, responsibilities, and needs of this part of the educational team. This also allows librarians to see and interact with students in different settings in order to instruct them in how to access information and develop related information literacy skills.

Involving Librarians in First-Year Seminars

One of the more effective ways to teach information literacy skills systematically to large numbers of students early in their college careers is to include librarians on the instructional team for first-year seminars. The Indiana University-Purdue University Indianapolis first-year seminar is taught by an instructional team that includes a classroom instructor, librarian, academic advisor, and student mentor. Through the instructional team, students become familiar with the subject librarian for their major area of study. This connection often continues through the undergraduate years with students contacting the same librarian for reference and research assistance in later courses.

At Wheaton College in Massachusetts, the first-year seminar (FYS) required of all students is staffed by a classroom faculty member, administrator mentor, librarian, and two preceptors who are junior- or senior-level students. All serve as advisors to FYS students. The classroom faculty member is the student's academic advisor throughout her or his first year, or until the student selects an academic major. Throughout orientation, new students meet daily with their preceptors either individually or in their advising teams. After orientation and throughout the students' first year, the preceptors work with the advisor and an administrative mentor to help students develop the academic and life skills they need. Wheaton students say that FYS prepares them to do college-level work, instills a sense of confidence and competence to meet academic challenges, and fosters meaningful relationships with peers, faculty, librarians, and staff. The team librarian plays a key role by acclimating students to library services and helping them find and effectively use information and other library resources to complete their research projects and assignments.

The first-year course at the University of Texas at El Paso (UTEP) (titled "Seminar in Critical Inquiry," though everyone there refers to it as UNIV 1301) is designed to facilitate students' transition to college by luring them into discovering the rewards of deep learning, or the ability to not only obtain substantive information but also to grasp the underlying meaning of the information (Biggs, 1987, 2003; Entwistle, 1981; Ramsden, 2003; Tagg, 2003). Students who engage in deep learning activities tend to earn higher grades, are more satisfied, and retain and integrate information more effectively (Biggs,1989; Ramsden; Tagg; Van Rossum & Schenk, 1984). The UTEP instructional team consists of a classroom faculty member, peer leader, and librarian, who emphasize active-learning techniques including open forums and group projects. All UNIV 1301 classes are small, about 25 students per section, making it possible for students to work more closely with others, get to know their classmates in a setting that values learning, and become familiar with the campus and its resources. UNIV 1301 classroom faculty members, along with the peer leaders, meet one-on-one with all students in their class twice during the fall semester to discuss their academic performance and are expected to inquire about student progress in the spring, as well.

Valuing Out-of-Class Interactions

Much of the literature on engaging students through meaningful encounters with librarians primarily focuses on learning communities, campus involvement, classroom sessions, and one-on-one meetings. Research shows that frequent, informal contact with both classroom faculty and other university support staff contributes to college success and to intellectual and emotional development in general (Regalado, 2003; Schackelford, Thompson, & James, 1999; Umbach & Wawrzynski, 2005). Frequent, sustained contact seems to work best in terms of keeping students engaged. Librarians can help students adjust to college life by orienting them to the library and library resources or just from personal contacts and close cooperation with classroom faculty members. Also, some evidence suggests that the library experiences of undergraduates are positively related to "select educationally purposeful activities, such as using computing and information technology and interacting with faculty members" (Kuh & Gonyea, 2003, p. 270). Spending time with students—in the classroom or at the reference desk—is essential in order to understand how students find, retrieve, and use information for their course and research needs (Manuel, 2002). These experiences are indispensable for selecting appropriate approaches to teaching information literacy.

Approaches to Teaching Information Literacy Skills to First-Year Students

Some evidence suggests that when institutions emphasize the importance of information literacy and encourage students to use computers and other information resources, students tend to report increased information literacy (Kuh & Gonyea, 2003). Furthermore, we believe that librarians can enhance information literacy among first-year students by collaborating with classroom instructors and student affairs staff members.

A key approach to introducing information literacy concepts to first-year students is fostering collaborations between librarians and classroom faculty to develop assignments leading to more effective use of information resources and technology throughout the student's academic career. Librarians and classroom faculty members working together to create class activities that incorporate library and other information resources, while supporting the content learning goals of the course, may be more effective than activities that either librarians or classroom faculty members design independently. For example, librarians likely know more about recent relevant acquisitions and resources. Yet, classroom faculty members may know more about how these resources support course goals. Similar collaborative efforts could include academic advisors and student mentors for first-year courses in offering additional support to faculty and students.

Because librarians interact with first-year students both in and outside the classroom, they come into contact with them in different venues on a variety of topics and issues. Through these contacts, librarians can introduce new college students to resources and information literacy concepts required for students' academic success. Librarians can become a resource to whom students return repeatedly, thus increasing the benefit of interacting with a key agent of socialization as they learn to navigate the college environment (Jacobson & Mark, 2000).

Many of the same educational activities that NSSE shows are positively correlated with student engagement, such as active and collaborative learning and student interactions with classroom faculty, can be incorporated into library information literacy initiatives easily and effectively. One can draw parallels between many of the NSSE questions and the Association of College and Research Libraries' (2000) *Information Literacy Competency Standards for Higher Education*. For example, survey questions intended to measure activities associated with active and collaborative learning asked how often students asked questions in class, contributed to class discussions, made a class presentation, or worked with other students outside of class to prepare class assignments. Mark and Boruff-Jones (2003) contend that, at a minimum, each of these questions relates to Standard 4 that defines "the information literate student" as someone who "individually or as a member of a group, uses information effectively to accomplish a specific purpose." By identifying the relationships between NSSE questions and the specific performance indicators and learning outcomes linked with each information literacy standard, librarians can use the NSSE results for their campus to identify areas of weak student engagement that may be addressed by concentrating information literacy instruction efforts on the corresponding standards, performance indicators, and learning outcomes (Mark & Boruff-Jones). For example, if first-year students score low on the questions regarding class presentations and working with other students to prepare class assignments, indicating that they participated infrequently in these activities, the librarian and classroom faculty might develop a group research project and presentation assignment that incorporates performance indicators and learning outcomes from the corresponding ACRL *Information Literacy Competency Standards* in order to strengthen student engagement in those areas.

More effective than one-time classroom visits for library instruction is incorporating meaningful information literacy instruction into the curriculum, using library-related assignments in first-year courses designed through collaboration with classroom instructors (Jacobson & Mark, 2000; Spence, 2004). Successful college-level research requires the use of academic resources, such as subscription databases, and developing the capacity to discern the differences in the quality of information found using scholarly library resources versus that found using an open web search engine. First-year students must first master the foundational skills of distinguishing between types of information sources, formulating search queries, and using reference sources (in any format) before acquiring more complex research competencies such as evaluating resources and using discipline-specific materials (Jacobson & Mark). This foundation cannot be laid in one class session but may be accomplished during multiple interactions in a first-year course.

Adapting Instructional Methods to Different Learning Styles

Dalrymple (2002) found that most librarians believe that learning style theory provides a useful conceptual approach to understanding and addressing differences among students. Well over half of the respondents to a survey expressed interest in learning more about how to use learning styles in their work, but they do not always act on this interest. According to Bell and Shank (2004), many academic librarians "are woefully deficient in their knowledge of how learning takes place, how structures for effective learning are designed, and how learning outcomes are assessed" (p. 3). For librarians to engage students more effectively, they must not only concentrate on content but also become familiar with and use instructional design concepts and pedagogies that take students' different learning styles into account.

Active and collaborative learning. A welcome trend in teaching is the shift from using the lecture as the dominant pedagogical approach to creating ways for more student responsibility for learning. Engaged, active, cooperative, constructive, and collaborative learning all are based on the idea that deep, meaningful learning requires more active involvement from students (Tagg, 2003). In addition, active and collaborative learning appeals to Generation Y—the current cohort of undergraduates (Stamatoplos, 2000). Students interviewed about a brainstorming exercise and collaborative learning in the library "liked participating, rather than merely watching or listening to a teacher, or reading from a book or handouts" (Stamatoplos). Also, librarians are well-advised to promote collaborative strategies because Gen Yers usually find peers more credible than teachers (Manuel, 2002).

Using Technology to Engage Students

To engage Gen Y or NextGen students more effectively, librarians should focus on how these students learn. One characteristic of NextGens, for example, is that the distinction between formats is not important (Abram & Luther, 2004). To this group, "Information is information and NextGens see little difference in credibility or entertainment value between print and media formats" (Abram & Luther, p. 34). To help students make distinctions between formats, librarians can show them how to distinguish between book and article citations and spend some time involving students in evaluating the content and validity of a variety of online sources such as library subscription databases and e-journals, general web sources, and open-source scholarly articles. Librarians can engage students through technology in three ways: (a) meeting Generation Y or NextGen students wherever they are physically, (b) using campus management systems to engage students with library resources, and (c) incorporating instructional and web site design more effectively in their presentations.

NextGens "expect information and entertainment to be available to them whenever they need it and wherever they are" (Abram & Luther, 2004, p. 35). Therefore, librarians need to incorporate the interactive technologies with which NextGens are familiar (e.g., laptops and Blackberries) into their teaching. NextGens play games collaboratively, use instant message features, take part in chat rooms, and have virtual classes. They are used to multi-tasking in the company of others. Academic librarians must adapt to these students by increasing real-time reference assistance and other creative ways of incorporating collaboration into reference services. One way might be to participate with a specific class when the students are required to use online discussion boards through classroom management systems. Another simple way of collaborating with students outside the classroom is to give them a librarian's e-mail address and encourage them to send electronic drafts, sources of which they are unsure, and other questions that crop up during the research process.

Librarians may also engage students by using course management systems (e.g., Blackboard) and other technologies to link to library resources and to create subject guides for specific courses (Coates, 2005; Reeb & Gibbons, 2004). Through course management systems, libraries can bring tutorials and other relevant information right into the classroom. Also, by linking online tutorials to the course, students are more likely to use time outside class to gain information literacy skills. Also, such systems mean that librarians are not tied to using class time for basic library instruction.

NextGens grew up playing video games and, as a result, prefer content-rich web pages as opposed to navigating the table-of-contents style web sites of which librarians are so fond (Abram & Luther, 2004). To keep students engaged, library-instruction web sites need to resemble the exploratory and discovery-oriented features of popular games. For example, the Southampton Institute Library made considerable effort, when re-designing their web site, to incorporate theory relating to user interface design, learning styles, and creative thinking with the goal of engaging students through multiple ways of exploring and discovering information resources on the library web site. The site design used a less formal navigation approach based on the metaphor of physical space and playful exploration (Collinson & Williams, 2004).

Drawing on techniques from behavioral, cognitive, and constructivist theories, instructional design is a growing area of information technology, with many campuses dedicating staff solely to assist faculty with improving the design and delivery of instruction (Bell & Shank, 2004). Often instructional design staff positions are housed in institutional teaching excellence offices and are readily available for consultations. Working together, librarians and instructional designers can combine their skills and knowledge of first-year students to draft assignments and other experiences that address dimensions of information literacy that students need to develop further.

Recommendations

Librarians would do well to connect with students in the early days of their first academic term to help them in the initial development of the research and information literacy skills and competencies they need to succeed in college. In addition, such personal connections establish rapport with students and contribute to a supportive campus environment, both of which appear to have salutary effects on student engagement and success. Through presentations in first-year orientation programs, team teaching in first-year seminars, and other collaborations with faculty and students, librarians can put themselves in a position to help students acquire information literacy skills through systematic integration into the curriculum.

Efforts to teach information literacy to first-year students will be more effective if librarians incorporate a variety of appropriate engaging pedagogies that complement the needs, interests, and learning styles of the current generation of undergraduate students. Librarians cannot do this important work alone. They must collaborate with classroom faculty to design assignments that require students to become familiar with information technology and with student affairs colleagues who have ongoing contact with students outside the classroom. In this way, libraries and librarians will become resources that students will use repeatedly.

References

Abram, S., & Luther, J. (2004). Born with the chip. *Library Journal, 129*(8), 34-38. Retrieved April 19, 2005, from http://www.libraryjournal.com/article/CA411572.html

Association of College and Research Libraries. (2000). *Information literacy competency standards for higher education.* Chicago, IL: Author. Retrieved July 14, 2005, from http://www.ala.org/ala/acrl/acrlstandards/informationliteracycompetency.htm

Astin, A. W. (1977). *Four critical years.* San Francisco: Jossey-Bass.

Astin, A. W. (1984). Student involvement: A developmental theory for higher education. *Journal of College Student Personnel, 25*(4), 297-308.

Banta, T. W., & Associates. (1993). *Making a difference: Outcomes of a decade of assessment in higher education.* San Francisco: Jossey-Bass.

Bell, S. J., & Shank, J. (2004). *The blended librarian: A manifesto for redefining the role of the academic librarian for 21st century higher education.* Paper presented as part of an ACRL/TLT Group Online Seminar.

Biggs, J. B. (1987). *Student approaches to learning and studying.* Hawthorn, Victoria: Australian Council for Educational Research.

Biggs, J. B. (1989). Approaches to the enhancement of tertiary teaching. *Higher Education Research and Development, 8,* 7-25.

Biggs, J. B. (2003). *Teaching for quality learning at university.* Buckingham: Open University Press.

Bostick, S. L. (1993). The development and validation of the library anxiety scale. In M. E. Murfin & J. B. Whitlach (Eds.), *Research in reference effectiveness* (pp. 1-7). Chicago: American Library Association, Reference and Adult Services Division.

Chickering, A. W. (1969). *Education and identity.* San Francisco: Jossey-Bass.

Chickering, A. W. (1974). *Commuting versus residential students: Overcoming educational inequities of living off campus.* San Francisco: Jossey-Bass.

Chickering, A. W., & Gamson, Z. F. (1987). Seven principles for good practice in undergraduate education. *AAHE Bulletin, 39*(7), 3-7.

Coates, H. (2005). Leveraging LMS to enhance campus-based student engagement. *Educause Quarterly, 28*(1), 66-68.

Collinson, T., & Williams, A. (2004). The alternative library. *Aslib Proceedings, 56*(3), 137-143.

Dalrymple, C. (2002). Perceptions and practices of learning styles in library instruction. *College & Research Libraries, 63*(3), 261-273.

Entwistle, N. J (1981). *Styles of learning and teaching: An integrated outline of educational psychology for students, teachers and lecturers.* Chichester: Wiley.

Ewell, P. T., & Jones, D. P. (1996). *Indicators of "good practice" in undergraduate education: A handbook for development and implementation.* Boulder, CO: National Center for Higher Education Management Systems.

Feldman, K. A., & Newcomb, T. A. (1969). *The impact of college on students.* San Francisco: Jossey-Bass.

Jacobson, T., & Mark, B. L. (2000). Separating wheat from chaff: Helping first-year students become information savvy. *Journal of General Education, 49*(4), 256-278. Retrieved April 20, 2005, from Project Muse database.

Kuh, G. D. (1981). *Indices of quality in the undergraduate experience.* Washington, DC: American Association for Higher Education.

Kuh, G. D. (2001a). Assessing what really matters to student learning. *Change, 33*(3), 10-17, 66.

Kuh, G. D. (2001b). College students today: Why we can't leave serendipity to chance. In P. Altbach, P. Gumport, & B. Johnstone (Eds.), *In defense of the American university* (pp. 277-303). Baltimore: The Johns Hopkins University Press.

Kuh, G. D. (2003). What we're learning about student engagement from NSSE. *Change, 35*(2), 24-32.

Kuh, G. D. (2005). Student engagement in the first year of college. In M. L. Upcraft, J. N. Gardner, & B. O. Barefoot (Eds.), *Challenging and supporting the first-year student: A handbook for improving the first year of college* (pp. 86-107). San Francisco: Jossey-Bass.

Kuh, G. D., & Gonyea, R. M. (2003). The role of the academic library in promoting student engagement in learning. *College & Research Libraries, 64*(4), 256-282.

Kuh, G. D., Kinzie, J., Schuh, J. H., Whitt, E. J., & Associates. (2005). *Student success in college: Creating conditions that matter.* San Francisco: Jossey-Bass.

Kuh, G. D., Schuh, J. H., Whitt, E. J., & Associates. (1991). *Involving colleges: Successful approaches to fostering student learning and personal development outside the classroom.* San Francisco: Jossey-Bass.

Manuel, K. (2002). Teaching information literacy to Generation Y. *Journal of Library Administration, 36*(1/2), 195-217.

Mark, A. E., & Boruff-Jones, P. D. (2003). Information literacy and student engagement: What the National Survey of Student Engagement reveals about your campus. *College & Research Libraries, 64*(6), 480-493.

Mellon, C. A. (1986). Library anxiety: A grounded theory and its development. *College & Research Libraries, 47*(2), 160-165.

National Survey of Student Engagement. (2002). *From promise to progress: How colleges and universities are using student engagement results to improve collegiate quality.* Bloomington, IN: Indiana University Center for Postsecondary Research and Planning.

Pace, C. R. (1982). *Achievement and the quality of student effort.* Washington, DC: National Commission on Excellence in Education

Pascarella, E. T., & Terenzini, P. T. (2005). *How college affects students: A third decade of research.* San Francisco: Jossey-Bass.

Ramsden, P. (2003). *Learning to teach in higher education.* London: Routledge Falmer.

Reeb, B., & Gibbons, S. (2004). Students, librarians, and subject guides: Improving a poor rate of return. *portal: Libraries and the Academy, 4*(1), 123-130.

Regalado, M. (2003). Competence, confidence, and connections: Aiding the transition to college. *College & Undergraduate Libraries, 10*(2), 89-97.

Schackelford, J., Thompson, D. S., & James, M. B. (1999). Teaching strategy and assignment design. *Social Science Computer Review, 17*(2), 196-208.

Spence, L. (2004). The usual doesn't work: We need problem-based learning. *portal: Libraries & the Academy, 4*(4), 485-493.

Stamatoplos, A. (2000). An integrated approach to teaching research in a first-year seminar. *College Teaching, 48*(1), 33-36. Retrieved March 1, 2005, from EbscoHost Academic Search Premier database.

Tagg, J. (2003). *The learning paradigm college.* Bolton, MA: Anker.

Umbach, P. D., & Wawrzynski, M. R. (2005). Faculty do matter: The role of college faculty in student learning and engagement. *Research in Higher Education, 46*(2), 153-184.

Upcraft, M. L., Gardner, J. N., & Barefoot, B. O. (Eds.). (2005). *Challenging and supporting the first-year student: A handbook for improving the first year of college.* San Francisco: Jossey-Bass.

Van Rossum, E .J., & Schenk, S. M. (1984). The relationship between learning conception, study strategy and learning outcome. *British Journal of Educational Psychology, 54*(1), 73-83.

Chapter 3

How First-Year College Students Use Their Time: Implications for Library and Information Literacy Instruction

Leticia Oseguera

Understanding the needs of America's college students is critical to providing services and programs that foster student learning and engagement. This chapter uses results from two national surveys to better understand the experiences of first-year college students. In particular, it examines how students use their time and how this may serve to hinder or support mastery of information literacy skills. The items selected for discussion relate to the characteristics and skills needed for effective information literacy. They include satisfaction with library facilities on campus, self-reports of students' computer skills, and time allocated for library and Internet research during the first year of college. In addition, possible implications of the findings for librarians and classroom faculty members who may want to integrate information literacy skills into first-year programs are discussed.

Overview of the Cooperative Institutional Research Program (CIRP) Freshman Survey and the Your First College Year (YFCY) Survey

The Cooperative Institutional Research Program (CIRP) Freshman Survey has been administered annually to entering first-year students since 1966. Housed at the Higher Education Research Institute (HERI) at the University of California, Los Angeles, this survey collects demographic and biographical information, high school grade point averages, standardized test scores, information on degree and career aspirations, measures of self-concept, and life goals. HERI administers the Freshman Survey during summer/fall orientation or during a course that is taken by all first-year students on a campus (e.g., the first-year seminar). The 2004 sample used for this study gathered responses from 289,452[1] students attending some 440 four-year colleges.

The Your First College Year (YFCY) Survey is in its sixth national administration. Also housed at HERI, YFCY was designed as a posttest to the CIRP, as more than one third of the items on the CIRP are measured again on YFCY after the first college year. That is, the instrument is intended to capture students' curricular and cocurricular experiences since entering college and, thus, enhance assessment of the first college year at the local and national level. For the 2005 administration, HERI collected data on 44,564 students at 144 two- and four-year colleges. For this chapter, I limited the sample to first-time, full-time students at four-year colleges and universities. Individual institutional response rates for this survey ranged from 8% to 100%, but for this study, sample results from institutions with response rates of less than 20% were eliminated.

To best capture the experiences of first-year college students, three types of analyses are included in this chapter: (a) 2004 CIRP Freshman Survey data only (*N* = 289,452), (b) 2005 YFCY data only (*N* = 38,178), and (c) matched 2004 CIRP/2005 YFCY data (*N* = 22,440). While the large number of students included in the analyses provides an excellent opportunity to assess the experiences of first-year students, some caution is offered about the generalizability of these data within and across institutions. Table 1 compares demographic characteristics in both surveys to gain a better understanding of the representativeness of the YFCY sample and the matched CIRP/YFCY sample against the normed entering CIRP first-year college population.

The YFCY sample and the matched CIRP/YFCY sample overrepresent women but come close to representing the ethnic/racial proportions found in the CIRP normative sample (Table 1). Similarly, the data underrepresent students from public colleges and universities and overrepresent students from private universities and nonsectarian, Catholic, and other religious colleges. While there are issues related to non-response bias and institutional participation patterns, these data are an important resource to researchers and campus personnel who are dedicated to the enhancement of the first-year experience.[2]

A Snapshot of the Final Year in High School (CIRP Only)

Years of High School Study

How well are first-year students prepared for their college experience? Table 2 displays the academic course-taking patterns of students in their final year of high school with respect to English coursework (e.g., language, literature, and composition) and computer science study, both of which may have some relationship to the development of information literacy. Nearly 98% of first-time, full-time students have completed four or more years of English language study. In terms of computer science study, 42% of students have taken between one semester and one year of computer science. On the other hand, an almost equal percentage (38%) of students reported not having taken a single course in computer science. However valid the perception some observers have regarding the computer proficiency of entering students, for a substantial portion of students, it does not appear to be the result of formal computer science study. In fact, the majority of students (both with and without formal computer science study) rated their computer skills average or lower (60% with formal study and 70% without formal study), suggesting a potential area for improvement among many first-year students.

While much has been written about the digital divide (Macias, Cutler, Jones, & Barreto, 2002; National Telecommunications and Information Administration, 2000), analysis of CIRP data found no evidence of one income group being more or less likely to have taken a computer course than others. Thus, librarians and first-year program faculty members cannot assume that most students have computer proficiency based on any formal course of study in high school. Moreover, the majority of students, irrespective of formal training, rate themselves as "average" at best in computer literacy, suggesting that formal instruction is imperative in the increasingly computer-based environment of higher education and business.

Table 1

Comparison of the 2004 CIRP Freshman Survey, the 2005 YFCY Survey, and the Matched CIRP/YFCY Student Samples

	Percent of first-time, full-time students at four-year institutions		
	2004 CIRP (N = 289,452)*	*2005 YFCY* (N = 38,178)	*2004 CIRP/2005 YFCY* (N = 22,440)
Gender			
Male	44.9	37.4	34.9
Female	55.1	62.6	65.1
Race/Ethnicity			
White/Caucasian	75.6	75.6	76.6
Black/African American	9.6	10.3	9.2
American Indian/Alaskan Native	1.9	1.8	1.6
Asian American/Asian	7.8	8.3	8.9
Native Hawaiian/Pacific Islander	0.8	1.0	1.1
Mexican American/ Chicano	3.5	3.0	3.1
Puerto Rican	1.1	1.4	1.3
Other Latino	2.4	3.2	3.0
Other	3.1	3.7	3.3
Institutional type			
Public universities	31.3	19.6	15.2
Private universities	8.5	22.2	24.4
Four-year colleges			
Public	34.5	15.5	16.3
Nonsectarian	12.1	15.1	18.8
Catholic	5.1	9.9	12.4
Other religious	8.4	17.7	12.8

Note. 2004 CIRP, 2005 YFCY, and 2004 CIRP/ 2005 YFCY.
*Weighted *N* = 1,258,333

Table 2

Academic Preparation During High School (N = 289,452)

	Percent of students completing:	
	English coursework	*Computer science study*
No years	0.1	37.5
1/2 year	0.2	13.6
1 year	0.2	28.1
2 years	0.4	13.5
3 years	1.4	4.2
4 years	95.0	2.7
5+ years	2.6	0.4

Note. 2004 CIRP.

Computer Use

Whatever their computer proficiency, a significant percentage of entering students report using a computer a great deal. When asked how often they used a personal computer in their final year of high school, 86% of students reported they used one frequently, 11% reported occasional use, and only 3% reported no computer use.

Entering students report extensive use of computers, not only for personal use but also for academic activities. When asked how often they used the Internet for research or homework during their final year of high school, 78% of the students reported engaging in this activity frequently, 21% reported occasionally using the Internet for research or homework, while only 1% reported no Internet use for research or homework during their final year in high school. Interestingly, students who completed computer science study were no more likely to report frequent computer or Internet use than those who did not. Roughly 85% of both groups reported frequent computer use, and roughly 78% of both groups reported frequent use of the Internet for research or homework.

Students may well enter college with some degree of knowledge of Internet search engines such as Google and Yahoo and view them as valid alternative information sources to the library. Nevertheless, if they are only developing superficial computer skills in searching for information, they may neither understand nor accept the need for instruction in developing more sophisticated information literacy skills, particularly those related to finding materials they perceive as less readily accessible, such as library print materials. Given students' self-ratings, librarians and classroom faculty members teaching information literacy skills in first-year programs may understandably be loath to view entering students as information literate. Too often, these neophyte scholars equate quantity of time spent with quality of use.

Although there was little evidence of the digital divide with respect to formal computer science study, differences in general computer use and Internet use for research or homework by income level[3] surfaced. Higher-income students were more likely to report frequent computer use than lower-income students. For example, 78% of low-income students reported frequent computer use while 90% of high-income students reported frequent computer use. Further, low-income students were three times greater than high-income students to report no computer use (see Figure 1). The digital divide also surfaced with Internet use for research or homework. Fewer than three quarters of low-income students reported frequent use of the Internet for

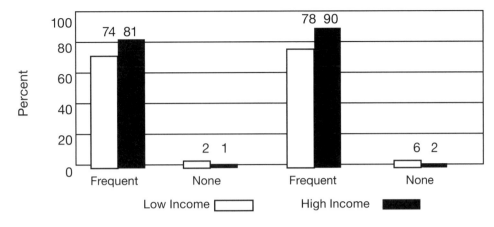

Figure 1. Internet and computer use during high school by income. Low income is family income less than $30,000 annually while high income is family income more than $100,000 annually.

research or homework while more than 80% of high-income students reported frequent use. Although both groups generally reported high levels of computer use, formal computer instruction, particularly as related to information literacy, may be especially important for students from low-income households. Researchers have shown that the quality of computer and technology proficiency varies by social class, thus, more attention is needed to bring computer literacy levels of lower socioeconomic students to that of higher socioeconomic students (Warschauer, 2003; Warschauer, Knobel, & Stone, 2004).

A Snapshot of the First-Year Experience (YFCY Only)

Satisfaction With Campus Facilities

If campus personnel want students to use the library and other campus resources to strengthen information literacy skills, they need to ensure student satisfaction with these services. YFCY asks students to rate their satisfaction on a variety of campus services at the end of the first year of college. When asked how satisfied they were with the library facilities on campus, 77% reported satisfaction and 6% reported dissatisfaction. Responses to satisfaction with the computer facilities on campus yielded a similar pattern: 76% of students reported that they were satisfied or very satisfied, and 7% reported they were dissatisfied or very dissatisfied.[4] With respect to tutoring and academic assistance, only 58% of first-year students reported satisfaction, and, perhaps even more significant, 30% of students actually reported no experience with tutoring and academic assistance. This finding highlights students' lack of experience with academic assistance options and may suggest that they are not aware of services available to them. This minimal use of general academic assistance likely corresponds with minimal use of specific assistance in training/support related to information literacy skills. Since we know from CIRP data that many students enter college with low self-assessments of their computer-skill level, librarians and classroom faculty teaching in first-year programs can introduce and promote campus resources, especially those related to computer training and information literacy.

Skill and Campus Success

YFCY also assesses students' feelings of success after their first year of college. Understanding the skill level students feel they have attained may help faculty and staff gauge a student's preparedness for long-term academic success and their potential for becoming information literate more accurately. Table 3 shows that fewer than one third of students feel completely successful at developing effective study skills, managing their time well, or using the campus services available to them. In fact, 11% of students feel unsuccessful in developing effective study skills, and 15% feel unsuccessful in managing their time well. Further, fewer than half of the students report feeling completely successful at adjusting to the academic demands of college.

According to students' self-assessments, time management, study skills, and academic adjustment are areas that need further development. Frequently, for example, use of the library for writing the typical research paper due near the end of the semester, involves students' planning ahead and structuring their own time without close guidance by others. First-year students may not develop the needed information literacy skills and make use of the abundant information resources available through the library if they cannot manage their time and adjust their study skills to the academic demands of college. Teaching information literacy skills without considering time management and study skills may be inadequate in developing the information-literate (and academically successful) student.

Table 3
Skill Development After the First College Year

	Percent reporting		
	Completely successful	Somewhat successful	Unsuccessful
Developed effective study skills (n = 37,943)	29	61	11
Adjusted to academic demands (n = 37,935)	41	54	6
Managed time effectively (n = 37,942)	27	58	15
Utilized campus resources (n = 37,905)	32	60	9

Note. 2005 YFCY; percentages may not sum to 100 due to rounding.

To further highlight first-year experiences, I explored the relationship between students' satisfaction with the library services available to them and their attendant strengthening of skill development after one year of college (see Table 4).[5] When skill development was examined by the level of satisfaction with library facilities, I found that those students reporting complete success at developing effective study skills were slightly more likely to report satisfaction with the library services. Not surprisingly, a higher percentage of students who reported success at using campus services also reported satisfaction with the library services on campus. Conversely, higher proportions of students who reported dissatisfaction with the library also reported being unsuccessful at developing effective study skills, adjusting to the academic demands of college, managing time, and using campus services. However, there were no meaningful differences among students who reported successful academic demand adjustment or successful time management by level of satisfaction with the library. Overall, equating satisfaction with a campus resource and skill development is of limited usefulness, since satisfaction alone does not indicate how or how much students are using the particular campus resource in question. In addition, other variables, such as academic ability, frequency and nature of use, and motivation, may influence the relationship between skill development and satisfaction with particular campus resources. Future research could help untangle the extent to which satisfaction with library facilities and services is related to skill development since these preliminary relationships point in that direction.

Table 4

Students' Self-Ratings of Success During the First Year of College by Level of Satisfaction With Library Facilities

	Satisfaction with library facilities		
	Percent dissatisfied or very dissatisfied	Percent satisfied or very satisfied	Sig. Diff
Developing effective study skills	(n = 2,111)	(n = 28,345)	
Completely successful	26	30	**
Unsuccessful	16	9	**
Adjusting to academic demands	(n = 2,113)	(n = 28,341)	
Completely successful	40	42	**
Unsuccessful	9	5	**
Managing time effectively	(n = 2,113)	(n = 28,347)	
Completely successful	27	28	
Unsuccessful	20	14	**
Utilizing campus services	(n = 2,108)	(n = 28,322)	
Completely successful	24	35	**
Unsuccessful	16	7	**

Note. 2005 YFCY; somewhat successful responses not reported.
$*p < .05. **p < .01.$

Research Avenues and Internet Usage

An additional area of interest for librarians and classroom faculty members teaching in first-year programs is students' Internet and library use as an academic aid. In particular, how does exposure and experience with library and information resources help inform changes in skill development during the first college year? Table 5 displays college students' overall pattern of Internet and library use for research or homework during their first college year. While, four out of five students reported frequently using the Internet for research or homework, only one third of first-year students reported frequently using the library for research or homework. In a comparative study of middle and high schools in the US, researchers found that faculty within these schools noted that the ease in retrieving information via the Internet often makes it difficult for students to sort through and evaluate the material for suitable incorporation into research assignments and also contributes to plagiarism, both of which can be minimized by obtaining information from trusted printed resources that are housed in the library (Warschauer, in press). Further, only a limited number of students within these schools reported using academic search engines such as WebQuest or NetTrekker (Thinkronize, 2006; Warschauer, in press) and instead opted for general search engines such as Google or Yahoo. Students' preferences for and use of search engines over library databases or indexes for coursework was also found among college students (Kaminski, Seel, & Cullen, 2003; Lippincott, 2005). The finding above, coupled with past research, may well confirm some librarians' and classroom faculty members' concerns that students are Googling more often than using the library in their search for information for research/homework. In addition, perhaps surprisingly, the relationship (i.e., the Pearson correlation coefficient) between the two activities is a modest .22, suggesting that those who prefer to use the Internet differ from those who prefer the library for research/homework.

Why some students primarily use the Internet rather than the library and vice versa for their research/homework raise several intriguing research questions for librarians and others. When and how is this pattern established? Is it established prior to or during the student's first year? Does the pattern stay constant throughout a student's college career, or do various methods of intervention, such as instruction in information literacy skills, affect the pattern?

Table 5
Frequency of Various Activities During the First College Year

	Percent reporting used the Internet for research or homework (*n* = 37,819)	Percent reporting used the library for research or homework (*n* = 37,861)
Frequently	82	34
Occasionally	17	53
Not at all	1	13

Note. 2005 YFCY; percentages may not sum to 100 due to rounding.

Given that most students have probably not cultivated sophisticated search strategies, it may be a problematic finding that the majority of them reported frequently using the Internet for homework and research purposes. Not only did more students report that they made more frequent use of the Internet than the library for research/homework, nearly 15% of first-year students reported not using the library *at all* for research or homework. This finding has implications for librarians and classroom faculty teaching in first-year programs as students are not making use of the physical library space. Rather, they appear to prefer to use the web for academic information. These extraordinarily high figures for Internet use suggest greater urgency for those teaching information literacy to foster advanced search strategies among students and train them to obtain accurate information from trusted academic sites. Classroom faculty and librarians who work with first-year students should identify ways to gauge a student's competence in navigating the Internet for research- and homework-related projects since the Internet (as opposed to the library) appears to be the preferred method to obtain academic information. Further, first-year programs may be one of the few places where students can be reached effectively, since a large percentage of students reports little or no library use for research or homework.

One might hypothesize that more skill in navigating resources on the Internet and/or in the library would help alleviate some first-year transition concerns. In fact, we see that frequent Internet users were far more likely to report completely successful adjustment to academic demands than non-users (42% vs. 29%, respectively) and less likely than non-users to rate their adjustment to academic demands as unsuccessful (5% vs. 18%, respectively; see Table 6). Conversely, students who reported no Internet use were twice as likely as frequent Internet users to report unsuccessful study skills development (20% vs. 10%, respectively).

Table 6

Skill Development and Satisfaction With Library by Internet and Library Use During the First College Year

	Used Internet for Research/Homework			Used Library for Research/Homework		
	Percent reporting frequently	*Percent reporting not at all*		*Percent reporting frequently*	*Percent reporting not at all*	
Developed effective study skills	(*n* = 31,029)	(*n* = 342)		(*n* = 12,688)	(*n* = 4,912)	
Completely successful	29	26	*	34	24	**
Unsuccessful	10	20	**	8	17	**
Adjusted to academic demands	(*n* = 31,023)	(*n* = 341)		(*n* = 12,685)	(*n* = 4,911)	
Completely successful	42	29	**	44	38	**
Unsuccessful	5	18	**	5	9	**
Satisfied with library facilities	(*n* = 30,099)	(*n* = 314)		(*n* = 12,633)	(*n* = 3,970)	
Satisfied	79	61	**	84	61	**
Dissatisfied	6	13	**	5	9	**

Note. 2005 YFCY; somewhat successful and neutral responses not reported.
*$p < .05$. **$p < .01$.

With respect to library use, those students who reported greater frequency in using the library for research/homework purposes also reported greater success with developing effective study skills (34% for frequent users and 24% for non-users) and adjusting to academic demands (44% for frequent users and 38% for non-users). Finally, perhaps not surprisingly, those students who frequently used the library (84%) were far more likely than non-users (61%) to be satisfied with the library facilities on campus. It may beg the question: Does increased satisfaction with the library result in greater use of library facilities? Among students who are satisfied with the library, 38% of them use the library frequently while only 28% of the dissatisfied students use the library frequently. Thus, these data suggest that increased satisfaction may result in greater use of the library—a relationship that future research can address systematically.

While these findings do not prove causality, they collectively highlight the positive outcomes that may result from increased skill in obtaining academic aid vis à vis the Internet and the library. That is, information-seeking students, whether via the Internet or the library, report higher success in adjusting to academic demands. Efforts to improve information-seeking skills, such as teaching information literacy in first-year seminars, may further enhance adjustment to academic demands.

In short, these results suggest that difficulties in making the transition to college academics might be reduced if students are exposed to and encouraged to use the Internet and the physical library as resources in their academic pursuits—an area that information literacy personnel can directly influence. These findings suggest the value of developing courses/workshops on navigating the Internet to help with first-year students' academic plans and progress. Such courses can entail refined means of searching and include such topics as what sites should be accessed for academic enrichment (i.e., electronic academic journals and academic research sites).

Time Spent Using Technology

Given the ubiquity of computers and their potential for both enhancing and inhibiting instructional efforts, it is important to examine general Internet and other computer-related use during the first year of college (see Table 7). The majority (66%) of first-year students surfed the Internet between 1 and 5 hours per week with an additional 15% surfing between 6 and 10 hours per week. Students' use of e-mail and Instant Messenger (IM) showed similar patterns, with 60% of students using these media between 1 and 5 hours per week. Nearly 20% communicated via e-mail/IM 6 to 10 hours per week. Students were less likely to use video games, with not quite half (48%) spending some time playing video/computer games. Further research is needed to better understand the impact these activities have on students' learning and intellectual development and strengthening of important skills, such as information literacy.

Table 7

Time Spent Using Computer Related Activities During the First College Year (N = 38,178)

Hours per week spent:	Surfing the Internet (%)	Communicating via e-mail, IM, etc. (%)	Playing video/computer games (%)
No hours	5	4	52
1 to 5 hours	66	60	39
6 to 10 hours	15	17	5
11 to 20 hours	9	12	3
Over 20 hours	4	7	2

Note. 2005 YFCY; percentages may not sum to 100 due to rounding.

Among the students who report long hours (e.g., over 20 hours per week) surfing the Internet, a lower percentage report frequent use of the library for research/homework (see Table 8). We see a slightly different pattern when we look at time spent using the Internet for research or homework. Students who spend 6 to 10 or 11 to 20 hours per week surfing the Internet report the highest percentages of using the Internet for research or homework (85% and 86%, respectively), but these figures decline among students who report surfing the Internet more than 20 hours per week. In other words, the rate of return decreases. These findings suggest that some surfing is necessary when students use the Internet for their academic work; but as use increases, students may surf for non-academic reasons. Perhaps, moderate users have developed the discipline to place a priority on academics over leisure activities.

The more hours students reported surfing, the less likely they were to report developing effective study skills (see Table 9). We see the same pattern for adjusting to academic demands and managing time effectively. These findings may support the assertion that with long hours of

Internet surfing, much of students' Internet use is non-academic and that excessive use detracts from academic performance. Frequent use of the Internet does not necessarily translate into productive searching. Thus, classroom faculty members and librarians must also attend to the quality of the use.

Table 8
Frequency of Use of Internet and Library for Research/Homework by Computer-Related Activities

	Percent surfing the Internet				
Used Internet for research/homework	No hours (*n* = 1,960)	1 to 5 hours (*n* = 24,343)	6 to 10 hours (*n* = 5,607)	11 to 20 hours (*n* = 3,426)	Over 20 hours (*n* = 1,526)
Frequently	69	82	85	86	83
Occasionally	28	17	14	13	14
Not at al	3	1	1	1	3
Used library for research/homework	No hours (*n* = 1,956)	1 to 5 hours (*n* = 24,344)	6 to 10 hours (*n* = 5,608)	11 to 20 hours (*n* = 3,427)	Over 20 hours (*n* = 1,525)
Frequently	38	34	31	31	29
Occasionally	50	54	54	53	52
Not at all	12	12	15	16	19
	Percent playing video/computer games				
Used Internet for research/homework	No hours (*n* = 19,028)	1 to 5 hours (*n* = 14,592)	6 to 10 hours (*n* = 1,755)	11 to 20 hours (*n* = 1,093)	Over 20 hours (*n* = 500)
Frequently	85	81	75	75	70
Occasionally	15	18	23	23	24
Not at all	1	1	2	3	7
Used library for research/homework	No hours (*n* = 19,019)	1 to 5 hours (*n* = 14,600)	6 to 10 hours (*n* = 1,755)	11 to 20 hours (*n* = 1,091)	Over 20 hours (*n* = 500)
Frequently	38	30	26	25	24
Occasionally	51	57	56	52	49
Not at all	11	13	18	23	27

Note. 2005 YFCY.

Table 9

Frequency of Use of Internet and Library for Research/Homework by Computer-Related Activities

		Percent surfing the Internet			
Developing effective study skills	No hours (n = 1,963)	1 to 5 hours (n = 24,372)	6 to 10 hours (n = 5,622)	11 to 20 hours (n = 3,431)	Over 20 hours (n = 1,526)
Completely successful	34	30	26	24	23
Unsuccessful	11	9	12	15	18
Adjusting to academic demands	(n = 1,961)	(n = 24,373)	(n = 5,617)	(n = 3,433)	(n = 1,527)
Completely successful	41	41	40	37	36
Unsuccessful	8	5	7	8	10
Managing time effectively	(n = 1,962)	(n = 24,378)	(n = 5,621)	(n = 3,431)	(n = 1,527)
Completely successful	32	28	24	23	23
Unsuccessful	14	13	17	20	24

Note. 2005 YFCY; somewhat successful figures are not reported.

A recent study found that by the time a student reaches age 21, he or she has spent "twice as many hours playing video games as reading (10,000 versus 5,000)" (Prensky, 2001 as cited in Oblinger & Oblinger, 2005, p. 2.14). Fittingly, the final variable highlighted in this section includes the time students spent during their first year playing video/computer games that detract from time that could be spent strengthening information literacy skills. Those students who reported more hours playing video/computer games were least likely to report frequently using the library or the Internet for research/homework. In terms of satisfaction with the library, those who spent more time on video/computer games were least likely to be satisfied with the library facilities.

Could their dissatisfaction really be a result of not liking the library, or are these students initially less likely to be satisfied with the library? Information literacy personnel must not only find ways to get students into the library, but they must also find creative ways to get students away from the more recreational and social use of the computer and encourage more educationally productive use of the computer. According to Oblinger and Oblinger (2005), "educators have to grab these learners with image-rich environments and opportunities to interact with each other" (p. 2.15).

To show additional relationships between computer-related activities such as surfing and gaming and educational outcomes, the final item highlighted is average letter grade changes (Table 10). Grade averages were higher for those students who reported less time surfing the web (53% of students who reported little or no surfing maintained a B+ or higher grade average compared to 45% of students reporting more than 20 hours of surfing per week). Video/computer game playing time followed a similar pattern: Overall grade point averages were lower among students who reported more time playing video/computer games. Although surfing and gaming may be a matter of personal preference (one which classroom faculty and librarians may not be in a position to alter), what they can do, as suggested by other researchers, is provide image-rich texts and even help classroom faculty integrate images and technology into their instructional practices as a way to engage and capture student interest (Manuel, 2002; Oblinger & Oblinger, 2005).

Table 10
First-Year Grades by Time Spent Engaged in Computer-Related Activities

	Percent surfing the Internet				
Grade average	No hours (*n* = 1,931)	1 to 5 hours (*n* = 24,259)	6 to 10 hours (*n* = 5,589)	11 to 20 hours (*n* = 3,407)	Over 20 hours (*n* = 1,504)
B+ or higher	53	53	50	47	45
B	24	27	29	30	29
C+/B-	13	12	13	14	15
C or less	10	8	9	10	11
	Percent playing video/computer games				
Grade average	No hours (*n* = 18,945)	1 to 5 hours (*n* = 14,532)	6 to 10 hours (*n* = 1,738)	11 to 20 hours (*n* = 1,081)	Over 20 hours (*n* = 491)
B+ or higher	56	48	42	39	40
B	26	29	28	31	29
C+/B-	11	14	17	16	18
C or less	7	9	13	14	14

Note. 2005 YFCY; percentages may not sum to 100 due to rounding.

Study Groups

Research has demonstrated that studying with other students facilitates the attainment of numerous positive educational outcomes, including mastery of abstract math concepts (Astin, 1993; Bosworth & Hamilton, 1994; Johnson & Johnson, 1989; Treisman, 1992). As such, it is useful for those teaching information literacy to determine whether a relationship exists between information literacy behaviors and studying with peers and to evaluate the potential value of providing instruction that draws on the strengths of group work. Therefore, in addition to asking students about the resources they used for homework, HERI asked students how often they studied with other students. Twenty-eight percent reported studying with other students frequently, while 12% reported never engaging in this activity.

Moreover, those students who spent more time studying with other students were more likely to report using both the library (47% of students who frequently studied with other students also reported frequently using the library vs. 26% of the students who reported not studying with other students) and Internet for research and homework (89% and 76%, respectively). This finding suggests that collaborative learners make more use of the library, which could result in students' greater ease navigating library resources and increased satisfaction with library services (see Table 11). Additionally, those students who reported studying with other students were also more likely to feel they had developed effective study skills, adjusted to academic demands, and used campus services. Library and information personnel may want to include more collaborative learning and group projects when designing the information literacy curriculum as it is reasonable to conclude from earlier research that the benefits of collaborative learning may also extend to mastery of information literacy concepts.

Table 11

Time Spent Studying With Other Students During the First College Year by Information Literacy Activities

	Studied with other students		
	Percent reporting frequently	Percent reporting not at all	Sig. diff.
Used library for research/homework	(*n* = 10,461)	(*n* = 4,458)	
Frequently	47	26	**
Occasionally	45	50	**
Not at all	9	25	**
Used Internet for research/homework	(*n* = 10,466)	(*n* = 4,461)	
Frequently	89	76	**
Occasionally	11	21	**
Not at all	1	3	

Note. 2005 YFCY; percentages may not sum to 100 due to rounding.
*p < .05. ***p* < .01.

Changes in Students From End of High School to End of First Year of College (Matched CIRP/YFCY)

The first two sections of this chapter provided a snapshot of first-year students as they entered college (via the CIRP) and at the end of the first college year (via the YFCY)—independent of one another. In this section, I discuss how students change over the course of the first year of college by examining responses from those students for whom HERI collected longitudinal data (i.e., at the beginning of college and again at the end of the first year of college). Here, I have highlighted those variables with implications for the development of information literacy skills during the first year of college.

Average Letter Grade and Self-Rating Changes

On the CIRP, students were asked to report their average high school letter grade. These same students were asked to report their average letter grade for the first college year on the YFCY. At the end of the first college year, 52% of the students reported a decrease in their average letter grade, while 13% reported an increase (see Table 12). The large numbers of students reporting a decrease in GPA may suggest that many students have an unrealistic expectation of the demands of college-level academic work.

Table 12
Changes in Average Letter Grade and Self-Ratings After the First College Year

	Average letter grade (n = 21,637)	Academic ability (n = 21,915)	Computer skills (n = 21,918)	Writing ability (n = 21,891)
Percentage of students who				
Increased	13	14	26	25
Stayed the same	36	62	59	55
Decreased	52	25	15	20

Note. 2004 CIRP/ 2005 YFCY; students were asked to rate the extent to which they had changed in selected areas over the course of the first year. Percentages may not sum to 100 due to rounding.

Students were also asked to rate themselves on a number of abilities, including general academic skills (see Table 12). Changes were assessed by calculating whether a student moved from one self-rating category to another (e.g., from "lowest 10%" to "average" or "average" to "above average") from the beginning to the end of the first college year. In terms of academic ability, the majority of students (62%) maintained their academic self-rating after the first year, while one quarter decreased their self-rating. The majority of students also maintained their self-ratings for computer skills and writing ability assessment. A positive sign is that a quarter of the students reported perceived increases in their computer skills and writing ability. Perceived writing ability increases may be due to the emphasis many first-year programs place on writing as well as the fact that more written work is expected in college than in high school—a speculation that merits further investigation. The pervasiveness of technology on many campuses may contribute to the perceived increase in computer skills. In fact, many campuses increasingly expect students to use computer technology for communication on administrative and instructional issues. This finding further highlights the critical need to assess students' actual computer skills competence at college entry and at the end of the first year. Are higher self-ratings really reflective of improved computer skills, or are they simply being bolstered by more time spent using computers on campus?

To get a sense of the relationship between academic performance and information literacy, I examined students' library and Internet use and their satisfaction with library facilities (see Table 13). For students who used the library or Internet frequently or who reported satisfaction with library services, there was not a significant relationship between these variables and earning higher grades in college. However, students who reported no Internet or library use were more likely to report decreases in grades after the first college year. Successful students may be more likely to avail themselves of a range of resources on campus. It is plausible that minor differences were uncovered because grade changes can result from a number of reasons that were not measured here (i.e., relationships with faculty, differences in college major, and interactions with peers).

As with grades earned in the first year, there were larger decreases in academic ability self-ratings among students who reported no use of the library for research or homework and among students who were dissatisfied with the library facilities on campus. A surprising and perplexing finding was that a larger percentage of students who did not use the Internet reported increases in their academic ability relative to those students who frequently used the Internet for research or homework. One possible explanation is that the frequency of use does not necessarily translate into quality use or sophisticated searching techniques. Thus, frequent use may not have been an asset for studying or completing assignments. Frequent use may also correspond to poor time management, which could have a negative impact on academic performance. Since past research on information literacy shows that availability of technology and extended use of technology alone is not sufficient to instill information literacy, professionally guided instruction for students is required to produce desired learning outcomes (Warschauer, 2003; Warschauer et al., 2004).

Table 13

Changes in Self-Ratings and Grades by Information Literacy Related Activities/Attitudes

Percent reporting	Used library for research/homework			Used Internet for research/homework			Satisfied with the library facilities		
	Frequently	Not at all	Sig. diff.	Frequently	Not at all	Sig. diff.	Satisfied	Dis-satisfied	Sig. diff.
Academic ability change	(n = 7,314)	(n = 2,764)		(n = 18,069)	(n = 168)		(n = 16,795)	(n = 1,154)	
Increased	15	13		13	23	**	16	13	*
Stayed same	62	60		62	51	**	63	62	
Decreased	23	28	**	24	26		21	24	*
Computer skills change	(n = 7,326)	(n = 2,768)		(n = 18,078)	(n = 168)		(n = 16,796)	(n = 1,151)	
Increased	28	24	**	26	28		26	27	
Stayed same	58	59		59	49	**	59	56	*
Decreased	14	17	*	14	23	**	14	17	*
Writing ability change	(n = 7,306)	(n = 2,757)		(n = 18,049	(n = 168)		(n = 16,785)	(n = 1,149)	
Increased	26	24		25	38	**	25	25	
Stayed same	54	54		56	35	**	56	54	
Decreased	19	22	*	20	27	**	20	21	
Grade average change	(n = 7,235)	(n = 2,733)		(n = 17,846)	(n = 161)		(n = 16,593)	(n = 1,122)	
Increased	13	11		12	12		12	16	**
Stayed same	37	33	**	36	31	**	36	36	
Decreased	50	56	**	51	57	**	52	48	**

Note. 2004 CIRP/ 2005 YFCY; percentages may not sum to 100 due to rounding.
*p < .05. **p < .01.

Perhaps because technology has become ubiquitous on college campuses, one quarter of students reported increased proficiency in their computer skills since starting college. Students who reported frequent library use were more likely to increase their self-rating on computer skills compared to those who reported no library use. Students who reported no library use were more likely to report decreases in their computer skills. Non-users of the Internet were more likely to be represented among students whose computer self-rating declined than frequent users. Regular Internet use (even if it is not necessarily experienced navigation) may play a role in how students perceive their computer proficiency. With respect to changes by library use, it is plausible that students are exposed to instructional staff who introduce students to the self-help tools and resources offered directly at libraries' computer search stations.

Finally, self-reported changes in writing ability do not appear to be related to frequency of Internet or library use. While information literacy is often connected to academic writing in the curriculum, frequent use of the library or the Internet may have little impact on writing. In fact, information literacy and writing may tap different skill sets for students. The ability to retrieve additional information resources may have little direct relationship to using them in writing better papers, particularly if no guidance is given to students on how to incorporate outside sources successfully into their written work. This emphasizes the need for close librarian and classroom faculty collaborations so frequently mentioned elsewhere in this monograph.

Conclusion

This chapter offers a profile of students attending higher education institutions across the country. The findings provide information as to how students perceive themselves during the first year of college. With the exception of the weighted norms, these findings should be used with caution because they may not generalize to all students and institutional settings. Nevertheless, the findings in this chapter attempt to paint the most complete portrait of first-time, full-time students attending four-year colleges and universities and what their information-related needs and experiences are across campuses in this country. Thus, I encourage librarians and classroom faculty to engage in further research and investigations at their individual campuses to determine the validity and applicability of my speculations.

The items selected for discussion relate to how first-year college students spend their time and how this relates to the characteristics and skills needed for effective information literacy. They include student activities related to library use, satisfaction with campus resources (including the library), readiness for computer and Internet use, and time spent engaged in academic activities. Of major significance is that the majority of students report using the Internet, but not the library, for their research or homework. While the Internet may well be the preferred method of information acquisition for this population of students, sophisticated use of this important resource also means the development of the ability to retrieve relevant information and make informed judgments as to its validity. The advent of the Internet has, in many ways, added to the challenge of developing the information-literate individual. While not overlooking the usefulness and convenience of the Internet resources, often made available to the academic community through paid subscriptions via the library, many, if not most, academic information resources remain in traditional formats within the library building. Although they may neither understand nor accept the need for instruction in developing more sophisticated information literacy skills, today's students, nonetheless, require continued professional guidance. The availability of technology and extended use of technology is not sufficient to instill information literacy.

Notes

[1] These data were then statistically adjusted to reflect the response of the 1.3 million first-time, full-time students entering four-year colleges and universities as first-year students in 2004 (see Sax, Hurtado, Lindholm, Astin, Korn, & Mahoney, 2004).

[2] For more information regarding the methods employed in the analyses, please contact the author directly.

[3] Parental income was divided into three groups. I established cutoffs based on national quintile guidelines for income. For 2004, the lowest income quintile fell into a CIRP category range of $25,000 through $29,999 while the highest income quintile most closely matched the $100,000-$149,999 category. As a result, for the year under investigation, low-income includes students who reported family incomes below $30,000, middle-income denotes students with family incomes between $30,000 and $100,000 (middle 3 quintiles), and high-income includes students with family incomes above $100,000.

[4] The Pearson correlation between these two items is .23, suggesting that students are discriminating between satisfaction levels. In other words, students are not simply responding to all items in the same way.

[5] Generally, correlation analyses, chi-square statistics, and contingency tables were used to describe relationships between the variables in the analyses. Future research can explore more sophisticated techniques to evaluate the validity of my speculations.

References

Astin, A.W. (1993). *What matters in college? Four critical years revisited.* San Francisco: Jossey Bass.

Bosworth, K., & Hamilton, S. J. (1994). *Collaborative learning: Underlying processes and effective techniques.* (New Directions for Teaching and Learning, No. 59). San Francisco: Jossey-Bass.

Johnson, D. W., & Johnson, R. T. (Eds.). (1989). *Cooperation and competition: Theory and research.* Edina, MN: Interaction Book Company.

Kaminski, K., Seel, P., & Cullen, K. (2003). Technology literate students? Results from a survey. *EDUCAUSE Quarterly, 26*(3), 34-40.

Lippincott, J. K. (2005). Net generation students and libraries. In D. Oblinger & J. Oblinger (Eds.), *Educating the net generation* (pp. 13.1-13.15). *Educause E-Book.* Retrieved August 3, 2006, from http://www.educause.edu/educatingthenetgen/

Macias, E., Cutler, R., Jones, S., & Barreto, M. (2002). *Promoting access to network technologies in underserved communities: Lessons learned.* Los Angeles: Tomas Rivera Policy Institute.

Manuel, K. (2002). *Teaching information literacy to Generation Y.* New York: Haworth Press.

National Telecommunications and Information Administration (NTIS). (2000). *Falling through the net: Toward digital inclusion.* Washington, DC: Author.

Oblinger, D., & Oblinger, J. (2005). Educating the net generation. *Educause E-Book.* Retrieved July 20, 2006, from http://www.educause.edu/educatingthenetgen/

Sax, L. J., Hurtado, S., Lindholm, J., Astin, A., Korn, W., & Mahoney, K. (2004). *The American freshman: National norms for fall 2004.* Los Angeles: University of California at Los Angeles, Higher Education Research Institute.

Thinkronize. (2006). *NetTrekker.* Retrieved August 3, 2006, from http://www.nettrekker.com/

Treisman, U. (1992). Studying students studying calculus: A look at the lives of minority mathematics students in college. *College Mathematics Journal, 23*(5), 362-372.

Warschauer, M. (2003). *Technology and social inclusion: Rethinking the digital divide.* Cambridge, MA: MIT Press.

Warschauer, M. (in press). Information literacy in the laptop classroom. *Teachers College Record.*

Warschauer, M., Knobel, M., & Stone, M. (2004). Technology and equity in schooling: Deconstructing the digital divide. *Educational Policy, 18*(4), 562-588.

SECTION 2

Chapter 4

Models of Library Instruction for First-Year Students

Debbie Malone & Carol Videon

Efforts to improve learning and success in the first college year take a variety of forms. Information literacy (IL) goals and instruction are increasingly embedded in these efforts. In 2003, we explored strategies for teaching IL in the first college year and identified hallmarks of successful efforts. We surveyed 153 respondents from 252 small and mid-sized college libraries and reported our findings in a CLIP Note (Malone & Videon, 2003). Based on the survey responses, we determined that successful IL programs usually fall into three basic categories: (a) those in which the goals and objectives of the program are integrated into the general education curriculum for first-year students, (b) those in which IL plays a pervasive role in first-year seminars, and (c) those in which stand-alone courses provide broad coverage of skills related to IL.

In all of these models, extensive collaboration between librarians and classroom faculty members plays a crucial role in the development of the programs. The type of faculty involvement varies widely from institution to institution, but librarians with clearly defined goals and objectives usually initiate and sustain the programs. Successful collaboration begins with librarians articulating a basic definition of what they seek to do and then working closely with classroom faculty members to be sure the faculty understand the various aspects of IL. These collaborations require skill, tact, and persistence in explaining the need for IL. As Gibson (1992) notes,

> The real challenge of the 1990s is for instructional librarians to develop the necessary political skills to convince faculty colleagues and administrators that there is a coherent set of intellectual skills in information-seeking that can be taught, evaluated, and dovetailed with the larger goals of the institution. (p. 103)

The programs discussed below are based on our 2003 research with the information updated in 2004-2005 through telephone and e-mail interviews with librarians and collaborating faculty members. From our original group of survey respondents, we selected six institutions with clearly defined IL goals that had been integrated into the curriculum for first-year students. We have also included one institution that was not in the original survey, Ulster County Community College, because they provide an innovative credit course for first-year students. Since 2003, these programs have expanded both in terms of the number of students they reach and the number of classroom faculty members who incorporate IL goals and skills in their courses.

Information Literacy Integrated Into the General Curriculum

Effective collaborative relationships between librarians and classroom faculty members are particularly important in institutions where IL for first-year students is emphasized in many different curricular areas and taught by a variety of classroom faculty members. Yet, librarians may be "invisible" to the faculty members who most need their assistance, making collaboration difficult, if not impossible. Service on campus committees can often raise the profile of librarians and offer them an opportunity to create successful working relationships with classroom faculty members across the curriculum. The programs at the two institutions below are examples of both effective committee work and exemplary relationship building.

Elmhurst College

At Elmhurst College, ongoing collaborations with librarians have encouraged faculty adoption of IL goals in their courses. As the instruction librarian notes,

> Many faculty members are on board with our information literacy initiative as a result of networking by many librarians over the past 20 years. Information literacy is an "institutional value" not a "top-down directive," and it is prevalent throughout the core courses. (S. Swords Steffen, personal communication, October 8, 2004)

However, it is an institutional value that is intentionally promoted by administrators. The appointment of a new dean, who strongly supported the embedding of IL concepts in the institutions' six "Common Experience" 100-level courses, expanded the longstanding IL program at Elmhurst College. The Common Experience courses range over a number of subject areas but share a common theme.

Although IL is not a required part of the general curriculum at Elmhurst, many Common Experience faculty members have incorporated IL goals into their courses due to the effectiveness of the material in helping students improve their research and writing skills. For example, an associate professor of geography includes "providing a basic level of IL as it relates to course content" as one of seven goals on the syllabus for his Common Experience course. He also includes enhancing students' research abilities as one of the goals of his assignments (M. Lindberg, personal communication, May 31, 2005).

Faculty members at Elmhurst College are open to incorporating IL goals in their courses because they have learned to value the assistance librarians can provide in enhancing their classes. For example, one professor notes,

> I work closely with the Head of Reference at our library to facilitate IL in two of my classes [one of which is a Common Experience course]. We collaborate on devising written research assignments that incorporate IL. I am not a writing instructor, yet I place a great deal of emphasis on writing in my classes. To have the assistance of professionals who are very familiar with the writing process as well as the research process is of great value to me, and I would be foolish not to take advantage of their availability. Cooperation and collaboration go hand in hand in this situation. (M. Lindberg, personal communication, November 11, 2004)

University of North Carolina, Asheville

At the University of North Carolina, Asheville, IL is a required part of the 2004 revised general education curriculum or Integrative Liberal Studies. Planning for this new model began with a general education task force that included a librarian. The library user instruction coordinator observed:

There had been a growing awareness on campus of the importance of information literacy. Now, every department on campus is required to participate in the general education curriculum. Students must enroll in two courses from Integrative Liberal Studies that are information literacy intensive. In addition, each department also needs a certain number of IL intensive courses for their majors. (J. Ferguson, personal communication, September 23, 2004)

In the planning stages for this new program, the director of the general education program requested that librarians teach IL workshops for classroom faculty members. To facilitate this teaching, the director awarded the librarians grant money to provide these sessions. The workshops included a definition of IL, ways to incorporate IL skills into courses, and ideas for crafting assignments that give students an opportunity to use these skills in their coursework.

The 2005-2006 University of North Carolina, Asheville course catalog describes these IL-intensive courses as ones in which the assignments, course work, or tutorials make extensive use of information presented in diverse formats from multiple sources. The learning outcomes for these courses, as stated in the catalog, include "the ability to select and evaluate relevant information using tools most appropriate for course-related information need" (p. 47). In achieving these learning outcomes, classroom faculty members will "introduce issues of plagiarism and academic integrity while fostering critical thinking skills" (p. 47).

Approval of an IL-intensive course begins with classroom faculty members submitting a proposal to a committee consisting of a librarian and two classroom faculty members. While classroom faculty members develop the course syllabus, they are encouraged by the committee to collaborate with their subject specialist liaison librarian who can help develop the assignments and serve as a consultant throughout the process. Examples of assignments are found in Appendices A and B.

Librarians have developed productive relationships with many classroom faculty members that allow them to tailor IL instruction to specific class assignments and research needs, making the value of IL skills more apparent to students. These librarians participate in designing assignments, identifying resources, supporting students, and teaching sessions. They also serve on committees that influence the basic structure of the general education curriculum for their institutions.

Information Literacy Within the First-Year Seminar

More than 68% of the 153 institutions whose librarians responded to our 2003 survey indicated that their institutions provide some form of first-year seminar (FYS) for incoming students. This high percentage of seminars for first-year students is confirmed in other studies as well. In 2003, the National Resource Center for The First-Year Experience and Students in Transition surveyed colleges and universities in the United States, and 83% of their 750 respondents reported offering a first-year seminar (Tobolowsky, 2005). These seminars, of course, vary in format and inclusion and in the treatment of literacy concepts.

At some institutions, librarians may have the opportunity to attend training sessions for the entire cohort of faculty members teaching the seminars. These sessions are an opportunity both to meet the instructors and to discuss with them the IL needs of their students. In the programs described here, librarians collaborate intensely with classroom faculty members to teach library sessions and to develop rich research assignments. Librarians provide guidance in locating appropriate materials as well as support for student research outside the classroom. This guidance and support enables classroom faculty members to include IL concepts in their seminars more effectively.

California State University at San Marcos

For many years, California State University at San Marcos (CSU San Marcos) was an upper-division-only institution with plans for a four-year program. In 1993, the institution convened a task force, which included an instruction librarian, to develop a new general education program. By April 1994, the College of Arts and Sciences began discussing the lower-division general education program, which was to include a library component. As a result, the CSU San Marcos librarians developed the goals and objectives of the IL program using the Association of College and Research Libraries' (ACRL, 1988) *Model Statement of Objectives for Academic Bibliographic Instruction.* These objectives functioned as the IL program's "course criteria" and formed the basis for discussions with classroom faculty members (Sonntag & Ohr, 1996). Such dialog with classroom members proved to be an essential component in the success of CSU San Marcos' IL program for first-year students. As part of the program, classroom faculty members develop research projects for the first-year seminars, and librarians design research syllabi that they teach for three weeks with a minimum of seven sessions. This unusually lengthy contact time with students allows the librarians to develop IL concepts within the context of the course research assignments. The assessment of IL skills involves evaluating projects students complete for the research section of the course including research journals, annotated bibliographies, and short-answer tests (G. Sonntag, personal communication, October, 2004). Librarians grade the assignments, but they also have the opportunity to observe students and reinforce areas where students encounter problems. Librarians have placed their syllabi for the GEL 101 library modules on their web site (California State University at San Marcos, 2005). An example of an assignment from the library unit is in Appendix C.

Librarians receive release time for their work in the seminars, and the library is reimbursed by the College of Arts and Sciences. Their first-year seminar courses now reach 50% of incoming first-year students. Of course, not every institution is able to support this model financially, but it has produced positive results for CSU San Marcos. Their own studies have shown that students enrolled in the first-year seminar have higher GPAs and better retention rates than students who do not take the course (Tobolowsky, Cox, & Wagner, 2005).

Oberlin College

The initial development period for a seminar on any campus provides an opportunity for librarians to become involved in the process. At Oberlin College, the administration offered classroom faculty members stipends to develop first-year seminars (FYS). The application for the stipends included questions related to IL. The library director provided additional grants for FYS development, giving the librarians a place at the table and allowing the embedding of IL, critical thinking, and research skills in the curriculum.

Using the *Information Literacy Competency Standards for Higher Education* (ACRL, 2000) as a springboard, librarians prepared a training handbook for FYS faculty members, which they used at FYS workshops and placed online. The handbook includes specific IL proficiencies and suggestions for assignments and activities to enhance learning (Oberlin College, 2003). Suggested goals or competencies for first-year students include:

1. Understanding the difference between scholarly and popular material
2. Recognizing primary and secondary resources
3. Understanding plagiarism and intellectual property issues
4. Understanding bibliographic citations
5. Knowing how to formulate a research strategy and understanding the process through which questions are refined

6. Determining which resources/databases are appropriate for the topic
7. Distilling research questions into searchable concepts or keywords
8. Critically evaluating the information

The handbook also refers to specific enrichment modules or lessons from an IL online tutorial that was created by the Five Colleges of Ohio, a consortium founded in 1995 that includes the College of Wooster, Denison University, Kenyon College, Ohio Wesleyan University, and Oberlin College (Five Colleges of Ohio, 2000).

Another factor in the success of the program at Oberlin is that a librarian serves on the first-year committee, which is the governance group for the FYS program. The librarians are, thus, aware of new topics being offered, and more important, they have a voice in the structure of the program as a whole. Many classroom faculty members have commented on the value of their collaboration with librarians. For example, one professor who taught a FYS suggests:

> I've learned more about searching during the library sessions for my students. The librarian was very helpful in the planning stages for the course in that she had more experience with my students' problems [in] doing research. She was instrumental in that she knew how to find things even though she was not necessarily familiar with my subject matter. (S. Faber, personal communication, October 15, 2004)

In another example, an associate professor of geology met with the science librarian to talk about IL goals and ways to incorporate them into the professor's courses. The librarian helped the professor create an assignment on evaluating web sources and recommended primary and secondary sources for use with the course assignments. Students in this course, and in other FYS sections, are encouraged by classroom faculty members to make an appointment to meet with a librarian on an individual basis. Many students take advantage of the opportunity (L. Moore, personal communication, November 5, 2004).

This close integration of subject matter and research skills provides an ideal situation for student learning. Librarians at Oberlin do more than teach specific sessions; they work closely with classroom faculty members to design assignments that effectively incorporate the achievement of IL skills into the goals of the professor's course (see Appendices D and E). Assessment of students' IL skills involves separate questions included on the regular FYS evaluations. The college also participated in the phase-three test of Project SAILS (Standardized Assessment of Information Literacy Skills) developed at Kent State University (2005).

College of Wooster

Institutions can expand the IL component of FYS by providing classroom faculty with stipends to encourage the addition of new goals in their syllabi. For example, the College of Wooster has more than 20 years of experience with FYS. Nevertheless, a Mellon grant designed to encourage librarian/faculty collaboration gave librarians an opportunity to incorporate more extensive IL instruction within the courses. In May 2003, the college held faculty workshops to discuss the design of research assignments. Classroom faculty members who created three redesigned assignments received a bookstore certificate. As a further incentive, a stipend was awarded to faculty members who collaborated with librarians more frequently and made more substantial changes to their courses. As a part of this effort, the reference and instruction librarians developed two key goals: (a) to develop more collegial relationships with faculty members teaching FYS and (b) to work toward 100% FYS faculty participation. Starting in the fall of 2003, each of the six teaching librarians was responsible for collaborating with six faculty members whom they contacted over the summer to work on instructional outcomes, expectations, collection resources, goals, assignments, desired faculty outcomes, and desired librarian outcomes. By fall 2004, almost all FYS faculty members had collaborated with librarians. Faculty members' responses to librarians' efforts are best described in their own words. One theater professor notes,

> The librarian worked with me then [after the workshop] and through the summer. She helped me find some of the material for my course. More importantly, she sat down with me and advised me on my syllabus. She noticed when assignments were not clear, and she helped me clarify them. I enjoyed having another pair of eyes looking at my syllabus and my students. I liked the interaction and the dialogue. (D. Seeds, personal communication, November 18, 2004)

Librarians defined the goals of the program for first-year students and made them available on their web site (College of Wooster, 2005). These goals include (a) defining a topic, (b) constructing a basic search strategy and accessing appropriate sources, (c) evaluating the sources chosen, (d) citing the material properly, and (e) using the material ethically.

Assessment of the College of Wooster program includes a four-question survey administered to each FYS student and another survey that faculty complete. Students comment on the most and least helpful aspects of the session and note areas where they still have questions. These formative assessments allow librarians to follow up with classroom faculty members and reinforce areas where students are having problems. Librarians also measure their success by the wide participation of FYS faculty members. In summary, while librarians at the College of Wooster provide workshops for faculty to assist them in the development of their FYS, much of the program's success is due to the congenial working relationships established between librarians and individual classroom faculty members.

Stand-Alone Information Literacy Courses

In our original survey, 16 (10%) of our 153 responding institutions provided stand-alone or for-credit IL courses for first-year students, making this the least common option. In many of these colleges, while the courses are recommended for first-year students, they are open to all students.

York College of Pennsylvania

York College of Pennsylvania (2005a, 2005b) has provided a two-credit IL course (Information Literacy 101 or IFL 101) for first-year students for more than 10 years. While it is a requirement in the core curriculum intended for all first-year students, some students enroll during their junior or senior years. In a phone interview, the library director explained that planning for the course began in 1995 with the college's general education task force (which included 10 faculty members, but no librarian). The dean was well aware of the American Library Association's (n.d.) work on IL and its application to the course.

The course has evolved over the years. At the start, very few people had e-mail accounts, so the course taught rudimentary skills. Now, the emphasis is on more sophisticated electronic communication. Online resources have greatly expanded since the mid-1990s making selection and evaluation of material difficult tasks. The librarian instructors now place much greater emphasis on ethical use of information (Appendix F), copyright, and plagiarism (S. Campbell, personal communication, October 18, 2005). Also, the curriculum includes instruction on major software packages such as Microsoft's Office Suite as well as IL concepts. In addition, students learn to use visual graphics to improve their oral presentations (S. Campbell, personal communication, September 10, 2004).

In order to link IL skills to the core curriculum more closely, the Honors English Composition course sections were team taught with IL faculty for a number of years. The director of composition and the IL faculty members together developed the syllabus, which included IL objectives. Two days per week, students worked on IL activities; and three days per week, they worked on composition. The research skills students learned were thus fully integrated into the course work for their English composition course. This coordination, however, was difficult to achieve when librarians tried to expand the coordination to all composition courses. Many sections of composition are taught by adjunct faculty whose schedules are not flexible enough to allow this type of close coordination of classes.

An interesting side note to the development of the library instruction program at the college is the change in the status of the library support staff. As the librarians sought to reach all first-year students, they found staffing the many IL sections needed the greatest challenge. Each semester, they had to hire numerous adjunct instructors. In order to respond to this challenge and to free librarians for increased instructional responsibilities, the library director upgraded clerical staff positions to allow them to handle some responsibilities previously held by librarians and technicians. As a result of this increase in responsibilities, the college recently granted the clerical staff administrative status.

Ulster County Community College

A thought-provoking adaptation of the credit-course model is the program developed by Ulster County Community College, which won the ACRL Innovation in Instruction Award in 1996. Their program is designed to overcome obstacles presented by numerous students taking a required course taught by a small library instructional staff. In the spring 2005, 15 day sections of LIB111, 8 online sections, and a number of evening sections were available. Each section enrolled about 20 students per class, which was too heavy a load for the relatively small library staff to carry alone. While other campuses hire numerous adjunct faculty members to staff these courses, Ulster County Community College recruits instructors from their own full-time faculty members. Thus, teaching faculty members are necessary to the success of the program.

In a phone interview, the coordinator of IL reported that, in 1992, the college administration proposed a two-credit course as part of an IL initiative. The institution found the model difficult to implement, as many departments could not support an additional two-credit course in their already-full curriculum. Moreover, some classroom faculty members believed that "information literacy was a 'skills' course that should not be offered as a credit course" (Walsh, 2003, p.14). The Ulster librarians met repeatedly with numerous administrators and classroom faculty members "until the librarians convinced the key people on campus that IL should be a high priority" (Walsh, p. 17). In 1994, the various stakeholders reached a compromise, and the institution approved a one-credit course.

Meanwhile, the director of the Teaching and Learning Center proposed that librarians offer workshops for classroom faculty members to learn about the electronic resources available to them through the library. After these two eight-hour sessions, librarians approached those faculty members who appeared especially interested in taking additional training to teach a section of LIB111, the one-credit IL course. The first three volunteers included a chemistry professor, a business faculty member, and an engineering faculty member.

Faculty members are trained to teach LIB111 either by taking the course in a section devoted to classroom faculty members only, or by taking a regular section of the course populated by students. These faculty members complete the course and then work one-on-one with a librarian. Ulster classroom faculty members from such diverse areas as nursing, communication, physical education, foreign languages, English, English as a Second Language, chemistry, business, and engineering have taught the course.

The general goals for the course underscore the value of learning fundamental concepts rather than specific tools that are subject to change. Such concepts include:

- How to ask a question
- How information is structured and accessed
- How to develop a successful search strategy
- How to evaluate the quality of information
- How to be informed consumers of information
- How to begin thinking about the educational, economic, social, and political implications of life in the Information Age (Ulster Community College, 2000)

At first, the institution only offered the course as an elective, but various departments soon adopted it as a requirement. The turning point came when the English department made LIB111 either a pre-requisite or a co-requisite for the second-semester English composition course, EN102. Other programs "piggy-backed" on the EN102 requirement; thus, the course became a requirement for graduation. Most students take the course in their first year. Administrative support for the library program is strong. In fact, the administration strongly suggests that EN102 and LIB111 be a part of any new program or major.

Faculty involvement in LIB111 helps instructors become more aware of what students need to know about research. One instructor notes that he spends considerably more time on concepts like source evaluation. He shows students how to use databases, but he also wants them to realize that some journals carry more scholarly weight than others. He thinks evaluation is an important skill in which many students are weak and that it needs to be emphasized in courses across the curriculum.

The obvious advantage of using classroom faculty to teach LIB111 is that it enables a small library staff to reach a larger number of students than would be possible if librarians had to do all the instruction. Also, the coordinator of information literacy reports that faculty members who teach LIB111 frequently incorporate IL concepts into their other courses, and they influence other departmental colleagues to more thoroughly embed IL in their classes. IL concepts are thus reinforced and expanded in a wider area of the curriculum in many disciplines. Librarians have a large, ongoing role to play in the design of the LIB111 course by keeping it up to date, training faculty, and providing assessment.

Conclusions and Recommendations

From our review of IL programs for first-year students at seven institutions, six essential principles emerge for building effective instruction for first-year students:

1. Library directors need to develop effective working relationships with deans and other administrators who are responsible for academic programs.

All the model programs described above demonstrate that strong administrative support is essential to launch and sustain a program. Effective working relationships between library directors, deans, and other administrators who are responsible for academic programs can be a critical factor in promoting an ongoing dialogue about the importance of IL for the first-year student. Providing administrators with published studies on the topic may facilitate this dialogue. Yet, face-to-face discussions with committed and knowledgeable library directors may be the best way to instill confidence in the academic administration that a new or updated program will be successful.

The examples of Wooster College, Oberlin College, Ulster County Community College, and other institutions demonstrate the importance of administrative support in providing workshops and stipends to faculty for redesigning their courses to include IL concepts or to design an entirely new course. Librarians at these colleges participated as instructors in faculty workshops that provided a means for getting to know instructors and for developing the rapport that often led to further collaborations.

2. Librarians should clearly define the goals of their program for first-year students.

The programs highlighted in this chapter have used ACRL's (2000) *Information Literacy Competency Standards for Higher Education* as the basis for their programs. While librarians are very familiar with the standards, classroom faculty members need to become familiar with them as well. However, all six of the regional accrediting associations have rewritten their standards to eliminate separate guidelines for library and learning resources and to integrate them into other sections with an emphasis on librarian and faculty collaboration. One of the most important results of these changes has been a new emphasis on student-learning outcomes (Nelson, 2004). Ratteray (2002) commented on the impact on IL resulting from the revised standards for Middle States Commission on Higher Education:

> The emphasis on information literacy as a meta-outcome could have an impact on higher education in at least three areas: long range planning, especially with regard to assessment; a change in the institution-wide dialogue about student learning; and increased collaboration woven into the campus culture. (p. 368)

Thus, librarians should closely watch recent changes in the accreditation standards for their areas and look for opportunities to build IL into program review and improvement efforts on their campuses.

3. Librarians should promote the essential collaborative relationships between librarians and classroom faculty members teaching first-year students through both formal and informal avenues.

All the models highlighted here credited the success of their programs to the role of effective collaboration between librarians and classroom faculty members. When IL is integrated within the first-year curriculum, the program reaches more students and offers them higher quality instruction. Once classroom faculty members from numerous disciplines have integrated IL concepts in their courses, librarians can play a reinforcing role by assisting with the design of assignments and providing supplementary exercises, materials, and database demonstrations. Partnering with faculty members in these efforts provides students with widespread opportunities to gain skills throughout their college careers. As Hunt and Birks (2004) note, librarians cannot be the only providers of IL instruction to students:

> In terms of information literacy, collaboration is the only way to achieve true integration with the curriculum. It is no longer the sole responsibility of the librarian or the library to ensure that students develop IL skills. In addition, faculty in other disciplines after working with librarians often will be inspired to advocate for IL, which frequently is not understood by discipline-based faculty. (p. 32)

This close collaboration between librarians and faculty members is a hallmark of successful IL programs for first-year students.

4. Librarians should serve on campus committees since such service can facilitate collaborative relationships by fostering mutual respect among librarians, classroom faculty members, and administrators.

Serving on influential campus committees dealing with curriculum issues can give librarians both insight into institutional planning and a forum for advocating the importance of IL for first-year programs of all types. For example, at University of California at San Marcos, an instruction librarian served on the task force that considered major changes in the general education program when the institution expanded to four years, and now librarians serve on all committees, even chairing some of them. At University of North Carolina, Asheville, a librarian sat on the general education task force that planned the new Integrative Liberal Studies program. At Oberlin College, a librarian serves on the first-year committee. At the College of Wooster, a librarian was appointed to the assessment committee. At Elmhurst College, a librarian and two faculty members form the committee that approves proposals for IL-intensive courses. Clearly, involvement on campus governance committees is an important factor in the development of IL programs and in sustaining their vitality.

Some of the programs described above were expanded because librarians were prepared to take advantage of major projects occurring on their campus, whether that was the construction of a new library building, the renovation of an older space, or a major change to the overall curriculum. These major projects can be opportunities to influence significant constituencies on campus about the importance of IL. Librarians need to prepare themselves to clearly articulate desired goals.

5. Librarians should consider seeking outside grants or institutional funding for stipends to classroom faculty members seeking to redesign their courses to include information literacy.

A number of our model programs received grant funds to provide successful faculty workshops on IL. We encourage librarians to develop working relationships with the grant writers on their campuses. Librarians need to clearly express the goals for which they are seeking funding and their ability to carry out a successful project. Stipends for faculty members to redesign their courses to include IL objectives may also be a part of grant applications. Including support for individual faculty can expand the IL program as well as provide evidence of the value an institution places on these changes.

6. One-on-one reference assistance by appointment can be a valuable and productive supplement to time spent in the classroom, especially for first-year students.

A number of institutions described here (Oberlin College, University of North Carolina, Asheville, the College of Wooster, and York College of Pennsylvania) use a reference appointment system to follow up with students after library instruction sessions. One-on-one reference assistance by appointment can be a valuable and productive supplement to time spent in the classroom because students and librarians already know each other, and the librarian is familiar with the assignments.

The widely different instructional models discussed in this chapter demonstrate that librarians across the country are collaborating with administrators and faculty members in new ways to more effectively embed IL concepts within the first-year curriculum. The programs highlighted here have evolved over time and adapted to changing campus needs, and no one template will serve all institutions equally well. Despite these promising initial efforts, more work is needed in this area. In particular, librarians and classroom faculty members interested in IL instruction should seek to answer a number of questions about these collaborations. First, do faculty members who work with librarians to include IL goals and activities in their courses encourage their colleagues to do the same? How do administrators influence faculty participation in these relationships? Finally, will the recent changes in accreditation standards provide the impetus for an increased emphasis on faculty/librarian collaboration for IL throughout the first-year student curriculum?

Author Note

The authors would like to thank the following librarians who kindly gave their time to talk with us about their information literacy programs for first-year students:

Susan Swords Steffans, Library Director at Elmhurst College

Janet Ferguson, User Instruction Coordinator, University of North Carolina, Asheville

Gabriela Sonntag, Coordinator for Information Literacy, California State University, San Marcos

Jessica Grim, Instruction Coordinator, Oberlin College

Elys Kettling, Reference and Instruction Librarian, The College of Wooster

Susan Campbell, Library Director, York College of Pennsylvania

Robin Walsh, Assistant Librarian and Coordinator of Information Literacy, Ulster County Community College

We would also like to thank the following faculty members who gave their time to talk with us about their experiences in collaborating with librarians at their institutions:

Michael Lindberg, Associate Professor of Geography, Elmhurst College

Sebastian Faber, Professor in Hispanic Studies, Oberlin College

Laura Moore, Associate Professor of Geology, Oberlin College

Dale Seeds, Professor of Theatre, College of Wooster

Rick Gelston, Acting Dean for Academic Affairs, Ulster County Community College

References

American Library Association. (n.d.). *Information literacy in the disciplines*. Retrieved September 19, 2005, from http://www.ala.org/ala/acrlbucket/is/projectsacrl/infolitdisciplines/index.htm

Association of College and Research Libraries (ACRL). (1988). *Model statement of objectives for academic bibliographic instruction*. Chicago: Author.

Association of College and Research Libraries (ACRL). (2000). *Information literacy competency standards for higher education*. Retrieved June 5, 2005, from www.ala.org/ala/acrl/acrl-standards/informationliteracycompetency.htm

California State University at San Marcos. (2005). *Subject and course guides*. Retrieved September 21, 2005, from http://library.csusm.edu/guides.asp

College of Wooster. (2005, August 25). *Recommended information literacy competencies for first-year seminar students*. Retrieved September 18, 2005, from: http://www.wooster.edu/library/instruction/competencies/fys/index.php

Five Colleges of Ohio. (2005). *Information literacy tutorial*. Retrieved June 6, 2005, from www.denison.edu/collaborations/ohio5/infolit/

Gibson, C. (1992) Accountability for BI programs in academic libraries: Key issues for the 1990s. In S. C. Blandy, L. E. M. Martin, & M. L. Strife (Eds.), *Assessment and accountability in reference work* (pp. 99-108). Binghamton, NY: Hayworth Press.

Hunt, F., & Birks, J. (2004). Best practices in information literacy. *portal: Libraries and the Academy, 4*(1), 27-39.

Kent State University. (2005, January 24). *Project for standardized assessment of information literacy skills.* Retrieved September 19, 2005, from: http://sails.lms.kent.edu/index.php

Malone, D., & Videon, C. (2003). *First-year student library instruction* (CLIP Note # 33). Chicago: Association of College and Research Libraries.

Nelson, B. (2004). SACS standards 2004: A compliance strategy for academic libraries. *Southeastern Librarian, 52*(3), 10-18.

Oberlin College. (2003, May). *Incorporating information literacy into Oberlin's first-year seminars: Faculty guide.* Retrieved June 5, 2005, from http://www.oberlin.edu/library/programs/fys/guide.pdf/

Ratteray, O. M. (2002). Information literacy in self study and accreditation. *The Journal of Academic Librarianship, 28*(6), 368-375.

Sonntag, G., & Ohr D. M. (1996). The development of a lower division, general education, course integrated information literacy. *College & Research Libraries, 57*(4), 331-339.

Tobolowsky, B. F. (2005). *The 2003 national survey on first-year seminars: Continuing innovations in the collegiate curriculum* (Monograph No. 41). Columbia, SC: University of South Carolina, National Resource Center for The First-Year Experience and Students in Transition.

Tobolowsky, B. F., Cox, B. E., & Wagner. M. T. (Eds.). (2005). *Exploring the evidence volume III: Reporting research on first-year seminars* (Monograph No. 42). Columbia, SC: University of South Carolina, National Resource Center for The First-Year Experience and Students in Transition.

Ulster Community College. (2000). *A course in information literacy.* Retrieved September 19, 2005, from http://ucc.sln.suny.edu/

University of North Carolina at Asheville. (2005). Information literacy intensives. *Catalog 2005-2006,* 40, 47.

Walsh, R. (2003). Involving faculty in BI-LIB111: Information literacy at Ulster Community College. *Community and Junior College Libraries, 12*(1), 11-20.

York College of Pennsylvania. (2005a). *General catalog, 2005 - 2007.* Retrieved February 7, 2006, from http://www.ycp.edu/admissions/catalog

York College of Pennsylvania. (2005b). *Information literacy e-text.* Retrieved February 21, 2005, from http://www.ycp.edu/library/ifl/etext/ethome.html/

Appendix A

Information Literacy Integrated Into the General Curriculum Model

University of North Carolina, Asheville

Finding Books and Articles for Your Research Journal

I. Identifying search terms for your topic:

Before beginning your research, think of all the keywords and concepts that describe your topic. Be sure to include synonyms. These terms can be combined to form a search strategy in electronic databases.

Example:

Topic: How does participation in a college team sport affect students' academic success?

Keyword/concept 1	Keyword/concept 2	Keyword/concept 3
College athletes	Academic achievement	
Team sports	Grades	
Intramural sports		

List your topic:

List keywords and concepts that describe your topic.

Keyword/concept 1	Keyword/concept 2	Keyword/concept 3

II. Identifying resources:

A. *Books (may include case studies, biographies, or diaries)*
- Search the library catalog using keywords or standard subject headings. Subject headings tend to be broader and more inclusive than keywords. For example, "College athletes" is an appropriate subject heading for the above topic.
- List the terms that you used to search the library catalog.
- Find a useful book and list the author, title, place of publication, publisher, and date below.

B. *Statistics/ reference books*

Statistical compilations, like those listed below, may be useful for some of your topics.

Statistical Abstract of the United States (Refdesk HA 202 2004)

Digest of Education Statistics (UNCA Fed Docs ED 1.326)

Reference books (encyclopedias, handbooks) such as these listed below may provide excellent background and overviews for a topic.

A to Z of Women in World History (Ref.CT3202.K84 2002)

Encyclopedia of Sociology (Ref.HM425.E5 2000)

Find a useful reference book and list the author, title, place of publication, publisher, and date below.

C. Journal articles. Use the EBSCOhost Academic Search Elite database.
- Go to the library home page
- Open the Quick Links drop-down menu.
- Select EBSCOhost.
- Check Academic Search Elite.
- Press "continue" to begin searching.
- Check to limit results to "scholarly (peer-reviewed) journals."
- Limit by publication date: from January 1995 to the present.
- NOTE: Select the "advanced search" option in order to combine keywords and concepts.
- List the author, article title, journal title, volume, issue, and date of one useful article.
- List other keywords that you found in searching the database. Be sure to identify the best or most useful terms.

NOTE: If you have trouble finding a useful book or article, please ask your instructor or the teaching librarian for assistance.

Please list comments, problems, or questions that you would like to discuss in the next class session.

Appendix B

Information Literacy Integrated Into the General Curriculum Model Web Evaluation

University of North Carolina, Asheville

- Locate the following Internet resources:
  1. Harvard School of Public Health Nutrition Source
     http://www.hsph.harvard.edu/nutritionsource/
  2. Global Warming Information
     http://www.globalwarming.org/
  3. WebMD
     http://www.webmd.com/
  4. Department of U.S. Homeland Security
     http://www.dhs.gov/dhspublic/
- Spend 15 minutes exploring the assigned web site with your small group in order to gather information and describe the site to your classmates. At the end of the 15 minutes, you and your partners will report your findings in a brief (five-minute) presentation to the class.
- Consider the following questions:
  Who created the site? What are their qualifications and credentials? Does the site have a profit motive? Does a profit motive impact the content?
  What is the purpose of the site? What types of information are available on this site? If data is available, what does a user need to know to successfully navigate through/find the data?
  Is the information presented from a biased point of view? How current is the information on the site? What type of language does the site use (e.g., scholarly, simplistic, informal, inflammatory)?
- What are the strengths of the site? What are the weaknesses of the site?
- Would you choose to use information from this site in your research paper? Why or why not?

Appendix C

First-Year Seminar
Model Assignment From Library Instruction Module
California State University, San Marcos

GEL101 Aronson/Meulemans Summer 2005
DUE DATE: Wednesday, August 9
NO LATE WORK ACCEPTED
POINTS: 25

A. Include:
1. A list of keywords and three search statements
2. A paragraph describing what kind of results you got with your search statements
3. A citation for an article you selected
4. An annotation for this article
5. The first two pages of the article.

B. Example:
1. These were my keywords:
    Haole*, Hawaii*, Caucasian*, "growing up"
2. These were my search statements:
    Haole* or Caucasian*, haole* and Hawaii*, haolc* and Hawaii* and female*
3. How I found my article:

Since I wanted an article on what it is like to grow up haole in Hawaii, my last search was the most effective. With my first search (haole* or Caucasian*) I got over 2,000 hits! This is because Caucasian is a widely used scholarly term. My 2nd and 3rd searches retrieved a few articles. I also tried these terms in Sociological Abstracts and found more than I did in Academic Search Elite. Sociological Abstracts had more detailed discussions of the haole experience. I even found some articles about the Portuguese in Hawaii. These articles may be useful for my project.

4. My selected article citation and annotation:

Medeiros, J. A. (2003). Haole in Hawai'i: The Caucasian as minority experience. *Journal of Race Studies* 34(5), 233-267.

Medeiros, an anthropologist at the University of Hawai'i and specialist in the field of minority studies, reports on a five-year study of attitudes shown toward haoles by non-Caucasians. Data was gathered through surveys and interviews on all islands. She argues that the "haole experience" is similar to that of a minority in the United States. Contrary to the argument in Burke's 1998 article, Medeiros disagrees that haoles experience true discrimination. Medeiros' thorough analysis of her data and systematic analysis reveal a blend of negative and positive attitudes towards haoles. This research will be invaluable as I attempt to describe, in my final project, the multiple ways of interpreting the haole experience in Hawaii. Medeiros' intended audience of other researchers who are interested in the minority experience will find the argument posed to be very different from previous and similar research.

Appendix D

First-Year Seminar
Model Information Literacy Assignment
Oberlin College

FYSP 168, Fall 2004
Assignment 4: Finding Images

The purpose of this assignment is to familiarize you with images from Tibetan religious culture and to help you develop a critical approach to searching the web.

1. Do a search in Google (or another general search engine of your choosing) in order to locate images of Tibetan religious culture on the web. Keywords might include thangka, Tibet, Buddhism, Dalai Lama, or some of the new glossary terms. You may also want to search image databases such as Corbis and the Fine Arts Museums of San Francisco (URL's follow):
   - http://pro.corbis.com
   - http://www.famsf.org/
2. Do the following subject search in OBIS: Art Buddhist China Tibet. Go to the Art Library to look at the images in a number of these books.

For class, consider these questions and jot down your thoughts for class discussion. How do the images you found online compare to the images found in print sources? Are there differences in what you learn from these two sources and how you learn it? What, if anything, does the exploration of images add to our study? How does it affect your understanding?

This assignment was created with the assistance of Jessica Grim, reference librarian. Reprinted with permission.

Appendix E

From: "Incorporating Information Literacy into Oberlin's First-Year Seminars"
Oberlin College

An information-literate, first-year student is able to:
Distinguish between primary and secondary resources in a given context and/or a given discipline; determine when it is appropriate to use these types of resources and why.

Strategy: Consider the context. Engage students in active thinking about what primary/secondary means in a given discipline and why, in making these distinctions, "context is everything."

Potential discussion topics:
- What might be some general "rules" about what constitutes primary and secondary sources in different fields of study (e.g., biology, English literature, and politics)?
- Why are the potential ambiguities and blurring of distinctions inherent in determining whether a source is primary or secondary dependent upon the question being asked, and when it is being posed (the time/date concept)?

- Ask students to consider a particular source (e.g., book, journal article, conference proceeding, web site) and think about whether there are circumstances under which it might be considered a primary source and other circumstances under which it might be considered a secondary source.
- Have students consider various kinds of writing they have done (e.g., autobiographical, experiential, essays, research papers) and discuss whether these materials would be considered primary or secondary sources, and under what circumstances

Potential exercises
- Give students several research questions/theses and have them make a list of the kinds of primary resource materials scholars might seek in each case.
- Have students evaluate a primary source, answering the following questions: What was the purpose/intent of the source? Who was its author/originator?
- "Determining the Information You Need" lesson from The Five Colleges of Ohio Information Literacy Tutorial at http://www.denison.edu/ohio5/infolit/a3determine/

Reprinted with permission from Oberlin College staff contact Jessica Grim.

Appendix F

"Stand Alone" Information Literacy Course Model Assignment

York College of Pennsylvania

Ethics Case Studies

For each case study, describe the main ethical dilemma posed and develop strategies for solutions. Use the YCP Student Handbook, Schmidt Library Acceptable Use Policy, Information Systems Policy, or any other resources as appropriate.

1. Three students, Ellen, Jeff, and Scott are working on a term project for their senior management seminar with Professor James. The project includes a 50-page report and an oral presentation. Dr. James expects extensive research, documentation, creativity, and initiative. She expects full and equal participation from the members of the group. In the early phases of conducting research on the management protocols of the White Rose Conglomerate, it becomes apparent that Scott will not do his share of the extensive work required to complete the project. Ellen and Jeff initially cover for him, but they become overwhelmed by the workload and angered by Scott's equal grades for unequal work.

2. Jones College is a small, rural institution committed to providing students with cutting-edge technology in all domains. One of their more imaginative art students, Eric, mounts a 24-hour/7-day a week live audio/video feed from his dorm room on his web page. The camera records everything which takes place in the room. College officials begin receiving complaints from students, parents, admissions, staff, and board members about the "obscene" nature of the web page. There is much media attention.

3.   Two Smithers University students, Pat and Chris, have extensive computer skills. They create an impressive looking web page on explosives that includes a "recipe" for making napalm in your kitchen borrowed from a friend's high school science fair project. In a distant state, two youngsters, ages 10 and 11, discover the recipe and attempt to make the napalm. It explodes in their faces, causing minor injury to both.

4.   Mike is no prude, but he is offended by pornography on the Internet. His roommate, Tom and some of their mutual friends are ardent net surfers. They frequently gather at Tom's PC and visit sites that Mike deems obscene and highly objectionable. They print pictures from these sites and post them in their rooms.

5.   Sam has a 10-page paper requiring 10 works cited due in his political science class tomorrow. He has had the assignment for a month, but he has done none of the work. A classmate, Derek, tells him about a web site where he can get a paper on almost any topic for free. A quick check, download, cut-and-paste, and Sam think he is home free. His professor, Dr. Roberts, quickly spots the plagiarized paper.

6.   Emily discovers the library's extensive CD collection and is eager to check some of them out. Unfortunately, she has a fine for overdue materials, and her borrowing privileges are temporarily revoked. This really irritates Emily, so she decides to take the CDs. Waiting until the library staff member on duty is busy with a patron, she stuffs 10 CD cases into her backpack. When she goes through the exit turnstile, Emily sets off the security alarm. The circulation staff member finds the CD cases and knows they are not checked out.

7.   Seniors Peter and Gretchen have been good friends since their first year. Both have developed extensive computer skills. They have worked together in classes and in the campus computer labs. Gretchen has been having some serious problems academically and has resorted to some things she should not have done to get by in her final year. Peter is oblivious to this. As a result of her bad judgment, Gretchen is denied network access. Claiming to forget her new network account password and to need access to files stored there for a project, Gretchen talks Peter into letting her use his. While in his account, she attempts to "hack" the campus grading system to change her grades.

8.   Adam and Megan dated all through high school. Megan broke up with Adam before coming to college this fall. Adam was very distraught. As soon as Adam went to another college, he began using his e-mail account to send Megan messages. At first, the messages were fairly innocuous. Megan either responded in a brief, perfunctory way that did not please Adam or ignored his messages. Adam increased the frequency of the messages, and there was a menacing tone to them. Megan was resentful at first, and then she became frightened.

Above case studies courtesy of Professor Susan Campbell.

9.   Lindsey, an enterprising new student, discovers the library's videocassette collection and checks out two of the newest releases. Over the weekend, she borrows her neighbor's VCR to dub copies of both movies. Lisa, the neighbor, wants copies too, so she gives Lindsey a blank tape. Soon, other people are asking Lindsey to copy tapes. Word gets out that Lindsey will dub movies if you give her $3 and a blank videotape.

10.   Fred, a first-year student at Smithers University, posts a personal web page providing links for free software downloads of programs he has purchased or been given. Fred allows anyone to download this software asking only that users "donate" copies of other software he does not have. An employee of Microsoft, performing a monthly check of the Internet for illegal copies of the company's software, finds Fred's page.

Above case studies courtesy of Professor Kimberley Donnelly.
Copyright©2005 York College of Pennsylvania (Reprinted with permission.)

Chapter 5

The Library and First-Year Seminars: In-Depth Analysis of a 2001 National Study

Colleen Boff & Kristin Johnson

"If everyone agrees that higher education should lead to lifelong learning, then learning how to navigate through information is key." (Watts, 2005, p. 346.)

First-year seminars can be an excellent venue to introduce students to the library and information literacy topics. John Gardner advocated for library integration into the first-year seminar 20 years ago, and he reiterated this sentiment at a recent national library conference (Gardner 2003; Gardner, Decker, & McNairy, 1986). Many first-year seminar faculty members and administrators are also advocates. As librarians and first-year seminar instructors at institutions that emphasize integrating the library into the first-year experience, we wanted to know if first-year seminar programs nationwide valued this as well. Therefore, in 2001, we conducted a nationwide survey to determine whether first-year seminar curricula at U.S. universities and colleges contained a library component and, if so, to what extent (Johnson & Boff, 2001).

Through our survey, we sought to establish baseline data from which we and others in the field could conduct research on the first year and library connection. Initially, we considered seeking information regarding the role libraries and librarians play in the total first-year experience (which could include first-year seminars, general education courses, and out-of-class programs), but, for manageability, we chose to examine this connection in first-year seminars alone. We first published the baseline data from our survey in *Reference Services Review (RSR)* (Boff & Johnson, 2002). In the *RSR* article, we reported how and the degree to which library topics were incorporated into credit-based, first-year seminars, as well as the depth of librarian involvement with the course.

For this chapter, we analyzed the qualitative data from that study in more detail to better identify and describe common practices, trends, and opinions regarding library and librarian involvement in first-year seminars. In particular, we focused on the open-ended responses to survey questions, especially those relating to (a) how much time was devoted to the library component, (b) who developed the library component, (c) how the component was taught, (d) what was taught, (e) whether training was offered, and (f) how the component was assessed.

Information Literacy

We did not include the phrase "information literacy" in the wording of our questions, and we did not attempt to measure anything specifically related to information literacy competencies through this survey (ACRL, 2000). We believe the inclusion of this language would have caused more confusion than clarification, as the respondents for this survey primarily consisted of administrators, directors, or coordinators of the seminar, not librarians or others more familiar with the scope and definition of information literacy. However, for this chapter, we will tie analysis of the data to larger issues related to information literacy when appropriate.

The primary purpose of this chapter, then, is to analyze first-year seminars in aggregate to identify common trends with respect to libraries and librarians that may be of interest to first-year educators. We will conclude with observations and recommendations for ways to maximize the impact of including a library component in a first-year seminar and institutional factors to consider when adding a library component to an existing or new first-year seminar.

The Survey

In October 2001, we collaborated with the National Resource Center for The First-Year Experience and Students in Transition to conduct this survey. The National Resource Center provided us with a mailing list of 749 respondents to their 2000 National Survey of First-Year Seminar Programs who indicated that their institution offered a first-year seminar. These institutions comprised the population for our study and represent a convenience sample, not a random sample; therefore, the results cannot be generalized to larger populations.

The web-based survey consisted of 15 questions. For several questions, the respondents could select more than one answer. We also provided respondents the opportunity to offer additional information through open-ended responses for 10 of the survey questions (see Appendix for the complete survey). We hoped that responses to the open-ended questions would reveal trends not obvious from the quantitative data, but we also sought to identify significant "minority opinions." We devote the remaining portion of the chapter to our analysis of these responses, including selected quotations when appropriate.

Survey Results

Presence of a Library Component

We received 368 usable responses to our survey for a response rate of 52%. Of those responses, the majority (315 or 86%) reported that a library component was part of the first-year seminar curricula. These 315 institutions provide the basis for the remaining analysis and statistics in this chapter. Of the institutions with a library component in the first-year seminar, most (210 or 67%) required the library component, while about one third of the schools (105 or 33%) made the component optional.

Time Devoted to Library Component

Two of the questions on our survey related to determining how much of a first-year seminar is actually devoted to a library component. We considered this important because the presence of a library component in these courses does not necessarily suggest its value to first-year educators. However, knowing how much time is devoted to library instruction would provide some insight into its value. Ultimately, we developed two similar questions. We asked respondents to estimate: (a) in-class time devoted to the component and (b) the percentage of the curriculum devoted to the component (see Appendix, questions 8 & 9).

Overall, very few schools devoted a large percentage of in-class time to the library component. When asked how much in-class time they devoted to the library component, the most frequent response was one hour. See Table 1.

Table 1
In-Class Time Devoted to Library Component (N = 315)

	Number of respondents	Percentage of respondents
1 hour	142	45
2 hours	88	28
3 hours	34	11
4 - 6 hours	27	9
7 - 9 hours	0	0
10 - 12 hours	2	1
12+ hours	7	2

Note. 15 respondents did not answer; 13 provided comment only.

Similarly, when asked to estimate the total percentage of the first-year seminar curricula devoted to the library component, slightly more than half reported that 5% or less of the curriculum was devoted to the library component. Only 11% estimated that they devoted more than 10% of seminar curriculum to the library. See Table 2.

Table 2
Percentage of Curriculum Devoted to Library Component (N = 315)

Range (%)	Number of respondents	Percentage of respondents
< 1	31	10
1 - 5	138	44
6 - 10	92	29
11 - 15	23	7
16 - 20	8	3
21 - 25	4	1
> 25	4	1

Note. 15 respondents did not answer; 8 provided comment only.

Responses to this question varied slightly from the former for two reasons. The percentage of the curriculum devoted to a specific topic may vary from in-class hours due to the length of the course. For example, two hours of in-class time for the library component may seem minimal for a three-credit course that meets throughout the semester, but for a one-credit course that meets once a week for half a quarter, those two hours increase the percentage of time spent on the library component significantly. Second, some schools may have delivered instruction outside of class meeting times (e.g., completing online tutorials outside of class time).

Although we specifically stated we were asking respondents for estimates, many of them found these questions difficult to answer and supplemented their answers with open-ended responses. The majority of these comments indicate that though an institution or department may have required the library component, classroom faculty members did not consistently include the component. Many of the responses indicated difficulty in estimating the percentage of the curriculum devoted to the library component because it varied widely among classroom faculty members. In other words, even with required components, classroom faculty members differed widely in how much time they devoted to a library component. Sample comments underscore this variability:

> I find answering these questions difficult. I think that most classroom faculty try to include some library work, but the amount and kind vary a lot.

> As much time as the faculty deem necessary.

> Varies from a low of 50 minutes to a high of 4 hours.

> Usually one or two class periods, but varies from class [to class] depending on research needs. Minimum has been half an hour; maximum has been 6 class periods at 75 minutes each.

> Depends on the classroom faculty. Some none, some a lot.

These comments suggest that classroom faculty have considerable flexibility in terms of course content. While institutions may value the library component in theory, in practice its inclusion and emphasis is often left up to the individual classroom faculty member.

We did not ask how learning goals or objectives determined or even influenced the amount of the course devoted to library instruction. However, one respondent indicated that a uniform curriculum dictated the amount of time devoted to library instruction and ensured consistency across sections:

> We have a set of library assignments that all students must complete. But we also require research throughout the semester on social topics, which require more work on 'library' issues. Thus, it is impossible to say precisely how much time is involved because some students are more proficient in conducting research than others. But I would say that each student probably spends at least 15 hours on what I would consider "library" work for the course.

Responsibility for Curriculum Development

While individual faculty members may have determined how much time was spent on library instruction at the majority of institutions, librarians developed the curricular content. At 80% of responding institutions, librarians were involved with curriculum development, whereas classroom faculty members developed the component at only 35% of responding institutions. As these responses indicate, responsibility for curriculum development is primarily borne by the librarian, but is shared at some institutions (Table 3).

Table 3
Who Develops the Library Component (N = 315)

Person	Number of respondents	Percentage of respondents
Librarians	253	80
Instructor of course	111	35
FYE director	76	24
Other	51	16

Note. Percentages exceed 100 because respondents could select more than one answer.

Indeed, analysis of the open-ended responses for this particular question indicates librarians, classroom faculty, and directors of the first-year seminars at some institutions collaborated on curriculum development. Of the 51 open-ended responses, only three first-year seminar directors reported that they developed the library component independently. The remaining responses indicated that a committee or the first-year seminar director in collaboration with the librarian developed the component.

The open-ended responses do not enable us to comment confidently on the extent to which librarians collaborate with classroom instructors and first-year seminar directors to develop the library component. Several respondents stated that a committee at their institution developed the library component, but they did not clarify if a librarian actually served as a committee member. We could not determine the degree to which librarians had been involved in the design of the library component, yet the involvement of librarians in the design of the component may well have an impact on its success.

As with the amount of time devoted to the component, several respondents provided comments to support the conclusion that classroom instructors have considerable flexibility in terms of course content:

Each of the 16 instructors in the course design their own content-oriented library assignment.

Faculty are not required to include a library component as part of the course, but many do. Most faculty require formal writing assignments that require research, so they include some sort of library orientation.

Although 'library skills' is a required component of the course, instructors are able to cover that area however they see fit. Some develop the component on their own; others ask librarians to cover the topic.

In two instances, the respondents referred to the use of learning objectives in developing the library component:

The objectives are instructor developed—the presentation is librarian developed.

The general core expectation was developed by the curriculum committee in consultation with the librarians. Each instructor may develop an assignment to meet the library expectations. In the pilot program, the librarians consult extensively with instructors to develop an integrated assignment that touches on the five ACRL *Information Literacy Competency Standards.*

Content of the Library Component

The content of the library component in first-year seminars was varied but centered on electronic resources. In particular, the majority of respondents reported that article indexes/databases and the online library catalog were included in the library component (see Table 4). Respondents also frequently reported that library tours and teaching students how to search the web were included in the content.

Additional instructional areas were noted by 67 respondents with some frequency, including information about locating reserve materials, ethical use of information (i.e., plagiarism, citation styles, academic integrity), and instruction on specific computer programs (e.g., e-mail, spreadsheets, presentation software, and word-processing packages).

Respondents cited the use of scavenger hunts infrequently, whereas two thirds of the reporting institutions included research assignments. Such responses are encouraging. Scavenger hunts tend to be paper-and-pencil exercises that require students to use a variety of library sources or to navigate the library building in the pursuit of information, oftentimes random facts or statistics. These exercises are typically unrelated to a research assignment and often require lower-order thinking skills. Moreover, if created without care, they can invoke a great deal of frustration for students and reference desk librarians. On the other hand, research assignments, which generally require higher-order cognitive skill sets, are more likely to foster a deep understanding of libraries and information literacy.

Table 4

Content of the Library Component (N = 315)

Content	Number of respondents	Percentage of respondents
Article indexes/databases	257	82
Library catalog	256	81
Web searching	247	78
Library tours	246	78
Research assignments	208	66
Web evaluation	114	36
Scavenger hunts	84	27
Other	67	21

Note. Percentages exceed 100 because respondents could select more than one answer.

While respondents were not asked if specific learning objectives or goals guided content development, a small number of the open-ended responses to this question identified information literacy standards or the *Information Literacy Competency Standards for Higher Education* (ACRL, 2000) as playing a part in curriculum development at their institutions:

> This web-based training, which is new this year, was modeled after the ACRL Standards and also discusses ethical use of information.

> [Curricular goals include] determining the nature and extent of an information need, interpreting citations, distinguishing between popular and scholarly sources, [and] the concept of academic integrity. This includes plagiarism and citing sources.

> Various information literacy principles, if appropriate to the specific assignment for the course, [are used].

Finally, analysis of the open-ended responses about what is typically covered in the library component again indicated that the institution often left the content up to the classroom faculty:

> Aside from the Library Tour, which is mandatory, each faculty instructor decides what to do.

> Depending on the instructor, it could include all (or conceivably none) of the above. I checked the ones that most classes cover.

> Library course elements are up to the individual instructor.

Thus, even though a library component may be "required," different content could be covered from section to section at some institutions. This, coupled with the minimal amount of in-class time and overall curriculum devoted to the library component, begs the question as to what students learn in this component.

Teaching Responsibility

While a range of people have responsibility for library instruction in first-year seminars, at the majority of institutions (264 or 84%), librarians taught the library component. Classroom faculty members taught the library component for this course at nearly one third of responding institutions (Table 5). At any given institution, librarians, classroom faculty members, and others may have responsibility for library instruction in different sections of the seminar.

Table 5

Who Teaches the Library Component (N = 315)

Person	Number of respondents	Percentage of respondents
Librarians	264	84
Instructor of course	102	32
Peer facilitators	23	7
Other	44	14

Note. Percentages exceed 100 because respondents could select more than one answer.

Some comments revealed other variables that impact the delivery of library instruction. For example, in addition to the traditional method of in-person instruction, some schools used self-paced methods of delivery. These included materials on a web site, online tutorials, print-based workbooks, videos, PowerPoint presentations, online courseware content such as Blackboard or WebCT, and library-sponsored drop-in workshops. Thus, at some institutions, the library component is essentially self-taught.

Training for Classroom Faculty

Through our experience as FYE librarians, we anticipated that some respondents would indicate that non-librarians taught the library portion of their first-year seminar. Thus, we asked whether librarians offered any training opportunities to instructors for them to teach the library component on their own. More than half of the respondents did not answer this question. This low response rate may be explained by the fact that at 84% of the schools, the librarian taught the library component. Several respondents, however, specifically used the phrase "not expected" when answering "no" to the classroom faculty training question, indicating the value campuses place on librarians as the primary teachers of this component. For example:

> Instructors are not expected to teach the library component themselves; only librarians teach the library component. If training were requested, it would be provided.

For those who did respond to the question, an almost equal number provided training (63 or 20%) as those who did not. Open-ended comments to this question revealed little about the variety of training delivery methods or the amount of time devoted to such training. Group workshops and individualized sessions seemed common. Several responses are included below:

> The librarians take the instructors through a training workshop and provide the instructors with detailed handouts and notes for instructing the students.

> During new faculty training for our Introduction to the University course, the librarian does training to assist instructors with the library component of the class. The component of the textbook that deals with the library is also an excellent resource tool for both instructors and students.

> The director meets each semester with library staff for updates and overviews.

> During faculty and peer advisor training, the library instruction coordinator takes time to explain and train [advisors on] the library curriculum.

One comment revealed that librarians did not provide training in person: "It is a taped segment prepared by the library staff." Another comment revealed that a grant made an extended training schedule possible at one institution:

Usually only one half-day session prior to the semester, but this year, an information competency grant paid for four six-hour days of training in a workshop format given by the two librarians who also teach the course.

While librarians appeared eager to offer training, varying levels of acceptance of training may explain why it was not offered more widely:

Training is offered. Some instructors accept it (usually new instructors), some don't (veterans).

Instruction was offered two years ago, but has not been offered since due to lack of faculty interest.

A small workshop is offered at the annual FYE training session on campus. Other than this, it is up to the instructors to seek out additional training from the librarians—who are always happy to do so.

Assessment

We asked two questions about assessment: (a) whether classroom faculty satisfaction with the library component was assessed, and if so, to rate the satisfaction level and (b) whether student learning from the library component was assessed, and if so, how. Regarding the first question, 39 respondents did not answer. Of the remaining 276, slightly more than half (55%) indicated that instructor satisfaction had been assessed. Of those, the majority (90%) indicated that classroom faculty were satisfied or very satisfied with the library component. Regarding the second assessment question about student learning, slightly more than half (57%) indicated that student learning had not been assessed, while 39% indicated that student learning had been assessed (Table 6).

Table 6
Assessment of Student Learning (N = 315)

	Number of respondents	Percentage of respondents (%)
Yes	122	39
No	174	55

Note. 19 respondents did not answer; 9 provided comment only.

The finding that more than half of the responding institutions were not assessing student learning, while disappointing, was not completely unexpected. Assessment of such learning may be a low priority considering that 73% of responding institutions only devote one to two hours of in-class time to a library component, and more than half devote 5% or less of the total curriculum to a library component. Another explanation, as the following comment suggests, may be that the librarians are assessing student learning separate from the first-year seminar directors whom we surveyed, as one indicated: "The library keeps data on this, I do not have the information."

We received more open-ended comments for this question than for any other on our survey, and through analyzing these responses, it became evident that respondents had a wide variety of interpretations of what constitutes assessment and of what they were actually assessing. The most common theme present in the responses indicated that many institutions had actually assessed *student satisfaction* (even though we specifically asked about student learning.) Of the 122 responses stating they had conducted assessment of student learning, exactly half (61) indicated they had measured *student satisfaction with the library component,* not *student learning.*

Many respondents cited using "student satisfaction surveys" in end-of-semester course evaluations that included questions about the library component as their method of assessing learning.

Through the question regarding assessment of student learning, we hoped to gather data that would highlight programs that had done something "well" or "right" for the purpose of improving teaching and learning of the library component and to share this information with first-year educators. In general, we were unable to do this, and we were surprised to see respondents cite student satisfaction instead of student learning. These comments may suggest that student learning is not being measured adequately and that further work is needed in this area.

Comments about assessment revealed low levels of satisfaction with the library component among students enrolled in the first-year seminar. Table 7 groups these comments into general themes.

Table 7

Students Perceptions of the Library Component

Theme	Perception of student attitude
General negative feedback from students	In the past years, we did a one-hour lecture introducing the library resources presented by a librarian. However, the feedback from the students was that this was not a help to them.
	Students are generally bored with the library tour, which is likely a function of the tour guide, a librarian.
	Most students were dissatisfied due to the inadequate job of the librarian.
Already know it	Students do not enjoy the library component—they claim it is repetitive and they already know about researching.
	Survey at the end of the course [used to measure student learning]....students have said the information was not anything new.
	Students answer a questionnaire at the end of the semester. Generally, students give the librarians high marks for the knowledge and presentation, but indicate that they already know the material (no[t] that they can actually use it!!!)
Mixed	General modal response has been that the library component is not popular, but is regarded as useful.
	Students have mixed responses. Some find the library component very helpful, others find it a waste of time. This is generally the mix we find on most of the questions.
	Students fill out a survey indicating their satisfaction with the various parts of orientation. In general, students 'agree' that they have learned useful information in the library component; however, many comments tend to indicate that students find this session somewhat "boring."

All of the above comments suggest improvements can be made to the library curricula in the first-year seminar; however, the comments under the "already know it" theme particularly concerned us. A widely held view among librarians based on hands-on experience with students is that students simply do not know what they do not know. They do not understand the difference between information available via a campus library versus information freely available on the Internet. This view is also supported by empirical evidence reported in the library literature. Frequently, when students self-report on their library or search skill knowledge, they tend to exaggerate or overestimate their abilities (Ivanitskaya, Laus, & Casey, 2004; Maughan, 2001; O'Hanlon, 2002; Wang & Artero, 2005). The exact reason for this disconnect between what students believe their skills to be and their actual skills is a subject of much interest to librarians. We believe the existence of this disconnect calls for better integration of library and information literacy topics into the college curricula, particularly in the first year.

First-year seminar curricula should not be influenced solely by student opinions. Curriculum decisions would be enhanced by using a combination of evaluative feedback from both students and classroom faculty members and by measuring student learning based on established learning outcomes. Responses to the student-learning assessment question indicate that some institutions have attempted more sophisticated evaluation methods. Where respondents ($n = 61$) listed specific strategies for measuring student learning, the most common methods cited included class presentations, papers, and journal entries (71%) and tests or quizzes (36%). The following are examples of the responses received regarding assessing student learning:

> Information literacy pre- and post-test, student feedback after library research seminar, student presentations during library research seminar, research paper in spring seminar, study of student bibliographies by librarians. The data is used to fine-tune the pre- and post-test instruments, to improve the various components of the teaching units, and to help instructors teach the spring seminar component.

> The library component is included on the final examination and is part of the course evaluation. Students learn 90% of the information presented about the library.

> The FYE librarian has used an end-of-semester assessment tool to gauge student learning of the library resources available on our campus. We have found that our initiatives have been beneficial to our students.

> We are just now implementing the interactive self-check test and don't yet have other evaluation procedures in place. We would like to assess the impact library instruction has on information literacy and research competence in terms of the overall academic environment.

> We're working on a method of looking at finished products to see what was and wasn't understood. It's a process under development. Eventually, we hope to have a rubric for making these assessments. Right now, we can generally tell that students at this level have difficulty differentiating scholarly from non-scholarly sources and documenting web sources in particular.

> We have assessed the freshmen seminars in their totality, i.e., on how effective they are in teaching writing and library literacy. In addition, we have begun a pilot project to assess digital information literacy, of which information literacy is a large component.

Conclusion

In *Challenging and Supporting the First-Year Student: A Handbook for Improving the First Year of College*, first-year-seminar textbook author and director of first-year programs, Margit Watts (2005), contributed a chapter on the topic of the library and first-year seminar. She asserts that "Information literacy is a nexus for the life experiences of the student, the academic world of scholarship, and the post-college real world of application of learning…it is core to the first-year experience" (p. 348). While information literacy does encompass concepts broader than simply "the library," libraries are intricately tied to information literacy at the college level. The findings of this study confirm that a library component generally does comprise some part of that "nexus" of the first-year seminar nationwide and that first-year experience professionals also seem to value the library as an important component to include in the first-year seminar.

Nevertheless, analysis of the data and the open-ended comments to this survey suggests that in many instances, the library component of the first-year seminar is not being implemented particularly well. Although further research is needed, areas of improvement include attention to formulating specific learning goals and objectives with respect to the library component, addressing the various ways in which the library component is or is not implemented on individual campuses, and the issue of assessment.

Recommendations

As librarians, we agree with Watts' assertion that the library and information literacy are "core" to a student's first-year experience and would like to see those topics comprise a significant portion of any first-year seminar. Yet, quantity seems less important than two major issues highlighted by our study: (a) consistency in terms of curricular content and (b) implementation of assessment.

First-year seminar professionals responsible for curriculum development (i.e., directors, librarians, classroom faculty) should not overlook the importance of developing formalized learning goals and objectives for the library component of first-year seminars. Whether the library component comprises a small or large portion of the curriculum, these goals and objectives are essential in order to create consistency between sections, to help classroom faculty members plan their curriculum, and, most importantly, to assess student learning.

Librarians have the potential to contribute significantly in this area, and the results of this survey confirm that this is happening at many institutions. Librarians on the reader's campus may well have spent a great deal of time examining the curriculum of first-year courses. Many librarians actively apply the ACRL *Information Literacy Competency Standards for Higher Education* to individual class needs, and they may well have developed assignments, activities, or tutorials for first-year students that correspond to these goals. If this is the case, we encourage readers to use their expertise to help inform the content of first-year seminars. In addition, it is important to know what students learn from library research in their other first-year courses so that stratified and meaningful learning can take place and redundancy between courses can be minimized.

In addition, we encourage directors of first-year seminars to carefully examine how consistently classroom faculty members incorporate the library component in the seminar. Our findings suggest that classroom faculty have a great deal of autonomy in determining what actually occurs in the classroom. If classroom faculty members do not want to teach a library component (and further research needs to be conducted to determine if this is the case), why do they not want to do so? Directors are encouraged to explore this issue and examine whether classroom faculty lack the preparation to teach this component or simply do not value it and, therefore, have dismissed it.

Finally, the results of this study suggest that institutions need to look more carefully at how they are assessing the library component, from both the perspective of student learning and student satisfaction. Assessment was an area highlighted by this survey as being inconsistently or incorrectly implemented, or, as at the majority of the institutions participating in this survey, not implemented at all. As stated earlier, curriculum decisions would be enhanced by using a combination of evaluative feedback from both students and classroom faculty members and by measuring student learning based on established learning outcomes. We recommend institutions examine their practices in this area.

We also recommend that librarians take more ownership of this process and formulate a library-assessment plan to present to the course coordinator. Even if the library component does not have a consistent presence in every section of the first-year seminar on campus, it is still a rich opportunity to assess student knowledge of information literacy skills. This course, in particular, could be a way to gather entry-level evidence of information literacy competencies (or deficiencies) and balance the skills taught in the students' other courses.

Maximizing the Impact

Including a well-planned and consistently implemented library or information literacy component in a first-year seminar can help students make the transition from navigating the information world at the high school level to being able to successfully display more rigorous, information-seeking behaviors at the college level. Planners should consider several factors when integrating a library or information literacy component in the first-year seminar curriculum: (a) the type of first-year seminar offered on the campus, (b) the size of the campus and resources available (including library resources), (c) the availability of other courses devoted to library skills or information literacy, and (d) the inclusion of library or information literacy instruction in first-year courses in the major. A comprehensive, environmental scan of the type of research experiences already built into the first-year curriculum is an important first step. For example, what kind of information-seeking skills do students learn in their English classes? What has been developed in the general education curriculum or the gateway courses? If the first-year seminar is required of all students, it might be an ideal place to infuse information literacy competencies.

In addition, collaborations are necessary to maximize the impact of this course. While learning how to find information and navigate the library as a place are essential components of library instruction, librarians' skills as educators go far beyond that of tour guides. Their professional expertise can provide an opportunity for a much richer collaboration in the areas of curriculum development and assessment. Clearly, librarians are not the only ones responsible for developing, teaching, and assessing the library component in this course; nor should they be. We believe that all first-year seminar stakeholders should participate in the process of helping first-year students learn how to use the library in order to increase their level of library and information literacy skills beyond what they traditionally have when they enter college. The very essence of the academy is continuous inquiry, research, and learning. Faculty, staff, and administrators can all contribute to the process of imparting these skills to their students in and outside the classroom and have an obligation to do so.

References

Association of College and Research Libraries (ACRL). (2000). *Information literacy competency standards for higher education.* Retrieved November 16, 2005, from http://www.ala.org/ala/acrl/acrlstandards/informationliteracycompetency.htm

Boff, C., & Johnson, K. (2002). The library and first-year experience courses: A nationwide study. *RSR: Reference Services Review, 30*(4), 277-287.

Gardner, J. N. (2003). *The reform movement for the first-year experience: What is your role?* Paper presented at the meeting of the Association of College and Research Libraries, Charlotte, NC. Retrieved June 7, 2005, from http://www.ala.org/ala/acrl/acrlevents/Gardner.pdf

Gardner, J. N., Decker, D., & McNairy, F. G. (1986). Taking the library to freshmen students via the freshman seminar concept. In G. B. McCabe & B. Kreissman (Eds.), *Advances in library administration and organization* (Vol. 6, pp. 153-171). Greenwich, CT: JAI Press.

Ivanitskaya, L., Laus, R., & Casey, A. M (2004). Research readiness self-assessment: Assessing students' research skills and attitudes. *Journal of Library Administration, 41*(1/2), 167-184.

Johnson, K., & Boff, C. (2001). *A survey to measure library components of first-year experience courses.* Retrieved November 16, 2005, from http://www.bgsu.edu/colleges/library/infosrv/cboff/fyelibrarysurvey.html

Maughan, P. D. (2001). Assessing information literacy among undergraduates: A discussion of the literature and the University of California-Berkeley assessment experience. *College & Research Libraries, 62*(1), 71–85.

O'Hanlon, N. (2002). Net knowledge: Performance of new college students on an Internet skills proficiency test. *The Internet and Higher Education, 5*(1), 55–66.

Wang, Y. M., & Artero, M. (2005). Caught in the web: University student use of web resources. *Educational Media International, 42*(1), 71–82.

Watts, M. M. (2005). The place of the library versus the library as place. In M. L. Upcraft, J. N. Gardner, & B. O. Barefoot (Eds.), *Challenging and supporting the first-year student: A handbook for improving the first year of college* (pp. 339-355). San Francisco: Jossey Bass.

Appendix

A Survey to Measure Library Components of First-Year Experience Courses

(Johnson & Boff, 2001)

When filling out this survey, you should be considering the answers to the questions from the point of view of an administrator, director, or coordinator of the course, not as an instructor of a specific section of the course.

Survey Questions

1. Is the FYE course on your campus a requirement or an elective?
   a.   requirement
   b.   elective

2. How many credits is the FYE course on your campus?
   a.   no credit
   b.   1 credit
   c.   2 credits
   d.   3 credits
   e.   4 credits
   f.   5 credits
   g.   other, please explain.

3. Is the course graded or offered on a pass/fail basis?
   a.   graded
   b.   pass/fail

4. What is the length of the course at your institution?
   a.   entire semester
   b.   entire quarter
   c.   six weeks
   d.   eight weeks
   e.   other, please explain.

5. Who is/are the lead instructor(s) of the course (check all that may apply)?
   a. faculty
   b. administrative staff
   c. classified staff
   d. graduate students
   e. undergraduate students
   f. librarians
   g. other, please explain.

6. Is there a LIBRARY component, whether optional or required, to the FYE course curriculum on your campus?
   a. no - please scroll to the bottom and click on the submit button
   b. yes - please continue

7. Is it optional or required for each instructor to include the library component?
   a. optional
   b. required

8. Approximately how much in-class time is devoted to the library component?
   a. 1 hour
   b. 2 hours
   c. 3 hours
   d. 4 - 6 hours
   e. 7 - 9 hours
   f. 10 - 12 hours
   g. more than 12 hours, please list hours.

9. Please estimate the percentage of the course curriculum devoted to the library component.
   a. less than 1%
   b. 1 - 5%
   c. 6 - 10%
   d. 11 - 15%
   e. 16 - 20%
   f. 21 - 25%
   g. more than 25%, please list percentage.

10. Who develops the library component (check all that apply)?
   a. a librarian
   b. the director of the FYE program/course
   c. the instructor of each section
   d. other, please explain.

11. Who teaches the library component (check all that apply)?
   a. librarian as a guest lecturer
   b. regular instructor for each course
   c. peer facilitator/mentor
   d. other, please explain.

12. If the instructors are expected to teach the library component themselves, and they are not themselves librarians, does a librarian offer training to course instructors to help them teach the library component?
   a. no
   b. yes, please explain.

13. What is typically covered in the library component (check all that apply)?
    a.   library tour
    b.   research assignment
    c.   scavenger hunt
    d.   library catalog
    e.   article indexes/databases
    f.   web searching
    g.   web evaluation
    h.   other, please explain.

14. If instructor satisfaction with the library component has been assessed, please rate the overall response to their experience.
    a.   has not been assessed
    b.   very satisfied
    c.   satisfied
    d.   neutral
    e.   dissatisfied
    f.   very dissatisfied

15. Has student learning from the library component been assessed?
    a.   no
    b.   yes, please explain the method of assessment used and the results.

Chapter 6

Information Literacy and the First-Year Experience in the California State University System

Ilene F. Rockman[1]

The California State University (CSU), the largest system of higher education in North America, has a long and strong tradition of supporting and educating students. CSU comprises 23 campuses and seven off-campus centers, with more than 44,000 faculty and staff serving more than 405,000 students. Campuses are in urban, rural, and suburban locations; serve residential and commuter students; and reflect both liberal arts and polytechnic curricula. The oldest campus (San Jose State University) was founded in 1857 and has more than 30,000 students. The newest campus (California State University, Channel Islands) opened in fall 2002 with fewer than 1,000 students. The system awards more than half of the bachelor's degrees granted in California.

CSU draws its first-year students from the top third of California's high school graduates. It is the nation's most diverse university system, with students of color comprising more than 53% of enrollment, twice the national average for four-year public universities. A recent survey showed 40% of CSU students come from households where English is not the main language, and more than one third consider themselves to be multiracial. Several CSU campuses are annually among the nation's leaders in the number of bachelor's degrees awarded to students of color. Almost every CSU campus has been commended in *Hispanic Outlook's* annual list of colleges and universities that excel in their service to Hispanic students (California State University, 2004b).

Although many students come to the CSU directly from high schools and community colleges, the average CSU student is older than 18, with many working full-time and having families. Despite the need for many students to balance multiple responsibilities, the CSU graduation rate (54% after six years) is 10% higher than the national benchmark of 44% (California State University, 2005).

The Chancellor's Office oversees the campuses, and each campus president reports directly to the Chancellor. Information literacy programs can be found on every campus, but campuses have autonomy in implementing local programs. Thus, no single approach to information competency exists in the CSU system. The system-wide Library Initiatives Office, within the

---

[1]Ilene Rockman died on November 26, 2006 after a long battle with cancer. We are grateful to her husband, Fred Gertler, for giving us permission to include her chapter in this monograph. Though she had completed several drafts of the chapter, I made final edits to the chapter, in conjunction with the editors at the National Resource Center for The First-Year Experience and Students in Transition. We have made every effort to preserve Ilene's original vision for the chapter. — Larry Hardesty

Chancellor's Office, operates with a full-time manager of the Information Competence Initiative. This office provides guiding principles, creates documents which can assist the campuses (e.g., rubrics for assessing information competency), offers incentives (e.g., grant programs), supports professional development opportunities (e.g., summer institutes, workshops, conferences), and works with various constituent groups (e.g., statewide academic senators, test officers, assessment council members, faculty development coordinators, academic technologists, first-year directors) to raise the visibility and importance of information competency on the campuses.

This chapter describes various strategies undertaken by CSU campuses to incorporate information literacy into first-year programs and system-wide efforts to support these endeavors. Campus descriptions include information about administrative support, faculty leadership and support, integration of information literacy into the curriculum, outreach services, librarian-faculty collaboration, partnerships between academic affairs and student affairs, establishment of closer relationships with English composition courses, assessment efforts, and the role of librarians (who have faculty status) in campus leadership. All these activities are helping students find a strong pathway to success as they pursue their degrees.

Overview of the Information Competence Initiative

The CSU Information Competence Initiative began in the early 1990s. The system's Commission on Learning Resources and Instructional Technology (CLRIT) developed and recommended policy guidelines to the chancellor to facilitate the effective use of learning resources and instructional technology on all the campuses. In January 1993, under the umbrella of CLRIT, the Council of Library Directors created a collective plan that would take the CSU libraries into the 21st century and began a strategic planning process. The Council identified information competency, considered by librarians to be a critical skill for all students, as one area for action. CLRIT approved the strategic plan of the CSU libraries and ranked the area of information competency as a high priority.

Over the years, system-wide efforts have focused on integrating information competency principles into the curriculum, especially as a student-learning outcome. One of the strategies pursued was the creation of a high-level committee (composed of administrators, classroom faculty members, and librarians) to drive the information literacy initiative from 1995 to 2001. Chaired by a library dean, the committee sponsored system-wide workshops, worked with academic senators to pass resolutions in support of information competency, and administered an active grant program to encourage faculty to create courses and assignments that reflected information competency principles.

In 2001, the CSU created a full-time management position to provide consistent guidance, expansion, and promotion of the initiative across the curriculum on the various campuses. The manager (a) serves as a strong advocate for information literacy within and across the national and international higher education community; (b) implements a grant program to develop information literacy projects on the campuses; (c) provides leadership for assessment strategies; (d) serves as a spokesperson about the importance of information literacy to other system-wide groups such as first-year experience directors, faculty development directors, assessment coordinators, and testing officers; (e) advocates for state-wide and local academic senate resolutions in support of information literacy; (f) edits a system-wide information literacy newsletter sent to presidents and other campus leaders; and (g) presents workshops in support of the continuing professional development of discipline and library faculty members. The information competency grants have resulted in the development of web-based instructional tutorials, summer faculty development workshops to reshape curricular offerings, outreach efforts to high schools and community colleges through teacher-librarian collaboration, support for an online information competency graduation requirement, the creation of various information competency courses and programs at the undergraduate and graduate levels, and the integration of information literacy into the learning outcomes of academic programs.

Then and Now

A generation ago, one would be challenged to find first-year experience programs in the CSU system. Most classroom faculty members expected students to come to classes already acclimated to university life, mature and academically ready to complete assignments, study effectively, write well, take tests, select a major, use the library, and pursue a career. While some library instruction existed, it was offered to a limited segment of the student population. Formal credit-bearing library instruction classes existed, taught by librarians and targeted to first-generation college or under-represented students through the Educational Opportunity Program (EOP). These programs were designed to improve retention, while the students participated in experimental "tracked classes" as part of a core general education curriculum (Rockman, 1978).

Now, a generation later, with a more academically diverse student population, learning communities, freshman interest groups, academic success programs, orientation, first-year seminars, and other initiatives targeting first-year students are prevalent on CSU campuses. A recent survey of CSU instructional librarians revealed that about half of the campuses have one or more such programs in place. Often, these programs consist of thematically linked quarter, semester-, or year-long general education programs in which students take classes together in small cohorts or learning communities intended to foster socialization and enhance peer mentoring and learning.

While the structures exist, not all campuses have successfully infused information literacy into interdisciplinary first-year or core general education programs. In addition, not all first-year programs are mandatory for all entering students. Thus, not all students have an opportunity to develop a sense of university identity or experience a supportive environment for learning how to find, use, evaluate, and apply information to problem solving and the communication of ideas.

In addition, some campuses report that no standard first-year curriculum (exclusive of the general education program) exists, including a standard information literacy skills curriculum. There are numerous reasons for a lack of a standardized curriculum, including (a) volunteer program directors or coordinators who change frequently, (b) lack of involvement by an appreciable number of tenure-track faculty members, (c) lack of librarian involvement in course or program planning, (d) recent budget problems, and (e) the perspective (by some) that first-year seminars are "non-academic." In addition, some campuses report that courses within the first-year seminar program do not contain a uniform syllabus, making it more difficult to deliver consistent information and content to the students and, thus, more difficult to assess.

However, there are bright spots on the campuses. Campus librarians (as faculty members) continue to partner with discipline faculty members to include information literacy in first-year seminars. They integrate information literacy tutorials into classes and teach stand-alone credit classes linked to the general education program. Librarians also advocate for information literacy as a graduation requirement and have become more involved in the first-year experience planning processes. Finally, they share their experiences with colleagues, both on and off campus. Each campus has autonomy in providing instruction to first-year students, and there is no system-wide mandate to implement a uniform strategy. Yet, the efforts of librarians strengthen common goals and demonstrate the impact of information literacy on student performance, academic achievement, and persistence to degree.

Factors for Success on the Campuses

Administrative Support—CSU Chico and Sonoma State University

Without a doubt, one of the key factors for success has been the support of senior administrators, both in the Chancellor's Office and on individual campuses. Although leadership occurs at all levels, administrators have the budget and clout to create and implement a meaningful program for the first year, which will grow and be sustainable over time.

At CSU Chico, the president and provost have set the campus tone for the first-year experience program, stating:

> . . . the University has approached the matter of student learning and student success intentionally and carefully, like the building of an arch. Each expression of this effort contributes to a strong and distinctive learning structure. The Freshman-Year Experience initiative reflects the integration of many efforts. (Zingg & McNall, 2005, p. 1)

A campus-wide focus on the first year makes such integration possible. Chico participated in the initial development of the aspirational principles of excellence in the Foundations of Excellence in the First College Year Project (Policy Center on the First College Year, n.d.). As a result of their involvement, a campus committee composed of classroom faculty and student services staff, two librarians, and the library director meets regularly to discuss the first-year experience offered to the students. Creating a task force on the first-year experience at Chico helped the entire campus understand a common philosophy and vision emanating from the top (the president and the provost), which nurtured student learning and encouraged academic rigor. As a result, Chico enjoys consistently high first- to second-year progression rates—over 80% (California State University, 2004a).

In addition, administrators see the library as an important player in the first-year experience by supporting librarian participation in the teaching of Introduction to University Life, a three-unit, graded course. The goals of the course are to increase student retention and increase students' academic skills (Blakeslee & Trefts, 2002). This course fulfills three of the 48-unit general education requirements (lifelong learning) and differs from most first-year courses in that half of the content is devoted to information competency (i.e., defining a research need, accessing information in the library and through electronic databases, developing effective search strategies, evaluating information, and presenting information). Devoting half the course to information literacy demonstrates administrative support and reflects positively on the library's role in educating students. The course, offered since 1997, is taught by instructors from various campus departments (both tenured and part-time lecturers), librarians, and support staff. Historically, the course has about 20 sections with 25 students per section (Blakeslee, Owens, & Dixon, 2001).

At Sonoma State University, the president is a contributor (along with 14 faculty members, including the library instruction and outreach coordinator) to the publication, *First-Year Experience Guide for Success* (Sonoma State University, n.d.). The guide includes a welcoming chapter from the president and a prominent chapter on information competency issues including library research and reference services, the research process, evaluating information, citing information, plagiarism, copyright, and remote access to library resources.

Between 1991 and 2003, Sonoma State faced numerous challenges due to a dramatic increase in the first-year student population and general changes in student demographics. To meet these challenges, the University produced a 38-page white paper, *The Whole University Supporting the Whole Student: Educational Foundations for New College Students* (Toczyski & Draper, 2004), which provides a new direction for general education by proposing a different design and rationale for the first-year experience. The document also includes a three-column chart, noting academic development, social development, and institutional knowledge with the first point under "academic development" being information literacy. The prominence of information literacy in the report is noteworthy, demonstrating the impact of the library on multiple content areas in the critical first year of college and that "foundational appreciation for research and scholarship in a variety of disciplines" is cohesively and intentionally woven throughout the curriculum (Toczyski & Draper, p. 10).

Faculty Leadership and Support—San Jose State University

San Jose State University's Metropolitan University Scholars Experience (MUSE) is a first-year learning community program, which began in fall 2002 (Matoush, 2003) and was designed to help students develop the skills necessary to complete the challenge of producing in-depth, university-level work. Research, information literacy, critical thinking, written work, attention to the rich cultural diversity of the campus, and active discussion are key parts of the experience. In recognition of the success of this course, in 2004, the academic senate passed a resolution, signed by the president, indicating that MUSE courses may fulfill core general education requirements.

Like many universities, San Jose State had information literacy programs in place well before the MUSE program. For example, the English 1B information literacy program, developed in 1979, targeted first-year students. Since no requirement mandated that students take English 1B during their first year, they often took it later in their academic careers. As a result, "students often went through many years of college without gaining an understanding of library research or developing necessary skills in finding, evaluating, and using information ethically and legally" (Matoush, 2003, p.78). To counteract this, the institution developed MUSE seminars, offered to first-year students during their first academic semester.

Within the intensive MUSE program, classes are limited to 20 students who are provided with critical information literacy skills early in their academic careers. Instructors use a variety of instructional strategies such as face-to-face presentations with a librarian in a small setting who uses active-learning assignments and discussion. They also use self-paced, interactive online tutorials. These tutorials teach students how to find books and articles and make them aware of information literacy issues such as plagiarism. Assessment data show that students are better able to search for and evaluate information after completing the MUSE sessions. In addition, students who took MUSE courses perceived themselves as better able to identify reliable information when doing research than students taking writing courses or other first-year courses (Matoush, 2003).

Data from fall 2003 found a greater retention rate in 2004 for MUSE students than for first-year students who had not taken a MUSE class. In addition, the cumulative grade point average of 2002 MUSE students was higher than for students who did not enroll in MUSE classes. These data paint an encouraging picture of the benefits of the MUSE program. Hopefully, the data will continue to show positive results for MUSE students.

Reaching out to Diverse Students—CSU Fresno

University 1 is a three-unit first-year seminar that has enjoyed a long tradition on the Fresno campus. It is geared to a diverse student population enrolled on an urban campus. The seminar includes the requirement that students complete a research paper, a personal essay, and an oral presentation.

In 1998, the CSU awarded an information competency grant to the campus instruction librarian who was charged with integrating information competency into the program. He proposed a multi-faceted system for teaching faculty members how to infuse these skills into first-year initiatives—through Summer Bridge (a program for economically and under-represented students who may be at risk), University 1 (an academic orientation course, at the time), and specific courses in the general education program (e.g., English, speech, and critical thinking). The instruction librarian invited 30 classroom faculty (instructors, librarians, and professors) in the Faculty Mentoring Program to attend a two-day information competency colloquium and workshop. He sought to demonstrate how information competency could contribute to teaching and learning throughout the curriculum. During the 2004-2005 academic year, the library instruction coordinator asked that all faculty members teaching University 1 have their students complete an information literacy tutorial and/or an in-person library workshop to gain a solid base for their future studies. Since faculty members also serve as curriculum advisors to students, they must understand and share responsibility for teaching these important foundational learning skills both inside and outside the classroom.

Partnerships Between Academic Affairs and Student Affairs—CSU Fullerton

CSU Fullerton is a large, diverse, urban, commuter campus with an enrollment of slightly more than 35,000 students in fall 2005. The percentage of first-time, first-year students accepted (11.2% in fall 2005) is typically small. Due to this small percentage, and the campus demographics in general, there is a need to foster a stronger sense of community, improve the first-year experience and retention rates, and provide students with the tools necessary to make a successful academic transition from high school to college.

In 1997, various CSU Fullerton campus entities including academic affairs (e.g., faculty, librarians, advisors, service-learning) and student affairs (e.g., EOP Summer Bridge, athletics, judicial affairs, Women's Center) partnered to develop and launch the Fullerton First Year (FFY) program to address these needs. In the first year of the program, 150 first-year students participated. Since that time, the program has grown and in fall 2005, 407 first-year students enrolled in a variety of first-year programs including Fullerton First Year, Compass, Live 'n' Learn, Freshman Future Teachers, and the Freshman Success Program. Common components in these initiatives include linked classes, mentoring, academic advising, study skills, academic field trips, service-learning, and instruction in library/information literacy. All first-year programs include a core University Studies (three-credit) course taught by instructional teams. Each team is comprised of a classroom faculty member, a student affairs professional, a peer mentor, and a librarian.

Due to the library's strong commitment to information literacy, librarians have been actively involved with the Freshman Programs office in the planning and implementation of the programs since 1997. A librarian sits on the Freshman Programs Advisory Board, and librarians present at annual Freshman Programs retreats and attend monthly instructional team lunches. Currently, three faculty librarians work closely with 16 University Studies instructional teams to provide a solid foundation in the information literacy skills necessary for student academic success. This collaboration includes ongoing dialogue and the creation of effective information literacy exercises, handouts, assignments, and structured library-instruction sessions.

First-year students who are enrolled in these programs are academically successful in numerous ways. Statistics indicate that 55% of Freshman Programs students who complete a full year of learning community participation graduate in four years, although the average campus time to graduation is six years. Freshman Programs students attain a higher GPA, 2.70 on average, as compared to 2.56 for the general CSUF first-year population. In addition, students who enroll in Freshman Programs are retained at higher rates (84% after the first year and 73% after the second year) than students not in learning communities (78% and 70%, respectively).

Learning Communities Linked to the General Education Curriculum—CSU East Bay, Humboldt State University, CSU Los Angeles, CSU Monterey Bay

Instruction in information literacy at the East Bay (formerly known as Hayward) campus became an explicit first-year requirement with the revision of the 1998 general education (GE) program, which linked GE to all first-year learning communities through a one-unit required course, Fundamentals of Information Literacy, taught by librarians. In fall 2004, a new two-unit course, Introduction to Information Literacy replaced the one-unit course. A cohort of students and classroom faculty members spend the year together exploring a common theme in a series of three-quarter thematically linked general education courses (Faust, 2001). In addition, librarians are actively involved in helping disciplinary faculty members develop assignments that support information literacy principles taught in the class.

The first-year learning community program was designed so that entering first-year students complete all lower-division GE in their first and second years (Kegley & Kennedy, 2002). In the past, students on this urban campus often took general education courses as seniors. Now, the "first-year clusters" consist of three discipline-based courses in the humanities, social sciences, or sciences; a composition class; a communication class; a general studies activity/support module; and an information literacy class. From 1998 to 2002, pre- and posttest assessment data have shown a marked improvement in student achievement. Students report that they have made gains in their ability to find, evaluate, and use information from a variety of sources (California State University, Hayward, 2002). In addition, the director of the general education program (a professor of communication) notes that the program has been successful in helping students make steady progress toward degree completion, especially when a separate information literacy class was included.

Humboldt State University (a campus near the Oregon border) has offered a variety of first-year experience and support programs for more than two decades. These have included orientation programs, themed living groups, learning communities (i.e., freshman interest groups or FIGs), and mentoring programs. First-year students have the option of enrolling in FIGs, clusters of about 25 students who take thematically linked courses. Not all first-year students enroll, but in fall 2002, more than half of first-year students participated in a FIG. Assessment data indicate that these students experienced higher retention and satisfaction rates than students who did not enroll (Conference on Student Success, 2003).

Another model linked to the GE program can be found at the CSU Los Angeles campus, which offers Introduction to Higher Education 101, a two-unit mandatory, quarter-long first-year seminar offered since 1996 and sponsored by the dean of Undergraduate Students Office and the school curricular deans. The course focuses on library and research, critical thinking, time management, and verbal/electronic/written skills. Approximately 1,300 first-year students take the course, which includes 90 minutes, or one class session, devoted to information literacy principles. The campus has a librarian dedicated to the seminar, and all subject librarians spend 10% to 15% of their time working on the course. Classroom faculty members report significantly better retention rates for students who take the course than those who do not take it.

CSU Monterey Bay has offered a four-unit, first-year seminar (FYS) since 1995 (the year that the institution was founded), as well as a Technology and Information Competence University Learning Requirement (ULR). ULRs are similar to general education requirements. In 1998, the first-year seminar course increased to six units to include the technology ULR. In the early years, each FYS class came to the library for an introductory session taught by the library instruction coordinator. As the number of seminars grew, one librarian could not teach them all. Therefore, in 2001, the library instruction coordinator offered a workshop for FYS instructors to familiarize them with library resources and basic information competency skills and to provide them with instructional materials that could be tailored to each section's research needs. Library faculty members are currently working with the FYS director to more fully integrate information competency skills into the course's writing and research assignments.

Other General Education Models—CSU San Marcos, CSU Sacramento

California State University, San Marcos, has offered a three-unit first-year seminar (lower-division general education credit course) since 1995. It includes a core information literacy component taught by librarians (Sonntag & Ohr, 1996). Web instruction is part of the course (Sonntag, 1999). The university's GE program mandates that information literacy be included in all lower-division GE courses. This inclusion has had a positive effect. Assessment shows that students in the first-year seminar have increased both grade point averages and persistence to degree (G. Sonntag, personal communication, September 30, 2004). Recent campus efforts are moving toward a comprehensive first-year experience program including the addition of learning communities.

At CSU Sacramento, the first-year seminar program (FSP) is the responsibility of the director of general education and is funded through academic affairs, the Educational Opportunity Program (EOP), and the departments and colleges offering the courses. The class is available to all incoming first-year students and satisfies a GE requirement. EOP students are required to take the class as part of a learning community. First offered during the fall semester 1999, the program had grown to 41 sections by fall 2004.

Since its inception, the FSP has had a strong information competency component because the initial FSP planning group included an associate dean of the library. From the beginning, the course syllabus included information competency under the course goals/learning outcomes. The director of general education noted that participation by the library faculty in FSP has allowed the program to successfully fulfill the university's information competency learning objectives.

Because librarians had worked with many of the faculty members teaching the first-year seminar before the course was developed, a good basis of trust and understanding already existed. The library's head of instructional services and the director of general education planned a workshop for first-year seminar faculty on information competency. Nineteen faculty members and nine librarians attended the half-day session held in January 2004. Concurrently, one of the instructional librarians received a faculty mini-grant to develop an online first-year seminar survival guide (CSUS Library Instructional Services, 2004).

The campus Office of Institutional Research has tracked all students who have taken the first-year seminar since its inception in fall 1999. Students who took this class have a higher retention rate and a higher GPA over a four-year period than the average student. EOP students in first-year seminars have a 6% higher retention rate than EOP students who entered CSU Sacramento before the seminar was offered.

Graduation Requirement—San Francisco State University

San Francisco State University (SFSU) implemented first-year seminars in 2000-2001, and more than 1,800 first-year students have participated since their inception. Librarians have been involved in planning the curriculum, introducing basic information literacy ideas, and designing the OASIS (Online Advancement of Student Information Skills) web tutorial. OASIS satisfies the campus' basic information competence graduation requirement, which was adopted by the Academic Senate in 1999 (superseding an earlier requirement) and which must be fulfilled by first-year students in their first year and transfer students in their first semester. Librarians conduct a class session on information literacy and OASIS in the first-year seminar. Faculty typically ask librarians to present these sessions early in the term. Librarians also "train the trainers" by instructing the classroom faculty members and graduate assistants who run discussion sessions in information literacy issues and resources available for students conducting research.

Elective Course—CSU Northridge, San Diego State University

California State University, Northridge, has continuously offered University 100 (U100), a first-year seminar, since fall 1999. It is an elective, letter-graded course offering three units of general education credit and introducing first-year students to the university as an institution, culture, and intellectual experience. Topics covered include academic skills, the value of higher education, becoming a lifelong learner, ethics in academic life, and diversity. The enrollment limit is 25 students per section, and about 10% of first-year students enroll in U100 per year. Since the beginning, librarians have been engaged in an information literacy instruction and assessment program with these students. They offer week long hands-on sessions (a.k.a. "Library Week") covering the basics of information literacy: (a) understanding the assignment, (b) topic selection, (c) keyword brainstorming, (d) Boolean logic, (e) resource types, (f) database selection, (g) search execution, (h) critical evaluation, (i) citation style, and (j) plagiarism. Students are then required to compile a short annotated bibliography on a topic using MLA style, which is graded by the course instructor. Assessment consists of a multiple choice pre- and post-test of information literacy concepts and skills. U100 students are required to take the tests and receive unit credit for their efforts. Preliminary analysis of the data indicates that the "Library Week" program has a positive impact on U100 students' information literacy skills, and additional analyses are currently underway.

In 2001, San Diego State University received a CSU information competency grant to assess information competency in a first-year orientation/transitions program. This program includes a course known as University Seminar, which is a one-unit, one-hour-a-week course designed to help students develop academic skills, learn about campus services, and explore the campus community.

The project developed a list of learning outcomes, including the skills of information competency, for the voluntary Freshman Success Program (FSP) that had been offered on the campus since 1991. The program enjoyed some success in that students who completed it have fewer academic probations, higher grade point averages, and higher retention rates (Harley, 2001). Commenting on the course from an instructor's perspective, Harley (also a librarian) believes that stronger connections could be made between critical thinking and information literacy. To confirm this, he co-taught the class with the FSP director. This experience "improved the FSP director's understanding of what librarians can contribute as participants in campus-wide programs for students" (Harley, 2001, p. 305).

Closer Relationship With English 101—Sonoma State University

As part of the Information Competence in the Freshman Interest Group (FIG) program at Sonoma State University, the library offered a training workshop for the educational mentoring teams teaching the FIG seminars in June 2001. The goals of the project included (a) increased information competency among classroom faculty who teach in the first-year seminar (University 102) and among students who serve as peer advisors in the program, (b) increased collaboration between the librarians and classroom faculty members, (c) enhanced student transition from high school to the university, and (d) a revised program curriculum to include information competency as a desired student learning outcome. Approximately 60 to 70% of Sonoma students enroll in a first-year seminar. The seminar includes various assignments, discussions, and hands-on workshops that culminate in a semester-long research project designed to help students develop effective research questions and select and evaluate information resources. According to one first-year seminar instructor,

> The information competency component has provided our freshmen students with the confidence to find information pertinent to their studies. Working closely with a librarian helped lower the anxiety of first-year students using the library. They became very engaged with their projects. I have no doubt this program is a vital part of their undergraduate experience. (Sonoma State University, n.d.)

Responses to the end-of-semester freshmen survey conducted over the past four years by the Office of Analytical Studies indicate that students who participated in the program experienced significant increases in skills related to locating, retrieving, and evaluating information as compared to those students who did not participate in the program. At the request of the library, in fall 2004, the information competency component was moved out of the seminar into English 101, the required first-year writing class, to reach the widest number of students possible and to ensure the direct connection between information competency and the students' academic coursework.

Factors for Success: CSU System-Wide First-Year Experience Workshop

As a result of a successful CSU grant to integrate information literacy into the first-year experience at Sonoma State University, the CSU Information Competence Initiative sponsored a system-wide workshop, "Information Competence in the First-Year Experience" in spring 2003 on the SSU campus. Discipline and library faculty from 17 campuses met at Sonoma State to learn about the successful information competency grant experiences of a librarian and modern languages faculty member (Brodsky & Toczyski, 2002). They also sought to share campus experiences and to participate in small-group discussions related to pedagogical strategies and ways to strengthen information literacy instruction in the first-year seminar. The workshop design deliberately focused on specific learning outcomes in the spirit of helping students become successful (Gardner, 1986).

The workshop leaders discussed their successful grant experiences and asked several of their students to join them on a panel to reflect on their learning experiences. Then, the manager of the information-competence initiative asked attendees to gather in small groups to discuss three key questions to stimulate conversations. Questions and responses are summarized below:

1. What are the important information competency learning outcomes for the first-year experience program?

Discipline faculty members indicated that they wanted guidance and assistance from librarians in designing effective learner-centered assignments for their courses. They realized that undertaking research is not always a linear process, and some of their assignments did not help their first-year students to learn. In addition, they expressed interest in strategies and ideas to help their students retain the knowledge acquired in courses about undertaking research and evaluating information so students could transfer it to future experiences. In addition, they wanted their students to be able to ask good questions, to recognize the existence of various formats of information, to be able to evaluate the quality of information retrieved, and to understand that the research process has multiple steps associated with it.

2. What types of assignments or experiences can foster information competency skills in the first year?

Discipline faculty noted that assignments linked to general education courses and/or programs can help improve information competency skills of first-year students. Similarly, open-ended assignments that were problem-, inquiry-, or performance-based were promising in enhancing these skills. These types of assignments, in particular, provide students with an opportunity to demonstrate and apply their information literacy skills. They also expressed the need for professors to model good research skills in class, including how to revise search strategies through the use of truncation, narrowing, or broadening of terms and using Boolean operators. "Smart" classrooms (those equipped with projection systems and computers) can help immensely by allowing professors to model the research process for students in real time.

3. What information competency skills and abilities should your students be able to build upon and transfer to other courses after the first-year experience?

Discipline faculty members wanted their students to know how to find a book and a journal article; to know the differences between keyword and subject searching in online catalogs, subscription databases, the web, and other sources; and to understand and demonstrate the ethical use of information with the proper attribution to the author.

Throughout the workshop, faculty members were stimulated by listening to their colleagues, gaining new ideas to try out on their local campuses, discussing problems and listening to/providing solutions to problems, and sharing success stories. By all accounts, the system-wide workshop exceeded expectations, and the participants provided extremely positive evaluations. Conversations continued on a system-wide listserv created especially for the participants.

Conclusion

After a decade of librarians partnering with discipline faculty to integrate information competency principles into specifically designed courses and throughout the first-year curriculum on many campuses of the California State University, faculty members and administrators clearly have greater awareness of and interest in these issues than before. In many cases, first-year programs are growing and helping students become more confident and successful in finding, using, evaluating, and applying information to fulfill academic and personal needs. In other cases, FYE programs are just beginning.

The integration of information literacy activities into first-year experience programs is gaining visibility, especially as retirements occur and new individuals join the CSU system. Discipline faculty members have recognized the importance of such integration. A recent document, *Academic Literacy: A Statement of Competencies Expected of Students Entering California's Public Colleges and Universities* (Intersegmental Committee, 2002), notes the importance of information literacy. The authors of the document are academic senate members from the California State University, the University of California, and the California Community Colleges.

In addition, libraries have partnered with academic affairs administrators, discipline faculty members, and student affairs professionals in a variety of settings to improve information literacy skills. Learning communities, for example, have been a popular model for introducing information literacy to first-year students. Through this model of cohort support and education, students have learned about information literacy in a nurturing, self-contained, mutually respectful, and trusting environment under the watchful eyes of faculty and peer mentors. Several campus librarians have also worked closely with assessment specialists to demonstrate the impact of the library on the first-year experience and have presented their findings at CSU-sponsored assessment conferences, summer workshops, and symposia on teaching and learning.

Recently, the CSU has taken a national leadership role as the lead charter client partnering with the Educational Testing Service and other higher education institutions to develop and implement a problem-based, web-based, valid, and reliable instrument to assess information and communication technology literacy (Rockman, 2005). Results help to strengthen the role of the library in both assessment and first-year efforts.

Although there is more work to do, and several campuses have yet to launch first-year experience programs, the future looks promising. Cross-campus communication is increasing due to campus and system-wide efforts, and the creation of a full-time Manager of the Information Competence Initiative (the first in the nation) has helped to accelerate the process. In addition, in some cases, campus efforts reveal a positive link between information literacy and student performance, academic achievement, grade point average, and persistence to degree—all priority goals of the universities.

Author Note

Appreciation is extended to all CSU information literacy librarians who provided valuable information for this chapter—Pam Baker, Sarah Blakeslee, Karen Brodsky, Suellen Cox, Kathy Dabbour, Judith Faust, Ned Fielden, Linda Goff, Kris Johnson, Ross La Baugh, Lynn Lampert, Toby Matoush, Kris Ramsdell, Gabriela Sonntag, and Alan Stein.

References

Blakeslee, S., Owens, J., & Dixon, L. (2001). Chico's first-year experience course: A case study. *Academic Exchange Quarterly, 5*(4), 128-132.

Blakeslee, S., & Trefts, K. (2002). Don't know much about Boolean: Training faculty to incorporate information literacy into a first-year experience course. In J. K. Nims & A. Andrew (Eds.), *First impressions, lasting impact: Introducing the first-year student to the academic library* (Proceedings of the 28th National LOEX Conference held in Ypsilanti, MI, May 19-20, 2000, pp. 27-32). Ann Arbor, MI: Pierian Press.

Brodsky, K., & Toczyski, S. (2002). Information competence in the freshman seminar: Teaching information literacy. *Academic Exchange Quarterly, 6*(4), 46-51.

California State University. (2004a). *Accountability 2004 biennial reporting. Campus summaries.* Retrieved March 28, 2006, from http://www.calstate.edu/AcadAff/accountability/index.shtml

California State University. (2004b). *Facts about the 23 campuses of the CSU.* Retrieved March 28, 2006, from http://www.calstate.edu/PA/2004facts/index.shmtl

California State University. (2005). *CSU retention and graduation rates exceed those at benchmark institution.* Retrieved March 28, 2006, from http://www.calstate.edu/pa/news/2005/gradrates.shtml

California State University, Hayward. (2002). *Information literacy (GE requirement G4).* Unpublished report.

CSUS Library Instructional Services. (2004). *The freshman seminar survival guide.* Retrieved March 28, 2006, from http://library.csus.edu/content2.asp?pageID=372

Conference on Student Success: Facilitating Transfer and Degree Completion in The California State University. (2003, December 4-5). Retrieved March 28, 2006, from http://www.calstate.edu/studentsuccess/firstyear.shtml

Faust, J. (2001). Teaching information literacy in 50 minutes a week: The CSUH experience. *Journal of Southern Academic and Special Librarianship, 21*(3). Retrieved July 24, 2006, from http://southernlibrarianship.icaap.org/content/v02n03/faust_j01.htm

Gardner, J. N. (1986). The freshman year experience. *College and University, 51*(4), 261-274.

Harley, B. (2001). Freshmen, information literacy, critical thinking, and values. *Reference Services Review, 29*(4), 301-305.

Intersegmental Committee of the Academic Senates of the California Community Colleges, the California State University, and the University of California. (2002). *Academic literacy: A statement of the competencies expected of students entering California's public colleges and universities.* Retrieved March 28, 2006, from http://www.academicsenate. cc.ca.us/Publications/Papers/AcademicLiteracy/main.htm

Kegley, J., & Kennedy, L. (2002, December). *Facilitating student success in achieving the baccalaureate degree.* (Report of the California State University Task Force on Facilitating Graduation). Retrieved March 28, 2006, from http://www.calstate.edu/acadaff/facilitatinggraduation.pdf

Matoush, T. L. (2003). Information literacy in a freshman learning community. *Academic Exchange Quarterly, 7*(3), 78-84.

Policy Center on the First College Year. (n.d.). *Foundations of excellence in the first college year participating institutions.* Retrieved March 28, 2006, from http://www.fyfoundations. org/participants/aspx

Rockman, I. F. (1978). *Library instruction to EOP students: A case study.* (ERIC Document Reproduction Services No. ED 174 211)

Rockman, I. F. (2005). Information and communication technology literacy: New assessments for higher education. *College & Research Libraries, 66*(8), 587-589.

Sonntag, G. (1999). Using technology in a first-year experience course. *College & Undergraduate Libraries,* 6(l), l-16.

Sonntag, G., & Ohr, D. M. (1996, July). The development of a lower-division, general education, course-integrated information literacy program. *College & Research Libraries, 57*(4), 331-338.

Sonoma State University. (n.d.). *First-year experience guide for success.* Retrieved March 28, 2006, from http://www.sonoma.edu/ge_initiative/pdf/firstyearexperienceguideforsuccess.pdf

Toczyski, S., & Draper, P. (2004, December 10). *The whole university supporting the whole student: Educational foundations for new college students.* Sonoma State University. Retrieved March 28, 2006, from http://www.sonoma.edu/ge_initiative/pdf/thewholeuniversitypdf.pdf

Zingg, P. J., & McNall, S. G. (2005). The freshman-year experience: Keynote of distinctiveness. *Chico State inside: A publication for the faculty, staff, administrators, and friends of California State University, Chico, 35*(5), 1-3. Retrieved March 28, 2006, from http://www.csuchico.edu/pub/inside/freshmanexperience.html

Chapter 7

Librarians With a First-Year Focus: Exploring an Emerging Position

Colleen Boff, Cheryl Albrecht, & Alison Armstrong

In 1998, the dean of University Libraries at Bowling Green State University (BGSU) proposed and successfully lobbied for an innovative position in the field of academic librarianship, the First-Year Experience (FYE) Librarian. The increased emphasis on new student recruitment, retention, and success, as well as the growing number of first-year student initiatives at BGSU, led to the creation of the position. In particular, the FYE librarian is dedicated to introducing beginning students and novice researchers to the library as a physical space and to relevant information literacy competencies that enhance first-year success.

Since that time, other academic libraries across the country have followed suit, creating library positions with a first-year focus. In this chapter, the authors offer an overview of these positions, describe specific institutional approaches to first-year library instruction, and make recommendations for the creation of future FYE librarian positions.

A Study Examining FYE Library Positions

The authors initially identified FYE librarian positions by reviewing job announcements in back issues of *College & Research Libraries News (C&RL News)* from January, 1998 to March, 2006. In order to identify positions filled internally, we posted inquiries to an academic library instruction listserv and searched the web. In total, we identified 15 FYE librarian positions and interviewed 14 of the 15 librarians. The FYE librarian position at Drake University was vacant at the time of our investigation, so we interviewed the chair of the search committee.

We developed a questionnaire with 40 questions focused on the key characteristics of each campus setting, characteristics of the library setting, and most importantly, the defining characteristics and responsibilities of the FYE positions. In an attempt to increase our sample size, we also asked each first-year librarian if he or she was aware of anyone else in similar job positions. Our participants were unable to identify additional FYE librarians.

Appendix A provides the institution, position title, and year established for FYE librarian positions included in this study. The majority of institutions with established FYE positions are from Carnegie Classification Research I and II institutions. Additionally 5 out of the 15 libraries have Association of Research Libraries status. See Appendix B for institutional data.

Position Characteristics

The primary reasons for creating specialized librarian positions were similar across institutions. Several librarians stated a growing interest in first-year initiatives on their campuses as a primary motivator to create new positions or revise existing ones. Another frequently stated reason for the creation of this type of position included the retention of students through their first year and beyond. Despite similar rationales for creating the positions, most institutions created their FYE position in isolation and seemed unaware of this type of position at other institutions.

Of the 15 libraries, 8 indicated their positions are new. Except at Emory University and Duke University, the librarians we interviewed for this chapter are the first to hold the positions since their inception. One third of the participants indicated that their institutions redesigned or reconfigured existing positions to create the FYE librarian position. The majority of the positions are 12-month, full-time positions with two exceptions: Ohio University has a half-time librarian, while the FYE librarian at Eastern Michigan University is on an eight-month appointment. Five librarians hold tenure-track faculty positions, and three positions have faculty status but are not tenure-track. Almost all positions (13) are permanent.

Nine positions require some previous library experience, while six positions are entry level. All but one institution require the traditional library degree, the Master of Library Studies (MLS) or the Master of Library and Information Science (MLIS). The exception was a position that calls for an advanced degree in instructional design. Marketing and promoting the library are key responsibilities of one of the positions. At least two of the positions have a heavy emphasis on recruiting new students to the institution including outreach and instruction to high school groups.

Reporting lines vary, though eight of the librarians report to a combination position such as the "Head of Technology and Instruction," "Head of Information Research Services Division," or "Head of Reference and Collections." Three librarians report to a head or coordinator of instruction, while two report to a head of reference. The majority of the positions do not have coordinator-level status in the traditional sense, but four librarians reported that they are responsible for coordinating instruction requests and assigning sessions in first-year courses to colleagues. None of the positions have supervisory responsibilities, but at least one FYE librarian does contribute to team member evaluations as the team leader.

At 10 institutions, FYE librarians have collections and additional liaison teaching responsibilities similar to those of other librarians in their institutions. However, at five institutions, FYE librarians do not have additional responsibilities for teaching or collections. More than half of the librarians reported having the same number of reference desk hours as their colleagues, but one third reported having reduced reference hours due to their heavier teaching loads. Only one librarian reported more reference desk hours than his or her colleagues. In addition to on-campus responsibilities, nine of the positions perform outreach to high schools. All librarians reported conducting some type of assessment.

When asked if the position had changed since their hiring, most of the librarians indicated that the position continues to be a work in progress. For example, it is not unusual for reporting lines to change. One position that originally reported to the coordinator of reference now reports to the coordinator of instruction because the FYE librarian's position is more closely aligned with classroom teaching than reference.

Position Highlights

The FYE librarians have a variety of responsibilities including new student orientation (campus-wide and/or to the library), library instruction for introductory composition courses and first-year seminars, a role in campus reading initiatives, representation on FYE-focused campus committees, and outreach to high schools. Since most of the FYE librarians have these responsibilities, what follows are descriptions of the unique aspects of the FYE librarian positions and the programs with which they work at selected institutions.

Bowling Green State University (BGSU)

In cooperation with the director of orientation and first-year experience, the FYE librarian at BGSU initiated a common reading experience for a portion of the incoming first-year class in 2001. Within five years, the program expanded to include all incoming first-year students (approximately 3,800). This program is unusual as it falls under the auspices of the University Libraries and is chaired by the FYE librarian rather than another unit on campus. The committee selects the book each year and plans programs related to the book's themes. In addition to students' discussing the book as part of their campus move-in and orientation experience, many of them work with the book in their courses during the first semester. The book or readings from it are typically embedded in the curriculum of the first-year seminar and in some sections of English composition.

Eastern Kentucky University (EKU)

A major emphasis of the first-year initiatives (FYI) librarian's responsibilities at EKU includes instruction and outreach to the Nova Program, a federal TRIO program designed to assist first-generation students in their transition to college life and to ensure success. The FYI librarian is also actively involved with the "EKU Reads Program," a common reading experience for first-year students. She participates in the book selection and coordinates library displays and library speakers related to the themes of the book as part of the campus effort.

Emory University (Emory)

Though the position title, instructional services (IS) librarian, is not reflective of a first-year focus, the librarian in this position is a liaison for first-year programs. In particular, the IS librarian works with the Freshman Writing Program (FWP) and with an advising program for first-year students. Thus, she is known as the first-year librarian on her campus.

The IS librarian's involvement with FWP is multifaceted. In addition to being the primary contact for FWP instructors, the librarian maintains an online tutorial and offers workshops to first-year students throughout the term. The IS librarian is also responsible for providing training sessions to the graduate students who teach in FWP. For those FWP instructors who feel more comfortable having a librarian teach students about research, the IS librarian also accommodates these requests. Because the FWP course is topical, individual preparation is required for each research session taught by the IS librarian.

All librarians, as members of the faculty, have an opportunity to become involved with Freshman Advising and Mentoring at Emory (FAME). A team of three, which includes a faculty member, a staff person, and a student advisor, are assigned to a group of 16 to 17 first-year students. The IS librarian is responsible for teaching a library session for the various FAME groups and is also encouraged to be a part of a FAME group as a staff person.

Kent State University (Kent State)

One of the primary responsibilities of the FYE librarian at Kent State is to work with area high schools. Through the grant-funded Institute for Library and Information Literacy Education (ILILE), Kent State and the FYE librarian are actively working toward the integration of information literacy into the K-12 curriculum and the pre-service teacher preparation curriculum throughout the state of Ohio.

More specifically, the FYE librarian has established a program called "Informed Transitions," which offers high school students an orientation to the University and an instruction session in a newly renovated high-tech classroom designated for high school outreach. During these visits, the FYE librarian helps students find information related to specific assignments, provides them with college-level research experience, and promotes higher education in general and Kent State in particular. Last year, more than 400 area high school students visited the library.

Northern Arizona University (NAU)

As a result of a recent library reorganization, the staff at NAU are now dividing instruction and collection development for various colleges on their campus among several different teams, each of which typically consists of three librarians and two staff members. The team that provides services for the majority of first-year students, the Arts and Letters Team, is also responsible for instruction and collection development for 15 schools and programs in one college. The Arts and Letters Team provides instruction to students enrolled in an English composition course and a first-year honors course. The team leader is also involved in the summer reading program. This team approach is an interesting model for several reasons. It allows for an exchange of ideas among colleagues when planning programs and instructional approaches for first-year students. It also disperses the workload of teaching gateway courses taken by the majority of first-year students among several library staff.

Ohio University (OU)

At OU, the University College is where most first-year initiatives are provided. The first-year librarian works closely with University College students. As this position is part-time and not a tenure-track position, the librarian is not required to fulfill obligations for tenure such as serving on committees, conducting research, publishing, giving presentations, or seeking grants. Rather, the librarian focuses entirely on coordinating instruction for several first-year classes, managing the collection development budget for her area, representing the library at campus outreach and orientation events, and participating in the first-year common reading program.

Plymouth State University (PSU)

The outreach and resource-sharing (ORS) librarian at PSU provides instruction and services to approximately 1,000 first-year students, but the primary focus is on instruction for first-year seminar students. While several librarians share the teaching responsibility for the first-year seminar, the ORS librarian coordinates it.

Tufts University (Tufts)

The coordinator of first-year library instruction at Tufts provides services to approximately 1,300 first-year students through the First-Year Writing Program, a two-semester, tiered program required of most students. Instructional preparation varies for each of the 90 sections of this course due to the flexibility in the curriculum, which focuses on a wide variety of controversial issues. Though other librarians assist with teaching, the coordinator teaches the majority of sessions each year.

University of Cincinnati (UC)

The FYE librarian is an active participant and contributor to the First Year Experience Liaison Group on campus that reports to the Center for First Year Experience & Learning Communities. This group is working toward a consistent and substantive first-year experience across all colleges. Service within this group has allowed the FYE librarian to develop relationships with key campus individuals and to create a greater awareness of the tremendous array of library resources and services available to meet the research and technology needs of first-year students.

The library has developed an integrated instruction model that connects the approximate 5,000 first-year students with library services, technology, resources, and applications both in the classroom and in the library. The FYE librarian coordinates and teaches a library component in a variety of first-year courses, teaching close to 100 sessions in all.

The FYE librarian also teaches a variety of workshops designed for faculty and students who want to incorporate technology into the learning experience. Staying abreast of new developments in this area allows the FYE librarian to quickly adapt to trends in learning and technology that affect first-year students. A current example is the use of e-portfolios, which allow new students to develop a "package" of their work that evolves as they continue through their undergraduate years.

University of Connecticut (UConn)

The responsibility of the undergraduate services (UGS) librarian is to increase library outreach to the entire undergraduate population, including first-year students. Because there is no coordinator of library instruction at UConn, coordination of the library instruction program falls to the UGS librarian and includes the development and assessment of a library information literacy plan. Students enrolled in sections of an English course have a required research assignment, and an in-person library session is provided to approximately 89 sections of this course each semester. Each session lasts an hour and 45 minutes. While some of the graduate services librarians help with this instruction, the bulk of the teaching is the responsibility of the UGS librarian. Due to the high level of activity, two more UGS librarian positions have been approved so that these three positions can work as a team to serve the library needs of the undergraduate population, most of whom are first-year students.

University of Montana (UM)

At UM, the FYE coordinator is also the instruction coordinator and the education librarian. The first-year population is large (3,000 students), and the responsibilities are extensive. The FYE coordinator is a member of the common reading experience committee and is successfully integrating library instruction into the freshman interest groups, first-year seminars, the honors program, first-year public speaking courses, and first-year composition. Due to the large number of requests for instruction for first-year students, the FYE coordinator has approached instruction using a train-the-trainer model. Teaching classroom instructors how to conduct the library component of their respective courses and initiatives frees the coordinator to focus on more specialized and unique sessions.

University of New Mexico (UNM)

The coordinator of first-year library instruction at UNM serves a population of approximately 3,500 first-year students. A library component is required in 120 sections of first-year English. The coordinator ensures that instruction sessions are provided upon request for additional freshman interest groups, first-year learning communities, and first-year residential communities. The coordinator receives support from her library colleagues to assist with this heavy teaching load.

Observations and Recommendations

While nothing can substitute institutional support, shared vision and direction, and clear lines of communication, the following recommendations are offered to ensure maximum success for the first-year librarian position.

Choosing a Title

Terminology and position title do matter. Words such as coordinator, department head, assistant librarian, adjunct, or part-time signal to both internal and external constituencies the priorities and importance related to the position. The job title may also indicate reporting relationships, seniority, authority, and permanence. Titles, which are used for internal human resources (HR) purposes, need not be the functional or working title of the position, especially if they are not descriptive of the position's primary focus or responsibility. Several of the first-year librarians in this study noted a common misunderstanding about their position titles: The term "first-year" is often thought to refer to the librarian's newness to the profession or to the temporary nature of the position. In other words, some people mistakenly believe that a first-year librarian position will terminate after the librarian's first year on the job. This suggests the need to craft positions more reflective of the audience served. Thus, "first-year student initiatives librarian" might more accurately identify the focus of the position than the titles we found.

Identifying Necessary Skills and Characteristics

In order to succeed, an FYE librarian should have experience communicating with campus colleagues, demonstrate initiative, be capable of innovation, and be able to give and take direction. This person needs to be able to navigate the political and bureaucratic landscape of the university and to be enthusiastic, innovative, and engaging in the classroom. Directives may come from more than one person, and the FYE librarian should be able to handle that reality. Positions included in this chapter tended to be closer to the entry level of the hiring spectrum, yet they often require a skill set that comes only with experience. Such skills include organizational, project, and time-management skills as well as a working knowledge of instructional design and assessment. These skills should be included in the requirements for the position as well as at least two years of academic library work experience.

Keeping It Fresh

A typical FYE librarian may teach nearly 100 sessions in a semester reaching more than 2,000 students. Most of these sessions have the same content. The general overview session is likely to be stale unless a concerted effort is made to have a series of standard, active exercises available for all classroom sessions. Therefore, strategies for keeping the teaching and learning fresh, lively, fun, and transferable are critical. Professional development opportunities, mentoring, and working as part of a cohort and in an environment conducive to risk taking will help the librarian remain up-to-date, excited, and engaged. Active-learning strategies are a must. Moreover, these strategies should be based on real-world experiences that will engage students more personally in the learning process. As with every instructional engagement, a research-related question or assignment provides the most authentic learning opportunity. Exploring alternative instructional models to reach the masses is another strategy that will help a person in this position avoid burnout while maximizing student learning. For example, well-designed online tutorials or self-paced activities are viable options.

Dealing With Assessment

All areas of the institution are being asked to assess their contributions to student learning, retention, and success, and the librarians in this study all reported doing assessment. While these librarians understood the value of conducting assessment, many reported a need for a more sustained effort. Such efforts would move beyond the typical approach of adding a few library-related questions to the end-of-term evaluation.

More sustained assessment efforts would also allow for intellectual engagement, the opportunity for research, publishing, presentations, and the feedback and reinforcement of a complex job well done. However, since many of these first-year-focused library programs are still relatively new, and often staffed by new professionals, librarians may need more training to engage in such efforts. Further, they will need support in terms of resources and release time to complete assessment projects. Libraries and institutions must work together to improve and implement assessment so data are available to track progress. A good classroom session will have measurable learning outcomes associated with it, and these outcomes are easier to identify with an active learning assignment than with a very broad "cover everything" session.

A Balancing Act

In addition to teaching responsibilities, first-year librarians must balance other responsibilities, including reference desk hours, committee assignments, and collection development. These other responsibilities can inform and enhance classroom performance; however, when teaching a heavy load, as most of FYE librarians do, a flexible approach to the number of hours and scheduling those hours is necessary. The same can be said for committee work. The FYE librarian is likely to serve on campus committees, and this may mean that he or she will have less time to commit to internal (library) committee work. Teaching library sessions, which are sometimes scheduled on short notice, can make attending meetings difficult. It might be unrealistic to expect this person to take on additional liaison duties such as reference desk and collection development. Adding these traditional responsibilities has the potential to fragment the person's time and compromise the specialized nature of this position. Yet, the FYE librarian should not become too specialized or work in isolation.

Creating Empowerment and Connections

Given the varied responsibilities of FYE librarians and the wide range of constituents they serve, feeling empowered and developing appropriate communication channels are critical markers for success. These attributes are essential as the person performs the crucial activities of marketing and public relations. This position needs credibility. It is important to make sure this person is fully integrated into the information loop so that he or she can fairly and accurately represent the library. There must be mechanisms to regularly report back to appropriate library personnel concerning the details of the campus initiatives and priorities, especially if the campus environment is fluid and flexible.

The librarian will also benefit from a cohort. Whether formal or informal, the cohort can serve as a sounding board and provide a sense of camaraderie. Moreover, the cohort can help the FYE librarian envision new and innovative ways to fulfill the responsibilities of the position. The department to which the FYE librarian belongs may be the primary cohort, but members of first-year experience committees, offices, or task forces might also fulfill this need.

Conclusion

The first-year librarian position is a new phenomenon, and while there are many similarities in the positions studied, there are also unique aspects of the positions tailored to meet specific campus needs. Our study found that the majority of these positions are in large Research I or II institutions where first-year students can easily get lost in the academic shuffle. Most were created in direct response to campus initiatives around student learning and retention. The positions studied focus on introducing first-year students to the library as a place and on using information literacy competencies to support student learning. Yet, they are also flexible "works in progress" as they strive to be relevant and integrated into the local campus environment. More sustained assessment is needed to determine the long-term effectiveness and impact of the first-year librarian on retention and student learning.

Appendix A

Librarian Positions With a First-Year Focus

Institution	Position Title	Year Established
Bowling Green State University	First-Year Experience Librarian	1999
Drake University	Librarian for First-Year Experience	2005
Duke University	Coordinator, First-Year Instruction and Outreach	1994
Eastern Kentucky University	First-Year Initiatives Librarian	2003
Eastern Michigan University	First-Year Experience Librarian	2005
Emory University	Instructional Services Librarian	2003
Kent State University	First-Year Experience Librarian	2004
Northern Arizona University	Librarian, Arts & Letters Team Leader	2003
Ohio University	First-Year Librarian	2005
Plymouth State University	Outreach and Resource Sharing Librarian	2003
Tufts University	Coordinator of First-Year Library Instruction	2002
University of Cincinnati	First-Year Experience Librarian	2000
University of Connecticut	Undergraduate Services Librarian	2000
University of Montana	First-Year Experience Coordinator	2003
University of New Mexico	Coordinator of First-Year Instruction Services	2003

Appendix B
Institutional Data Summary

Institution	Full-time Equivalent	Control	Type	Carnegie Class	ARL Status*
Bowling Green State University	20,361	Public	Four-year	Research II	No
Drake University	5,160	Private	Four-year	Masters I	No
Duke University	12,181	Private	Four-year	Research I	No
Eastern Kentucky University	15,951	Public	Four-year	Masters I	No
Eastern Michigan University	24,419	Public	Four-year	Masters I	No
Emory University	11,654	Private	Four-year	Research I	Yes
Kent State University	24,242	Public	Four-year	Research I	Yes
Northern Arizona State	18,824	Public	Four-year	Research II	No
Ohio University	19,962	Public	Four-year	Research I	Yes
Plymouth State University	4,994	Public	Four-year	Masters I	No
Tufts University	9,400	Private	Four-year	Research I	No
University of Cincinnati	27,601	Public	Four-year	Research I	No
University of Connecticut	26,629	Public	Four-year	Research I	Yes
University of Montana	13,091	Public	Four-year	Research II	No
University of New Mexico	25,793	Public	Four-year	Research I	Yes

*Membership in the Association of Research Libraries

Chapter 8

Strategies for Designing Assignments to Support Information Literacy Initiatives

Larry L. Hardesty

Given the long history of efforts to involve students in productive use of the library dating well back into the 19th century (Hardesty, Schmitt, & Tucker, 1986; Hardesty & Tucker, 1989) and the increased sophistication of current goals in developing information literacy (see chapter 1), one might assume that the academy would have developed a useful pedagogy for teaching first-year students library skills. Such pedagogy, however, remains in varying degrees an elusive aspiration. This fact should become evident to readers as they examine the various case studies in the second half of this monograph. Several authors describe false starts and unsuccessful efforts before embarking on their current programs. Pedagogy, or the science of teaching, remains a complex subject and encompasses numerous variables ranging from student-learning styles and levels of intellectual maturity to classroom structure and types of evaluation. As such, the definitive pedagogy in any area, not just information literacy, is difficult to determine as we seek approximate solutions to address the ever-changing and multifaceted challenges of facilitating successful and appropriate learning. No doubt, we can benefit from determining what does work, but often we can also benefit considerably from understanding the challenges to successful pedagogy and what does not work. While much of this chapter may be applicable to the development of information literacy skills at other levels, I have focused on those challenges and strategies most related to the development of information literacy in the first year of college.

Challenges to Effective Instruction and Assignment Design

The challenges to successful library assignments come from many areas. Some challenges are related simply to practical concerns, such as the logistics of numerous first-year students attempting to use the library. The sheer number of students may overwhelm the library staff and its resources, but the problem is compounded because many of these students are neither adequately informed about how to use the library nor motivated to do so. Other challenges relate to a lack of communication between librarians and first-year classroom faculty. Each group may have different goals in mind, may be unclear about their own or each other's goals, or may disagree about appropriate instruction and guidance (Tiefel, 1982). Moreover, librarians and classroom faculty may misunderstand or be completely unaware of the guidance or instruction given to students by the other. Both librarians and classroom faculty may enter the experience without sufficient awareness of the challenges of information literacy instruction and adequate preparation to address them.

For example, instructors of first-year courses are often drawn from the ranks of relatively new classroom faculty, graduate assistants still developing their teaching skills, and adjuncts often new to both teaching and the institutions. Even when experienced classroom faculty teach first-year courses, they are often drawn from disciplines not highly dependent on the library in undergraduate teaching. Or, these experienced classroom faculty members are from disciplines that typically involve only their upper-level students in use of the library. Further, doctoral education does not adequately prepare them for undergraduate teaching. In graduate school, they learn the content of the discipline, develop an expertise in a specialization, and learn how to conduct research as presented in their dissertation (Gaff, Pruitt-Logan, Weibel, & Participants in the Preparing Future Faculty Program, 2000).

Because of their preparation and socialization in their doctoral studies, most classroom faculty leave graduate school for the undergraduate classrooms of community colleges, liberal arts colleges, and comprehensive universities of the nation without a sufficient understanding of the relevance of undergraduate use of the library to the courses they are teaching or how to make such use relevant. Several observers, mostly librarians (Branscomb, 1940; Farber, 1974; Hardesty, 1991, 1995; Knapp, 1965, 1966; Merrill, 1979), have long noted that classroom faculties are not very well-prepared to make effective use of the library in their teaching. Former Earlham College library director Farber suggested that the attitudes classroom faculty learned in graduate school interfered with their ability to see librarians as partners in the educational process and the role of the library in undergraduate education. As a result, Knapp (1965) concludes that "Sophisticated understanding of the library and increasing competence in its use as a goal of general education is not accepted, perhaps not understood by most of the faculty" (p. 262). Yet, classroom faculty are being asked to play a role in teaching first-year students how to make effective use of the library. As such, they are being required to take on responsibilities for which they are not adequately prepared either by socialization or education.

In addition, one can also argue that many librarians are also not prepared to play a role in teaching first-year students how to make effective use of the library. Some, by temperament and preference, do not want to teach in the classroom. Others, while willing teachers, have little preparation through their graduate education since exposure to the concepts and implementation of information literacy is usually only a small part, if any, of graduate library school preparation. Finally, probably most librarians do not have extensive classroom teaching experience, even as teaching assistants in graduate school.

Perhaps less obvious, but no less problematic, are the challenges relating to the intellectual readiness of first-year students to make sophisticated use of the library. Whether one refers to the earlier Bloom's (1956) taxonomy of cognitive skills or its more recent revision (Anderson et al., 2001), a review of library assignments reveals that they often require students to use a higher level of cognitive skills than they have fully developed. Frequently, first-year students are required to compare and contrast information from multiple sources, to make determinations as to the validity of information, and to synthesize this information using their own words. The intent of such assignments is, of course, quite desirable—to improve the intellectual capabilities of first-year students.

Nevertheless, Perry (1970) suggested that first-year students may not be intellectually ready to make such sophisticated discriminations among ideas. In his study of undergraduates, students described past experiences of a dualistic approach to thinking (i.e., the belief that all questions have one right answer that is known to authorities) at the end of their first college year (Perry), suggesting that some students may enter college as basic dualists. Building on Perry's work, Baxter Magolda (1992) explored gender-related differences in intellectual development. She found considerable evidence of absolute knowing (closely related to dualism and briefly defined as a view that knowledge is certain and that absolute answers exist in all areas of knowledge) among first-year students.

If classroom faculty and librarians do not pay attention to the intellectual development of first-year students in designing library-related assignments, the result can be a very frustrating experience for all concerned. For example, a typical library-related assignment might require students to use the library to find several journal articles on a topic and then evaluate how well the various authors addressed that issue. Such an assignment may completely baffle a first-year student in the early stages of intellectual development. Some students may think, "There is clearly a right answer" and approach the reference desk, asking, perhaps obliquely, "Where is *the* book that has the *right* answer to this question?" Other students may see a variety of answers as being possible, but they do not distinguish between the credibility of those answers. Similarly, these students may view all published materials, whether journals or popular magazines, as authorities. In more recent years, such students have treated the Internet with greater deference than printed pages as they readily use popular search engines to find information for their assignments. While we may want students to use higher-level cognitive skills to analyze and evaluate a variety of answers, Perry found students in the early development stages often rejected such tools of "critical analysis, reflection and critical thinking" (p. 73) as they sought "the answer" from authorities.

This presents us with an interesting quandary. As we challenge first-year students to develop their information literacy skills, we risk some students becoming frustrated and forming long-lasting, negative attitudes towards the library and the research process. How can those involved in the first-year experience (i.e., classroom faculty, librarians, student affairs personnel, and others) design assignments that help students develop needed information literacy skills without creating counterproductive attitudes towards the library? How can we foster in students both the *ability* and the *desire* to use the academic library and other information resources effectively?

Despite these challenges, designing effective library assignments is a critical task for classroom faculty and one that is as complex as designing assignments to develop any other sophisticated ability in our students, such as competence in writing or mathematics. While there may be no easy or "right way" to develop good library assignments, there are some general characteristics of effective library-assignment design upon which instructors may rely. The rather practical recommendations in the following section suggest that helping first-year students develop information literacy skills can be a positive experience for all concerned when there is good communication and cooperation among all parties involved; careful structuring of assignments; clear, relevant guidance and instruction; and frequent feedback.

Characteristics of Effective Assignments

How to design effective library assignments is one of the most popular topics among college and university librarians today. A recent Google search for "effective library assignments" returned almost 10,000 hits. The characteristics described below were gleaned from some of the web sites I reviewed as a result of this search, but they also come from the literature and from conversations with other librarians (see Appendix). Effective library assignments have the following characteristics:

1. They are clear.

Perhaps the first step in creating an effective library assignment is clarity. In plain language, the assignment should identify its connection to course goals, the expectations of the instructor, how students are to meet those expectations, and how the instructor is going to evaluate the assignment. These need to be clear not only to the students in the course but also to the librarians who may be providing instruction in the classroom or assistance at the reference desk.

Simple directions such as "Go to the library and look in the periodical stacks. Find three good articles in scholarly journals in X discipline on Y topic and compare them." can baffle and frustrate the first-year student. First, students are probably unfamiliar with the term "periodical stacks" and other library jargon. More important, they may not know the difference between scholarly journals and popular magazines. Neither are they likely to know which periodicals in a discipline are considered scholarly, which are not, and why. Perhaps even more challenging, they are being asked to discriminate among several "authorities" without any guidance or instruction in understanding or appreciating the criteria to be used for such analysis. Thus, instructors may want to take time to define terms unfamiliar to students—either in the assignment itself or during their in-class review of it. Instructors may also want to include a list of specific library resources for students to use in the assignment description.

One useful technique for testing the clarity of an assignment is by having one or more students read through it and provide feedback. For example, research and writing strategies may seem obvious to the instructor, who is also an experienced researcher, but may be largely unknown to the first-year student. Discussing these strategies with students helps the instructor discover what students do not know about successfully completing an assignment.

2. They are relevant to course goals.

Understanding how to make the library relevant to both the general goals of undergraduate education and to individual course goals is important. Without a concerted effort to make the library relevant to the goals of the course, students will see the library assignment, as Knapp found, "as sheer high school busy work" (1966, p. 89). Various actions by instructors help convey the relevance and importance of library assignments to course goals. Students quickly sense from a classroom instructor's behavior (e.g., not attending the library instruction session) and attitude (e.g., making observations or asking questions that elaborate on or support points made by the librarian providing instruction) whether a library assignment is an add-on or essential to success in the course. From sensing the assignment and instruction is not relevant to the course, it is a short step for first-year students to developing lasting negative attitudes about the library. For example, Hostrop (1966) found that instructors who considered knowing how to use the library an important course objective and who followed up on assignments, informing students of their progress, made the greatest use of the library in their courses. Presumably, the value they placed on the library was also clear to students.

Ideally, library assignments should be so relevant to the goals of the course that students do not perceive them as anything other than an integral and necessary element to the successful completion of the course goals. The library assignment should have a specific purpose that is clearly articulated by the instructor, comprehended and reinforced by librarians, and fully understood by the students.

The failure of some commonly used first-year assignments (i.e., scavenger or treasure hunts and orientation tours) to engage students intellectually underscores the importance of relevant assignments. Tours of the library teach about as much about the use of the library as tours of the chemistry lab teach about chemistry. Without follow-up assignments, little of the information provided is seen as significant, understood, or remembered. Scavenger hunts teach students little about conducting independent research or evaluating and synthesizing information. Many times, such assignments become exercises in futility as items are misplaced or disappear. Often, the librarian ends up hunting for the information for the students one at a time. Rather than helping students master relevant research skills, such assignments promote learned helplessness, and students come away viewing the library as one huge source of isolated fragments of information without a coherent framework (Knapp, 1966).

3. They specify the source materials to be used.

Concerns about plagiarism and the quality of sources students use in their research and writing lead some instructors to specify the kinds of sources students can use or to ask students to turn in copies of the sources used. As noted earlier, first-year students may have difficulty evaluating the credibility and relevance of the literature in a field. After all, it may have taken their instructor years of graduate study to understand the hierarchy of the quality of journals in the discipline and the various nuances and perspectives of each. Thus, a list of scholarly journals in a discipline, even if it is not exhaustive, can help students avoid some frustrations. Such a list should have complete, unabbreviated titles to avoid confusing those unfamiliar with the discipline. A resource commonly known among scholars in the discipline may have a different "official" name in the library's catalog. Instructors may also want to verify the availability of sources on the list to avoid sending students to find a print resource that is now only available electronically. If certain reference works are to be used, complete citations with call numbers are useful.

Some instructors may prohibit the use of general web sites. From a student's perspective, this may mean not using such scholarly resources as JSTOR, Project Muse, and an increasing number of other high-quality electronic resources. Providing some definition as to what is meant by Internet sources and a list of electronic sources appropriate for student use may alleviate this problem. At the same time, students need to be cautioned about expecting too much from Internet resources. The Internet can be a great resource and often includes information not available in print. However, despite occasional pronouncement by the uninformed to the contrary, not all information is available on the Internet. Much remains available only in print—a situation that is likely to exist for the foreseeable future. Both Internet-based and traditional print resources provide useful information, and students need guidance as to the appropriate use of each. In fact, specifying the format to be used (i.e., a certain number of sources from print materials, microforms, and the Internet) can result in a rather contrived assignment since given a particular topic, any one of these formats may provide the best sources of information while others are not helpful at all.

Finally, asking that students turn in original source materials (e.g., photos, advertisements, illustrations, articles) may appear an innocuous requirement as part of an assignment. Unfortunately, such a stipulation sometimes leads to students' stealing or mutilating library resources. Photocopies, particularly with the increasing availability of color photocopiers, may quite adequately serve this requirement.

4. They are feasible, both in terms of the library's resources and the scope of the topic chosen.

If an assignment requires first-year students to make extensive use of interlibrary loan, it may create or reinforce the impression of inadequate institutional library resources. First-year students may carry this attitude with them throughout their academic careers at the institution. Thus, making assignments that can be completed with available library resources is important. Likewise, when numerous sections of a course have the same or similar assignments, available resources may be strained. If numerous students are searching for the same book or journal, there is a good chance it will disappear or be temporarily misplaced—either accidentally or deliberately—which will frustrate both the library staff and other students. Because the assignments are also likely to have similar due dates, students will probably show up at the library all at once. Frequently, librarians have little chance to prepare to help students and to staff the reference desk accordingly. If multiple students need to use the same resource, it is a good idea to put it in the reserve collection or, if possible, make it available electronically. Because some electronic resources allow only a limited number of simultaneous users, it may be a good idea to schedule a time when students can use these resources as a group.

Selecting and developing an appropriate topic, as most classroom faculty should recall from their dissertation days, are very important elements in the research process. Too often, without guidance, neophyte scholars will select an overly broad topic (e.g., global warming, women in American history, cures for cancer) and be frustrated by the huge amount of information available and their inability to distill it into a quality paper. On a related note, such broad topics, particularly if they have great social significance, may outstrip locally available resources.

At other times, students will readily choose a very narrow topic that is very current or very local (e.g., bird flu in Turkey or the impact of global warming on Sandhill cranes in the Platte Valley of Nebraska) and covered in yesterday's newspaper. In this case, they may well experience the frustration of not finding enough information in the library. Topics readily narrowed or expanded by an experienced scholar may present a frustrating challenge to the first-year student without guidance. Sometimes, requesting a preliminary bibliography and/or proposal statement can help the student focus the topic appropriately. Asking students to list the number of articles found in particular databases and search terms used can help alert the instructor to the need to limit or broaden a topic.

5. They are designed with and/or previewed by librarians.

Working together and sharing their perspectives and knowledge, librarians and classroom faculty can do more to create positive library experiences for their students than either group working separately. Librarians are usually very willing to discuss the assignment with the classroom instructor and provide feedback before the assignment is finalized. The preview allows librarians to alert classroom faculty to potential problems with the availability of resources and to suggest alternatives that will achieve the same goal. The librarian can help to ensure the accuracy of the descriptions and locations of needed library resources and make sure the resources are available when students need them. The librarian can also provide instruction suitable to the assignment at an appropriate time. Sometimes, the cooperation is as basic as helping librarians to anticipate that numerous students will be coming to the library to complete an assignment.

In addition, it is a good idea to provide the library with a copy of the final assignment. Sometimes, the descriptions of the assignments offered by students to librarians have little resemblance to the explanations (however clearly and carefully made) provided in the classroom the day before. If librarians have the assignment ahead of time, they are better prepared to help students and reinforce the purpose of the assignment.

6. They have been tested by instructors before being given to students.

Often, if the instructor works through the assignment and analyzes what is needed to complete it, he or she can make it clearer. Still, this requires instructors to put themselves in the shoes of first-year students who do not have the benefit of advanced study in a discipline and several years of teaching and researching experience. Some years ago, at a library instruction workshop I hosted (Hardesty, Hastreiter, & Henderson, 1993), an Earlham College political scientist shared with the attendees that she had developed a library assignment that she thought her students could complete in two or three hours. However, when she tested the assignment, it took her eight or nine hours to complete. Given her students' inexperience with the library, they probably would have taken even longer. Modeling assignments, while often time-consuming, can help the classroom instructor discover unexpected challenges in completing them.

7. They have been broken down into a series of shorter, sequenced tasks or assignments.

Often, first-year students can be overwhelmed by the totality of a library assignment and not consider it attainable. Pacing or staging assignments may encourage students to see the assignment as a series of discrete, but manageable projects. Since time management probably is not a well-developed skill of many first-year students, staged assignments can help students grow in this area and give the instructor multiple opportunities for feedback. Staging library assignments can include such requirements as writing a preliminary bibliography, formulating a thesis statement, developing an annotated bibliography, making oral presentations of works in progress, and writing preliminary drafts of the paper. Such staging may also help reduce problems with plagiarism (Miller, 2006). Students may feel less overwhelmed by the process and less tempted to resort to copy and paste material from a convenient source. In addition, the instructor has multiple check points integrated into the assignment to determine whether the student is doing his or her own work and to intervene when further guidance is needed.

8. The assignments are linked closely in time to instruction.

Most students are motivated to learn what it takes to complete the current assignment but not for some possible assignment they may or may not have two years from now. Often, the more that one attempts to teach, the less students learn. In any case, students are not going to learn all they need to know about the library in one class session. However, librarians are often tempted to pack too much into one or two class periods of instruction during the first year, in part because they may be uncertain they will have opportunities to provide more advanced instruction to students at a later time.

Further, instruction provided too far in advance of an assignment may well mean librarians will be repeating the instruction individually to students as they come to the reference desk when they start on the assignment. It may well also mean a steady stream of students to the instructor's office for guidance provided earlier (and forgotten).

In some cases, an assignment is made without accompanying instruction. The (often unstated) assumption is that students will somehow pick up the knowledge of how to use the library or that they already know it. The sink-or-swim approach often results in a very frustrating and negative experience for students and for instructors who are disappointed by the completed assignments they receive.

We need to keep in mind that information literacy assignments (and accompanying instruction) in the first year are only starting points in developing more sophisticated information literacy skills as students progress though college. Successful mastery of information literacy skills, like writing and other complex skills, involves a series of increasingly complex assignments with feedback for improvement, probably extending throughout a student's undergraduate career.

9. They are appropriately challenging.

Incorporating the right amount of challenge in assignments for first-year students is sometimes difficult to achieve. What may be a modest library project for upper-level students can be a substantial and overwhelming challenge for first-year students who may not have developed the intellectual ability and time-management skills to complete the assignment successfully.

Left to their own devices, many first-year students can readily confuse quantity of information and the accumulation of descriptive information with quality of thought. And some, of course, are quite ready to accept convenient information, whatever its quality, over information that requires more time and effort to retrieve, analyze, evaluate, and synthesize. Nevertheless, through carefully constructed assignments, most students come to understand the benefits of coursework that goes beyond accumulation of descriptive information and engages them in intellectual tasks appropriate to their skill level.

Understanding the appropriate level of challenge is not always easy. Typically when asked, most first-year students will say they have written library papers in high school or even junior high and that they know how to use the library. This does not mean they have gone beyond compilations of descriptive and unevaluated information, nor does it indicate they know how to use an academic library with its more sophisticated resources. Mellon (1986) contends students may not acknowledge that they do not use the library because they have "library anxiety" and are reluctant to admit what they do not know. The same misleading information may be offered when students are asked if they know how to use the Internet. They may know how to download music files, participate in chat rooms, and do basic Google searches. However, this does not mean they know the terminology of a discipline, basics of Boolean logic to construct sophisticated searches, or how to evaluate the information they find. First-year students often overestimate their understanding of the library, which becomes obvious both at the reference desk and in the quality of their work from library assignments.

Conclusions and Recommendations

As emphasized at the beginning of this chapter, helping first-year students develop library skills so they can become information literate men and women involves significant challenges. These challenges are due to many factors. First-year students may overestimate their skills or be reluctant to admit their lack of skills. They may not be intellectually mature enough to handle complex library assignments that require the application of higher-order cognitive skills. They may not have the motivation or the time-management skills needed for independent use of the library. Often, first-year programs deal with a large number of students and with a relatively small number of classroom instructors and librarians. Neither librarians nor classroom faculty come into their positions fully aware and adequately prepared to meet these challenges.

Nevertheless, if we believe that the first year, and perhaps even the first few weeks of the first year, is critical in developing appropriate academic attitudes and skills among students; if we believe that knowing how to retrieve, analyze, evaluate, and synthesize information is critical to an educated person in today's society; and if we believe ethical use of that information is equally important, then we must begin developing library-related skills and attitudes in the first year—no matter how demanding the challenges. Librarians and first-year classroom faculty share the common goal of enhancing students' success. Working together and pooling their perspectives and knowledge, librarians and first-year classroom faculty can do more to create positive library experiences and ensure students' success than either group working separately. Frequent and good communication is the key to a positive library experience in the first year.

References

Anderson, L. W., Krathwohl, D. R., Airasian, P. W., Cruikshank, K. A., Mayer, R. E., Pintrich, P. R., Rath, J., & Witttrock, M. C. (Eds.). (2001). *A taxonomy for learning, teaching, and assessing: A revision of Bloom's taxonomy of education objectives* (abr. ed.). New York: Longman.

Baxter Magolda, M. B. (1992). *Knowing and reasoning in college: Gender-related patterns in students' intellectual development.* San Francisco: Jossey-Bass.

Bloom, H. S. (1956). *Taxonomy of educational objectives: Handbook I: Cognitive domain.* New York: David McKay.

Branscomb, H. (1940). *Teaching with books.* Chicago: Association of American Colleges, American Library Association.

Farber, E. I. (1974). College librarians and the university-librarian syndrome. In E. I. Farber & R. Walling (Eds.), *The academic library: Essays in honor of Guy R. Lyle* (pp. 12-17). Metuchen, NJ: Scarecrow Press.

Fink, D. (1986). What you ask for is what you get: Some dos and don'ts for assigning research projects. *Research Strategies, 4*(2), 91-93.

Gaff, J. G., Pruitt-Logan, A. S., Weibel, R. A., & Participants in the Preparing Future Faculty Program. (2000). *Building the faculty we need: Colleges and universities working together.* Washington, DC: Association of American Colleges & Universities.

Hardesty, L. L. (1991). *Faculty and the library: The undergraduate experience.* Norwood, NJ: Ablex.

Hardesty, L. L. (1995). Bibliographic instruction and faculty culture. *Library Trends, 44*(2), 339-367.

Hardesty, L. L., Hastreiter, J., & Henderson, D. W. (Eds). (1993). *Bibliographic instruction in practices: A tribute to the legacy of Evan Ira Farber.* Ann Arbor, MI: Pierian Press.

Hardesty, L. L., Schmitt, J. P., & Tucker, J. M. (Eds.). (1986). *User instruction in academic libraries: A century of selected readings.* Metuchen, NJ: Scarecrow Press.

Hardesty, L. L., & Tucker. J. M. (1989). An uncertain crusade: The history of library use instruction in a changing educational environment. In J. V. Richardson & J. Y. Davis (Eds.), *Academic librarianship: Past, present, and future* (pp. 97-111). Littleton, CO: Libraries Unlimited.

Herro, S. (1996, January). Tips for effective library assignments. *The Beacon: A guide to faculty development at St. Norbert College.* Retrieved October 29, 2006, from http://www.lib.berkeley.edu/TeachingLib/Tips.html

Hostrop, R. W. (1966). *The relationship of academic success and selected other factors to student use of library materials at College of the Desert.* Unpublished doctoral dissertation, University of California, Los Angeles.

Knapp, P. B. (1965). The meaning of the Monteith College library program for library education. *Journal of Education for Librarianship, 6*, 117-127.

Knapp, P. B. (1966). *The Monteith College library experiment.* New York: Scarecrow.

Mellon, C. (1986). Library anxiety: A grounded theory and its development. *College & Research Libraries, 47*(2), 160-165.

Merrill, M. (1979). *Regular and irregular library use by faculty members at three universities.* Unpublished doctoral dissertation, University of Pittsburgh.

Miller, W. (2006). Enhancing students' academic honesty and respect for research. *Library Issues, 25*(6), 1-4.

Mosley, P. A. (1998). Creating a library assignment workshop for university faculty. *The Journal of Academic Librarianship, 24*(1), 35-37.

Perry, W. G., Jr. (1970). *Forms of intellectual and ethical development in the college years: A scheme.* New York: Holt, Rinehart and Winston.

Tiefel, V. (1982). Libraries and librarians as depicted in freshman English textbooks. *College English, 44*(5), 494-505.

Appendix

Print and Online Resources for Effective Library Assignments

To develop the recommendations in this chapter, I reviewed numerous academic library web sites. A Google search using the phrase "effective library assignments" returned almost 10,000 hits, which, of course, is larger than the number of academic institutions in this country, and some evidence that it is a topic of considerable and widespread interest among librarians. In reviewing the sites, I have found many similarities with occasional attributions to other sites and, less frequently, a note that the information on the web site has been adapted from another source with permission. In fall 2005, I spent some time trying to trace the origins of the various "effective library assignments" lists, assuming a path would lead me back to the original source. That effort led me in a number of directions, and the information gathered in that search has been incorporated in the chapter. However, I encourage readers to explore these sources for themselves and highlight some of the most prominent here.

John Kupersmith, reference librarian at the University of California, Berkeley, provided me with a document titled "For Effective Library Assignments" that he developed in May 1983, which is the earliest document I could locate. However, when I asked John to examine some of the other sites, he found some similarities in purpose and content but quite different structure and wording. He concluded: "I think what you have here is a number of people working earnestly on a topic and coming up with somewhat similar results" (personal communication, November 2, 2005). Deborah Fink (1986) also wrote an article 20 years ago on the topic intended as a guide for classroom faculty with elements of successful, effective research assignments and those that lead to dissatisfaction.

Steve Herro (1996) originally published "Tips for Effective Library Assignments" in *The Beacon: A Guide to Faculty Development at St. Norbert College*. The campus-specific treatment has since been modified for a wider audience and is now available at http://www.lib.berkeley.edu/TeachingLib/Tips.html.

Several web sites acknowledge the contribution of Pixey Mosley (1998) in shaping the design of effective library assignments. Currently, Mosley serves as the director of access services at Texas A&M University's Evans Library. The faculty guide she helped create can be downloaded from the library's web site at http://library.tamu.edu/portal/site/library/. Readers should search the library's site for "creating effective library assignments."

Another list often cited and developed relatively more recently is the "Guidelines for Effective Library Assignments" created collectively by members of the California Clearinghouse on Library Instruction, Southern Section (CCLI-South) in 2000. CCLI-South is now an interest group of the California Academic and Research Libraries (CARL) and is now the Southern California Instruction Librarians (SCIL). A source for this document is available at http://gort.ucsd.edu/dtweedy/EffectiveAssignments.html.

Other commonly sited sources for "Effective Library Assignments" documents include:

- Bowling Green State University
  http://www.bgsu.edu/colleges/library/infosrv/lue/effectiveassignments.html
- California State University, East Bay
  http://www.library.csuhayward.edu/library_assignments.htm
- Delta College
  http://www.delta.edu/library/Efflib.html

- Duke University
  http://www.lib.duke.edu/services/instruction/assignments.htm
- Instruction Section of the Association of College and Research Libraries, "Share Your Teaching Tool Kit: Best Practices in Library Instruction Bibliography" http://www.ala.org/ala/acrlbucket/is/conferencesacrl/midwinter001/bibliography.htm
- St. Louis Community College
  http://www.stlcc.edu/ls/assign.html
- University of Maryland
  http://www.lib.umd.edu/guides/assignment.html
- University of Minnesota
  http://www.lib.umn.edu/libdata/page.phtml?page_id=972
- University of New Brunswick
  http://www.lib.unb.ca/instruction/assignments.html
- University of Notre Dame
  http://www.library.nd.edu/instruction/svcsteaching/efflibassign.shtml
- University of Oregon
  http://libweb.uoregon.edu/instruct/assignments.html
- University of Texas
  http://www.lib.utexas.edu/services/instruction/faculty/creatassignment.html
- University of Washington
  http://www.lib.washington.edu/help/guides/design.html

Chapter 9

Engaging First-Year Students: Developing Library-Related Cocurricular Activities That Impact and Empower Students

Ellysa Stern Cahoy & Loanne Snavely

Cocurricular activities are defined as those student experiences that take place outside the formal classroom setting and may include student clubs and organizations, athletics, and living-learning programs. Though often thought of as nonacademic, some out-of-class activities (e.g., international or study abroad experiences, service-learning, and internships) offer course credit. Moreover, student involvement is increasingly in the areas of "academic clubs, service-learning, work, undergraduate research, and community service" rather than more traditional campus activities (Kuh, Palmer, & Kish, 2003, p.1). While the literature on cocurricular activities infrequently addresses library-related activities, librarians can use general studies to inform the development of out-of-class, library-based activities. Moreover, because cocurricular activities are among the most important and influential aspects of a student's college education, their connection to library instruction may have synergistic effects on student learning. This chapter describes the importance of cocurricular activities in the library environment. The authors examine the results of a national survey of libraries providing cocurricular activities and use examples from the survey and from the literature to provide models for cocurricular programming for libraries and first-year programs.

Cocurricular Activities: What the Research Tells Us

In a review of research on the effects of out-of-class experiences on students' learning and cognitive development, Terenzini, Pascarella, and Blimling (1999) examined multiple sources of influence, including those occurring in a student's place of residence (e.g., off-campus housing, campus residence halls, Greek housing, themed residence halls, living-learning centers), in fraternities and sororities, in intercollegiate athletics, in employment, and in faculty and peer interactions. Peer interactions that involved educational or intellectual content such as tutoring or discussing racial/ethnic issues produced the most positive and beneficial effects, while time spent purely socializing with peers was found to have a negative impact. Terenzini et al. concluded that a wide variety of out-of-class experiences have a positive influence on academic and intellectual development, especially those in which academic and nonacademic aspects are integrated. The key to experiences that enhance learning is active student involvement. Additionally, they found, "the most powerful source of influence on student learning appears to be the students' interpersonal interactions, whether with peers or faculty (and one suspects, staff members)" (p. 619). Terenzini et al. suggested that these effects are cumulative and that a variety of experiences over time produced the most significant impact on students' overall academic success.

In another article tracing the value of educationally purposeful out-of-class experiences, Kuh et al. (2003) reached a similar conclusion, noting: "One thing about college student experience is certain: Students learn more when they are engaged at reasonably high levels in a variety of educationally purposeful activities, inside and outside the classroom, over an extended period of time" (p. 1). They surmise that both classroom and cocurricular experiences are required to help students develop the full range of abilities that they will need to succeed in our ever-changing and complex society and that educators should look for ways to intentionally create the conditions to enhance these experiences. Kuh et al. examined a variety of out-of-class activities and associated them with gains in the following domains: (a) cognitive complexity (i.e., critical thinking, quantitative reasoning, reflective judgment, and intellectual flexibility), (b) knowledge acquisition and application, (c) humanitarianism, (d) interpersonal and intrapersonal competence, and (e) practical competence (i.e., the ability to identify and solve problems, manage time effectively, and make good decisions). In addition to producing gains in these areas, educationally purposeful out-of-class activities enrich the undergraduate experience and enhance student learning, persistence, and educational attainment.

In a third article, Gellin (2003) presented a meta-analysis of eight studies and examined the effect of undergraduate student involvement on critical thinking. He found overall involvement in a variety of out-of-class activities including Greek life, clubs and organizations, faculty and peer interactions, living on campus, and employment correlated positively with gains in critical thinking. Involvement in out-of-class activities accomplishes this by providing a variety of new perspectives and learning experiences that students can compare and contrast with their own points of view. Such involvement can also create opportunities for applying in-class learning to real-world situations, which may, in turn, increase the student's appreciation for their in-class learning.

Such findings diverge from earlier views of cocurricular activities that considered them to be taking time away from studying and other important activities that contribute to academic achievement (Black, 2002; MacKinnon-Slaney, 1993). Recent research, however, has shown that cocurricular activities do not have a negative impact on academic involvement (Huang & Chang, 2004).

Attitudes about cocurricular activities may vary by country of origin or ethnic group. International students, in particular, may avoid cocurricular activities fearing that cocurricular involvement could negatively affect their academic involvement (Shieh, Gong, & Huang, 1992). Parental and societal attitudes may contribute to this view by prizing academic performance and degree attainment and being wary of other factors that may, at least superficially, seem to detract from these goals. However, a number of studies reveal these fears to be unfounded. In addition to those studies discussed above, House (2000) reported that academic self-concept was positively correlated with student involvement, and Pritchard and Wilson (2003) correlated students' social (including cocurricular) and emotional health with their success, as measured by GPA and retention.

Indeed, cocurricular activities can benefit students even after graduation. Increasingly, in the US, when students enter the job market, college grades may not be the only important factor in enhancing a person's marketability. Interpersonal skills and leadership ability, which are often at the top of the recruiter's list of most valued characteristics, are often judged through involvement in cocurricular activities (Dunkel, Bray, & Wofford, 1989; Rubin, Bommer, & Baldwin, 2002).

Cocurricular Activities Help Students Develop Positive Emotional Feelings About the Library

New to campus and to academic research, first-year students may view the traditional academic library as an overwhelming place. The typical first-year student's experience is based on a high school library with a relatively navigable collection and one or more readily known librarians, or a high school without any library at all. Thus, he or she may feel overwhelmed by the vast array of collections, services, and staff that an academic library presents. Mellon (1986) found that 75% to 85% of college students surveyed consistently used words like "scary, overpowering, lost, helpless, and confused" to describe the way they felt in the library (p. 162). Such feelings are defined formally in the literature as library anxiety, for which Mellon identified four causes including (a) library size, (b) not knowing "where things are located," (c) not knowing how to begin, or (d) what to do (p. 162).

Similar to math anxiety and test anxiety, library anxiety develops when students perceive their skills as poorer than those of their peers but, fearing ridicule, hide their ignorance (Mellon, 1986). Mellon concluded that many first-year college students are so anxious about their first research projects that they are unable to complete them successfully. More recent research has corroborated the importance of Mellon's claim that library anxiety significantly reduces students' ability to use the library and its resources successfully (Jiao, Onwuegbuzie, & Lichtenstein, 1996; Westbrook & DeDecker, 1993).

The development of in- and out-of-class activities that focus on feelings about the library can successfully alleviate the anxieties that many first-year students harbor about academic libraries and the research process. Information literacy instruction typically emphasizes cognitive skills, as they are concretely linked to conducting an effective search or retrieving appropriate resources. Less obvious, but just as important, are students' attitudes while they are attempting to perform a specific task. Several research studies have shown that students who are not confident library users are often less successful in finding the information needed to complete an assignment (Mellon, 1986; Nahl, 1996). As a precursor to traditional library skills instruction, cocurricular activities can provide the context students need to eradicate their anxieties and become proactive, confident library users throughout their academic careers.

The Role of Cocurricular Activities in the Library

Academic librarians have developed many outstanding information literacy programs that help students become empowered information users in their daily lives, overall academic pursuits, and chosen disciplines. Orientations, term paper clinics, tours, course-related and integrated instruction, and credit courses have all been successfully used as means to reach students. In general, librarians have concentrated many of their efforts primarily on integrating library instruction, in whatever form it may take, into the curriculum. Recently, this has included integrating the library into first-year seminars and other first-year experience programs, many of which are described throughout this monograph.

Working through the curriculum is an excellent method for helping students master information-seeking strategies and achieve information literacy competency standards. However, this method is not the only one that we should consider. For example, Terenzini and Pascarella (1994) remind us that "as much as 85 percent of a student's waking hours are spent outside the classroom. Common sense should tell us that educational programs and activities that address only 15 percent of students' time are needlessly myopic" (p. 31). This balance of time alone suggests that carefully developed cocurricular programs might have a valuable place in a library's outreach efforts. Libraries are in a unique position to reach students at both the curricular and cocurricular level and can help bridge the gap between in- and out-of-class experiences.

Examples of Model Cocurricular Programs and Survey Findings

The authors designed and conducted a national survey to assess college and university libraries' involvement in providing cocurricular programs to first-year students. In conducting this survey, the authors hoped to gain a national overview of the types of cocurricular activities currently being offered by academic libraries, the perceived benefits of such activities, and the internal barriers that possibly prevent development of cocurricular library-related activities. The authors designed the survey to complement a study conducted by Boff and Johnson (2002), which examined the level and type of traditional library instruction within first-year seminars. The authors' survey is the first of its kind to examine the level and scope of cocurricular programming that libraries are developing for first-year students.

Methodology

The authors designed a 17-question, web-based survey. The first section of the survey contained questions about library orientation, a common library-related cocurricular activity. The second section of the survey included questions about additional forms of library-related cocurricular activities. Finally, the authors asked respondents to provide descriptive information about their existing programs, including project web sites, program assessment, longevity, and contact information. The examples in this chapter are drawn from this descriptive information, as well as from examples found in the literature. (See Appendix for survey instrument.)

The survey was publicized in various library instruction listservs, including ILI-L (Information Literacy Instruction listserv), LIRT-L (Library Instruction Round Table listserv), and the discussion list for the Association of College and Research Libraries (ACRL) Immersion Institute Alumni. We also contacted librarians in leadership roles within ACRL, encouraging them to ask the appropriate librarian(s) at their institutions to complete the survey.

Survey Respondents

Of 155 people who responded to the survey, 56.2% represented four-year universities with graduate study; 32.4% represented four-year colleges; 7.6% represented community colleges, and 3.8% represented other types of post-secondary institutions.

Survey Findings

Library orientation. Traditionally, library orientation has centered on acquainting new students with the library's physical layout, resources, and services. One of the most common functions of library orientation is to increase students' comfort in navigating and using the library (Marcus & Beck, 2003). Indeed, Marcus and Beck's extensive study of the structure of library orientation tours found that students who participated in a self-guided library orientation had a marked increase in positive feelings about the library and library staff.

For the purposes of this survey, the authors defined library orientation as activities for first-year students that introduce them to the libraries' resources and services. An overwhelming majority of the survey respondents (83.9%) indicated that their school provided some type of library orientation activity for first-year students. At these institutions, the orientation took a number of different forms with some campuses reporting more than one type of orientation program. These included hands-on (computer-based) library instruction (68%); formally guided tours (44.1%); formal, lecture-based library instruction (44.1%); an "information fair" or "open house" where students explore and learn about the library informally (37.3%); and self-guided tours (23.5%). One third of respondents identified some other type of library orientation including online library-focused tutorials, scavenger hunts, or "murder mystery" programs.

Cocurricular activities. Survey respondents were asked to describe additional types of cocurricular activities (other than orientation programs) currently offered by their libraries. Examples of other library-related cocurricular activities designed for first-year students include, but are not limited to, campus reading programs, residence hall-based outreach, peer mentoring, and more.

More than 44% of respondents indicated that their library provided cocurricular activities beyond orientation for first-year students. The survey asked respondents to identify important reasons to provide library-related cocurricular activities. Increasing students' comfort with asking for help in the library (90.5%) was the most frequently cited reason. They also identified enriching students' knowledge of what the library can provide (87.6%) and helping students develop positive emotional feelings about the library, its resources, and services (76.2%) as important reasons to offer these activities. Finally, 73.3% of respondents believed that such activities were important because they enabled students to develop positive attitudes about the use of libraries for lifelong learning. Only 1% of survey respondents found cocurricular activities unnecessary.

Comments from respondents on the value of providing cocurricular library-related activities varied and, in general, reflected a desire to offer such programs:

> Cocurricular activities could give faculty a better understanding of the need for information literacy throughout the curriculum.

> It is hoped that reaching students via cocurricular activities will help them see the connection between research and learning beyond their text books and provide them with a richer university experience.

However, several respondents worried that adding on new cocurricular activities might negatively impact existing library instruction initiatives:

> Our only concern is that some faculty will feel students are now getting all the library instruction they need in the orientation class and will stop sending their students for more specialized, subject-based instruction.

Of those libraries not currently providing cocurricular programs (including any type of library orientation program) for first-year students, 19% had future plans to add such programs, while 17.2% did not. Where cocurricular activities were not offered, respondents were asked to relate why their libraries chose not to do so. Table 1 summarizes these responses.

Table 1

Reasons Libraries Did Not Offer Cocurricular Activities (n = 87)

Reason	n	Percentage
Question does not apply to my library	28	32.2
Lack of library faculty/staff time to provide programs	15	17.2
Lack of institutional (outside the library) interest	15	17.2
Other	10	11.5
Lack of student interest	7	8.0
Lack of funding	6	6.9
Lack of library faculty/staff interest	6	6.9

Developing Library-Related Cocurricular Activities: Model Programs

The survey data indicate that cocurricular and orientation programs continue to be essential elements in many libraries' programs and that they are becoming more varied and interesting than the traditional formats for library orientation, with new and exciting programs being implemented to create an information-literate student body. To complete the picture, and to reveal a more in-depth view of what these programs are like, survey respondents were encouraged to send additional information on their own programs. This information, combined with program ideas gleaned from the literature, provides a portrait of the types of cocurricular programs being offered by librarians around the country to acquaint students with specific aspects of library services, spaces, collections, staff, and/or other areas as defined by the needs of the individual institution. The strategies profiled here include library orientation, common reading programs, residence life initiatives, and peer mentoring.

Library Orientation

As noted earlier, most library orientation programs focus primarily on increasing students' comfort level in navigating the library, while communicating basic library skills information to them. Descriptions of three programs that embody this philosophy follow.

CSI Meets the Library: A Murder Mystery Orientation. Since 2003, the University of Wisconsin Oshkosh has hosted a murder mystery for first-year students. The students' mission is to solve a crime, following strategic clues placed throughout the library. As students track the clues, they also learn about the library, including the location of specific types of materials, how to find a particular call number or material on course reserve, and where to ask for help. Numerous library staff members (posing as murder suspects) are available throughout the library to offer assistance (University of Wisconsin Oshkosh, 2004). A 'Murder Mystery' orientation removes the barrier between library faculty, staff, and first-year students. Immersed in solving the mystery, students' anxieties about the library itself are relieved.

The Open House: A Self-Guided Library Orientation. Since fall 2001, the University Libraries at Penn State's University Park campus have hosted a two-day open house that annually attracts more than 4,000 students. Library faculty and staff created this library orientation as a fun, welcoming event where students could interact with librarians and staff in a non-threatening atmosphere designed to ease library anxiety. Each open house has a party-like theme (e.g., luau, winter carnival), and library faculty and staff dress in costume and design games and other activities for students to enjoy. Students decide which areas of the library they would like to visit (to complete the event, students must visit at least eight separate areas) and, along the way, receive many prizes and giveaways, meet librarians, play games, and hopefully walk away from the event feeling like the library is a friendly, navigable place (Cahoy & Bichel, 2003). At the conclusion of the event, students complete a survey asking what they thought of and gained from the event. In one survey respondent's words, "This was very stimulating and rewarding for a student who is not accustomed to a large facility such as this. Because I took part in this activity, I feel more confident in coming to the library."

LibraryFest. Millersville University (PA) presents another variation on this style of orientation in their library each fall. Approximately 500 students attended the 2004 LibraryFest. Participating students take a self-guided tour of the library's main areas, enjoying snacks, free giveaways, and music. Students who visited all of the featured stations received a special library mug and were entered into a drawing for additional prizes. LibraryFest organizers noted that some students expressed such enthusiasm about the event that they brought friends back with them to take the tour again later in the day (M. Parrish & M. Warmkessel, personal communication, July 11, 2005). In many ways, the "open house" orientation event conforms to Mellon's (1986) vision of a "warmth seminar" in which "the primary goal is to help students see the library as a great place with fascinating information and welcoming, friendly people available to help them" (p. 164).

Common Reading Programs

Over the course of the last decade, campus-wide common reading programs, in which the entire first-year class reads and discusses a specific book, have become more prevalent. Indeed, 26.9% of survey respondents noted that their library participates in this type of program. Other respondents indicated that plans were underway on their campus to develop such a program with library participation. Common reading programs enable discussions between students and faculty about issues impacting society today. Traditionally, the books selected as common readings are thought-provoking works designed to encourage dialogue and critical thinking. The importance of providing such programming is illustrated by a finding from the 2004 National Survey of Student Engagement (NSSE) that nearly 40% of first-year students never discussed concepts or ideas from classes or readings with a faculty member outside of class (Indiana University Center for Postsecondary Research, 2004).

Many libraries support institutional efforts to promote the importance of reading and appreciating literature in the first year. The University of Montana's First-Year Reading Experience selects a specific book each year that all new students read (University of Montana, 2005). The library promotes the initiative by hosting a web site with information about the program, including a related reserve readings list. Similarly, Plymouth State University's Lamson Library participates in the first-year common reading program by featuring an exhibit of relevant books from the library's collection and creating a web page designed as a central source for program information (Plymouth State University, 2005). Librarians also can participate in common reading programs by creating research guides and hosting workshops for faculty facilitating the common reading program or book discussions for the entire campus community. Hosting speaker events in the library on topics relevant to the common book is another way to participate in a campus-wide reading initiative.

Libraries can benefit from participating in common reading programs by reinforcing the library's role in literacy on campus and encouraging students to view the library as a source for leisure reading, not just a repository for research materials. Common reading programs provide opportunities for librarians to become actively involved in electronic or in-person book discussion groups, to participate in cross-campus book selection teams, and to encourage a love of literature and reading in students, faculty, and staff.

Residence Hall Outreach

Residence hall outreach efforts center on the idea of taking the library to the students—where they live. This form of outreach includes special library collections and reference areas, and library instruction sessions in the residence halls. Fully 25% of survey respondents indicated that their library provides programs or services in residence halls.

Through the Michigan learning communities, the University of Michigan has extended its services for first-year students far beyond the physical library, offering research sessions in residence halls and providing individual satellite libraries for each learning community's living quarters. A housing librarian provides direction for residence hall initiatives and oversees student workers trained in providing research and technology support to on-campus residents (University of Michigan, 2005).

The University of Illinois Urbana Champaign (UIUC) manages eight residence hall libraries tied to subject and/or discipline-specific learning communities within the university's first-year experience program. While the school's Housing Division administers and operates the libraries and they are not formally tied to the UIUC libraries, collaborative programs are in place to link the libraries with the Residence Hall Library System (RHLS). Collections in the RHLS are geared toward the focus of each learning community and also include recreational reading and listening choices. Library instruction sessions are provided in the residence halls, with a focus on presenting personalized sessions tailored to the needs of the learning community residents (University of Illinois Urbana Champaign, 2005).

In the Duke University Libraries, an initiative called "Librarian in the House" brings librarians, equipped with laptops, printers, and research guides to the first-year residence halls and to a popular campus cafeteria. There, librarians provide reference and research assistance in an environment that is convenient and comfortable to students (Dougan, Holloway, Lawton, & Werrell, 2005).

Residence hall libraries can function as a confidence-building service for first-year students. Catering to undergraduates, residence hall libraries present a smaller, more navigable environment for students. Encouraged by positive experiences in their residence hall library, students may be more receptive to focused exploration of the traditional library collections and services available on campus.

Peer Mentoring

Some libraries provide instruction not only for first-year students but also for upper-level students serving as peer advisors to first-year students. Of the survey respondents, 11.5% indicated that their library participates in peer-mentoring programs. At Penn State University (PSU), the Learning Edge Academic Program (LEAP) features mentors living in the residence halls with students in their pride (learning community) and helping them with their class work, organizing out-of-class activities, and providing one-on-one help with computing and library resources. The mentors attend a semester-long class in the spring, designed to prepare them for their mentoring role. Included is a session held in the PSU libraries. Led by instruction librarians, the session orients the mentors to the library resources most frequently used by LEAP students and encourages the mentors to consider and discuss the feelings and challenges that they themselves once faced regarding library research during their first year of college. Each pride also includes a designated LEAP librarian, related to the discipline of the pride. Later in the summer, after the LEAP librarians have worked with their prides, the mentors help facilitate the connections between students and the pride librarians (Penn State University, 2005).

Washington State University devised a similar program, teaching first-year seminar peer facilitators about the library and research skills through an eight-week credit course, GenEd 300, Accessing Information for Research. Lindsay (2003) describes the focus and scope of the course:

> Not only do they (peer facilitators) need to learn how to do research in educational resources for their training as facilitators, but they also need to learn how to conduct research for the popular topics that (first-year seminar) students often select. In addition, they need to know how to help their future students with research problems. (p. 26)

Lindsay concludes, "The librarians' involvement with training upcoming peer facilitators has added to the importance and value of the libraries' involvement with the educational process" (p. 27).

Powerful Learning Environments:
Integrating Curricular and Cocurricular Activities

The most influential learning environments are those that "integrate the curricular and the cocurricular activities in meaningful ways" (Winston, 2003, p. 18). Kuh et al. (2003) conclude, "The positive effects of out-of-class experiences on desired learning and personal development outcomes could be enhanced through partnerships between academic and student affairs that induce students to engage more frequently in educationally purposeful activities" (p. 13). However, Terenzini et al. (1999) also call attention to the fact that classroom faculty and academic affairs personnel are traditionally more concerned with students' academic and cognitive development while student affairs personnel are more concerned with the affective, emotional domain. This division of labor may conflict with the more holistic approach called for by research, which reveals the interconnected impact of both in-class and out-of-class activities on student learning and development. Librarians can (and many do) work actively to establish curricular partnerships among the various groups and integrate information literacy into the curriculum. While continuing these efforts, librarians can simultaneously develop and provide related and relevant cocurricular learning opportunities that engage students and create enhanced learning environments. This combination allows librarians to create a dynamic learning atmosphere that helps students develop both cognitively and emotionally. Specifically, librarians may seek to enhance student learning by designing out-of-class experiences that encompass a wide variety of interactions, including those:

- Between students and library faculty and staff members
- Between student peers on library and information-seeking related issues and topics
- Involving students actively in non-threatening, library-based activities

Conclusion and Recommendations

Kuh and Gonyea (2003) emphasize the importance of the library to academic success, noting that the "students who make the greatest gains…attend institutions that communicate the importance of information literacy and engage in activities and practice the skills that lead to information literacy" (p. 268). The first step toward achieving this goal is to introduce the library as a positive, engaging place for a variety of learning activities, both curricular and cocurricular. Library-related activities can be ideally integrated with other activities for first-year students, such as campus-wide orientation events, learning communities, and other first-year centered initiatives. Separate from the curriculum, yet important in developing positive emotional outcomes, cocurricular activities provide a foundation upon which curricular learning activities can be launched. The programs and initiatives outlined in this chapter can serve as models for future program development. According to members of Duke University's Lilly Library East Campus Outreach Committee, cocurricular activities "challenge too narrowly defined perceptions of the library, and may increase the impact of traditional library services that are included in the academic curriculum or are available at the library itself" (Dougan et al., 2005, p. 5)

Bolstered by successful cocurricular experiences, especially near the beginning of their first year, students are better prepared to benefit from the formal library instruction they receive within academic courses, to use scholarly resources during their academic careers, and to use libraries throughout their lives for continued learning. Developing cocurricular activities that reinforce the library's place on campus—a place where students feel comfortable and want to be—can be an important step in establishing positive attitudes toward libraries and information literacy. It promotes and builds a readiness to learn about the resources and services the library offers in support of the curriculum.

References

Black, S. (2002, June). The well-rounded student. *American School Board Journal, 33-35.*

Boff, C., & Johnson, K. (2002). The library and first-year experience courses: A nationwide study. *Reference Services Review, 30*(4), 277-287.

Cahoy, E. S., & Bichel, R. M. (2003). A luau in the library?: A new model of library orientation. *College & Undergraduate Libraries, 11*(1), 49-60.

Dougan, K., Holloway, C., Lawton, K., & Werrell, E. (2005). Creating community: Duke's East Campus libraries reach out to first-year students. *Duke University Libraries, 18*(2/3), 2-5.

Dunkel, N., Bray, K., & Wofford, A. (1989). *Training and raising awareness in career knowledge.* Gainesville: University of Florida, Division of Housing.

Gellin, A. (2003). The effect of undergraduate student involvement on critical thinking: A meta-analysis of the literature 1991-2000. *Journal of College Student Development, 44*(6), 746-762.

House, J. D. (2000). The effect of student involvement on the development of academic self-concept. *Journal of Social Psychology, 140*(2), 261-264.

Huang, Y.-R., & Chang, S.-M. (2004). Academic and cocurricular involvement: Their relationship and the best combinations for student growth. *Journal of College Student Development, 45*(4), 391-406.

Indiana University Center for Postsecondary Research. (2004). *National Survey of Student Engagement—2004 overview.* Retrieved March 18, 2006, from http://nsse.iub.edu/2004_annual_report/pdf/annual_report.pdf

Jiao, Q. G., Onwuegbuzie, A., & Lichtenstein, A. (1996). Library anxiety: Characteristics of "at-risk" college students. *Library & Information Science Research 18*(2), 151-163.

Kuh, G. D., & Gonyea, R. M. (2003). The role of the academic library in promoting student engagement in learning. *College & Research Libraries, 64*(4), 256-282.

Kuh, G. D., Palmer, M., & Kish, K. (2003). The value of educationally purposeful out-of-class experiences. In T. L. Skipper & R. Argo (Eds.), *Involvement in campus activities and the retention of first-year college students* (Monograph No. 36, pp. 1-18). Columbia, SC: University of South Carolina, National Resource Center for The First-Year Experience & Students in Transition.

Lindsay, E. B. (2003). A collaborative approach to information literacy in the freshman seminar. *Academic Exchange Quarterly, 7*(3), 23-27.

MacKinnon-Slaney, F. (1993). Theory to practice in cocurricular activities: A new model for student involvement. *College Student Affairs Journal, 12*(2), 35-40.

Marcus, S., & Beck, S. (2003, January). A library adventure: Comparing a treasure hunt with a traditional freshman orientation tour. *College & Research Libraries, 64*(1), 23-34.

Mellon, C. (1986). Library anxiety: A grounded theory and its development. *College & Research Libraries, 47*(2), 160-165.

Nahl, D. (1996, October). Affective monitoring of Internet learners: Perceived self-efficacy and success. *Proceedings of the 59th Annual Meeting of the American Society for Information Science, Baltimore, Maryland* (pp. 100-109). Medford, NJ: Information Today.

Penn State University. (2005). *LEAP (Learning Edge Academic Program).* Retrieved April 5, 2005, from http://www.psu.edu/summersession/LEAP/

Plymouth State University. (2005). *First Year Common Reading Program.* Retrieved April 5, 2005, from http://www.plymouth.edu/library/?home/firstyear/

Pritchard, M. E., & Wilson, G. S. (2003). Using emotional and social factors to predict student success. *Journal of College Student Development, 44*(1), 18-28.

Rubin, R. S., Bommer, W. H., & Baldwin, T. T. (2002). Using extracurricular activity as an indicator of interpersonal skill: Prudent evaluation of recruiting malpractice? *Human Resource Management, 41*(4), 441-454.

Shieh, H. P., Gong, Y. W., & Huang, S. Z. (1992). An investigation on the current status of cocurricular involvement among college students. [Translated from Chinese] *Research in Moral Education, 319*(3), 39-56.

Terenzini, P. T., & Pascarella, E. T. (1994, January/February). Living with myths: Undergraduate education in America. *Change,* 28-32.

Terenzini, P. T., Pascarella, E. T., & Blimling, G. S. (1999). Students' out-of-class experiences and their influence on learning and cognitive development: A literature review. *Journal of College Student Development, 40*(5), 610-623.

University of Illinois Urbana Champaign. (2005). *University Housing Residence Hall Libraries.* Retrieved April 5, 2005, from http://www.housing.uiuc.edu/living/library/index.htm

University of Michigan. (2005). *Michigan learning communities.* Retrieved April 5, 2005, from http://www.lsa.umich.edu/mlc/overview.asp

University of Montana. (2005). *First-year reading experience.* Retrieved April 5, 2005, from http://www.lib.umt.edu/firstyear/readingexperience.htm

University of Wisconsin Oshkosh. (2004). *Murder in the stacks: A Shakespearean murder mystery.* Retrieved July 13, 2005, from http://www.uwosh.edu/library/news/2004/sept04.html#mystery

Westbrook, L., & DeDecker, S. (1993). Supporting user needs and skills to minimize library anxiety: Considerations for academic libraries. *The Reference Librarian, 40,* 43-51.

Winston, R. B., Jr. (2003). Stimulating and supporting student learning. In G. L. Kramer & Associates (Ed.), *Student academic services: An integrated approach* (pp. 3-26). San Francisco: Jossey-Bass.

Appendix

**Library-Related Cocurricular Activities for
First-Year Students**
Survey Instrument

Survey Introduction

Cocurricular activities enrich and extend students' academic experiences. Examples of library-related cocurricular activities designed for first-year students include but are not limited to: orientation programs, campus reading programs, residence hall-based outreach, and more.

This survey is being conducted as part of a planned chapter on cocurricular library-related activities in the monograph, *The Role of the Library in the First College Year.* The chapter authors seek to find out the scope and frequency with which libraries are currently providing cocurricular programs and initiatives for first-year students. If you serve students at the first year of college level, we are interested in your experiences and feedback, whether or not you have provided cocurricular programming to date. If you have any questions regarding this survey, please contact the authors, Ellysa Stern Cahoy (esc10@psu.edu) or Loanne Snavely (lls11@psu.edu).

1. Does your library currently provide a library orientation program(s) for first-year students?
   ____ Yes
   ____ No

Library Orientation Questions

If your library provides library orientation program(s), please answer the following questions below. Otherwise, please scroll to the bottom of the page, and click on the "Next" link to skip to the next set of questions.

2. Identify below the basic structure of your library orientation program(s) for first-year students (Please check all that apply.)
   ____ A formally guided tour
   ____ A self-guided tour
   ____ Formal, lecture-based library instruction
   ____ Hands-on (computer-based) library instruction
   ____ An "information fair" or "open house" where students can informally explore and learn about the library
   ____ Other (please specify)

3. Please briefly describe your orientation program(s) for first-year students, including the longevity of your program(s).

4. Please tell us about the setting for your library orientation program(s) for first-year students. (Please check all that apply.)
   ____ Program is held as part of a larger, institution-wide orientation program for new and first-year students
   ____ Program is held as a fully separate orientation offering for first-year students
   ____ Program is held in the library
   ____ Program is held outside of the library
   ____ Other (please specify)

5. Approximately what percent of your institution's first-year students do you reach via your library orientation program(s) each academic year?

    ____   0 - 25%

    ____   25 - 50%

    ____   50 - 75%

    ____   75 - 100%

6. Please identify the goals of your library orientation program(s). (Select all that apply.)

    ____   Introduce students to the library, its resources, and services.

    ____   Introduce students to librarians and library staff.

    ____   Help students learn how to navigate the library's physical layout.

    ____   Help students learn how to use the library's print resources.

    ____   Help students learn how to use the library's electronic resources.

    ____   Reduce students' anxiety about using the library and its resources.

    ____   Communicate to students that librarians and library staff are friendly and happy to help them.

    ____   Help students feel more comfortable asking for help with using library resources and services.

    ____   Other (please specify)

Additional Cocurricular Library Programs for First-Year Students

7. Does your library currently provide or maintain involvement in any other cocurricular programs (other than library orientation programs) for first-year students?

    ____   Yes

    ____   No

8. If you answered "yes" to the question above, please tell us about your library's other cocurricular programs for first-year students. Does your library provide or maintain involvement in: (Choose all that apply.)

    ____   A campus-wide reading program for first-year students

    ____   Residence hall-based outreach for first-year students

    ____   Service-learning projects for first-year students

    ____   Participation in first-year student learning communities

    ____   Peer-tutoring programs for first-year students

    ____   Other (please describe)

Additional Questions

Please answer the following questions regarding the entire scope of your library's cocurricular programs for first-year students (including orientation programs).

9. If your library does not currently provide a library orientation program or other cocurricular activities for first-year students, please explain why. (Choose all that apply.)

    ____   Lack of funding

    ____   Lack of library faculty/staff time to provide programs

    ____   Lack of library faculty/staff interest

    ____   Lack of student interest

    ____   Lack of institutional (outside the library) interest

    ____   This question does not apply to my library.

    ____   Other (please specify)

10. If your library does not currently provide a library orientation program or other co-curricular activities, does your library have any future plans for providing such programs for first-year students?

    ____ Yes

    ____ No

    ____ This question does not apply to my library.

Additional comments:

11. What do you feel are the most important reasons to provide library-related cocurricular activities (including library orientation programs) for first-year students? (Choose all that apply.)

    ____ Cocurricular activities help students develop positive emotional feelings about the library, its resources, and services.

    ____ Cocurricular activities help students feel more comfortable asking for help in the library.

    ____ Cocurricular activities enrich students' knowledge of what the library can provide.

    ____ Cocurricular activities prime students to make the most out of the formal library instruction that they receive.

    ____ Cocurricular activities enable students to develop positive attitudes about the use of libraries for lifelong learning.

    ____ I do not feel that cocurricular library-related activities are necessary.

    ____ Other (please specify)

Special Student Groups

12. In addition to the cocurricular programming addressed in the above questions, does your library do special programming for the following first-year student groups?

    ____ Programs for first-year returning adult students?

    ____ Programs for first-year international students?

    ____ Programs for first-year / first-generation (first in the family to attend college) students?

    ____ Programs for first-year at-risk students?

    ____ Programs for first-year students with remedial needs for college-level work?

    ____ Other (please specify)

13. If you serve any of the groups listed in the question above, please briefly describe your program(s) below.

Final Questions

14. Please identify your educational institution type:

    ____ Community college

    ____ Four-year college

    ____ University (bachelor's and graduate study)

    ____ Other (please specify)

15. Please identify the size of your institution's student population:
    ___   0 - 2000 students
    ___   2000 - 4000 students
    ___   4000 - 10,000 students
    ___   10,000 - 20,000 students
    ___   Over 20,000 students

16. Do you have any additional information on your library's cocurricular activities to share with the authors? Please include assessment results, impact, program web site(s), etc.

17. If you have provided information above on your library's cocurricular programs for first-year students, please consider providing your name and e-mail address so that the authors can contact you for additional information, if necessary.

Thank you for your participation in this survey! We appreciate your feedback! If you have questions about this survey, please do not hesitate to contact Loanne Snavely or Ellysa Cahoy, Penn State University Libraries.

SECTION 3

Chapter 10

Assessing Library Instruction in the First College Year

Robert Fitzpatrick & Randy L. Swing

Academic libraries directly contribute to an institution's overall plan for first-year students in myriad ways, whether through direct contact and services with students or through electronic connections. For some first-year students, libraries provide a quiet place to study or a gathering spot for group study. For many others, they are the front line for personalized research assistance. However, there should be no question that librarians play a central role in building student skills in information literacy. The first-year library instruction program establishes a foundation for student success. Because of its critical importance, libraries must take the assessment effort seriously. Briefly, this chapter endorses the core assumption that assessment will lead to the improvement of library instruction and to the confirmation of existing practice.

Assessment is an engaging process built on the intellectual curiosity of librarians and their commitment both to building future generations of information-literate citizens and to establishing an appropriate alignment of the library and institutional missions. While well-planned and executed assessments produce data suggesting improvement or confirmation of existing practices, poor assessments simply fill bookshelves with unread reports and undigested data—a waste of time for all involved. This chapter suggests ways to achieve the former and avoid the latter.

High-quality assessment distinctively grounds its conclusions in evidence that goes beyond intuitively knowing that something is or is not working. In many ways, assessment skills are simply a natural extension of the skills of professional librarians who find, critically evaluate, and cite sources of evidence. Certainly, librarians would not let their students proclaim that they "just know" some fact. Likewise, they themselves should not be overly confident in their own opinions: "I know what students need to know. I don't have time to assess what I'm doing." Good practice requires the evaluation of success based on more than instinct or gut feelings; it requires real evidence that students are learning.

A carefully designed library-instruction assessment program is not just useful; it is essential. Making use of assessment results can enhance enthusiasm, instill justifiable pride in the program's accomplishments, confirm successful existing practices, and guide management's budget and personnel decisions toward continued support. Even in a supportive institution, there is value in highlighting the library's contribution to the first-year experience; in aligning with the institution's mission; and in demonstrating the library staff's willingness to gather and use feedback. Indeed, gathering purposeful data regarding instructional services to new students encourages fine-tuning and improvement, thereby adding value to the overall educational experience. The use of assessment has the potential to improve a library's efforts and imbue it with vitality and legitimacy.

This chapter stresses the inextricable link between good assessment and the institution's educational mission. Being able to articulate a direct connection among institutional and departmental missions and the specific mission and goals of the library-instruction program is an educational and, often, a financial imperative. The perennial battles and increased competition for resources, due to stagnant or reduced general funding, only add to the importance of the effort. If asked today, what could the typical librarian provide as either quantitative or qualitative evidence of a library-instruction program's furtherance of the institution's mission? Could the typical librarian explain how its efforts successfully contribute to the institution's strategic plan? Increasingly, the payoff for a good library-instruction assessment program justifies the effort. For those desiring a more detailed discussion of this particular issue, Nelson and Fernekes' (2002) *Standards and Assessment for Academic Libraries: A Workbook* offers an excellent justification for a mission-driven approach to assessment.

What Assessment Is Not

Traditionally, library assessment has relied too heavily on counting. In the case of library instruction, counting the number of classes taught each semester serves to make us think more is better—as if we were justifying our roles by working harder. Libraries seem to count everything and then compare these data to other libraries as if they illustrate something about learning outcomes. Mere numbers, whatever their real usefulness, tell us little about the quality of instruction, the quality of learning, the progress toward the institution's mission, or why the numbers are what they are. At worst, "bad" numbers lead to laments over why the numbers are a disappointment. At best, "good" numbers lead to self-congratulatory and quite possibly misguided optimism. In either case, counting seldom answers the "why" questions, so the numbers leave us not knowing what to change when we do not like them or what not to change when we do. If assessment has a single guiding principle, it is this: If you do not or cannot make use of the data you collect, there is probably very little reason to collect them.

What Assessment Is

Types of Assessment Data

Two types of assessment data provide meaningful information: quantitative and qualitative. In general, quantitative data, usually in the form of numbers, establish statistical relationships among variables. Qualitative data, usually in the form of words and visual representations, identify themes and non-statistically derived relationships among variables. Both are meaningful tools. For example, a quantitative tool is the right choice for comparing pretest scores to posttest scores on a test of library knowledge or on a survey of student satisfaction with library instruction. On the other hand, the qualitative input of a focus group is often the best choice to examine why students sometimes prefer an online-learning experience to a classroom experience.

Sometimes, both types of assessment data are useful for the same assessment procedure and, when used together, they form a richer and more complete picture of reality. For example, both qualitative and quantitative data used in combination might help document that test scores (quantitative data) are better as a result of an online approach to library instruction even though student comments (qualitative data) suggest that they prefer an in-class experience.

Assessment Structures

Most often, librarians use some combination of the three assessment structures: (a) criterion-referenced, (b) value-added, and (c) benchmarking. What follows is a brief primer on assessment. Mastering these techniques will make planning future assessments easier.

Criterion-referenced assessment. A criterion-referenced structure measures performance against an established baseline or norm. For example, a test of library skills might have an established or expected "passing" score set at 85 out of a possible score of 100. Institutions most frequently use criterion-referenced assessments to differentiate students who are ready for regular college work from those who are not likely to be successful without special assistance. The best use of criterion-referenced assessments is in evaluating the skills of individual students as part of a needs analysis—perhaps as way to funnel the most high-risk students into special library instruction programs. Nevertheless, even as individual assessments, criterion assessments have limited use. They cannot explain *why* students did not perform as well as hoped. This form of assessment might be very important in an overall plan for library instruction, but it has limited use in program-level assessment intended to improve the library-instruction program.

Value-added assessment structures. Value-added assessment, based on the work of Astin (1991), is the most frequently used form of assessment, but it is also the most labor intensive. The use of *input, environment,* and *outcome* data form the I-E-O model. Simply stated, in the I-E-O model, some outcomes are directly caused by inputs (e.g., characteristics, knowledge, or experience students bring with them to college). Some outcomes are directly caused by environments and experiences colleges provide to students. In addition, some outcomes are caused by the interaction of input and environment elements, a process also known as conditional effect.

Value-added assessment is often the best approach for library instruction, because it can give the clearest evidence for how to improve a teaching program. For example, to evaluate the success of instruction in the concepts of Boolean logic, the first step and the last step might involve testing student knowledge. A pretest would establish what students know before the intervention (instruction) is delivered, and a posttest would tell us what students know after the intervention. The middle element of this process requires documenting what happened between the pretest and posttest. If the period between the pretest and posttest was short, then the intervention would likely account for any change in outcome knowledge, since that was the main student experience between the two test points. When the intervention is more than a brief event, such as instruction spread over several days, weeks, or an entire academic term, then the "E" data must account for other elements that could have an impact on the outcome. For example, a student taking a computer logic class could encounter instruction in Boolean logic that would also explain an increase in the outcome measure related to library instruction. Likewise, the effort students give to the subject likely shapes the impact of long interventions. Therefore, assessment may require measurement of student effort or participation to understand fully any change in the outcome. The following questions are examples of environment/experience measurements.

1. In how many courses—other than this library instruction class—have you been taught Boolean logic this term?
2. How many sessions of library instruction did you attend this term?
3. How would you rate your overall effort in the library instruction class?

Initial data analysis in an I-E-O model consists of comparing input data to outcome data in order to determine if a change occurred.

The I-E-O model can also be easily adapted to compare various intervention strategies. For example, one class might cover a particular library skill on its own via purely online instruction (method A). A second class receives instruction about the same skill through a traditional in-class presentation (method B), and a third class simply reads a handout on Boolean logic and completes a worksheet (method C). This example employs three different environments of learning. A comparison of the posttest scores of the three classes will reveal any difference in the effectiveness of these methods.

To be fair, to measure all possible elements of input (I), environment (E), and outcome (O) is nearly impossible. Therefore, developing the perfect value-added assessment plan is unlikely. Evaluators should acknowledge limitations in methods, but they should not use the lack of a perfect plan as a reason to delay any assessment efforts.

If the primary reason for assessment is to produce institutional change, then assessment reports should include recommendations for using the results. Examining the outcomes of the three different teaching methods would provide hard evidence to make decisions about the most appropriate choices for future instruction. If all three methods produced the same post-test score, the library might appropriately opt to save class time and assign the task of learning Boolean logic using the online or worksheet approach. If the in-class method produced the greatest learning, then professional judgment determines if the additional cost of that effort justifies the amount of increased learning it created. Experimenting with the environments provides evidence to make a decision with confidence.

Benchmarking. A third assessment structure, benchmarking, is a variation of the value-added model. The easiest way to understand benchmarking is to consider the following two examples. In the first example, students from several institutions with very different kinds of students and different approaches to library instruction complete a standardized test of library skills. However, comparisons of outcomes across institutions are extremely difficult to interpret and provide little useful information. In the second example, several institutions that recruit similar students agree to compare aggregate scores on the standardized test. Because of the careful selection of peers (meaning institutions that have similar inputs), any difference in outcomes (scores) is likely the result of variations in the teaching method. Benchmarking, while not offering as precise an assessment as those produced with the value-added model, still provides evidence about the relative quality and effectiveness of campus efforts. Benchmarking affords the advantage of evaluating efforts without conducting a pretest, thereby reducing the time students engage in testing (rather than learning). Additionally, it can be quite motivational to discover that another institution with similar students is capable of producing better outcomes.

It is also possible for a single campus to conduct benchmarking. One campus might, on its own, establish internal peer groups and compare the aggregate outcome scores among them. For example, if students in various sections of first-year seminars were similar in terms of library knowledge when they enrolled, then it would be possible to benchmark the outcomes across sections. Identifying the high-performing section would allow the researcher to conduct further investigations to establish the best practices used by that section but not used in lower-performing sections. Similarly, studying low-performing sections could provide information about what did not work.

Criterion-referenced, value-added, and benchmarking assessments comprise the most common assessment structures. Value-added assessment, with its input, environment, and outcomes data, is probably the best assessment choice whenever possible, because it provides the greatest amount of usable information. The goal of assessment is to improve the program. When the "pay off" is increased student learning and/or improved efficiency, assessment is an investment in the future well worth the effort.

Eight Qualities of Effective Assessment

Just as it is unlikely to have a good instruction program without careful attention to the qualities of a good learning experience, it is also unlikely that a library will design a good assessment plan without paying attention to the qualities of effective assessment. Before shifting from the discussion of assessment to a discussion of designing a specific assessment plan, identifying these qualities is useful. This section examines eight qualities of effective assessment (Swing, 2004).

If a library identifies making its web site easier to use as a major goal for the coming semester, how should it go about collecting the information needed to improve the site?

1. Focus on what matters most. There are always numerous interesting questions, but assessment is not simply an intellectual exercise. High-quality assessment springs from an organization's well-defined goals, objectives, and mission. Clarity about desired outcomes is the first step in successful assessment. A good assessment plan focuses on what matters most. In this example, ease of use of the library's web site is the most important goal.

2. Pay attention to the elements you can control. If a library budget cannot support buying access to more online periodical databases, there is little point in asking students if they would like more. However, if most students report they are having trouble finding the periodical databases, then that is something a library should address.

3. Help stakeholders understand the value of assessment. If students believe their input will result in change or will help them in some way, they are more likely to take the assessment process seriously and provide useful information. Assessment efforts that are properly timed, orchestrated, and explained to participants are more likely to produce trustworthy data and outcomes.

4. Measure the same experiences in a variety of ways. A simple survey may elicit information about how students interact with a web site, but convening a focus group might uncover valuable information that no one thought to ask on a survey. Assessment seldom meets the rigorous standards of controlled experimentation, but it can produce credible results when establishing information by corroborating studies using multiple measures and methods.

5. Include input from all stakeholders. In the case of the web site, classroom faculty might have some valuable input about how they see students using the library's resources that would have an important impact on decision making. By identifying off-campus students as a special target group, valuable information about how the site works from remote locations may emerge. Externally mandated and contrived assessment is less likely to produce meaningful change than assessment created by and for those directly involved in the assessed activity. It is tempting to be an "input snob" seeking input only from the most sophisticated users (e.g., the librarians or graduate students), but input from the most naive user cannot be ignored.

6. Place findings in an appropriate context. If the reference librarians wanted to know what students considered the best features of the web site and which services they used most frequently, a longitudinal study would be suitable. A longitudinal study would show whether certain features gained or lost popularity over time and would provide the librarians with the information needed to make appropriate changes. For example, a decline in popularity might suggest the need to increase efforts to alert students to the value of underused resources, or it might lead to the elimination of some resources altogether. Comparative benchmarks, longitudinal data, and/or professional judgments often provide necessary context for assessment findings.

7. Summarize the results of assessment initiatives in a format that will be most useful. Identifying the audience for an assessment summary is a key step in reporting data. If librarians only want to recommend changing the placement of some resources on the web site, there is little point in a wordy report discussing who, what, where, when, and why. The systems librarian would probably prefer a simple prioritized list of desired changes. Further, librarians should write assessment reports in language accessible to each target audience. Finally, they should write reports at the appropriate level of specificity for each target audience (e.g., executive summary, concise edition, or full report). A general rule of thumb is to disseminate aggregated data widely, but treat data that could identify a specific individual with the highest level of confidentiality.

8. Make use of the results. If an assessment did not deliver any useful, actionable results, it probably should not have been undertaken. Useful results, however, are worth sharing with the individuals who shape the desired outcome, and decision makers should cite the use of assessment data that inform program decisions.

The reader will find a more detailed account of these structures and qualities in Swing's (2004) *Proving and Improving, Volume II: Tools and Techniques for Assessing the First College Year.*

Getting Started

The four structures and the eight qualities of good assessment provide background for designing an assessment program with confidence. Too often, the excuse of not knowing where to begin delays or even prevents the creation of an assessment plan. Feeling overwhelmed and trying to take on too much at once are the most common deterrents. Keeping initial efforts simple and maintaining flexibility are both essential when taking the first steps. While, clearly, a library's specific mission and goals dictate different approaches, it is wise to keep in mind the points discussed so far when devising assessment tools:

- Select the most appropriate assessment structure for a particular need.
- Focus efforts on gathering only information that will be used.
- Review the technique to be sure it contains the eight qualities of good assessment.
- Start by assessing the most important issues—do not try to do it all at once.
- Commit to accepting and using the results to improve your program.

Assessment and the Library-Instruction Program

Libraries and the Internet are filled with valuable information regarding the design of library-instruction programs and assessment procedures. However, showing congruence between institutional behavior and the institution's mission are essential. Showing how an institution uses assessment results to support improvements that further the institution's mission are emerging as the sine qua non of assessment. Indeed, as Dugan and Hernon (2002) mention throughout their article, "Outcomes Assessment: Not Synonymous With Inputs and Outputs," accrediting bodies are increasingly demanding evidence for mission-driven assessment as part of the accreditation process. Accrediting bodies stress the importance of congruence among an institution's various missions, vision statements, and goals. They are no longer looking for evidence of assessment alone; they are looking for evidence that the use of assessment to improve performance is consistent with the institution's mission. The Appendix to this chapter offers a list of necessary and useful resources for initiating a dynamic assessment plan.

Putting It All Together

Information Literacy

As mentioned at the beginning of the chapter, a goal of many college libraries and entire undergraduate higher education curricula is the development of information literacy. Information literacy is an intellectual framework (ACRL, 2000) requiring students to "recognize when information is needed and have the ability to locate, evaluate, and use effectively the needed information" (ACRL, 1989). The American Library Association, through the Association of College and Research Libraries, differentiates information literacy from information technology skills and provides a set of standards, *Information Literacy Competency Standards for Higher Education,* comprised of five competencies (ACRL, 2000). See the Appendix to this monograph for the complete document.

The competency standards are excellent examples of outcomes assessment criteria that might serve to measure a library's contribution to the development of students' skills in information literacy. However, they present a challenge for assessment in the first college year, because they leave the instruction librarian with the task of associating them with specific student experiences or learning environments. The instruction librarian must clarify how far a student should progress in each of the standard's five competencies.

To incorporate these outcomes into a meaningful student assessment effort would require some knowledge about the level of skills students bring with them to campus at the start of their college experience. Likely, that would require some pretest rather than a student self-report, because students cannot be expected to rate their own skills accurately in an area where they do not know what constitutes a high level of achievement. In other words, entering college students could not know what they do not know about information literacy. Here, it is useful to note the distinction between evaluation, the mere gathering of information to determine "whether or not a system does what it is designed to do in an efficient and effective manner" (Dugan & Hernon, 2002, p. 378), and assessment, the measure of value-added outcomes with inferences drawn from the differences between pretests and posttests.

Assessing Congruence Among Missions

Demonstrating congruence among the three levels of institutional missions—the missions of the institution, the library, and the library-instruction program—is an important goal. Congruence among the missions is so crucial to an effective assessment plan that it requires some discussion of how they relate to each other before outlining a library-instruction assessment plan. At the most basic level, the library-instruction mission must have a direct and profound relation to the library mission. In turn, the library mission must demonstrate a direct and profound relation to the institutional mission. An assessment plan should provide ample proof that each mission is succeeding.

The institutional mission. A quick search through most institutional mission or vision statements will yield a plethora of phrases easily related to library goals. Indeed, failing to show a clear connection between the two indicates an alarming lack of understanding of the institution's aspirations. Culling apt phrases from the institutional mission statement is a good first step. Nelson and Fernekes (2002) and Breivik (1998) further describe essential elements of the process in detail. These highly recommended sources serve as the basis for much of the following.

The library mission. Fortunately, the role of the library is so integral to the mission of the institution that it is easy to extract wording from the institution's mission and echo it in the library mission. Indeed, it is prudent to show the library's vital contribution to the institutional goals. Reviewing the ACRL's (1987) "The Mission of a University Undergraduate Library: Model Statement" will facilitate writing a mission statement that reinforces the library's support of the institutional mission.

The library-instruction mission. Armed with information about the institutional mission, the library mission, and personal experience, a complementary library-instruction mission provides the final step toward preparation of the library-instruction assessment plan. Each institution's library-instruction mission statement takes into account the unique needs of its clientele in order to best prepare students for their educational goals. It takes into account its resources in order to design realistic goals and expectations. Furthermore, it considers its institutional mission in order to ensure that it operates in conjunction with the institution's aspirations. Because the library-instruction mission grows from the institution's mission, one can still easily draw parallels among the three levels of mission statements. A side-by-side comparison of the missions (Table 1) shows how the mission statements can work together and complement each other.

Table 1

Comparison of Institutional, Library, and Library-Instruction Missions

Phrases From the Institution's Mission Statement	The Library Mission Statement	Mission Statement and Goals of the Library-Instruction Program
• Meet the educational needs of our students, region, and state • Provide a learning environment supporting the development of mind, body, and spirit • Base our educational philosophy on concepts of learner-centered teaching and experiential learning • Encourage students to be active agents in the education process with faculty, staff, and community • Encourage faculty and administration to support the educational philosophy through a commitment to excellence in teaching • Design programs of study to engage students and prepare them for gratifying and productive careers • Give students a broad perspective on ideas and an awareness of the diversity of human experiences and cultures through the general education program • Strive to be the best at what we do • Evaluate and assess our success using the results to improve the learning experience	• The library selects, acquires, organizes, and distributes information and resources in support of the college mission and its curricular and social goals • Through our collection of resources, our service orientation, and our various programs and displays, we strive to provide organized access to the record of human discovery and achievement and to the diversity of human experience and culture. • Our services, including reference and library instruction, serve to foster and develop student skill and confidence in finding, using, and critically evaluating print, media, and electronic information resources. • Our goal is not only to assist students with their immediate needs but also to empower them with the skills and enthusiasm necessary for lifelong learning. • We design, facilitate, and encourage electronic access to our resources not only to patrons in the building, but also to on-campus constituents in their residence halls and offices and to those at remote locations. • We share our resources and expertise with members of the campus, the library profession, our community and region, and our state. • We work closely with the faculty of other departments to assure congruence among the college mission, curricular needs, and library goals. • We provide a comfortable physical environment conducive to individual and group study and instruction. • We evaluate and assess our efforts and use the results to improve our service.	The mission of the library-instruction program is to support the library and college missions by instructing students in selecting, locating, and evaluating the most appropriate print and electronic resources necessary for completing their assignments. Furthermore, we hope to instill the information skills necessary for self-enrichment and lifelong learning. *Instruction Goals:* 1. Librarians identify and teach the specific and changing skills needed for research literacy at appropriate instruction levels from first-year to graduate students. 2. Librarians design instructional sessions in which students learn by doing, develop skill and confidence, come to appreciate the need of research skills for lifelong learning, and critically evaluate information resources. 3. Librarians communicate with teaching faculty regarding the need and value of library instruction and to develop engaging pedagogies that contribute to excellence in teaching. 4. Librarians design course guides, handouts, bibliographies, and other instructional materials as needed and deliver them where they are needed. 5. Librarians continue to develop their own skills and foster the reputation of the instruction program by participating in conferences and other learning activities. 6. Librarians evaluate and assess the effectiveness of the instruction program through a variety of methods. 7. Librarians use the results of evaluation and assessment to improve the instruction program.

Note. Based on Nelson and Fernekes, 2002.

Table 1 illustrates a direct connection among the institutional mission, the library mission, and the mission and goals of the library instruction program. For example, the institutional mission is to encourage "faculty and administration [to] support the educational philosophy through a commitment to excellence in teaching." In turn, the library mission claims, "We work closely with the faculty of other departments to assure congruence among the college mission, curricular needs, and library goals." Finally, the library instruction mission (goal three) claims, "Librarians communicate with teaching faculty regarding the need and value of library instruction." Therefore, by communicating with teaching faculty, librarians look for opportunities to mesh library instruction goals with faculty course goals. Working together, librarians and faculty are more likely to develop engaging pedagogical approaches with synergistic results. With this clear outline of purpose, the library can identify how it contributes to the institutional mission of "excellence in teaching." Further, librarians can demonstrate their effectiveness with a clearly stated evaluation and assessment plan showing how specific activities contribute to the whole.

Deciding What to Assess

With the mission and goals of the library instruction program firmly decided, and building upon the foundation of both the institution and library missions, it becomes easier to look at each goal and decide what skills to teach, where to teach them, and how to either evaluate or assess the results.

Table 2 contains a list of sample knowledge outcomes and skills an academic library might want to instill in first-year students. In this example, the library has at least three points of access with first-year students: (a) a "skills" session embedded in a first-year seminar, (b) a "Periodicals and Books" session embedded in English composition, and (c) an "Online and Internet" session also embedded in English composition.

Some skills lend themselves to assessment more readily than others. For example, although it would be possible, it might not be worth the effort to design an assessment method for orientation to the building. Similarly, if one assumes that first-year students have little or no knowledge of the Library of Congress classification system before enrolling in the institution, there is little point in designing a method of assessing a "value-added" learning outcome. In this case and others, a simple evaluation might be sufficient.

On the other hand, it might well be worthwhile to design an assessment tool to measure what students know about searching the Internet when they enter their first year of college and then to compare it to the "value added" learning outcome as a result of the library instruction program. Selecting what to evaluate as opposed to what to assess is a significant element of an efficient assessment program.

Assessment Fatigue

An important key to assessment success is not to overdo it. As mentioned earlier, attempting too many assessment measures may turn others off to both the program and to ongoing assessment efforts. Selecting the most important knowledge or skills to assess and starting small will not only contribute to the success of the assessment program but also provide valuable experience to apply to other assessment projects. It is not necessary, for example, to assess every section of English composition. A random sample of sections, generally those with professors who also see the value of assessment, will yield as much of the needed information as a more time-consuming and labor-intensive assessment of every section. Further, it is good practice to vary assessment techniques every semester or every year. Adding variety will also add interest and enthusiasm.

Table 2
State Library's 31 Desirable First-Year Student Skills

Skill Number	Session	Skill Name
1	Orientation 1	Orientation to the building
2	Skills 1	Library of Congress classification
3	Skills 2	Basic online catalog searching
4	Skills 3	Locating materials (location codes)
5	Skills 4	Reading bibliographic citations
6	Skills 5	Orientation to the library web site
7	Skills 6	Circulation policies
8	Skills 7	Online access to student library accounts
9	Skills 8	Reserves
10	Skills 9	Interlibrary loan
11	Per/Books 1	When to ask a librarian
12	Per/Books 2	Use of encyclopedias, bibliographies
13	Per/Books 3	Boolean search concepts
14	Per/Books 4	Online catalog advanced searching
15	Per/Books 5	Primary v. secondary sources
16	Per/Books 6	Print periodical indexes
17	Per/Books 7	Newspaper indexes
18	Per/Books 8	Print/fiche/film periodical formats
19	Per/Books 9	Style guidelines: MLA, APA
20	Online I 1	Review of library web site
21	Online I 2	Internet resources: fee v. free
22	Online I 3	Online bibliographic citation database
23	Online I 4	Online full-text periodical database
24	Online II 5	Online full-text newspaper database
25	Online II 6	Online information database
26	Online II 7	Online encyclopedia
27	Online II 8	Planning a research strategy
28	Internet I 1	Advanced search engine techniques
29	Internet I 2	Internet directories
30	Internet II 3	URL's
31	Internet II 4	Evaluating Internet sites

Further Considerations

Even with a pretest of information literacy skills and a posttest at the end of the first college year, a full student assessment model is only present if evaluators have information about how students participated in the educational environment so that change (or lack of change) in skills can be connected to specific activities. Certainly, a number of educational activities could contribute to increased information literacy. Evaluators may never fully accomplish the disaggregation and identification of the library's unique impact on information literacy, but useful information still will emerge. In fact, often the most important outcome of assessment is refining the questions that will guide future assessment efforts.

An alternative approach to assessing the library's contribution to information literacy bases assessment on an institutional self-study rather than a student outcomes approach. The Policy Center on the First Year of College has successfully piloted self-studies based on an aspirational model for the first year as an alternative to focusing on student outcomes (Barefoot et al., 2005).

In such a model, librarians could develop or adopt an aspirational model using both direct interaction with first-year students and interaction with those who teach and counsel them outside the library. Although outside the scope of this chapter, one can easily conceive of professional development opportunities built around working with advisors, classroom faculty members, student affairs personnel, financial aid counselors, and others. Such interaction could identify previously overlooked issues such as when first-year students need information, the difficulties they have in locating that information, and how they evaluate and use it. Once the librarians identify the opportunities, they can evaluate how well they are serving the needs of students in each area. Such an audit is likely to show that many opportunities to encourage information literacy arise from non-classroom aspects of the first year of college as students plan travel, seek summer jobs, explore career options, participate in clubs and organizations, and manage the normal decisions of life.

Using Assessment to Support the Mission

Finally, the most important element of a good assessment program is using the information one gathers to improve a program. Assessment often yields surprising results. We sometimes find students have a very clear grasp of the knowledge we previously assumed they lacked. Conversely, we sometimes discover that skills we had assumed were obvious actually baffle students completely. Assessment provides real data to either confirm or refute assumptions. Table 10.3 shows an abbreviated diagram of an assessment plan as suggested by Nelson and Fernekes (2002). A fully developed plan might incorporate all the elements of good assessment mentioned in this chapter. Specifically, it could give a clear indication of how the library accomplishes its instruction goals and supports the mission of the institution.

In Table 3, the essential column between "Evaluation Procedure" and "Use of Results" outlines the specific outcomes, or assessment criteria, desired for each goal—the specific skills to be acquired—in this case, the skills listed in Table 10.2. These desired outcomes form the basis of the assessment instruments. Appendix E of Breivik's book (1998) contains an especially good example of an assessment plan including examples of assessment criteria.

Nelson and Fernekes' (2002) work illustrates a systematic process for putting the library-instruction program and its assessment component into a format that is clear to colleagues, faculty, and administrators. Best of all, because it prescribes specific review periods, it builds into the program a requirement for ongoing assessment, so that the assessment component does not fall prey to being something "we started a few years ago but haven't kept up."

Table 3

An Assessment Plan Outline [Excerpts]

Purpose and Relevance to the Institutional Mission[a]	Goals Listed by Department or Function[b]	Assessment Activities and Frequency	Assessment Criteria	Use of Results
Our services, including reference and library instruction, serve to foster and develop student competence and confidence in finding, using, and critically evaluating print, media, and electronic information resources. Our goal is not only to assist students with their immediate needs but also to empower them with the skills and enthusiasm necessary for lifelong learning.	Library-Instruction Goal One: Librarians identify and teach the specific and changing skills needed for research literacy at appropriate instruction levels from first-year to graduate students.	Library-Instruction Goal One: Evaluate or assess, as appropriate, first-year students to see which of the 31 desirable library skills they have mastered. (Annually) Include general skills questions in class evaluation forms. (Periodically among randomly selected classes at all levels)	Desired Outcomes Goal One: Skill #1: Students are able to find major areas of the library, e.g. circulation desk, reference desk, [etc...] Skill #2: Students understand the Library of Congress system and can use it to find materials in the library. Skill #3: [etc...] Skill #19: An examination of random bibliographies from random classes shows students understand and can appropriately use either MLA or APA bibliographic format. Skill #22—#26: An examination of bibliographies from random classes indicates an ability to find and use appropriate online resources. Skill #30: [etc...]	Instruction Goal One Use of Results: Revise first-year instructional environment according to the results of surveys or assessment. Revise instruction according to results.

cont. p. 151

Table 3, cont.

Purpose and Relevance to the Institutional Mission[a]	Goals Listed by Department or Function[b]	Assessment Activities and Frequency	Assessment Criteria	Use of Results
Phrases taken from the institution's mission and vision statements supported by this portion of the library mission statement and guide the library-instruction program's instructional approach: —Provides a learning environment that supports the development of mind, body, and spirit —Bases its educational philosophy on concepts of learner-centered teaching and experiential learning —Encourages students to be active agents in the education process with faculty, staff, and community	Library-Instruction Goal Two: Librarians design instruction sessions in which students learn by doing, develop skill and confidence, come to appreciate the need of research skills for lifelong learning, critically evaluate information resources.	Library-Instruction Goal Two: Library-instruction librarians periodically attend sessions of other instructors and discuss levels of hands-on experience, practicality of assignments, and instructions (bi-annually)	Desired Outcomes Instruction Goal Two: Librarians demonstrate an ability to connect with students and communicate the desired goals of particular instructional sessions Librarians demonstrate engaging pedagogic strategies appropriate to the desired goals of the instructional sessions. [Etc.]	Library-Instruction Goal Two Use of Results: Librarians use discussions for personal development.
	Library-Instruction Goal Six: Librarians evaluate or assess the effectiveness of the instruction program using a variety of methods as they deem appropriate.	Library-Instruction Goal Six: As described in library mission statement paragraph #2 [....] (Specific goals are assessed and reported annually on a predetermined and rotating basis.)	Desired Outcomes Instruction Goal Six: Librarians can produce reports including qualitative and quantitative evidence demonstrating successful achievement of library-instruction goals.	Library-Instruction Goal Six Use of Results: Librarians discuss evaluation and assessment results to plan future strategies and improve the instruction program

Note. Based on Nelson and Fernekes, 2002 and Breivik, 1998.
[a]Excerpt from the library mission statement
[b]Experpt from the library-instruction mission statement

Conclusion

This chapter does not attempt to downplay the time and institutional resources needed to conduct assessment; rather, it attempts to build the case that librarians have a significant base to stand on as they undertake assessment activities. Librarians, individually, and through their professional associations, have built a commendable set of reference materials to guide their assessment practices. Truly, there is no need to re-invent the wheel or to feel that one must "go it alone" at this point. The resources in this chapter, and those listed in the Appendix, provide both a primer on assessment structures and a map to many of the significant tools readily available for adoption or adaptation. Useful assessment to improve the experiences of first-year students is within the reach of librarians at institutions large and small.

The authors hope this chapter will focus the reader's attention on two major themes: purpose and mission. First, the purpose of assessment is either to confirm existing practices or to create action for improvement. Efforts that produce unused findings are not examples of high-quality assessment and generally just waste valuable resources and time. Second, assessment activities should align with the mission of the library-instruction unit, the library's overall mission, and the mission of the institution. By focusing on those efforts that advance the ultimate goals of the institution, librarians will assess what matters most.

A third, but less obvious theme is the advantage of focusing on institutional efforts—what institutions do—rather than simply focusing on what students do. The latter mentality can lead to a simplistic belief that the outcomes would improve if only the institution had "better" students. Institutions should not ignore how library instruction changes what students do. However, they should recognize that there is much to gain from assessments focusing on how institutional efforts support and challenge students to move in the direction of desired learning outcomes.

References

Association of College and Research Libraries (ACRL). (1987, October). *The mission of a university undergraduate library: Model statement.* Retrieved March 27, 2006, from http://www.ala.org/ala/acrl/acrlstandards/missionuniversity.htm

Association of College and Research Libraries (ACRL). (1989, January 10). *Presidential committee on information literacy: Final report.* Retrieved March 27, 2006, from http://www.ala.org/ala/acrl/acrlpubs/whitepapers/presidential.htm

Association of College and Research Libraries (ACRL). (2000). *Information literacy competency standards for higher education.* Retrieved March 24, 2006, from http://www.ala.org/ala/acrl/acrlstandards/informationliteracycompetency.htm

Astin, A. W. (1991). *Assessment for excellence.* New York: American Council on Education, Macmillan Publishing.

Barefoot, B. O., Gardner, J. N., Cutright, M., Morris, L. V., Schroeder, C. C., Schwartz, S. W., et al. (2005). *Achieving and sustaining institutional excellence for the first year of college.* San Francisco: Jossey-Bass.

Breivik, P. S. (1998). *Student learning in the information age.* Phoenix: Oryx Press.

Dugan, R. E., & Hernon, P. (2002). Outcomes assessment: Not synonymous with inputs and outputs. *The Journal of Academic Librarianship, 28*(6), 376-380.

Nelson, W. N., & Fernekes, R. W. (2002). *Standards and assessment for academic libraries: A workbook.* Chicago: ACRL, a division of American Library Association.

Swing, R. L. (Ed.). (2004). *Proving and improving, volume II: Tools and techniques for assessing the first college year* (Monograph No. 37). Columbia, SC: University of South Carolina, National Resource Center for The First-Year Experience and Students in Transition.

Appendix

Assessment Resources

The following resources introduce the tools and basic steps of designing a new assessment plan or of reviewing or reconfiguring a plan currently in use. Others have already done a great deal in the area of library-instruction program assessment. Furthermore, this chapter does not presume to include everything an instruction coordinator will want to know about assessing the first-year library instruction program. However, reviewing the readily available resources listed here will certainly supply ideas and confidence to anyone designing assessment tools for specific needs or institutions. A good example is the chapter by Carter "Outcomes Assessment in a College Library: An Instructional Case Study," appearing in *Outcomes Assessment in Higher Education* (Hernon & Dugan, 2004). She describes a case study involving five assessment projects. The chapter even includes reproductions of the assessment tools used. With a little modification, many of the ideas and processes described in the following sources will serve as models for practically any assessment need.

Given the importance of mission-driven assessment, materials specific to the institution's missions are important resources. These include:

- The institution's mission statement
- The library's mission statement
- The library-instruction program's mission statement
- Association of College and Research Libraries. (1987, October). *The mission of a university undergraduate library: Model statement.* Retrieved March 20, 2006, from http://www.ala.org/ala/acrl/acrlstandards/missionuniversity.htm

Guidelines for Program and Assessment Design

- Association of College and Research Libraries (ACRL). (1998, June 27). *Task force on academic library outcomes assessment report.* Retrieved March 20, 2006, from http://www.ala.org/ala/acrl/acrlpubs/whitepapers/taskforceacademic.htm
- Association of College and Research Libraries (ACRL). (2000). *Information literacy competency standards for higher education.* Retrieved March 27, 2006, from http://www.ala.org/ala/acrl/acrlstandards/informationliteracycompetency.htm
- Association of College and Research Libraries (ACRL). (2001, January). *Objectives for information literacy instruction: A model statement for academic libraries.* Retrieved March 22, 2006, from http://www.ala.org/ala/acrl/acrlstandards/objectivesinformation.htm
- Association of College and Research Libraries (ACRL). (2003). *Characteristics of programs of information literacy that illustrate best practices: A guideline.* Retrieved March 27, 2006, from http://www.ala.org/ala/acrl/acrlstandards/characteristics.htm
- Association of College and Research Libraries (ACRL). (2005). *Guidelines for university library services to undergraduate students.* Retrieved March 27, 2006, from http://www.ala.org/ala/acrl/acrlstandards/ulsundergraduate.htm

Sources With Assessment Guidelines and Sample Assessment Documents

- Hernon, P., & Dugan, R. E. (Eds.). (2004). *Outcomes assessment in higher education: Views and perspectives.* Westport, CT: Libraries Unlimited.
- Malone, D., & Videon, C. (2004). *First-year student library instruction programs* (CLIP Note #33). Chicago: Association of College and Research Libraries.
- Merz, L. H., & Mark, B. L. (2002). *Assessment in college library instruction programs* (CLIP Note #32). Chicago: Association of College and Research Libraries.

Assessment Design

- Nelson, W. N., & Fernekes, R. W. (2002). *Standards and assessment for academic libraries: A workbook.* Chicago: ACRL, a division of American Library Association.

Web Resources

- National Forum on Information Literacy, http://www.infolit.org/

Listserv

- American Library Association. INFOLIT. [To subscribe, send an e-mail to listproc@ala.org with the following line as the only line in the message body: "subscribe INFOLIT firstname lastname"]

Chapter 11

*Research on Student
Retention and Implications
for Library Involvement*

Cindy Pierard & Kathryn Graves

Only 63% of students who enroll in a four-year college complete a bachelor's degree at that or any other institution within six years (Berkner, He, & Cataldi, 2002). The first year is particularly important in determining a student's overall persistence in college. This is the time when a student's commitment to an institution is weakest and when the difficulties of separation from past associations and the transition to new environments are most pronounced. As many as 25% of the students who eventually leave college depart during their first year or prior to their second year (U.S. Department of Education, 2001). Therefore, many institutions have developed specific programs for these students in the hopes of encouraging them to persist to graduation. The research on student persistence and institutional retention provides insight into the challenges students encounter during their transition to college and the interventions that may help them succeed.

Successful retention efforts reflect a collective commitment to student success and not "the sporadic efforts of a few officially designated members of a retention committee" (Tinto, 1993, p. 212). The contemporary library offers many possibilities for supporting student success through effective collaborations with other campus groups. This chapter reviews the research on student persistence during and beyond the first year, highlighting the work of Astin, Tinto, and others. Further, the chapter examines retention literature on special student populations (i.e., adult and minority students) and institution-specific settings, such as community colleges and online programs. The recommendations section outlines the role the library can play in supporting student persistence and success. Other chapters of the monograph also offer rich and detailed examples of specific institutional practices with the potential for enhancing student success and retention.

Today's Students

Americans participate in postsecondary education at higher rates than ever. In 1900, only 4% of all 18-year olds attended college. In 2004, 66.7% pursued some form of postsecondary education (U.S. Department of Labor, 2005). The student body is also increasingly diverse. Consider the following statistical portrait of today's undergraduates, as reported by Horn, Peter, and Rooney (2002):

- 56% are women
- 33% are minorities

- 39% are 25 years old or older
- 27% are parents
- 39% are enrolled part-time
- 44% are enrolled at two-year colleges

These figures demonstrate that the traditional undergraduate student—defined as one who has earned a high school diploma, enrolls in college on a full-time basis immediately after completing high school, depends on parents for financial support, and either does not work or works part-time during the school year—is no longer the norm. Almost three quarters of today's students are considered nontraditional in some way.

Moreover, this increasingly diverse student body may be at greater risk of not persisting to graduation. A study of students who began their college education in the mid-1990s found that only 55% of the students who attended four-year institutions graduated from that same institution within six years; 63% completed a degree overall (Berkner et al., 2002). African American and Hispanic students were less likely to complete degrees than White or Asian/Pacific Islander students. Lower-income students had lower completion rates in comparison to other students. Women were more likely to persist to graduation than men.

Of the students who intended to attain a bachelor's degree at any institution, factors negatively affecting their completion rates included delayed enrollment after high school, part-time attendance during the first year of school, parenthood, and full or part-time employment during the first year. Students with greater numbers of "negative persistence" characteristics were decreasingly likely to complete their degree (Berkner et al., 2002). Among those students attending two-year institutions whose goals included completion of an associate's or bachelor's degree, only 31% graduated within six years.

Research on first- to second-year persistence as well as graduation rates indicates that these factors have remained steady over the past three decades (Adelman, 2004). Furthermore, baccalaureate completion rates have been consistent since the start of the 20th century (Tinto & Lentz, 1986), even though the amount of time needed to complete a degree has increased. The consequences of failing to graduate, however, have become more serious. The financial and personal costs to students who enroll and then prematurely depart should be a matter of great concern to not only the students and their families but also administrators of higher education and society at large. Over their lifetimes, college graduates now earn an average of 1.8 times as much as those who only completed high school, and nearly one third more than those who completed some college, but did not achieve a four-year degree (Day & Newburger, 2002). The unemployment rate for individuals with a bachelor's degree was 6% in 2003, compared to 14% for those with a high school diploma or less (Lotkowski, Robbins, & Noeth, 2004). The gap in both employment and earnings between those with college degrees and those who lack a four-year degree is likely to widen as the United States transitions to a knowledge economy in which employers widely view a four-year degree as a necessary credential (Carey, 2004). In addition to the economic costs for individuals, institutional losses are also significant. Student departures create significant problems for colleges and universities through unstable course enrollments and uncertain tuition revenues, resulting in both short- and long-term budget difficulties.

Challenges of Retention Research

Student retention has long challenged educational researchers and practitioners. The many variables affecting a student's decision to persist in college and the difficulty of demonstrating causal relationships between those variables and academic persistence make it an incredibly complex problem. Part of the challenge consists of defining what is meant by retention and determining how it may best be tracked. Porter (2003-2004) writes that practitioners and administrators have typically viewed retention as a stay-or-go decision when the reality is considerably more complex: "some students decide to stay, others to transfer, some simply take some time off, and others decide to discontinue their education altogether" (p. 53). Yet another practice that adds to the challenge of determining retention rates, particularly at two-year colleges, is for students to "opt out" or leave an institution before graduating, simply because they never aspired to do more than take a few classes (Bonham & Luckie, 1993). Therefore, variations in student motivations and student attendance hamper understanding of retention issues.

Retention Characteristics

Numerous studies have attempted to identify student and institutional characteristics that contribute to student persistence. In general, students who are most likely to persist have high school backgrounds characterized by strong academic preparation and involvement with extracurricular activities. They perform well on standardized tests and enroll in college immediately following high school. Once at college, these students typically attend on a full-time basis, live on campus, and have fairly clear career and educational goals, including graduation. Institutions that are most likely to retain students offer graduate degrees in addition to four-year degrees; are selective in their admission students; and have a student body that is predominantly full-time and residential (Astin, 1993; Tinto, 1993).

Of course, knowledge of these general characteristics alone is of little help to college administrators who hope to improve their student retention rates, unless colleges plan to admit only a very select group of students. Therefore, researchers and practitioners have sought to understand interactions between students and postsecondary institutions to learn how college affects diverse groups of students and to identify those practices successful in encouraging persistence in a variety of settings. While it is beyond the scope of this chapter to review the enormous body of literature on the college student experience, and specifically student departure, we will examine the work of two highly influential theorists, Alexander Astin and Vincent Tinto.

Theories of Student Involvement and Departure

Astin (1984) developed his theory of student involvement in an attempt to determine which attributes of the college environment could best promote student success. He reviewed traditional ideas of what students need in order to succeed—exposure to appropriate educational content, access to high-quality faculty, access to well-equipped labs and libraries—and found such traditional ideas lacked an emphasis on student engagement. Astin wrote:

> [H]aving established a multimillion-volume library, the administration may neglect to find out whether students are making effective use of that library . . . having successfully recruited a faculty 'star,' the college may pay little attention to whether the new faculty member works effectively with students. (1984, p. 300)

Instead, Astin recommended that colleges emphasize and support those educational policies and practices that are proven to enhance the quantity and quality of student involvement. He concluded, "The greater the student's involvement in college, the greater will be the amount of student learning and personal development" (1984, p. 307).

In order to identify characteristics of the college environment with positive or negative effects on student persistence, Astin (1993) applied his theory to several decades of data on American college students, using an Input-Environment-Output model to study the characteristics students had upon entering an institution, their experiences while at college, and the effects of college on students after they left. Environmental factors that increased student involvement such as interaction with faculty members and student peer groups were positively associated with learning, improved academic performance, and persistence. Factors with a negative effect on student development and persistence included those that "either isolate the student from peers or remove the student physically from the campus: living at home, commuting, being employed off-campus, being employed full time, and watching television" (Astin, 1993, p. 395). Other research has supported Astin's theory on the connection between student engagement and academic achievement, satisfaction, and persistence (Pascarella & Terenzini, 1991; Tinto, 1993).

Tinto (1993) incorporated the work of the sociologist Emile Durkheim (1951) and the anthropologist Arnold Van Gennep (1960) in his model of student departure. Specifically, he employed Durkheim's model of suicide—in which individuals commit suicide because of an inability to make connections with their larger social system and a lack of peer support—to explore the question of why students leave college. Tinto explained that "both forms of behavior can be understood…to represent a form of voluntary withdrawal from local communities that is as much a reflection of the community as it is of the individual who withdraws" (1993, p. 99). He also integrated Van Gennep's rites of passage theory, indicating that successful navigation of any rite of passage necessitates that an individual separates from past associations, transitions to and interacts with the new environment, and ultimately integrates into the new community.

Tinto's model is a longitudinal one, in which students enter college with various characteristics (i.e., family background, academic preparation, goals) that influence their commitments to remaining at that institution and graduating. Ultimately, however, his theory is interactional and grounded in the idea that the experiences and interactions a student has at an institution—both formal and informal, social and academic—play the greatest role in influencing decisions to persist or depart:

> Though the intentions and commitments with which individuals enter college matter, what goes on after entry matters more. It is the daily interaction of the person with other members of the college…and the person's perception or evaluation of the character of those interactions, and of those that involve the student outside the college, that in large measure determine decisions as to staying or leaving. (1993, p. 136)

Tinto shared Astin's belief that involvement is key: the greater the student's level of social and academic integration, the more likely she or he is to persist.

Astin, Tinto, and other researchers have argued against the idea of retention for the sole purpose of keeping students in college. Although institutions should take responsibility for the students they have admitted, education is a mutual responsibility of both the student and the institution (Tinto, 1993). Astin (2000) has also cautioned against the approach of comparing institutional retention rates as a measure of quality. Institutions with high retention rates may simply admit more students exhibiting factors associated with persistence. More important is the ability of a college or university to work within its mission to help admitted students fulfill their potential.

Expansions of Retention Theory:
A Closer Look at Specific Student Populations and Settings

Both Astin's and Tinto's theories have undergone criticism as well as calls for revision and expansion. A central concern is that these theories may not adequately address the challenges faced by minority students since many early retention researchers based much of their work on more homogeneous student populations, largely composed of White, male students (Hurtado & Carter, 1997; Tierney, 1992). Some (Jalomo, 1995; Terenzini et al., 1994) have called for revisions to Astin's involvement theory, arguing that many nontraditional students may find involvement difficult in programs directed at traditional student populations. Others have asserted that Tinto's work should be revised to incorporate the role that environmental factors, particularly personal finances, play in student-departure decisions (Cabrera, Stampen, & Hansen, 1990).

Braxton, Hirschy, and McClendon (2004) have provided one of the most significant critiques of Tinto's model. They found it inadequate in its approach to student-departure patterns among different racial and ethnic groups and within two-year and commuter college settings. Considering the data on today's increasingly diverse student body as well as growing enrollments at community colleges and online education programs, it is also important to investigate retention as it applies to these students and settings.

Racial and Ethnic Minority Students

Researchers caution against pigeonholing racial and ethnic minority students. As Tinto (1993) has noted, "It would be a serious mistake to assume that all group members are alike in their experience of higher education" (p. 72). Nevertheless, the attrition rates for many minority students far surpass those of White students. Many non-White students attend institutions where they are a distinct minority, thus facing greater challenges to academic and social integration. Among the most significant barriers to persistence for racial and ethnic minority students are concerns about financing their education and the difficulty of experiencing social integration or finding groups of students who share similar beliefs and goals (Braxton et al., 2004).

Research indicates that the attrition rate among African American students is disproportionately high compared to attrition among White students, particularly at predominately White colleges and universities (Jones, 2001). Although an increasing number of African American students have the advantage of being second-generation students with support from their parents' educational experience and perhaps parental finances (Somers, Cofer, Hall, & Vander Putten, 1999), socioeconomic factors may still inhibit retention for many. A 2004 report (Persisting Racial Gap) noted that 69% of African American students who left college cited student loan debt as the underlying cause for their departure. As with minority groups in general, African American college students are more likely to persist if they encounter an inclusive environment, financial assistance, student-support services, as well as campus- and culture-centered student activities and organizations (Jones).

A similar retention situation exists for Hispanic students. As the fastest growing minority group in the United States, Hispanics represent an increasing segment of the college population, with 40% to 55% of Hispanic undergraduates enrolling in community colleges. Despite their total enrollment figures, however, this group still exhibits low graduation rates from four-year institutions in comparison to White students. Similar challenges that face African American students may also confront Hispanic students: They may be first-generation, older students, and/or working part-time. Hispanic students may also come from low-income families, who are sometimes recent immigrants. They may not speak fluent English, and close family ties may inhibit children from leaving home to pursue an education (McGlynn, 2004). The support factors noted by Jones (2001) for helping African American students may enhance retention among Hispanics as well.

While minorities represent approximately 23% of postsecondary education students, Native Americans comprise only .9% of that number, making them one of the least represented minorities on a traditional college or university campus (Aragon, 2004). Native American students are often first-generation students from single-parent household whose families and communities face high unemployment rates (resulting in poverty), high morbidity rates (including a high number of alcohol-related deaths), drug use, and high suicide rates (Heavyrunner, 2002; O'Brien, 1992). These students may have difficulty focusing on academics, experience anxiety over and accept little responsibility for educational tasks, and feel low self-confidence about their ability to succeed academically (Aragon). Despite these challenges, researchers have found certain actions and programs relate positively to retention of Native American students. An institution that advocates both mainstream and Native social competencies and cultures will retain Native American students at higher rates than those that do not (Laughlin, 2001). Implementing student success courses, hiring culturally conscious faculty members, and providing continuous faculty involvement on a personal basis are also positive retention practices (Aragon).

Researchers who have studied the challenges faced by racial and ethnic minority students (e.g., Braxton et al., 2004) take issue with the notion of college as a rite of passage as it appears in Tinto's model of student departure. Instead of leaving behind past associations, minority students need programs and services that encourage linkages between individual and organizational identity (Tierney, 2000). Indeed, colleges that are effective in retaining minority students emphasize an inclusive campus community, which recognizes and respects the different cultures represented among students and staff. An institutional commitment to building and sustaining campus communal groups is also imperative and strongly linked to the recruitment and retention of a diverse faculty, staff, and student body.

Adult Students

Adult students face particular transition challenges. They frequently have more demands on their time than do traditional 18- to 24-year-old students, including work and family. They may require information about childcare, financial aid, and health insurance and may have little patience with peripheral issues such as academic bureaucracy, class schedules, or parking. Because many adult students enroll to change careers or advance in a current career, they may focus more on the practical applications of knowledge than the intellectual pursuits of education.

Because they may or may not have degree completion as a goal, adult students may periodically stop out before returning at a later point. Their academic integration and retention are tied to social connectivity with the campus as well as perceptions of the relevance of their educational experience (Tweedell, 2000).

Because of their need for flexible scheduling, adult students may turn to evening, weekend, or online education programs. They may need special assistance in working with online educational technologies (Nelson, 1999). Academic advising and support groups, both in person and online, will strengthen retention. Such groups counteract the isolation these students may otherwise feel because they lack available time to connect with other students and faculty. Also important to these students is that institutions must provide timely and convenient access to student services. As with the other student populations discussed in this chapter, adult students need attention, follow-up, feedback, and support to sustain their motivation and retention (Tinto, 1993; Wonacott, 2001).

Two-Year College Students

The typical two-year or community college student may be a recent high school graduate or, more frequently, an adult student. Community college students are often the first in their families to attend college, and their external commitments include full- or part-time employment and family responsibilities, which means they are attending college part-time. This combination of characteristics means that retention is a prevalent concern for two-year institutions. The first-semester community college student is at particular risk, with reported attrition rates at 67%. Minority students and those with low socioeconomic status enrolled at two-year colleges experience the highest first-semester attrition rates (Rendón, 1995).

To improve retention, community colleges must emphasize facilitating a student's transition to college and making connections, both with faculty/counselors and with peers (Rendón, 1995).

Providing support for students who then transfer to another institution, particularly if the student plans to pursue a four-year degree, is also important. In this instance, retention may not be an appropriate goal if it is better for the student to continue studies elsewhere (Tinto, 1993).

Two-year college students may lack clear educational goals or doubt their ability to reach those goals. They may be intimidated by the system. Thus, retention-enhancement strategies at two-year colleges are similar to those for other institutions: strengthening the first-year experience, offering opportunities for collaborative and active learning; facilitating student involvement with faculty; and setting clear, high expectations. Also important, institutions should provide faculty-development opportunities related to working with diverse students (Rendón, 1995).

Online/Distance Education Students

Online/distance education programs offer a relatively new approach to achieving a post-secondary degree and are an option that appeals to an increasing number of nontraditional students in the United States. Motivation and self-direction are important individual factors related to persistence in online courses, but the institution must also provide support.

Retention figures, however, are low for online education (O'Brien & Renner, 2002). Some administrators have estimated that course-completion rates for online courses are 10% to 20% lower than face-to-face offerings (Carr, 2000). Online/distance education students frequently experience disconnectedness and lack a sense of community because there is no face-to-face interaction with faculty or classmates. Rovai (2003) recommends a model program in which students come to campus for one or more face-to-face sessions with their peers and instructors as a way to strengthen feelings of personal integration with the institution. Other needs identified by Workman and Stenard (1996) include consistency and clarity of online programs, policies, and procedures; development of self-esteem (which can be built through orientation programs); identification with the school (issuing an ID card); social integration (even if this may take place online); and easy access to support services including libraries, study-skills, and technology training.

A Role for Libraries: Lessons From the Research on Persistence and Retention

In previous sections of this chapter, we focused on the problem of student retention, the challenges students face in persisting to a baccalaureate degree, and some particular issues for retention practices with specific student populations and institutional settings. In this section, we turn our attention to the role of the library. What lessons does the literature on student persistence and institutional retention hold for libraries? In particular, we discuss three lessons for libraries that are supported by available research. These lessons are: (a) integrating libraries into institutional retention efforts; (b) employing information literacy as a means of promoting student engagement; and (c) re-engineering library spaces as centers for student learning and community.

Lesson #1: Integrating Libraries Into Institutional Retention Efforts

Retention researchers are in agreement that uncoordinated retention programs will not be effective. Kuh (2001-2002) states that no single campus entity can promote and ensure student success; rather, collaborative campus efforts can project a supportive, affirming environment. Others speak to the necessity of ensuring that all campus entities recognize the desirability of student success, and thus a higher rate of retention, and understand the roles that they play in that process (Braxton et al., 2004). Yet, the data also suggest that few campuses coordinate their retention efforts effectively. A 2004 survey (Habley & McClanahan) found that only 51.7% of responding institutions had identified an individual with responsibility for coordinating retention efforts, and fewer than half had goals or plans for improving student retention between the first and second years, or for improving degree-completion rates.

If they are to be effective in enhancing students' success, librarians must be part of campus conversations on student retention at the levels of planning, implementation, and assessment. Librarians who are involved with retention committees, for example, will have a clearer understanding of student needs and institutional retention goals. Librarians who are active in planning and implementing general education or academic support services related to student success will be more effective in ensuring that library services complement curricular goals, embrace progressive teaching methods, and provide appropriate academic support.

Assessing the role of the library in the first-year experience is important, as discussed elsewhere in this book (see Chapter 10). The first-year experience has been frequently evaluated. In fact, Upcraft (2005) noted that "perhaps no other area in higher education has been more subjected to assessment than efforts to promote first-year student success" (p. 469). Yet, we found a paucity of data demonstrating connections between student use and knowledge of how to use libraries and their academic success and persistence, either during or after the first year. Successfully demonstrating these connections presents librarians and others with some daunting challenges. For example, commonly used self-report instruments may lack sufficient validity to establish any definite connections. Students may also report satisfaction with services they rarely use. For example, Gardner and Hardesty (2004) have noted that although 81% of student respondents to the 2002 Your First College Year survey reported satisfaction with library services and resources, half indicated that they perceived no changes in their levels of library-research skills during the first year. Students may not know what services are available or what they have the right to expect. In addition, Manuel (2002) has cited several studies in which students' self-assessment of their research abilities far surpassed their actual skills.

In addition to the various evaluation and research methods discussed elsewhere in this monograph, Kuh and Gonyea (2003) have suggested several possibilities for further investigation of the role the library plays in promoting student success. These possibilities include inquiring as to how students use what they have learned in interactions with librarians, reviewing teaching methods that appear effective in promoting student engagement, and identifying "best practices" that can be tried in multiple settings to determine if such practices consistently lead to improved student persistence and success. Recent projects such as the Project for Standardized Assessment of Information Literacy Skills (SAILS) may prove useful in this regard (Blixrud, 2003).

Lesson #2: Employing Information Literacy as a Means of Promoting Student Engagement

As discussed earlier in this chapter, Astin, Tinto, and numerous other retention researchers have all noted the importance of student engagement as a necessary condition for persistence, while recognizing the difficulty that many students have in seeing the relevance of a college education to their lives. In what ways can the library promote student engagement?

Although many educators would agree that libraries support the goals of higher education, identifying those institutions at which the library plays an active role in supporting student success during or beyond the first year is challenging. A recent study (Boff & Johnson, 2002) found that, among responding institutions with first-year seminars, only 67% included a required library-instruction component, and nearly 50% indicated that this component consumed no more time than an hour class period. Only 17% of the student respondents to a 1996 study at Kent State University indicated that they were required to use the library either often or very often (Kunkel, Weaver, & Cook, 1996). Fister (1992) and Kuhlthau, Turok, George, and Blevin (1990) reported that students express frustration and anxiety in describing their experiences with library research projects. Perhaps this frustration and anxiety comes from the lack of consistent emphasis on building research skills. Certainly, we doubt that such anxiety and frustration is conducive to student success and persistence.

Nevertheless, few institutions apparently foster a culture in which student engagement through research is more than a peripheral part of the undergraduate experience. In 1998, The Boyer Commission issued a report, *Reinventing Undergraduate Education: A Blueprint for America's Research Universities*, in which the authors concluded, "Many students graduate having accumulated whatever number of courses is required, but lacking a coherent body of knowledge or any inkling as to how one source of information might relate to others" (p. 4). Among their recommendations, they proposed that universities "make research-based learning the standard" (p. 15) and "construct an inquiry-based freshman year" (p. 19) that forms the foundation for subsequent student learning. Student engagement is clearly an important element in student success and retention.

Therefore, we contend that librarians can help foster student success and retention in several ways. They can help build a culture of engagement with research and inquiry by leading campus efforts to integrate information literacy into the curriculum and cocurriculum, particularly during the first year. Along with librarians, classroom faculty members, student affairs staff, educational technologists, and librarians can all play a role in designing curricular and cocurricular experiences that develop students' abilities of finding, evaluating, and applying information. The values and practices of information literacy directly support the type of engaged, integrated educational model supported by research on student persistence. Specific examples of the ways in which libraries are collaborating with others to foster campus information literacy efforts may be found both within this text as well as through the Association of College and Research Libraries (2003) information literacy web site at http://www.ala.org/ala/acrl/acrlissues/acrlinfolit/informationliteracy.htm.

Lesson #3: Redesigning Libraries as Centers for Learning and Community

In his Input-Environment-Output model, Astin (1993) found support for the idea that environments that promote interactions—between students and faculty as well as students and peers—positively affect student persistence. Creating these types of environments, particularly on nonresidential or even virtual campuses, can prove especially challenging. The library is one environment where such interactions might take place; however, the notion may be greeted with surprise by some. Yet, Demas (2005) has noted that people value libraries because they are comfortable and quiet, provide a place for learning interactions, and promote serendipity and opportunities for learning and inquiry (¶ 10). Libraries on college campuses often are located centrally, are highly networked, and offer extensive hours of operation.

Although libraries have frequently been referred to as the "heart" of the university, they were not traditionally designed for the purpose of fostering an active and dynamic learning center: "Despite their handsome exteriors, the interior spaces were often dim and confining, the buildings were difficult to navigate, and specialized services and collections were inaccessible to all but the serious scholar. Libraries were revered but...comparatively static buildings" (Freeman, 2005, ¶ 2). Contemporary college and university libraries are increasingly being designed with not only collections but also people and academic objectives in mind. Bennett (2003) conducted a study of those responsible for planning library renovation and construction projects between 1992 and 2001 and found that the need to respond to new student-learning styles was one of the driving forces behind such projects.

Consideration must also be given to the nature and types of services offered in these spaces. Levitz and Noel (1989) have warned that "retention efforts that do not put student needs first will not work…we must extend quality programs, services, and people to the freshmen we are here to serve" (p. 81). The same is true when designing learning environments. Many projects have been centered on the idea of an "information commons" defined by the *Online Dictionary for Library and Information Science* as:

> a new type of technology-enhanced collaborative facility on college and university campuses that integrates library and computer applications services (information, technology, and learning) in a single floor plan, often equipped with a wireless network, and, in some cases, equipment for multimedia production. (Reitz, 2004)

Examples of learning or information-commons models may be found at institutions such as Dartmouth College, Brookdale (NJ) Community College, Iowa State University, and the University at Waterloo. However, those who have studied the move in library planning towards information commons or learning commons note that the desire to increase building usage will not lead to the creation of better learning environments—in libraries or anywhere else. Instead, the goal must be to "qualitatively enhance the library as a resource and to create an atmosphere conducive to sustained, serious academic work" (Demas, 2005, ¶ 30).

Thus, library facilities that have been reengineered as information or learning commons and that are increasingly also home to complementary services such as writing centers, computer labs, seminar rooms, art galleries, and cafés may promote the types of behaviors—talking with peers or instructors outside of class, viewing exhibits, studying in groups or alone, seeking assistance from librarians or other academic support service providers, exploring new resources—that are positively correlated with student persistence. Although there is currently no empirically based evidence that relates the offering of such services in libraries to student success and persistence, anecdotal information suggests students do positively respond to these services, especially specific populations such as adult students and two-year students, who value the convenience of co-located services, who need to build community with peers, and who appreciate flexible hours of service delivery (Tinto, 1993; Tweedell, 2000; Wonacott, 2001). Kuh and Gonyea (2003) found that students who frequently used the library had a serious work ethic and were more likely to engage in academically challenging work. More research is needed to determine the nature of this relationship. For example, do students who frequent the library develop a serious work ethic, or did they already have this serious work ethic prior to establishing a pattern of college library use?

As we have already noted, students involved in online degree programs face particular challenges in persisting to degree completion due to the difficulties with developing institutional connections and a sense of community. We propose that the library can help to support these students by offering welcoming and well-designed virtual spaces wherein useful and appropriate resources are made readily available—perhaps via course web sites or courseware programs—and where help, in the form of e-mail, chat-based, or toll-free reference services, is provided in a friendly, functional, and convenient manner (Workman & Stenard, 1996).

Summary

Student success and their resulting retention are significant concerns on many campuses. The research indicates that the first year is a particularly critical time for fostering those student skills and attitudes that lead to persistence and success. The research also indicates that many institutional practices can effectively promote this success and retention. To be effective, institutional efforts must be collaborative and student-focused. We contend that librarians and libraries can play an important role in such efforts. To do so, however, librarians must become more actively engaged with campus conversations about student persistence and success. We believe information literacy is a particularly important strategy for promoting student engagement with ideas and information. Librarians, in collaboration with others in the academic community, should play a leadership role in ensuring that students develop these skills. Library spaces should also be redesigned to foster the types of enriching interactions and collaborations that are key to encouraging and sustaining student engagement and the resulting student success.

References

Adelman, C. (2004). *Principal indicators of student academic histories in postsecondary education, 1972–2000.* Washington, DC: U.S. Department of Education. Retrieved April 25, 2006, from http://www.ed.gov/rschstat/research/pubs/prinindicat/prinindicat.pdf

Association of College and Research Libraries (ACRL). (2003). *Information Literacy* . Retrieved April 25, 2006, from http://www.ala.org/ala/acrl/acrlissues/acrlinfolit/informationliteracy.htm

Aragon, S. (2004). Learning and study practices of postsecondary American Indian/Alaska Native students. *Journal of American Indian Retention, 43*(2), 1-18.

Astin, A. (1984). Student involvement: A developmental theory for higher education. *Journal of College Student Personnel, 25*(4), 297-308.

Astin, A. (1993). *What matters in college? Four critical years revisited.* San Francisco: Jossey-Bass.

Astin, A. (2000). The civic challenge of educating the underprepared student. In T. Ehrlich. (Ed.), *Civic responsibility and higher education* (pp. 124-146). Phoenix: Oryx Press.

Berkner, L., He, S., & Cataldi, E. F. (2002). *Descriptive summary of 1995-96 beginning postsecondary students: Six years later, NCES 2003-151.* Washington, DC: U.S. Department of Education. Retrieved April 25, 2005, from http://nces.ed.gov/pubs2003/2003151.pdf

Bennett, S. (2003). Libraries designed for learning. In *The library as place: Rethinking roles, rethinking space.* Washington, DC: Council on Library and Information Resources (CLIR Publication No. 129). Retrieved April 25, 2006, from http://www.clir.org/pubs/abstract/pub129abst.html

Blixrud, J. (2003). Project SAILS: Standardized assessment of information literacy skills. *ARL Bimonthly Report, 230/231,*18-19. Retrieved April 25, 2006, from http://www.arl.org/newsltr/230/sails.html

Boff, C., & Johnson, K. (2002). The library and the first-year experience course: A nationwide study. *Reference Services Review, 30*(4), 277-287.

Bonham, L. A., & Luckie, J. I. (1993). Community college retention: Differentiating among stopouts, dropouts, and optouts. *Community College Journal of Research and Practice, 17*(6), 543-554.

Boyer Commission on Educating Undergraduates in the Research University. (1998). *Reinventing undergraduate education: A blueprint for America's research universities.* Stony Brook, NY: State University of New York.

Braxton, J. M., Hirschy, A. S., & McClendon, S. A. (2004). *Understanding and reducing college student departure.* San Francisco: Jossey-Bass.

Cabrera, A. F., Stampen, J. O., & Hansen, W. L. (1990). Exploring the effects of ability to pay on persistence in college. *Review of Higher Education, 13*(3), 303-336.

Carey, K. (2004). *A matter of degrees: Improving graduation rates in four-year colleges and universities.* Washington, DC: The Education Trust. Retrieved April 25, 2006, from http://www2.edtrust.org/NR/rdonlyres/11B4283F-104E-4511-B0CA-1D3023231157/0/highered.pdf

Carr, S. (2000, February 11). As distance education comes of age, the challenge is keeping the students. *The Chronicle of Higher Education*, p. A39.

Day, J. C., & Newburger, E. C. (2002). *The big payoff: Educational attainment and synthetic estimates of work-life earnings* (Current Population Reports, Special Studies, pp. 23-210). Washington, DC: Commerce Department, Economics and Statistics Administration, Census Bureau. Retrieved April 25, 2006, from http://www.census.gov/prod/2002pubs/p23-210.pdf

Demas, S. (2005). From the ashes of Alexandria: What's happening in the college library? In *The library as place: Rethinking roles, rethinking space*. Washington, DC: Council on Library and Information Resources (CLIR Publication No. 129). Retrieved April 25, 2006, from http://www.clir.org/pubs/abstract/pub129abst.html

Durkheim, E. (1951). *Suicide* (J. A. Spaulding and G. Simpson, Trans.). Glencoe, IL: The Free Press. (Original work published 1897).

Fister, B. (1992). The research process of undergraduates. *The Journal of Academic Librarianship, 18*(3), 163-169.

Freeman, G. T. (2005). The library as place: Changes in learning patterns, collections, technology, and use. In *The library as place: Rethinking roles, rethinking space*. Washington, DC: Council on Library and Information Resources (CLIR Publication No. 129). Retrieved April 25, 2006, from http://www.clir.org/pubs/abstract/pub129abst.html

Gardner, J. N., & Hardesty, L. (2004). The reform movement for the first-year experience: What is the role of librarians? *Library Issues: Briefings for Faculty and Administrators, 24*(5), 1-4.

Habley, W., & McClanahan, R. (2004). *What works in student retention? All survey colleges.* American College Testing. Retrieved April 25, 2006, from http://www.act.org/path/postsec/droptables/pdf/AllColleges.pdf

Heavyrunner, I. (2002). Family education model: Meeting the student retention challenge. *Journal of American Indian Education, 41*(2), 29-37.

Horn, L., Peter, K., & Rooney, K. (2002). *Profile of undergraduates in U.S. postsecondary institutions 1999–2000.* (NCES 2002-168). Washington, DC: U.S. Department of Education, National Center for Education Statistics, U.S. Government Printing Office. Retrieved April 25, 2006, from http://nces.ed.gov/pubsearch/pubsinfo.asp?pubid=2002168

Hurtado, S., & Carter, D. F. (1997). Effects of college transition and perceptions of the campus racial climate on Latino students' sense of belonging. *Sociology of Education, 70*(4), 324-345.

Jalomo, R. E., Jr. (1995). *First-year student experiences in community college: Making transitions, forming connections, and developing perceptions of student learning.* Draft. (ERIC Document Reproduction Service No. ED 387 291)

Jones, L. (2001). Creating an affirming culture to retain African-American students during the postaffirmative action era in higher education. In L. Jones (Ed.), *Retaining African Americans in higher education: Challenging paradigms for retaining students, faculty, & administrators* (pp. 3-20). Sterling, VA: Stylus Publishing.

Kuh, G. D. (2001-2002). Organizational culture and student success: Prospects and puzzles. *Journal of College Student Retention, 3*(1), 223-239.

Kuh, G. D., & Gonyea, R. M. (2003). The role of the academic library in promoting student engagement in learning. *College & Research Libraries, 64*(4), 256-282.

Kuhlthau, C., Turok, B., George, M. W., & Blevin, R. J. (1990). Validating a model of the search process: A comparison of academic, public, and school library users. *Library & Information Science Research, 1*(1), 5-32.

Kunkel, L. R., Weaver, S. M. & Cook, K. N. (1996). What do they know? An assessment of undergraduate library skills. *The Journal of Academic Librarianship, 22*(6), 430-434.

Laughlin, W. (2001). Recruitment of Native Americans: A counselor's perspective. *The Journal of College Admission, 171*, 3-4.

Levitz, R., & Noel, L. (1989). Connecting students to institutions: Keys to retention and success. In M. L. Upcraft, J. N. Gardner, & Associates, *The freshman year experience* (pp. 65-81). San Francisco: Jossey-Bass.

Lotkowski, V. A., Robbins, S. B. & Noeth, R. J. (2004). *The role of academic and non-academic factors in improving college retention.* ACT Policy Report. Iowa City, IA: American College Testing, Inc. Retrieved April 25, 2006, from http://www.act.org/path/policy/pdf/college_retention.pdf

Manuel, K. (2002). Teaching information literacy to generation Y. *Journal of Library Administration, 36*(1/2), 195-217.

McGlynn, A. P. (2004). Nurturing Hispanics to four-year degrees. *Education Digest, 69*(5), 51-56.

Nelson, L. M. (1999). *Increasing retention of adult learners in telecourses through the incorporation of learning-centered instructional strategies and the use of multiple modalities for content delivery and instruction.* EdD Practicum Report, Nova Southeastern University. (ERIC Document Reproduction Service ED 438 469)

O'Brien, B. S., & Renner, A. L. (2002). Online student retention: Can it be done? In *ED-MEDIA 2002 World Conference on Educational Multimedia, Hypermedia, & Telecommunications.* Proceedings, 14th, Denver, CO. (ERIC Document Reproduction Service No. ED 477 076)

O'Brien, E. M. (1992). *American Indians in higher education.* Washington, DC: American Council on Education, Division of Policy Analysis and Research. (ERIC Document Reproduction Service No. ED 387 291)

Pascarella, E. T., & Terenzini, P. T. (1991). *How college affects students.* San Francisco: Jossey-Bass.

The persisting racial gap in college student graduation rates. (2004). *The Journal of Blacks in Higher Education, 45,* 77-85.

Porter, S. R. (2003-2004). Understanding retention outcomes: Using multiple data sources to distinguish between dropouts, stopouts, and transfer-outs. *Journal of College Student Retention, 5*(1), 53-70.

Reitz, J. (2004). *ODLIS: Online dictionary for library and information science.* Libraries Unlimited. Retrieved April 25, 2006, from http://lu.com/odlis

Rendón, L. I. (1995). *Facilitating retention and transfer for first-generation students in community colleges.* Paper presented at the New Mexico Institute, Rural Community College Initiative, Espanola, NM. (ERIC Document Reproduction Service No. ED 383 369)

Rovai, A. P. (2003). In search of higher persistence rates in distance education online programs. *Internet and Higher Education, 6*(1), 1-16.

Somers, P., Cofer, J., Hall, M., & Vander Putten, J. (1999, November). *A comparison of the persistence of African American and White students using NPSAS: 96.* Paper presented at the 24th Annual Meeting of the Association for the Study of Higher Education, San Antonio, TX.

Terenzini, P. T., Rendón, L. I., Upcraft, M. L., Millar, S. B., Allison, K. W., Gregg, P. L., & Jalamo, R. (1994). The transition to college: Diverse students, diverse stories. *Research in Higher Education, 35*(1), 57-73.

Tierney, W. G. (1992). An anthropological analysis of student participation in college. *The Journal of Higher Education, 63*(6), 603-618.

Tierney, W. G. (2000). Power, identity, and the dilemma of college student departure. In J. M. Braxton (Ed.), *Reworking the student departure puzzle* (pp. 213-234). Nashville: Vanderbilt University Press.

Tinto, V. (1993). *Leaving college: Rethinking the causes and cures of student attrition* (2nd ed.). Chicago: University of Chicago Press.

Tinto, V., & Lentz, B. (1986). *Rates of system departure from higher education: 1890-1980.* Paper presented at the Annual Meeting of the American Educational Research Association, San Francisco.

Tweedell, C. B. (2000). *A theory of adult learning and implications for practice.* Paper presented at the annual meeting of the Midwest Educational Research Association, Chicago, IL. (ERIC Document Reproduction Service No. ED 446 702).

Upcraft, M. L. (2005). Assessing the first year of college. In M. L. Upcraft, J. N. Gardner, & B. O. Barefoot (Eds.), *Challenging and supporting the first-year student: A handbook for improving the first year of college* (pp. 469-485). San Francisco: Jossey-Bass.

U. S. Department of Education. (2001). *The condition of education.* Washington, DC: National Center for Education Statistics.

U. S. Department of Labor. (2005). *College enrollment and work activity of 2004 high school graduates.* Washington, DC: Bureau of Labor Statistics. Retrieved April 25, 2006, from http://www.bls.gov/news.release/hsgec.toc.htm

Van Gennep, A. (1960). *The rites of passage.* (M. Vizedon and G. Caffee, Trans.). Chicago: University of Chicago Press. (Original work published 1909).

Wonacott, M. E. (2001). *Adult students: Recruitment and retention* (Practice Application Brief No. 18). Columbus, OH: ERIC Clearinghouse on Adult, Career, and Vocational Education (ERIC Document Reproduction Service No. ED 457 405)

Workman, J. J., & Stenard, R. A. (1996). Student support services for distance learners. *DEOSNEWS, 6.* Retrieved April 25, 2006, from http://www.ed.psu.edu/acsde/deos/deosnews/deosnews6_3.asp

Chapter 12

The Convergence of Information Literacy and the First-Year Experience: Looking to the Future

Larry L. Hardesty

At the risk of stating the obvious, this monograph is neither the first nor the last word on teaching information literacy skills in the first college year. It examines the association between two movements—the first-year experience and information literacy—without tracing either back to their origins. The modern development of both library instruction (which has evolved into the teaching of information literacy) and the first-year experience dates back to the 1970s, and both, as pointed out elsewhere in this monograph, have their antecedents much further back in the history of higher education. Separately, the movements have accomplished a great deal in the past three decades and are early in their exploration of a common purpose. So, as we look to the immediate future, it is difficult to predict with certainty where the relationship between these two movements is headed and what shape their convergence might take.

With that in mind, the goal of this monograph is to advance the convergence of these two movements so they can, working together, more readily facilitate the academic success of first-year students. It does so by describing and analyzing the current situation from the perspective of librarians, classroom faculty members, administrators, and researchers. In addition, it provides practical information through case studies written jointly by librarians and classroom faculty members that illustrate and, hopefully, facilitate collaborative efforts.

Challenges

In 2006, progress toward this convergence has been uneven. As Kirk's (chapter 1) analysis of the recent history of information literacy standards suggests, the theoretical framework for understanding information literacy is far ahead of the implementation of programs that successfully teach information literacy. At the same time, there is a growing awareness outside the library profession (see Gardner & Koch's preface; Kuh, Boruff-Jones, & Mark, chapter 2) of the importance of students' developing information literacy skills early in their academic careers. However, as Boff and Johnson (chapter 5) conclude, based on their national study of first-year seminar courses, these efforts have not always been well implemented. Further, in developing this monograph, I found it challenging to locate examples of library initiatives in the first college year that exhibited mature efforts (i.e., long-running programs with strong, widespread institutional support and evidence of sophisticated evaluations and assessments). While I did not exhaust all possibilities in seeking exemplary programs, I believe my failure to identify such programs at a variety of institutions reflects the current situation of information literacy in the first year of college.

There are, to be sure, some substantial efforts, as indicated by the results of the two national surveys included in this work (Johnson & Boff; Malone & Videon, chapter 4) and the description of the California State University experiences (Rockman, chapter 6). There are also efforts that go back many years, such as those at Dickinson College (Bombaro & Stachacz, case study 1) and Earlham College (Baker & Kirk, case study 9). However, most of the efforts described in this monograph go back only a few years. I received numerous proposals for contributions that described in glowing terms programs in their first or second years. This may indicate an increasing number of recent efforts, but these efforts have not stood the test of time in terms of either institutional acceptance or rigorous evaluation. While there is evidence of increased and successful involvement of the library in the first-year experience, the effort is far from mature.

Therefore, while there appears to be an interest among enthusiasts from both movements for closer convergence, the fledgling status of most current efforts prevents any predictions about their long-term success. In fact, the individual histories of these movements suggest anything but a sure, clear path to success. Gardner and Koch pointed out the waning of the first-year orientation seminars in the 1930s. A similar waning in library-instruction efforts also occurred earlier in its history, particularly in the post-World War II period as the number of students simply overwhelmed many of the even well-established programs (Erickson, 1949). By the late 1960s, Phipps' (1968) investigation into librarians' involvement in user instruction found them frustrated, disappointed, and demoralized because of "lack of staff, lack of time, lack of money for experimentation, lack of cooperation and interest from the faculty and the administration" (pp. 411-412). Kirk (1977) has provided a cogent analysis of the earlier programs and their failure to thrive, and we, perhaps, can learn from them. Nevertheless, the problems discovered by Phipps almost 40 years ago are, no doubt, quite familiar to librarians now involved with information literacy efforts and the first-year experience. They are, in fact, well-documented in this monograph. One thing we can learn with certainty from past efforts is that the successful convergence of information literacy and the first-year experience is not predetermined. Nevertheless, this monograph provides some promising examples from which the readers can glean useful information to apply to their situations.

Elements of Successful Programs

Close Collaboration Among Librarians, Classroom Faculty Members, and Others

Establishment of successful programs requires a long-term effort with constant vigilance and study. Even when information literacy programs are well established, such as at Earlham College, changes in technology, styles of teaching, faculty composition, and the curriculum can necessitate considerable flexibility, political acumen, and assertiveness on the part of librarians. Close collaboration with classroom faculty members is essential, as evidenced at numerous institutions. Kirk (2002) reported on the quality of collaborations between classroom faculty and librarians as the primary predictor of success in information literacy programs. Mutual trust, respect, and sharing of common goals between librarians and classroom faculty are obviously basic to the establishment and long-term success of information literacy programs. Therefore, several of the contributors describe the extensive efforts librarians make in involving classroom faculty. Contacts are made early in course development, workshops are offered, grants provided, stipends awarded, and other inducements used, including free meals. Other groups and individuals are also important. IUPUI, for example, developed the concept of instructional teams that include, in addition to classroom faculty members and librarians, academic advisors and student peer mentors. At Wartburg College (see case study 5), the president provided an impetus for an information literacy program by announcing "all Wartburg College students will be information literate upon graduation" (Vogel, 1997).

Innovative Staffing Patterns

Obviously, information literacy programs are labor-intensive enterprises. The continued cultivation and renewal of positive collaborative relationships is time-consuming. Once a program is established, additional time is needed for librarians to prepare and provide instruction, and then follow up with evaluation and application of that evaluation. One might readily expect staffing challenges at large institutions, such as at IUPUI where burnout among librarians became a serious threat. Yet, even at small colleges (e.g., Macalester College, case study 4; York College of Pennsylvania, chapter 4; and Grinnell College, case study 8), contributors reported significant staffing challenges.

In response to these challenges, some institutions reported implementing new staffing patterns. For example, York College of Pennsylvania (see Malone & Videon, chapter 4), which has provided a stand-alone information literacy course for more than 10 years, has upgraded all the clerical staff to administrative status as they assumed responsibilities once held by librarians and technicians. This has allowed librarians to be more involved in teaching library skills. IUPUI (Orme & Jackson, case study 3) moved away from traditional departmental divisions and created a team-based configuration, including instructional teams. Some academic libraries have employed librarians with specific responsibilities for the library's role in the first-year experience. While academic libraries may experiment more with staffing patterns in the future, to date, the efforts have been fairly modest and not widely adopted.

Creative Use of Technology

The overarching question about the role of technology in information literacy is, how can it be used to revolutionize and expand the efforts of librarians teaching students information literacy skills. Several institutions in this monograph reported exploring innovative instructional methods involving technology to alleviate staffing challenges and to assist in teaching information literacy. Certainly, during the past 10 to 15 years, technology has revolutionized how libraries provide information. Yet, historically, the use of technology to address inadequate staffing and resources in teaching students how to use the library has had mixed results (Givens, 1974). Nevertheless, unlike earlier technologies (e.g., transparencies, slide-tapes, videos, films), the computer offers ways to engage students actively in the learning process. The cases presented in this monograph highlight lab-based models, wired classrooms, and web-based instructional guides. Lab-based models and wired classrooms offer opportunities to move beyond "show and tell" demonstrations to involve students in hands-on, interactive learning experiences. Web-based tutorials offer the opportunity to reach large numbers of students. Generally, technology has been used to expand the efforts of librarians beyond face-to-face classroom instruction and to overcome staffing deficiencies.

Still, much of the successful use of technology depends on the cooperation between librarians and classroom faculty. The most sophisticated hands-on experience may not overcome student apathy if students do not see the relevance to course assignments. Without classroom faculty support, even the best-developed, computer-based information literacy tutorial can languish unused (see Chu, case study 11). In some ways, technology can be a distraction from developing sophisticated information literacy skills. Oseguera (chapter 3) suggests that the ease with which students can retrieve information from the Internet may give them a misplaced confidence in their ability to analyze and use that information effectively. In other cases, students may use the Internet for recreational purposes with little educational value. Technology, if it is to be used successfully, must be carefully incorporated into the learning process, not as a goal unto itself, but as an avenue to facilitate the achievement of educational goals.

Recommendations

Increased and More Sophisticated Assessment Efforts

To date, most institutional information literacy assessment efforts have also been relatively modest and have dealt largely with student satisfaction. Useful to a degree, satisfaction surveys are sometimes suspect because they are skewed toward the positive. More important, satisfaction surveys are subjective measures that deal largely with students' immediate response to the instructional experience. They are not objective measures of short- or long-term learning. More promising are recent efforts highlighted by Kirk (chapter 1). These include the use of the *Information Literacy Competency Standards for Higher Education*, Project SAILS, ACRL's efforts to get information literacy represented in such national surveys as CSEQ and NSSE, and the development of Information and Communications Technology (ICT) Information and Communication Technology Literacy Assessment.

While assessment has long been a concern of librarians involved in instruction (Association of College and Research Libraries, 2006; Hardesty, Lovrich, & Mannon, 1979, 1982; Maki, 2002; Maughan, 2001; Meulemans, 2002; Riddle & Hartman, 2000), the challenges of finding time, getting access to students, developing appropriate methodologies, and successfully using the results continue to be impediments to examining the outcomes of instruction. Nevertheless, there is no shortage of the need for further evaluation efforts.

Increased Basic Research

Oseguera's report on data from the Higher Education Research Institute raises several questions worthy of further research. We really know little about how students perceive information literacy, how their cognitive development impacts their progress in becoming information literate, and the long-term impact of information literacy on academic success and retention. The pioneering works of Mellon (1986) on library anxiety and of Kuhlthau (1991) on students' information-seeking behavior need further exploration to improve our understanding of student behavior and attitudes toward information literacy.

Such large-scale national studies are of tremendous value and importance, but campus-based research efforts also can provide important insights into the factors supporting information literacy efforts in specific contexts. For example, Knapp's (1964) sociological and anthropological study of efforts to implement a library-instruction program in the Monteith College of Wayne State University in the early 1960s provided keen insight into the attitudes of faculty members and students. It remains, more than 40 years later, a "must read" for anyone involved in information literacy efforts. More of these large-scale, national and individual, campus-based studies are needed.

Increased Awareness of Methods to Promote Information Literacy Programs in the First-Year Experience

As described in the Macalester College case study (Fishel, Hillemann, & Beccone, case study 4), librarians have to make an intentional effort to become change agents in promoting information literacy. In order for librarians and others to become successful change agents, they must become familiar with the diffusion and adoption of innovation literature from sociology and education. For example, Rogers' (1962) classic, now in its fifth edition, *Diffusion of*

Innovations, provides a conceptual framework for understanding the diffusion and adoption of ideas and their implementation. Such an understanding coupled with case studies exploring dynamics of establishing information literacy programs in the first college year are critical if these innovations are to become permanent fixtures in higher education.

Increased Collaboration With Others in Higher Education

There is evidence, as indicated in this monograph, of increasing acceptance of a role for information literacy in the first-year experience by accreditation agencies, senior administrators, and classroom faculty members. This does not mean the perennial challenges of lack of time, money, mutual goals, and expertise do not remain as substantial impediments to the development of mature programs. In his contribution, Kirk put forth a provocative call for ACRL to join with other higher education associations to provide a mechanism for addressing a wide range of information literacy issues. In many ways, information literacy is too important to be left to librarians. While the efforts will not succeed without librarians, the efforts cannot succeed if only librarians are involved. Librarians need the support, perspectives, collaboration, and cooperation of numerous other groups, including classroom faculty members, administrators, student affairs personnel, accreditation agencies, and professional associations.

Establishment of a National Center on Information Literacy

I will be bold enough to expand on Kirk's call. I have been very impressed by the individuals involved with the National Resource Center for The First-Year Experience and Students in Transition (http://www.sc.edu/fye/) and their role in promoting positive experiences for first-year students. I would suggest that ACRL look specifically at the National Resource Center as a model to emulate. Within the library profession, ACRL's Institute for Information Literacy (http://www.ala.org/ala/acrl/acrlissues/acrlinfolit/professactivity/iil/welcome.htm) and the National Forum on Information Literacy (http://www.infolit.org/activities.html) serve very important roles. However, both efforts are largely carried out by volunteers with other responsibilities and very limited resources. A key element in the success of the National Resource Center has been a staff dedicated to identifying, conducting, and facilitating research and assessment of student transition issues and disseminating the results of this research through conferences and publications. I believe ACRL would do well to adopt a model with similar practices and staffing patterns to promote information literacy efforts in the first-year experience. The joint distribution of this book by both organizations is one modest initial step in that direction.

Through either a separate National Center for Information Literacy or as part of the ACRL Institute for Information Literacy, ACRL could provide much-needed on-site assistance to individuals seeking to establish and evaluate information literacy programs at individual institutions. Too often, librarians in the trenches are so involved in day-to-day information literacy efforts that they do not have time to analyze current practice, identify goals for the future, plan how to achieve those goals, and assess those efforts. Such assistance would fill an important need—a critical need that must be met if information literacy is to move steadily forward. Despite the progress made to date, it still remains on an unsteady foundation at many institutions.

Conclusions

I am optimistic about the successful convergence of information literacy with the first-year experience movement. I believe most of the participants in both movements have primarily the interests of students in mind, and they share an overlapping goal—the immediate and long-term success of first-year students. While we are only midcourse and the future is uncertain,

I hope this monograph provides the impetus for increased collaboration between librarians and those involved in the first-year experience. I share the late Ilene Rockman's optimism (to whom I have dedicated this book), "The future looks promising." However, it is only promising if we continue to work with the dedication and tireless efforts that Ilene exhibited in her pursuit to develop needed information literacy skills in our students. With such efforts, perhaps within a decade, someone can publish a follow-up monograph describing an abundance of mature first-year experience information literacy programs in a wide range of institutions.

References

Association of College and Research Libraries. (2006). *Research agenda for library instruction and information literacy.* Instruction Section, Research and Scholarship Committee. Retrieved August 20, 2006, from http://www.ala.org/ala/acrlbucket/is/iscommittees/webpages/research/researchagendalibrary.htm

Erickson, E. F. (1949). Library instruction in the freshman orientation program. *College & Research Libraries, 10,* 445-448.

Givens, J. (1974). The use of resources in the learning experience. In M. J. Voight (Ed.), *Advances in librarianship* (Vol. 4, pp. 160-164). New York: Academic Press.

Hardesty, L., Lovrich, N. P., & Mannon, J. (1979). Evaluating library-user instruction. *College & Research Libraries, 40*(4), 309-317.

Hardesty, L., Lovrich, N. P., & Mannon, J. (1982). Library-use instruction: Assessment of the long-term effects. *College & Research Libraries, 43*(1), 38-46.

Kirk, T. G. (1977). Past, present, and future of library instruction. *Southeastern Librarian, 27,* 15-18.

Kirk, T. G. (2002, June 11-13). Unpublished notes from ACRL Institute for Information Literacy's Best Practices project conference, Atlanta, GA.

Kuhlthau. C. C. (1991). Inside the search process: Information-seeking from the user's perspective. *Journal of the American Society for Information Science, 42*(5), 361-371.

Knapp, P. B. (1964) The methodology and results of the Monteith pilot project. *Library Trends, 13*(1), 84-102.

Maki, P. L. (2002). Developing an assessment plan to learn about student learning. *The Journal of Academic Librarianship, 28*(1/2), 8-13.

Maughan, P. D. (2001). Assessing information literacy among undergraduates: A discussion of the literature and the University of California-Berkeley assessment experience. *College & Research Libraries,* 62(1), 71-77.

Mellon, D. A. (1986). Library anxiety: A grounded theory and its development. *College & Research Libraries,* 47(2), 160-165.

Meulemans, Y. N. (2002). Assessment city: The past, present, and future state of information literacy assessment. *College & Undergraduate Libraries,* 9(2), 61-74.

Phipps, B. H. (1968). Library instruction for the undergraduate. *College & Research Libraries,* 29(5), 411-423.

Riddle, J. S., & Hartman, K. A. (2000). "But are they learning anything?" Designing an assessment of first-year library instruction at the College of New Jersey. *College & Undergraduate Libraries, 7*(2), 59-69.

Rogers, E. M. (1962). *Diffusion of innovations.* New York: The Free Press.

Vogel, R. (1997, November 13). *Wartburg College faculty meeting minutes.* Waverly, IA: Wartburg College.

SECTION 4

Campus Case Studies

Case Study 1

The Library and the First-Year Experience Over Time at Dickinson College

Christine Bombaro & John C. Stachacz

Institutional Description

Dickinson College, a small liberal arts college in Carlisle, Pennsylvania, was founded in 1783 with a mission to disseminate and promote the growth of useful knowledge (Gerencser & Osborne, 2002). In the continued fulfillment of that mandate, Dickinson initiated a required research and writing seminar program for first-year students in the fall of 1981. An essential component of this successful seminar program is required library instruction. Dickinson's program is among the oldest, continuously running programs for first-year students in undergraduate academia in the United States.

The first-year seminar experience at Dickinson has necessarily evolved and changed over the years, particularly with the constant introduction of new classroom and database technologies. Despite some challenges, including the steady growth in size of the first-year classes, the College's administration continues to support and promote the library-instruction element of the program as an integral link to the first-year students' success throughout their liberal arts education and beyond. The library-instruction program at Dickinson College has existed for more than a quarter of a century due to the unequivocal support of the administration, the collaborative efforts of the faculty and librarians to make the program challenging and meaningful, the constant examination of the outcomes of the library component, and the positive effects the program has had on the students.

Dickinson College enrolls approximately 2,000 full-time students and employs approximately 200 faculty members. The size of the first-year class ranges between 480 and 650 traditional-aged students each year. The College offers between 36 and 42 first-year seminars each fall, with no more than 17 first-year students enrolled in each seminar. A representative number of faculty members from all three educational divisions—the humanities, social sciences, and natural sciences—is required to participate in the seminar program each year. Because the seminars do not have a common theme, the subject content varies from seminar to seminar.

To enhance communication between the librarians and faculty members, each academic department is assigned a library liaison for research help, collection development, and to assist in teaching information literacy. As an extension of the library liaison program, the librarians divide the first-year seminars among themselves and assume responsibility for teaching the information literacy sessions for the classes they choose. Usually, but not necessarily, the librarians will choose to work with faculty members from departments to which they are already assigned as liaisons. At the inception of the first-year seminar program, Dickinson College employed eight librarians who participated in teaching the library-instruction component. Each librarian was required to work with four or five seminars. A restructuring of the library's organization in 2003 resulted in a reduction of the liaison staff. Since then, four librarians have been responsible for teaching the library component of 8 to 10 first-year seminars.

History of the Library Component in the First-Year Seminars

The idea that first-year students should be required to participate in a class designed to teach research strategies and library skills began to take shape in the late 1960s. The current first-year seminar program had two precursors, Humanities 101, offered from 1968 through 1978, and the Nisbet Scholars Program, offered from 1978 through 1989. Humanities 101, an "interdisciplinary examination of Western literacy," (Dickinson College, 1970-1972), was an elective course for first-year students only, co-taught by librarians and faculty members. The course's format included discussion, small-group work, and writing assignments. These activities highlighted the need for early instruction in library research, leading to the development of the Nisbet Scholars Program, a selective, intense four-year program designed as "an alternative to . . . graduation requirements" (Dickinson College, 1978-1980). The Nisbet Scholars Program consisted largely of a four-year plan of independent research, which began with a seminar focused on research and writing skills. Librarians participated in the Nisbet program by teaching some of the seminars and providing at least one library-instruction session for each seminar.

In the late 1970s, the faculty started discussing the idea of creating a first-year program that would include all first-year students. In 1978, the Department of Library Resources, now called Library and Information Services (LIS), presented a formal memo in support of this endeavor to Dickinson College's administration. In their "Position Paper for Requiring Instruction to Insure That All Freshmen Possess Minimal Library Skills," the Department of Library Resources advised:

> Library instruction should be a part of a course or courses [for] all freshmen [and] should include: 1) information on library reference works and research strategies, 2) assignments in library use which are integrated into the process of preparing course required research papers, 3) a provision for testing out of the program early in the year, 4) a means for enforcement of this college requirement. (Department of Library Resources, 1978)

Shortly after the department submitted this memo to the Academic Program Committee (APC), the College administration, faculty, and librarians organized a retreat, during which they designed the basic structure of the current first-year seminar program.

To the dismay of the librarians, however, the earliest proposals did not include mandatory library instruction. This omission prompted the College's archivist, then a standing member of the APC, to draft a memo to the committee clarifying what the librarians meant when they recommended the inclusion of library instruction in the first-year seminar curriculum. The library session she proposed would "include a class assignment integral to the class' other work which will be a required part of the course, though evaluated by the librarian" (Slotten, 1979). Upon reviewing this memo, the APC further recommended that library instruction "be tied into the subject matter of the freshman seminars" (Committee on Academic Programs, 1979).

The faculty voted on a proposal to create the first-year seminar program at Dickinson College during a faculty meeting in May 1980 and "concluded that a freshman seminar program is both desirable and within the College's capabilities" (Dickinson College Faculty, 1980). The seminars became a graduation requirement for all students who entered the College as first-year students. The classes were to emphasize on an individual level the importance of critical thinking, writing, group discussion, presentation, and library research skills and were to have a small enrollment (no more than 16 students in each class). In fall 1981, Dickinson College first required new students to take a first-year seminar, where librarians delivered library instruction at least once to each seminar.

Assessing the Library Component of the First-Year Seminars

At the conclusion of the fall semester of 1981, the librarians immediately conducted a brief survey of students who had taken a first-year seminar to determine the effectiveness of the library instruction. About 95% of the first-year students who entered Dickinson College that fall reported having had "some experience or introduction to [the] library and ha[ving] met a librarian" (Bechtel, 1982). The survey also compared the type of library instruction that students received in different seminars. Some of the librarians had developed their instructions around course-based assignments, while others offered a more general introduction to the library. In evaluating the library-instruction portion of the seminar, librarians and faculty members "independently concluded that while the general introduction is useful, the library projects that contributed to the course content and were important to the progress of the course were the most successful," and that "[i]nstruction conducted in the library rather than in the classroom was more effective" (Bechtel).

The administration of Dickinson College planned to conduct the first formal evaluation of the first-year seminar program between 1983 and 1984. However, between the inception of the first-year seminar and the completion of this first evaluation, librarians began to notice a shift in the way students were using the library. In a report from the library staff following the first semester in which the College required first-year seminars, the librarians described

> a dramatic change in library usage following the introduction of the seminar program. Now the library is used more heavily in the fall than in the spring, and this high use begins immediately upon the opening of the academic year. Before freshman seminars, the second semester had seen the heaviest library use, and in the fall heavy use did not begin until after the middle of the semester. (General Education Committee, 1989)[1]

The librarians viewed the shift in library usage as significant. They concluded that students were becoming familiar with the library's resources earlier in their academic careers and that they saw value in using the library to complete their assignments.

The assistant dean and the librarian who was an ex-officio member of the APC led a formal evaluation of the first-year seminar program during the 1983-1984 academic year. The evaluators invited faculty members and students to comment on the library component of the seminar experience. A frequently mentioned problem on the evaluations was one that the librarians had already acknowledged: Some students received only a general introduction to the library while others received instruction directly related to course projects. This inconsistency prompted the faculty to request, and the College to require, that all seminar instructors participate in a "more stimulating faculty orientation" before the beginning of the fall semester (General Education Committee, 1989).

In order to improve the first-year seminar, the librarians continued to lobby the APC and the General Education Committee to clarify and make consistent the requirements of the research component. As a result, the APC voted in 1984 to include in each seminar "at least one project based upon library research which aims to define and focus a topic, to enable students to discover what has been said on a subject, and to enter a conversation on that topic through writing or discussion" (General Education Committee, 1989). Both students and faculty members deemed instruction integrally related to an assignment as the most successful type of instruction (Bechtel, 1982). Students reported that practicing library skills after an instruction session was useful not only for assignments in their first-year seminar, but also in completing projects for other classes. The librarians further recommended that faculty members be present at the library-instruction sessions. Not only did the presence of the faculty members emphasize the importance of the instruction, but it also gave students the opportunity to witness the librarian and the faculty members discuss various research options and strategies. With the implementation of improvements to the first-year seminar program as a whole, as well as the recommended changes to the library component, the APC voted in 1984 to continue the program into the future (General Education Committee).

During the 1988-1989 academic year, the General Education Committee conducted a second large-scale evaluation of students who had participated in the first-year seminar. The evaluators randomly selected 25% of the students who had been enrolled in first-year seminars in any of the previous three academic years and asked them to complete evaluation forms about the program. Students who participated in the survey reported that they found the research and writing aspects of the program to be very important to their college experience. Some of the students reported being surprised at the challenges they faced while completing their research-based assignments and thought it would be helpful to future students if more library projects were integrated into the seminars (General Education Committee, 1989).

In addition to these college-wide evaluations of the first-year seminars, the librarians have conducted brief, informal annual surveys to examine the effectiveness of the library-instruction component. Students have been asked such questions as what new concepts they learned from the librarian, in what ways they thought the instruction would be helpful to them, and whether they thought that additional library sessions in other classes would be useful for other class assignments. Librarians have been using this information to assess the effectiveness of the librarian and the relevancy of their instructions. The librarians also use this feedback to plan information literacy sessions throughout the curriculum so as not to repeat concepts as they work with higher-level classes within each major field of study.

Implementation and Impact of First-Year Library Instruction

The librarians and faculty members who envisioned and designed the library component of the first-year seminar never intended the instruction to be a generic overview of the library but rather an introduction to the basic research skills that are important in beginning any academic inquiry. Since the purpose of the seminar is to orient first-year students to the liberal arts, content is less important than teaching them to think critically, write well, enhance their speaking skills, and conduct research. The content of each first-year library instruction is tailored to the individual seminar topics, which have included such diverse themes as "food and wine," "war and peace," and "literature and film." The role of the librarian in the first-year seminar is to begin the students' education in information literacy in a way that flows seamlessly from the content of the seminar. The librarian may, for example, lead the seminar toward a subject-specific database and focused reference materials, while also introducing the library catalog and general-purpose databases covering a broad range of subject areas. The library session is adapted to each seminar to provide students the knowledge and skills needed to complete an assignment successfully, such as an annotated bibliography, a biography assignment, or a short research paper. At Dickinson, the faculty member and the librarian often collaborate to design such assignments.

The librarian's partnership with the faculty member ensures that the course is relevant and that it meets the needs of the students and the requirements of the first-year seminar. At the same time, this allows the librarian to contribute his or her expertise to the research experience by choosing appropriate resources and teaching their use at a level appropriate to first-year students. Additionally, the frequent contact that the librarians have with these small classes allows them to develop individual working relationships with students that are often sustained throughout their careers at Dickinson.

Longevity of Library Instruction

Numerous crucial factors contribute directly to the longevity of the mandatory library-instruction program at Dickinson College. These factors include the clearly articulated goals of library instruction, the willingness of the librarians to adapt instruction to each individual seminar, close collaboration between faculty members and librarians, the unequivocal support and interest of the College's administration, and the librarians' direct involvement with campus governance. Because of the constant vigilance and ongoing study, the library component of the first-year seminar at Dickinson College has necessarily changed over the course of its long history. Librarians made changes partially in response to formal studies conducted by academic committees, partially in response to the less formal feedback received from first-year students and faculty members at the conclusion of the fall semester, and partially as a result of the new technologies that Dickinson and other academic institutions and their libraries are continually acquiring.

Each year, Dickinson College librarians re-examine the content and delivery of the first-year seminars. This usually begins in the summer, often immediately after graduation. The librarians also participate in the annual workshop designed to help faculty members who will be participating in the first-year seminar program to accomplish the goals of the program. These sessions give the librarians an opportunity to meet with the participating faculty members and inform them about the library's services early in the process, usually before the faculty members set their syllabus and assignments. Throughout the summer, the librarians and faculty members often meet to discuss the particulars of library instruction and to create appropriate and challenging assignments.

The longevity of the first-year seminar is also due to the fact that, after 25 years, the faculty members have come to expect a certain level of participation by the librarians. Each seminar class is required to visit the library at least once during the fall semester (General Education Committee, 1989). However, it has not been unusual for seminar classes to meet their librarian as a group multiple times or for the librarians to schedule individual consultations with students as necessary. In 2005, the Academic Programs and Standards Committee (APSC) recommended and the Dickinson College faculty approved a motion to make it a requirement for each first-year seminar to visit the library at least twice. The content of second session, which may be decided upon between the faculty member and the librarian, may include evaluating Internet resources, in-depth training on effective search strategies, creating appropriate citations, and using primary resources.

Conclusion

Information literacy sessions have been integrated into first-year seminars at Dickinson College since their inception in 1981, although information literacy had become part of the curriculum in an unofficial manner many years before that. Through their experimental integration of library instruction in courses such as Humanities 101 and the Nisbet Scholars Program, the library staff proved to the Dickinson faculty and administration the necessity and significance of information literacy and that such training upheld the mission of the College. The proactive approach the library staff took in lobbying the appropriate committees that created the program is the main reason for the inclusion of library instruction in first-year seminars. Ongoing assessment of the program and constant dialogue with administrators and faculty members nurtures and secures the important role that library instruction in general plays at the College. They are the prime reasons for the longevity of librarians' involvement with the first-year seminar program. By keeping the program fresh and modern through innovation, and by being open to new ideas and practices, an important continual library presence in the first-year seminars at Dickinson College is ensured.

Notes

[1]The General Education Committee memo of 1989 quotes the results of studies conducted on the first-year seminars during 1983 and 1984. The original documentation of those earlier studies has been lost.

References

Academic Programs and Standards Committee. (2005). *Resolution to approve the expectations for first-year seminars.* Carlisle, PA: Dickinson College, Archives & Special Collections.

Bechtel, J. (1982). *Evaluation of the library component in freshman seminars. Carlisle*, PA: Dickinson College, Archives & Special Collections.

Committee on Academic Programs. (1979). *Minutes of the meeting of the college.* Carlisle, PA: Dickinson College, Archives & Special Collections.

Department of Library Resources. (1978). *Position paper for requiring instruction to insure that all freshmen possess minimal library skills.* Carlisle, PA: Dickinson College, Archives & Special Collections.

Dickinson College. (1970-1972). *Bulletin, 61*(9). Carlisle, PA: Dickinson College, Archives & Special Collections.

Dickinson College. (1978-1980). *Catalogue.* Carlisle, PA: Dickinson College, Archives & Special Collections.

Dickinson College Faculty. (1980). *Minutes of the faculty meeting.* Carlisle, PA: Dickinson College, Archives & Special Collections.

General Education Committee. (1989). *Memo regarding the evaluation of freshman seminars.* Carlisle, PA: Dickinson College, Archives & Special Collections.

Gerencser, J. W., & Osborne, J. M. (Eds). (2002). The charter of Dickinson College - 1783. *Encyclopedia Dickinsonia.* Retrieved August 22, 2005, from http://chronicles.dickinson.edu/archives/charter_orig/

Slotten, M. (1979). *Memo to the Academic Program Committee.* Carlisle, PA: Dickinson College, Archives & Special Collections.

Case Study 2

Collaborative Curriculum Building at Millikin University: The Critical Role of Faculty/Librarian Collaboration

Susan Avery & Nancy DeJoy

Institutional Description

Millikin University, established in 1901 in Decatur, Illinois, is a comprehensive private university with schools of Arts and Science, Nursing, Fine Arts, and Business. It has a student body of 2,400 students, 140 full-time faculty, and an average class size of 23 students. The first-year class averages 650 students. Millikin University has five librarians, and all but one (i.e., the University Librarian) provide library instruction.

Program History

In 1995, Millikin's faculty voted in a new "Program of Student Learning" that included a series of sequential interdepartmental (IN) courses that form the core of a shared curriculum for all undergraduate students. All students take IN 150 and IN 151, Critical Writing, Reading, and Research (CWRR) I and II, in their first two semesters. The new curriculum replaced a one-credit required course titled "Library Research Methods" and integrated library studies into the first-year writing, reading, and research courses.

IN 150 concentrates on introducing students to generative and analytic practices that help them meet faculty expectations for college-level writing. For example, students learn how to evaluate argumentative texts by examining their structures and the contexts within which they emerge. This practice of critical reading helps students judge the ways that external matters affect the authority of particular pieces of discourse. Students are also introduced to a variety of invention, arrangement, and revision strategies that encourage them to create increasingly sophisticated pieces of academic prose. In the second course in the sequence, IN 151, students study and practice a variety of research methods as they create an original piece of academic research.

Piloting the New Program

During the pilot year of the IN 150 and 151 courses, a committee of English faculty members worked together to create shared goals, expectations, and grading guidelines for the courses. The director of the program also invited a research librarian to join the committee so the library components would be integral in the development of shared goals and expectations for the two courses. This approach enhanced the perception among committee and program faculty members that library components are central to the courses. This integrated approach allowed the committee members to shape the courses in new ways, to think specifically about the integration of library skills related to these courses, and to continue to provide assurance to the faculty at large that a core set of research skills would be taught to all students. Further, the integration allowed assessment of the effectiveness of the library components of the course as well as the effectiveness of the relationship between those components and more general course goals. In fact, discussions of needed changes in the library components of the two courses have often initiated more general revisions to the curriculum.

Faculty had been resistant to the curricular changes in the first-year program, but the librarians' quick and direct response to the changing needs of faculty and students in the first-year writing program inspired faculty to give the program a new chance in their classrooms. This significantly benefited the program, which had considerable faculty turnover for the first five years of its existence. The work faculty and librarians have done each year to maintain the integrity of the relationship between library components of the course and the critical writing, reading, and researching goals has helped maintain consistency across sections of the course and initiate discussions about changes needed to improve the program.

Building the Curriculum

The initial steps in building information literacy into the curriculum presented some challenges, in part due to the differences in the cultures commonly associated with classroom faculty and librarians. Classroom faculty members most often work autonomously, while librarians are accustomed to working collaboratively. Merging these two cultures would be crucial to the success of the information literacy initiative in the first-year writing program.

The librarians confronted the difficult situation of identifying what aspects of the previous stand-alone course should be included in the new courses. They identified an abbreviated set of goals and objectives from the original "Library Research Methods" course, and the CWRR program director determined that librarians would teach three class sessions for IN 150 and two for IN 151. For the first year of the new program, librarians taught these sessions when the sessions best fit individual faculty members' schedules. The librarians prepared generic instruction sessions and follow-up assignments they used in all course sections. However, the librarians and the program director identified a problem: Students failed to see the relevance of the generic assignments in each individual course section, which, in turn, hindered the growth of a community of learners (students and faculty) with a shared research vocabulary.

Focusing on Common Goals

Librarians recognized that identifying common goals across the CWRR courses and for the related library instruction was an essential task in building successful collaborations among those responsible for the classes. While creating shared goals, librarians and CWRR faculty discovered they already had many of the same instructional goals for the first-year students, but needed a shared vocabulary for naming those goals.

A meeting of the instruction librarians and CWRR faculty facilitated by the director of the CWRR program provided another major step in sustaining the success of the collaboration. This meeting focused on the common research and information literacy goals shared by librarians and classroom faculty. In many ways, it served as a turning point in the integration of information literacy into the CWRR curriculum. We cannot emphasize strongly enough the importance of identifying common goals as a starting point for collaboration. The process served as an opportunity to open a continuing dialogue about the specific content and actual placement of the library-instruction sessions in IN 150 and IN 151. These goals included:

- Developing research questions and a subsequent search strategy
- Successfully retrieving relevant information
- Successfully evaluating information for academic content

Although identification of common goals served as a crucial first step in creating effective assignments, further revisions have been particularly important in establishing the relevancy of the library instruction in meaningful ways for students. From the perspective of the librarians, the generic assignments used in the initial integration had failed to elicit satisfactory efforts by many of the first-year students. Redesigning library instruction to integrate it with course assignments and to connect them directly to the course syllabus became an obvious step in creating relevance for the students. It also required an increased level of communication between classroom faculty and librarians, thereby encouraging classroom faculty members to request library-instruction sessions in a more timely manner each semester. The logistical components of the integration became easier and more effective once faculty understood the importance of discussing the library components with librarians before the start of classes.

Continuing the Dialogue

An initial meeting of CWRR faculty and librarians early in the fourth year of the program led to the inclusion of instruction librarians at monthly CWRR faculty meetings. This change became another factor in the growing success of the program. The meetings provide a valuable forum for discussing information literacy integration and for continuing the dialogue regarding both placement of library instruction and relevance of the assignments associated with this instruction. This more inclusive involvement, moving beyond the program coordinators and including all classroom faculty and librarians, has resulted in major changes to the program.

In addition to facilitating the integration of the information literacy instruction, the program coordinators serve as resources for other classroom faculty and librarians teaching the course. This includes taking the lead in curricular changes and design of information literacy-based assignments and serving as intermediaries when instructional issues arise. Collaboration between the director of the CWRR program and the library instruction coordinator facilitates the annual assessment of the role of the library instruction in the course. By becoming partners in the classroom, and by including classroom faculty in discussions regarding the role of integrated library instruction in the program, directors can address concerns related to the specifics of the integration of the library instruction on multiple levels: experientially, programmatically, and conceptually. This collaboration has allowed the librarians to create assignments that, while reflecting the general program goals, are relevant and meaningful to the content of each individual course section.

Assessing the Integration's Success

We have used several approaches to assess library instruction in the CWRR courses at Millikin University. The quantitative and qualitative assessments have focused on evaluating the effectiveness of the assignments themselves and the placement of the library components in the course. For example, librarians reviewed generic assignments used during the first two years of the program and assigned points based on the identification of specific criteria in each student's completed assignments. These criteria included items such as (a) identification of appropriate keywords from a search statement, (b) selection of an appropriate database for the topic, (c) subsequent identification of appropriate controlled vocabulary in initial searches (e.g., noting the subject terminology and expected punctuation in each database), and (d) selection of relevant articles from the search results (see the Appendix for assignment details and grading rubric). Students also completed a similar assignment that required them to search for, evaluate, and select sources using an Internet search engine. There was, however, a lack of consistency in how each of the CWRR classroom faculty members weighted these assignments. This, in turn, affected the effort many students put into completing the assignments.

Revising Assignments

In the third year of the program, the librarians revised the library assignments, moving away from generic toward more course-specific structures. Although the instructional goals and content remained largely the same, the in-class demonstrations and assignments focused on the subject-based content of each individual section. For example, if a section focused on the subject of literacy and technology, librarians focused on that subject in their demonstrations. If a faculty member elected to focus on literacy and popular culture, then librarians would use that subject during demonstrations. This served two important purposes. First, it provided another opportunity for dialogue between librarians and CWRR faculty. Second, it made the assignments more relevant for students. At the encouragement of the librarians, many of the CWRR faculty included a follow-up assignment directly related to the library instruction.

The bulk of the assessment related to actual writing assignments was, therefore, qualitative. In this case, individual faculty members assessed the relevance and appropriateness of students' sources. In addition, as a component of a Title III grant awarded to Millikin, the University's assessment officer provided support for a quantitative assessment of assignments for two semesters. We used student assignments (similar to the generic assignments discussed earlier), designed and graded by the librarians. Librarians assigned points based on suitable keyword and database selection and relevance of selected sources from initial database searches. The assessment provided quantitative data for each individual section and first-year students as a whole, which demonstrated that, by and large, students failed to use information resources in the most effective manner. This assessment confirmed the suspicions of both librarians and CWRR faculty: Students lacked adeptness at analyzing the citations they retrieved, understanding the subject headings associated with each record, and selecting the most relevant articles.

The librarian and faculty's discussions led to the placement and focus of the library instruction in the CWRR course sequence. Through reviewing assignments and course objectives, librarians determined that certain components of the library instruction would better serve the students if much of the material covered in the first semester was moved to the second semester and vice versa. Initially, for example, one first-semester session focused on the differences among magazines, journals, and trade publications. This instruction, however, is more relevant in the second semester when all students must complete a significant piece of formal academic research. Given that all students are required to write a research paper as a culminating activity in the second semester, this allowed librarians to tie the library instruction more directly to the research project.

Integration Outcomes

Our classroom faculty/librarian collaborations have had positive outcomes for classroom faculty, librarians, students, and, more generally, for the CWRR program. From the start, our collaborative efforts helped faculty understand and respond to the fact that the two courses are about more than just their individual work in isolated classrooms. Integrating library components reminds faculty that the courses are a part of the larger curriculum and that successful achievement of information literacy requires integrated and interdisciplinary approaches to teaching and learning. We have created a common ground where faculty can discuss reading and writing in an increasingly information-based literacy context. On a practical level, it has also ensured that a group with high turnover rates has opportunities to meet people outside their departments who can help improve teaching and learning and assist them as they pursue their scholarly interests.

Integration of library components into the first-year writing program helps students understand that writing, reading, and researching are interrelated activities they will continue to perform throughout college. Because the library components of the course are sometimes the only shared part of the curriculum in IN 150 and IN 151 courses, they also create a common ground upon which students can discuss the courses and their projects. Library sessions include not only skill- and resource-based activities, such as how to access and use databases, but they also include readings emphasizing the important role of accessing and evaluating information in our culture. Two sources that are useful for this purpose include the still timely Shapiro and Hughes (1996) article "Information Literacy as Liberal Art" and Curran and Adams' (1999) "Galloping New Ignorance, Watchdogs, and the Enlightenment Syndrome." The library session pushes students to think of themselves as more than users and consumers of information retrieved via technologies but also as critical thinkers as they engage in advanced literacy activities. (See the introduction to Selfe's 1999 book, *Technology and Literacy in the Twenty-First Century: The Importance of Paying Attention* as an example of a discussion that can be used in this context.)

Obviously, faculty/librarian collaboration has contributed significantly to the success of the first-year writing program at Millikin University. Individual classroom faculty members and librarians have presented and published together, improving the profile of the program inside and outside the university. Because the library assignments are the same from one section of the course to another, the program has also gained a level of consistency across course sections that had not occurred previously. The library component of the course creates a common ground in the curriculum, which encourages classroom faculty members to understand that the courses exist in a larger framework, with a responsibility to the core curriculum specifically and more generally to the institution and its constituents.

Conclusion

Millikin University's integration of library instruction into first-year writing courses clearly illustrates that such activity opens new opportunities for cooperation and collaboration between classroom faculty and librarians. The integration of library components into writing courses helps all participants develop a more sophisticated understanding of the relationship between advanced levels of literacy and information literacy. The process invites everyone involved—classroom faculty, students, librarians, and institutional research administrators—to think of themselves as more than mere consumers of information. Perhaps most important, the collaboration encourages librarians and classroom faculty to work across the institutional boundaries that too often isolate us from one another. Such collaboration encourages us to work together in confronting the growing challenges and opportunities in the 21st century in achieving information literacy.

The continually changing face of information access that confronts us each year dictates collaboration among those responsible for the education of our first-year students. As illustrated in this case study, clearly, communication is at the heart of any successful librarian/faculty partnership. Searching for and identifying the common goals can serve as an excellent starting point for discussion. Through such efforts, collaborative relationships flourish and grow. Developing a practice of collaboration serves both librarians and faculty well, particularly as they move on to new positions at new institutions (as the authors have). These prior foundations then provide the basis for the development of new collaborations and encourage relationships in new settings. Regardless of location or situation, faculty and librarians can successfully collaborate to the advantage of the students in their classrooms.

References

Curran, C., & Adams, D. (1999). Galloping new ignorance, watchdogs, and the enlightenment syndrome. *American Libraries, 30*(10) 46-50.

Selfe, C. (1999). *Technology and literacy in the twenty-first century: The importance of paying attention.* Carbondale: Southern Illinois University Press.

Shapiro, J. J., & Hughes, S. K. (1996). Information literacy as liberal art. [Electronic version.] *Educom Review, 31*(2). Retrieved March 7, 2000, from http://www.educause.edu/pub/er/review/reviewarticles/31231.html

Appendix

Generic Information Literacy Assignment

Students were each randomly given one of six generic research topics and asked to perform the tasks that follow. They were also instructed to include a printout of the first set of articles retrieved from each search, their search histories, and the first page of the article selected.

1. *Keyword Selection.* Using the assigned research topic, select appropriate search terms/keywords.
2. *Database Selection.* Select an appropriate database from database listings (alphabetical and subject) available on the library's web page.
3. *Search Results.* Perform and refine a search in the selected database that yields a manageable number of results relevant to the question. (Students were instructed to refine the search if their initial search yielded more than 100 or fewer than 6.)
4. *Article Selection.* From the articles returned, select the article that is the best, most relevant article with regard to the assigned research topic.

Assignment Revisions

The assignment revision maintained the same tasks, as illustrated below, but provided a topical focus relevant to the current class discussions and readings for the students' searches. Examples:

Course theme: Gender roles
Assignment: Locate articles that discuss how the depiction of women in advertising influences teenage girls.

Course theme: Media in society
Assignment: Locate articles that discuss the impact of television on an aspect of our culture.

Scoring Rubric

Research Skill	*Criteria*	*Scoring*
1. Selection of search terms	Appropriate keywords selected from assigned topic statement Refinement of search terms/language as warranted by initial results	0-2
2. Database selection	Nature of database: subject-specific, discipline-based, general Relevancy of database to subject focus of question	0-2
3. Search results	Number of results retrieved Evidence of refinement based on number of results	0-2
4. Article selection	Article directly addresses research question Relevancy of article: Does the article address the specific topic in question or merely contain the search terms?	0-2

Case Study 3

Transformations: Librarian/Faculty Collaboration in First-Year Programs at IUPUI

William A. Orme & Barbara D. Jackson

Institutional Description

Indiana University-Purdue University Indianapolis (IUPUI), established in 1969, is an urban campus of 29,000 students that provides two- and four-year programs as well as professional programs business, dentistry, law, and medicine. Most students are commuters, with the bulk of the population coming from the nine-county Indianapolis, Indiana metropolitan area. Students receive degrees from either Indiana University or Purdue University, depending upon the program in which they are enrolled.

In the mid-1990s, a variety of town hall meetings on campus revealed a need for a centralized unit that would serve as a common gateway to the various academic programs offered on campus. As a result, in 1997, IUPUI created University College, a new academic unit, to serve as a center for innovative approaches and a showcase for best practices for enhancing the success of first-year students. Using the graduate school faculty model, University College drew faculty members from academic units across campus, including the library. University College provides new student orientation, first-year seminars, thematic learning communities, critical inquiry courses, Summer Bridge Academy, learning and resource centers that offer supplemental instruction, and an academic advising center.

This case study will focus on the various University College programs for first-year students that promote faculty/librarian collaboration, specifically as members of instructional teams. University Library, which is the primary undergraduate library on campus, moved into a new building in 1994. This new building is home to the campus' most comprehensive information technologies and provides access to these technologies on a wider scale than was possible in the previous library environment. Public computer clusters with complete Internet access share space with traditional library stacks and print materials. New leadership within the library regards focusing on instructional services and curricular engagement as critical for ensuring that IUPUI puts the library's new technologies to maximum use in the service of student success.

Collaborative Programs Within University College

First-Year Seminars and Learning Communities

"Students have changed more than universities have."[1] This simple statement evokes many possible responses, and IUPUI has been seriously working on institutional change for more than a decade. Campus librarians have been significant partners in this work, particularly as it affects first-year students.

IUPUI introduced a first-year seminar (U110) on its campus in the mid-1990s after an annual teaching seminar featured John Gardner as a guest speaker. The campus had been experiencing unacceptably low retention rates, and the course was designed in response to this concern. It also addressed the need to provide an introductory experience for new students, many of whom were the first generation in their families to pursue higher education. The seminar was the first course offering from IUPUI's University College. Later, the first-year seminar was embedded in thematic learning communities (TLCs). A TLC consists of several introductory courses (e.g., anthropology or psychology) administratively linked to create a learning community that encompasses the bulk of a student's first-semester course load. As the name suggests, a common theme is emphasized across the courses to provide a common focus. Participation in the TLC ensures that a student in a first-year seminar is part of a cohort that spans more than one introductory course.

Critical Inquiry

In 2000, University College developed Critical Inquiry (U112) as a support course for conditionally admitted students. Designed to take the place of a pre-existing study skills course, U112 was not intended for students with narrowly defined risk factors in reading or writing. Rather, course developers envisioned it primarily as a spring semester course for students, identified by first-year seminar faculty, who were most likely to benefit from an additional academic support course.

The fundamental concept behind Critical Inquiry is that the university should provide transitional academic support so that students can meet the challenges of college-level work. As with U110, Critical Inquiry is administratively linked to a three-credit disciplinary course. All work in Critical Inquiry is at the college level and is similar to the requirements of first-year general education courses. Discipline-based reading assignments or supplemental texts of a similar nature allow students to develop the skills needed to succeed academically in other courses. The key skills developed through the Critical Inquiry course are critical thinking, writing, information literacy, and learning strategies.

Summer Bridge Academy

In 2001, University College developed the Summer Bridge Academy to provide students a head start on acclimating themselves to a college campus. The Summer Bridge Academy begins two weeks before the start of the fall semester. Academic units have the opportunity to participate in Bridge, which is administered by University College. Bridge targets younger students who are no older than 19 and live within the nine-county Indianapolis metropolitan area. Bridge candidates have already been admitted to the University and have expressed an interest in a program of study from one of the units participating in Bridge.

Instructional Teams at IUPUI

What Is an Instructional Team?

First-year seminars, Critical Inquiry, and Summer Bridge Academy all incorporate the instructional team model of teaching. An instructional team is a group of people who have different roles on campus and who come together to plan and implement a course. The team approach recognizes that a successful transition to higher education requires more than student-faculty interaction. New students need a variety of perspectives and areas of expertise to help them succeed in meeting their academic goals. Thus, instructional teams include faculty members, academic advisors, student peer mentors, and librarians.

How Does an Instructional Team Function?

Instructional team members begin meeting well before the course is offered. In fact, course development often takes place over a span of months. Individual team members may or may not be present at all planning sessions. Although the team jointly develops and implements the course and shares in the responsibility for the success of students in the course, not every member's expertise is needed throughout the entire semester.

The instructional team typically includes several members, who each play an important and distinctive role in the processes of conceptualizing, developing, implementing, and assessing the course. The faculty member is the instructor of record, functions as the team leader, and is responsible for setting the team in motion and guiding its progress. Academic advisors are resources for students because they are knowledgeable about the policies, procedures, and bureaucracies of the campus and provide more traditional guidance concerning course selection and progress in degree programs. Advisors also may provide practical tips on time management or study techniques that will help ensure that students make the most of their educational opportunities. The student mentor plays a crucial role in identifying student concerns and helping to ensure that the academic environment is conducive to student success. Because the student mentor is on the instructional team to serve as a knowledgeable peer rather than as an instructor, he or she—unlike other instructional team members—has no responsibility for assigning student grades. Librarians provide an introduction to a new information landscape and to new information resources, many of which were not previously accessible to students. As an example, most student are familiar with the Internet and may use one or more search engines to satisfy their information needs outside school, but they are typically not familiar with the concepts of peer-review and refereeing or with the fact that there are specialized resources made available to them by the campus through licensing agreements.

At the end of every spring semester, University College hosts a colloquium for new instructional team partners. The organizers intend these colloquia primarily for new team members, but they include all instructional team partners and provide opportunities for teams to share experiences and approaches. As a result, the Spring Colloquium has become an important information-sharing vehicle and developmental tool. It is known as the launching pad for the first-year template and is the arena where librarians can collectively share their vision of their educational contribution and how to best realize that contribution.

The Impact of Librarian Involvement on Instructional Teams

Before the creation of these instructional teams, the library centered its instructional services on two writing courses: (a) a speech course and (b) the aforementioned study skills course. Librarian liaisons to academic units also provided instructional services to other academic units. Use of those services depended primarily on the entrepreneurial spirit of the librarian and the receptivity of individual faculty members. These courses provided librarians broad access to first-year students, but instructional activities within these courses focused on the preparation of student products such as research papers or persuasive speeches. Although IUPUI intended these courses for first-year students, often students delayed taking these courses until later years.

The creation of new courses that focused on first-year students and their adjustment to a postsecondary environment provided an opportunity for the librarians to rethink their instructional services. The University Library administration, which had recently abandoned traditional departmental divisions for a team-based configuration, created an internal instructional team. This newly created library unit took as its first task the development of a set of learning objectives for first-year students. These learning objectives were of two types: (a) one type focused on critical thinking skills (library independent) and (b) the other focused on resources and services unique to the campus library (library dependent).[2] The development of learning objectives by librarians illustrated one transformative effect of this new collaboration: Librarians now considered the educational impact of their work not only in the context of how it affected a student's performance on a specific task, but also how it impacted a student's success as a member of a new community. The library began a subtle move away from marketing new library services toward instructional design. Our partners on the IUPUI campus assisted this transformation. IUPUI created a Center for Teaching and Learning and housed it in the newly constructed library building, providing librarians access to instructional designers and pedagogical resources that were previously unavailable. As a result of these developments, librarians became more fully integrated as members of the campus community and began to see themselves in new roles.

Eventually, a University College task force of classroom faculty members, advisors, mentors, and librarians developed learning objectives based on larger campus objectives called the "Principles of Undergraduate Learning" and incorporated these learning objectives into a template for first-year seminars. Significantly, the resulting document is a University College rather than a library document, demonstrating that the library's instructional mission has become an integral part of the academic mission of University College.

Although University College put a template of objectives in place, no overarching approach to achieving those objectives exists, as different schools develop different approaches to achieving them. For example, the School of Science developed a course separate from University College, and while that school followed the instructional team approach, it functioned quite differently from most University College sections. The library's instructional team coined the slogan "one size fits none" to remind itself that no set, standard approach could respond effectively to this type of innovative endeavor.

Library instruction gave way to information-skills instruction. The marketing of library services continued, but librarians complemented it through an increasing focus on the nature of academic communication and the differences between the information landscape that students encountered prior to college and the one that a college student needed to navigate. This task was most strikingly evident in students' reactions to components of the "invisible web," those resources made available only to university students and only through university licensing and subscription agreements. While librarians traditionally tried to acquaint students with distinctions between popular periodicals and scholarly journals, it became even more important for students to understand the qualitative difference among resources available from free Internet search engines, public libraries, and academic libraries.

Librarians had already been moving away from demo and lecture models toward more active-learning approaches. Because classroom faculty members and librarians now worked together from the beginning of course development, exercises and plans could now be collaboratively designed. Information-skills instruction could be more closely tied to overall course objectives and placed in the sequence of a semester in a more rational and pedagogically sound manner. In some cases, these collaborations became very elaborate and time-consuming. Science faculty members and librarians almost immediately became strong partners, with librarians filling roles that traditionally had not been assigned to them. Librarians not only became involved in developing exercises but also in assessing student performance on those exercises. Some classroom faculty members assumed that a teaching role for librarians implied constant course involvement throughout a semester regardless of whether the librarian contributed anything to weekly class sessions. The demands on librarians increased, but not all of these proved to be productive.

Impact of the Program on Librarians

Within three short years, from fall 1996 to fall 1999, first-year experience courses alone increased from 23 to more than 100 sections, all of which used the instructional team approach. This rapid growth strained the human resources available for the project. Schools could enlist additional faculty members; however, the library could not justify a proportional increase in the number of librarians on campus since instructional services were essentially seasonal. Eventually, the library instructional team increased in size from five members to nine, yet the library's team suffered from an exponential increase in demand for services. Burnout became a serious threat. In response, the team investigated alternative ways of contributing to the course.

The librarians early on established the principle that a librarian's expertise, not a librarian's presence, mattered most. They formulated this principle to rebut arguments for having a librarian in every session of a 15-week class even when they had no role in the class. With that in mind, librarians looked to technology for assistance. The campus developed a courseware package called Oncourse that included a wide range of functions such as the posting of syllabi and schedules of events; e-mail, chat, and discussion groups; and browser-friendly pointers to a variety of information sources. Although the librarians ultimately deemed it unfeasible for them to develop their own web-based tutorial to place within Oncourse, the librarians did arrange with the University of Texas (Austin) to use its award-winning tutorial, commonly known as TILT (Texas Information Literacy Tutorial). The objectives of the TILT program modules significantly overlap the objectives in the campus template for first-year seminars.[3] Use of TILT freed librarians to provide more in-depth individualized assistance and to participate in a larger number of course sections without undue strain. Subsequent research revealed that TILT was an effective teaching tool and it, therefore, seemed an adequate solution to the problem of librarian overload (Orme, 2004). Eventually IUPUI's librarians adapted TILT to address the specific campus environment and named the resulting product "inflite," a name derived from collapsing the words "information" and "literacy."

Librarians continue to play important roles in the development of first-year initiatives on campus. A librarian served as a member of the founding faculty of University College and continues to serve on its executive committee. Librarians helped draft the first-year template, the campus-wide Principles of Undergraduate Learning (upon which the template objectives were based), and a librarian served as chair of the Critical Inquiry Curriculum Committee during the development of the Critical Inquiry course. Librarians remain active contributors to first-year seminars, Critical Inquiry courses, and the Summer Bridge Academy.

Assessment and Outcomes

One of the first questions the library's instructional team posed was, "What difference does it make that librarians are involved in this class?" This question not only framed the way librarians thought about learning objectives, but also raised the issue of assessment.

In some ways, the nature of the instructional team approach makes it difficult to assess the impact of individual team members. If the team is acting as a fully integrated unit, student performance may seem to be the result of the whole rather than of any one member. Also, the overarching goal of the first-year seminar is to acclimate students to an academic environment. Determining the extent to which this has occurred is problematic since acclimation is a gradual process and may not be fully realized in the first semester or during a single course.

University College has undertaken a variety of assessments to determine the impact of not only the program, but also of those contributing to it. The U110 first-year experience course has been the most studied of the University College courses. Some longitudinal data are available that describe student perceptions of the course, including their views of the instructional team concept, the benefit of having a librarian on the team, and self-reports about confidence in the ability to use the library and its resources. Data show clear support for the instructional team concept, the perceived benefit of having a librarian as a member of the team, and student recognition of the value of the course in providing an introduction to information and critical-thinking skills, particularly as these concern the ability to retrieve and select credible sources appropriate for academic work.

Conclusion

Students appear to like and benefit from the expertise of a variety of campus professionals afforded by the instructional team concept. Classroom faculty members obviously provide an introduction to a discipline and more subtly but distinctively provide an introduction to the world of the scholar. Advisors provide guidance in the working of the campus, particularly in the processes of course registration but also in other areas critical to student success such as time-management and note-taking skills. Student mentors provide a knowledgeable peer who not only can provide pragmatic advice for surviving that critical first semester, but who can also serve as a sounding board for student issues and concerns. The librarian's role is perhaps less distinct. Librarians introduce students to information resources they have not used before and to strategies for critical thinking and resource evaluation. By discussing the scholarly peer review process and the need for adherence to standards of academic integrity, librarians also reveal the information landscape of the scholarly world with its various conventions and rules that govern the creation, dissemination, and distribution of scholarly communication.

More work needs to be done in order to more fully and accurately assess the attainment of fundamental skills intended by the course templates and the campus Principles of Undergraduate Learning. If information literacy is indeed the basis for lifelong learning, the librarians on instructional teams need to provide recognizable benchmarks that chart a student's progress throughout his or her college career, not simply during their first semester of college. We need to go beyond our first-year objectives and establish rubrics and benchmarks for the entire post-secondary experience.

Notes

[1]Unidentified student panelist. 11th International Conference on The First-Year Experience. Dublin, Ireland. 1998.

[2]A complete set of learning objectives for IUPUI's first-year seminars is available at http://uc,iupui.edu/uploadedFiles/Learning_Communities/LC%20Template.pdf. Hard copies are available upon request from the authors.

[3]IUPUI's revised version of TILT (known as inflite) is available at http://inflite.ulib.iupui.edu/. Each section of the tutorial begins with its own set of learning objectives.

References

Orme, W. A. (2004). A study of the residual impact of the Texas Information Literacy Tutorial on the information-seeking ability of first-year college students. *College & Research Libraries, 65*(3), 205-215.

Case Study 4

Teresa Fishel, Beth Hillemann, & Jean Beccone

Librarians as Change Agents:
The Evolution of a
First-Year Information
Fluency Program at a
Small Liberal Arts College

Challenges

Librarians at Macalester College have traveled along the same path as many other college and university librarians, seeing the need to transform a traditional course-integrated library instruction program into a comprehensive information literacy program. A successful transformation requires the collaboration and active support of faculty and staff throughout the college. However, in our case, many roadblocks stood in our way. Information fluency, as we call it, is one initiative among many competing for faculty and administrative attention. We have a small library staff, lack faculty status, and are not routinely involved in curricular discussions. To gain allies and support for the integration of information fluency in the college's curriculum, we needed to find a way to attract and hold faculty and administrative attention. While several initiatives have led to progress toward our goal, we discuss in detail the development of a collaborative workshop for faculty teaching first-year courses. Collaboration has proven to be the key for unlocking barriers and allowing us to effect change across the campus.

Institutional Description

Macalester is a small, liberal arts institution in St. Paul, Minnesota, with approximately 1,900 undergraduate students. The DeWitt Wallace Library staff includes six librarians who provide library instruction. Course-integrated library instruction has been part of our campus culture for more than 25 years. We became involved in information literacy discussions by attending conferences, participating in the Institute for Information Literacy Immersion Program sponsored by the Association of College and Research Libraries, and reading the professional literature on this topic. We realized that if we wanted to carry our vision for information fluency beyond the library's walls, we needed to infiltrate other areas of campus, communicate with faculty, demonstrate our abilities beyond one-shot library instruction sessions, and create allies.

The First-Year Program

In 1997, we decided to increase our focus on the needs of first-year students who were coming to college with varying levels of technological and information-seeking proficiencies. The first-year program at Macalester consists of department-based courses taught by rotating faculty who are also the entering students' advisors. Some of these courses are designed to feed directly into the study of a particular field (such as "Introduction to Psychology"), and others are designed to be more of an introduction to academia and the process of scholarship. All first-year students are required to take a first-year course in their first semester. Working with members of the Computing and Information Technology department (CIT), we developed a two-session program for the first-year courses introducing students to the campus network and basic library resources. Faculty members teaching first-year courses had the option to include these sessions in their course, but the curriculum did not require them to do so. We started with five of 32 first-year courses participating in our program. By 2002, all first-year classes participated and have continued to do so each subsequent year. Concurrently, members of the library staff and CIT formed an information literacy task force. We created a draft definition of "information fluency" at Macalester (see Appendix) and worked on several initiatives to communicate that definition to the campus and to provide instruction.

Pilot Lab: Beyond the Two-Session Model

While we had achieved modest success in persuading some faculty members of the importance of library and technology instruction within the first-year course, the first-year two-session model did not meet all the objectives we envisioned for an information fluency program. In 2002, the library director served on a strategic planning task force consisting of administrative staff and faculty members, with one of their objectives being to look at the first-year experience at Macalester. From this task force came the idea of using a lab-based model for information fluency, similar to the labs attached to science courses. The following year, an opportunity to try out this idea arose when one faculty member, serving on a grant-funded working group to study writing requirements, became interested in working with the librarians to develop a more in-depth first-year information fluency experience. Working closely with this faculty member, and with the help of grant money for information literacy programs received from the Associated Colleges of the Midwest (ACM), we created a pilot project by attaching a weekly, one-hour lab session to the faculty member's first-year course. During the 15-week semester, we covered crucial information-fluency concepts in detail and worked with Macalester's writing center (MAX Center) for added emphasis on writing in the first year.

We evaluated the pilot lab using pre- and post-course surveys, campus course evaluations, and the faculty member's and librarians' observations. While student reactions to the lab varied from enthusiasm to indifference, the post-course survey revealed that students had achieved most of the learning goals we had set for the lab. We decided to expand the program the following year into two lab courses, and the post-course surveys for those labs revealed similar positive results in relation to the learning goals. However, with a small library staff, we could not further expand weekly lab courses without increased funding and staffing. In addition, any curricular change, such as an added lab, would have to be approved by the faculty. We wanted to find a sustainable program that faculty members would support without formal changes. Once again, collaboration became the key.

"Entering the Community of Inquiry" Workshop

Encouraged by our success with the pilot labs, we approached MAX Center staff and faculty and staff from our Center for Scholarship and Teaching (CST) to propose a three-day workshop for first-year course faculty. We considered the support of CST critical because it is a conduit to faculty. Faculty listen when the CST promotes programs and ideas on campus. To our good fortune, the director of the CST became an early and vocal advocate for information fluency. The workshop proposal brought together different, yet complementary, perspectives and goals.

The MAX Center wanted to improve writing instruction in the first-year courses. The librarians wanted to introduce and expand on the concept of integrating information fluency into the curriculum. The CST sought to promote these ideas and improve the first-year experience for students and faculty. We concluded a collaborative workshop would be an appropriate way to achieve our goals. We applied for and received a $10,000 ACM information literacy grant, and the CST provided additional funding. We used the funding to provide reading materials, workshop handouts, food and beverages, and a small stipend as an added incentive for faculty members to attend. The CST, along with our long-time ally, the academic dean who oversees the first-year program, helped promote the workshop among faculty members teaching first-year courses.

In choosing a name for our workshop, we wanted to emphasize one of the aspects of the first-year courses—to introduce students to their new community. We called it "Entering the Community of Inquiry" to represent the ways in which our academic community members actively engage in exploring, constructing, and sharing knowledge—often in written form. We also wanted to make explicit to faculty the needs of novice scholars entering our academic environment. One of the underlying goals of our workshop was to give faculty members an opportunity to step outside their disciplines and discuss how first-year students ought to be introduced to our community.

We developed outcomes and goals for the workshop along with an assessment tool. Our goals included (a) introducing faculty to information fluency and writing standards, (b) discussing the unique needs of first-year students, and (c) constructing effective assignments. We asked faculty members to read selected materials to stimulate discussion about information fluency concepts and writing standards. We set up pages in our course management software that included links to readings, the ACRL information literacy standards, and other web resources. Our selected readings focused on the research and writing characteristics of incoming students and their transition to a scholarly community. We used small and large groups to facilitate discussion and to help faculty members design assignments appropriate to their first-year course. We invited experienced faculty members to participate in a panel discussion of their first-year course assignments and experiences. The dean of academic programs spoke about expectations for the first-year course program and characteristics of incoming students. We also discussed the "Google factor" (i.e., the tendency for students to choose Google as their first and only resource) and traits of Millennial students (who have grown up with technology and the Internet), especially those observed at Macalester. Each faculty member in the workshop developed a specific assignment incorporating library research and writing. We used the technique of pair-and-share to give faculty members the opportunity to work with each other to improve their assignments. In addition, we took the opportunity to introduce faculty members to new resources at Macalester such as RefWorks (i.e., a web-based citation database for creating bibliographies and notes in papers) and Moodle (i.e., an open-source course-management system). Naturally, we offered faculty members food and beverages throughout the workshop, and at the end, we asked the faculty members to complete an assessment survey.

Assessment

We first offered the workshop in June 2003, and eight faculty members attended. We offered it again in 2004 and 2005, following modifications based on faculty feedback, and each year about a third of the first-year course faculty members attended. The first workshop attracted mostly new faculty members; the second and third workshops included a mix of new and long-term faculty members. They represented all disciplines, from the fine arts to the sciences, which greatly enhanced the sharing of ideas and discussion.

The participating faculty members provided overall feedback and assessment. We based the assessment survey on the goals and outcomes we created for the workshop. These goals have evolved based on feedback from the assessment but have included helping faculty members

- Understand the recommended expectations for a common experience for first-year courses at Macalester
- Understand the importance of introducing students to the Macalester network and resources available to them
- Understand the standards of information fluency and how to incorporate them into assignments
- Understand how to make the academic research process (construction of knowledge) explicit to students to help initiate them into an academic community of inquiry
- Understand that teaching the evaluation of resources is an important element of academic inquiry
- Start a list of desired student outcomes for writing assignments in the first-year course
- Outline one research-based writing assignment for their first-year course
- List criteria for responding to, assessing, and evaluating writing assignments
- Understand the services and support available from the MAX Center
- Become aware of an established network of faculty and staff members to consult for course design and teaching

We have revised the survey tool as we modified the goals for the workshop, making comparisons between years difficult. At the end of the fall semester 2004, we held a focus-group discussion with past participants of the workshop to solicit additional ideas to improve the workshop. Of the respondents to the 2005 survey, 80% agreed or strongly agreed that we met all the goals of the workshop. Faculty members have generally been enthusiastic about their experiences and have recommended the workshop to their colleagues. The experience of one faculty member proved typical. She somewhat dreaded the coming workshop, since we had scheduled it right after commencement, a time when most of us in academia feel tired and drained. She found herself, however, so inspired by discussions with her colleagues that she stayed up late developing her assignment for additional discussions at the workshop. Several faculty members at the 2006 workshop mentioned a new-found eagerness for their classes to begin in September. The best feature of our workshops, according to faculty members (and from our observations), are the structured discussion opportunities that have led to the rich exchange of ideas and have invigorated the participants. Indeed, after the 2004 workshop, faculty members created a lunch-discussion group under the sponsorship of the CST, which met regularly throughout the summer and fall semester to continue conversations related to their first-year courses. This group invited all first-year course faculty and librarians to participate in these lunch discussions.

Future Directions

From the librarians' perspective, we have seen improved assignments for the first-year students. We have developed a closer working relationship with faculty members teaching first-year courses, and they are more aware of the expertise that librarians bring to teaching information seeking skills to their students. As a result, we are developing more robust instruction modules for first-year courses based on information fluency concepts. These modules, direct descendants of the pilot labs, will require more collaboration and commitment from faculty members, but they will reach more students, cover more information fluency topics, and will be sustainable even for a small staff.

Perhaps our greatest success, however, has been the infiltration of information fluency concepts into the faculty discussions about curricular renewal. For the past two years, Macalester faculty have been engaged in reviewing the curriculum. A current proposal for the first-year course program states:

> In addition, all FYCs [first-year courses] will be expected to cooperate with staff to ensure a minimal level of library instruction, and explicitly discuss how to properly access and analyze sources of information appropriate to the discipline(s) covered by the course.

The proposal appropriated the title of our workshop, calling the redesigned first-year program "Entering the Community of Inquiry." We believe the mandate in the new first-year course proposal reflects our efforts and points to a new and growing understanding among faculty of the importance of information fluency and its place in the curriculum.

Conclusion

Collaboration proved the key ingredient for us to begin to develop a true information fluency program at Macalester. We still have a long way to go, and there will be additional roadblocks and detours. Nevertheless, we are excited by the success of our collaboration with the CST and the MAX Center and by the expanding discussions on campus. Developing collaborative relationships is not as easy as it seems when reading about a successful program. Our collaborative efforts took years to develop and equal amounts of patience. We cultivated relationships by serving on committees and discussing our ideas in public and private conversations. We took advantage of some opportunities, such as participating in campus task forces and curricular discussions, and created others, such as the pilot labs and the workshop, to effect changes to our environment. Commitment and dedication on the part of individual faculty members and staff members proved absolutely critical. Through perseverance and the ability to see how disparate needs might be harnessed for common goals, we pooled our resources and our talents to reach out to faculty members teaching first-year courses and, as a result, influence the first-year experience at Macalester. Through the Entering the Community of Inquiry workshop, librarians have managed to sow and cultivate ideas about information fluency beyond the library. We have gained faculty advocates across campus and have watched discussions blossom into campus-wide proposals. We intend to continue our workshop, build slowly, and expand our information fluency program, carrying it beyond the first-year program. Macalester's curriculum is changing and will continue to change over the next few years. Nevertheless, our experiences and collaborative efforts have given us both the means and ability to not only respond to these changes but also to influence them.

Appendix

Definition of Information Fluency at Macalester College

At Macalester, "students should develop the ability to use information and communication resources effectively, be adept at critical, analytical, and logical thinking; and express themselves well in both oral and written forms." This excerpt from the college's Statement of Purpose and Belief sets the stage for discussions on the definition of information fluency at Macalester. In addition, as a liberal arts institution, we see the greater value in asking and determining questions, as opposed to simply supplying answers.

Rigorous exploration of important questions starts with determination of the questions, a basic information need. Exploration requires a strategy for identifying and critically sifting through the wealth of information available, using technology effectively, and understanding the complex ethical and legal issues surrounding the use of information. Results are then developed, shared, and evaluated, leading to new information and new knowledge. New questions emerge, and the cycle begins again.

Revealing this iterative process to students within a disciplinary context is critical to ensure their successful participation in scholarly discourse. Understanding the conceptual frameworks of this process provides a foundation for developing abilities to transform information into knowledge. Embedding this process into the curriculum empowers all students to become life-long learners. The library web site (http://www.macalester.edu/library) includes more details on our information fluency efforts as well as a list of readings that have been used with the faculty for our workshops.

Case Study 5

Developing a First-Year Information literacy Program: The Contexts and Challenges of Change

Randall Schroeder & Judith Griffith

Contexts of Opportunity and Change

The development of an information literacy curriculum seldom occurs in a perfectly calm and stable environment. Three positive but challenging circumstances coincided in 1999 to create a perfect information literacy storm at Wartburg College, a confluence of change that might easily have resulted in failure. First, the president announced a new initiative that "all Wartburg College students will be information literate upon graduation" (Vogel, 1997). Second, the faculty approved the sweeping revision of a 16-year-old general education program, wiping out old courses and sequences and creating new ones. Third, a new library building opened and created campus-wide excitement that placed the librarians at the center of attention. The combination of these events resulted in an opportunity for librarians and classroom faculty members to set a new course for information literacy, a course that would successfully move beyond the old contexts of past practices and resistance to change and forward into the challenges of new curricula and facilities.

The Challenge to Change

There had been clear signs that information literacy efforts faced major difficulties in the old curriculum. The previous general education requirements contained no formal information literacy goals, and past courses reflected little thoughtful integration of information literacy skills. Individual classroom faculty members' requests for instructional support almost always resulted from informal conversations between individual classroom and library faculty members. Furthermore, any given student might have similar instruction about reference sources in three different classes because three different classroom faculty members might request the same instruction from librarians. Students frequently had repetitive lessons regarding the library with no logical sequence. As a result, students often complained, justifiably, that they had already had the same library session in another class (or classes). This situation frustrated students, classroom faculty members, and library faculty and prevented the effective presentation, development, and assessment of information literacy skills. Moreover, the institution had no data about what students learned, retained, and applied. The new curriculum and library provided a perfect, although challenging, opportunity in which to address these information literacy issues.

The College Context

Wartburg College is a four-year, private liberal arts college affiliated with the Evangelical Lutheran Church in America (ELCA) and located in Waverly, Iowa. The 150-year history of the college has been coupled with much recent change and growth in both academic areas and in the physical plant. Wartburg is in its ninth consecutive year of record enrollment, with approximately 1,850 students in the 2005-2006 academic year. This enrollment increase is part of a general Wartburg renaissance that includes new faculty members and curricula. In addition, campus renovation and construction projects affected the library, chapel, fine arts center, football stadium, student center, student housing, and science building. While these are all positive modifications, the pervasive atmosphere of change created a challenging context for information literacy innovation.

The completion of the Robert and Sally Vogel Library, opened in September 1999 and described as a "learner's library," provided the most critical factor in this renaissance. The College deliberately designed a library that would facilitate active learning instead of serving as a warehouse for books or a glorified computer lab. The Vogel Library contains two classrooms dedicated to information literacy sessions. The library is currently staffed by five full-time librarians and one part-time librarian, three of whom are full-time information literacy librarians. This reflects a reorganization plan implemented in 1994 by the new library director, who moved from a traditional staffing paradigm to a staff that reflected a focus on information literacy instruction. Additionally, library building planners designed the new facility for use in innovative ways to promote Information Literacy Across the Curriculum (ILAC). The library and its faculty were prepared for these changes; however, classroom faculty had to be assured that their curricular needs would be met in this new context.

Curricular Contexts

The new library facility and staffing patterns provided potential for information literacy innovation, but the curricular context could have been a stumbling block. After the adoption of the new (and thoroughly debated) general education program, the faculty created a core of classes required of all students. The core courses required in the first year were designed to serve a critical role in the development of information literacy skills (i.e., accessing, selecting, evaluating, and integrating sources into individual student research). Early in the course development process, the information literacy coordinator for group instruction participated in an intense weeklong faculty retreat to create a new first-year seminar class. The retreat resulted in the creation of a course titled Inquiry Studies 101: Asking Questions, Making Choices (IS 101), which had the goal of introducing students to the information universe. During the course development, the ILAC coordinator assured the classroom faculty members that every ILAC skill lesson could be modified to work with any faculty-chosen theme. The promise of genuine cooperation between the classroom and library faculty proved persuasive. Classroom faculty members agreed to include ILAC skills in the IS 101 course because they concluded that ILAC did not restrict the content or continuity of their courses. Protection of course content proved a primary factor in the acceptance and successful implementation of ILAC. The collaborative development of this course provided the first opportunity for librarians and classroom faculty members to work together on embedding information literacy goals in the new curricular context.

The IS 101 seminar is half common content (material taught by all instructors in all sections) and half thematic content (determined by individual instructors and completely different for each instructor's theme). Each year, at least 20 different instructors teach this course. Thus, the library's information literacy coordinator works with a course that has a potential for 20 different foci each year (see Appendix A for a sample list of themes for one term). IS 101 is strongly infused with information literacy lessons, but those lessons must be flexible enough to be placed in either the common content or in the classroom faculty member's thematic material. This seminar is only one of five sources of information literacy in the early core courses. The other courses include composition, Inquiry Studies 201 (focus on diversity), historical Bible, and a scientific reasoning course, all of which must be completed in a student's first two years at Wartburg. Each of these classes addresses a specific ILAC goal (see Appendix B for course specific goals); but for most students, the first significant use of the intellectual resources of the Vogel Library takes place in IS 101. Each classroom faculty member includes at least two days of information literacy activities in his or her syllabus and most request further information literacy activities related to the class theme. Over time, IS 101 became the foundational class for an ILAC program that eventually spanned all four years and all disciplinary majors.

All IS 101 information literacy activities, as well as those in other ILAC classes, are designed in collaboration with a librarian, involve active learning emphasizing critical thinking skills, and are delivered in the library's dedicated classrooms by a library faculty member with the classroom faculty member present. These requirements—collaboration, active learning, instructor presence—are crucial to success. Sessions begin in the dedicated classrooms, but after relatively brief direct instruction, students move quickly into the information laboratory, reference collection, and book stacks to work on their individual assignments. This model relies much less on instruction (lecture) than on active learning and ensures that students apply the skills they learn in class almost immediately. Students come to know that this focus on active and individualized learning is an integral part of all information literacy sessions, and faculty members trust that the sessions will be lively and tailored to their specific content.

For instance, the theme for one IS 101 is cinema, and the students view the film *Citizen Kane*. During the information literacy session, students locate credible and authoritative print and electronic sources to support the hypothesis that *Citizen Kane* is one of the great films of American cinema. During the direct instruction portion of this session, students use the "Earned Scholarly Average" (ESA) worksheet (see Appendix C). The exercise compels students to use the intellectual resources of the library while reflecting critically on the authority and usefulness of those sources. Whatever theme is addressed in these sessions, students can apply the evaluative skills that have been taught in the context of information literacy. Classroom faculty members have reported the usefulness of these same skills throughout IS 101 and in upper-division general education and major courses. Post-testing in the sophomore and senior years also validates this transference of skills from IS 101 to other courses.

The Context of Individual Courses

During the creation of IS 101, the ILAC coordinator assured classroom faculty that the information literacy skills would be universal and could be taught in any context. Faculty members wanted instruction that fit naturally into their syllabi and that did not interrupt the flow of their instruction. So, information literacy sessions were adapted to address specific lesson plans, whether those plans occurred in the common content or in the individual thematic material. The librarians and the faculty members collaborated over coffee or by e-mail to design flexible activities that simultaneously addressed ILAC and course goals. One example of this flexibility is found in the ESA exercise mentioned above (Appendix C). The ESA can be modified by librarians to support almost any content.

Such flexible activities promote logically sequenced information literacy experiences linked to specific classes. Classroom faculty members and students feel secure knowing that a specific and goal-focused information literacy session will not be repeated, except by instructor request at a higher level of difficulty or in a specific disciplinary context. This new consistency allows for effective, scaffolded ILAC skills acquisition, and it ensures support from classroom faculty members, who can now design instruction with specific skill sets in mind. This consistency also provides information literacy librarians with opportunities for effective formative assessment done in multiple ways at multiple points.

The Context of Standards

While Wartburg's standards and goals for information literacy assured internal consistency of instruction, we also found that they were closely aligned with national standards. The Association of College and Research Libraries' (2000) *Information Literacy Competency Standards for Higher Education* appeared concurrent to Wartburg's early ILAC development. The national standards could easily be divided up as goals and, to the delight of the library and classroom faculty members who reviewed both sets of material, the Wartburg and national standards matched closely. This congruence provided additional security to classroom faculty members and librarians who were concerned about the validity of institutional goals in the larger context of national postsecondary curricula.

Faculty could also count on the establishment of baseline information literacy competencies in students' first-year courses, such as IS 101. These baseline competencies provided classroom faculty members the freedom to design additional ILAC instruction specific to the literatures of their disciplines. The basic tools of information literacy are taught in the first and second years. Classroom faculty members in all departments could be confident that their second-year students had addressed:

*   The taxonomy of overview/finding/fact sources in a search strategy
*   Differences between popular and scholarly materials and how to distinguish between them
*   Effective evaluation of print and Internet sources
*   Recognition of author bias
*   Inclusion of different voices in a bibliography

Knowing that students had basic skills, faculty teaching upperclass students in the major, could confidently focus on information literacy skills for specific disciplines.

The Context of Assessment

Keeping the ILAC promises to IS 101 classroom faculty about consistency and flexibility requires constant vigilance in the form of ongoing assessment. Frequently, curricular and technological changes displace specific information literacy teaching methods. Databases disappear and portals change, and the IS 101 *Reader*, the class text, is revised every two years. Every year, one third of the IS 101 faculty is new to the course, having never taught it before. These new faculty members need an orientation to the information literacy program. Therefore, the ILAC coordinator works directly with the IS 101 team and the associate dean for faculty development to reinforce program continuity. Experienced IS 101 faculty members sometimes wander from the ILAC plan when they change texts, syllabi, themes, or schedules, and frequently these changes occur without the ILAC coordinator's knowledge. The instructor who selected Early Film Comedy as a theme last year might choose to focus on Sociological Implications of Hip Hop next year. The burden for ILAC maintenance in IS 101 falls primarily on the library faculty, and assessment and communication are the primary means of keeping everyone on course.

IS 101 offers some excellent examples of how assessment provides rationales for appropriate instructional change. Assessment data from pretests (administered in September to entering students) have helped direct IS 101 instruction to the appropriate levels of prior knowledge.

The IS 101 lesson is in its third iteration in five years because pretest results indicated that student understanding of the information universe is changing.

For example, the first lesson in IS 101 was about an Internet toolkit, but it became apparent over time that students had become sufficiently familiar with the Internet before coming to college. Therefore, the librarians abandoned this focus. The need for this change may seem obvious now, but the Internet has a very short history and even a few years ago, student access to the Internet at either the home or school (and resulting familiarity with the Internet) could not be assumed.

Pretest results indicated another gap: Students had trouble selecting good subject headings for searches. The IS 101 lesson changed to teach the role of overview sources and thesauri in choosing subject headings. Initially, instruction tried to connect the authority and credibility of campus speakers to this lesson. However, because of the lack of information resources for many speakers, the lesson did not work as hoped. Additionally, some IS 101 faculty members did not want to use guest speakers as the focus of the information literacy lesson; they preferred a lesson linked more closely to their individual syllabi. Pretest data also showed that, while students frequently used the Internet and felt confident of their Internet searching abilities, they exhibited incomplete understanding of the information universe beyond the Internet, especially in the areas of print and scholarly resources.

In our view, assessment is the final mechanism that self-corrects the program to keep it relevant to students and classroom faculty. Librarians' willingness to constantly monitor changes in contexts and to make appropriately responsive instructional modifications ensures the ongoing success of an information literacy program. Flexibility based on collaboration is the foundation of the program. The library and classroom faculty recognize the context and challenges of change and understand that responsive learning environments are seldom stable. If library and classroom faculty are comfortable with a program, that is a sure indication that it is time to consider change.

Authors' Note

Many of the documents and tools discussed in this case study can be found at http://www.wartburg.edu/library/infolit/. Readers are freely given permission to use and adapt materials found at the above web site for their own purposes. All the authors ask in return is notification that the materials have been used and perhaps a copy to see what improvements the reader has made to the original.

Reference

Association of College and Research Libraries (ACRL). (2000). *Information literacy competency standards for higher education.* Chicago: Author.

Vogel, R. (1997, November 13). *Wartburg College faculty meeting minutes.* Waverly, IA: Wartburg College.

Appendix A

IS 101 Common Content, 2005-2006

The IS 101 *Reader* contains the common textual referents for the course and the Norton Critical Edition of *Frankenstein* is this year's cohort book. Instructors use this material for about half the course, and they are free to select any other individual theme for the other half.

IS 101 Foci, 2005-2006

The list of titles below represents the themes selected by individual instructors in the 2005-06:

Education and Social Change
The Plural "I": Popular Culture and the Shaping of Identity
Banned Books Does Anybody Know What Time It Is?
A Few Great Flicks
Identity on Stage
Futurism
Communication and Interpretation
Faith and the Questioning Mind
1968: The Year that Rocked the World
Deconstructing the Simpsons
Coding and Code Breaking
Discovering Your Vocation Through Learning
Ragstock to Pulp Fiction
Why People Believe Weird Things

Appendix B

Five Foundational ILAC Courses and Their Goals
(Wartburg Plan of Essential Education, Years One and Two)

Inquiry Studies 101 (Asking Questions, Making Choices)

Search Strategy Part I: Using overview sources to choose good search terms, to select appropriate databases and indexes, and to evaluate the quality of sources.

English 112 (Intermediate Composition)

Search Strategy Part II: Using and finding fact sources to create a bibliography in support of a hypothesis.

Inquiry Studies 201 (Focus on Diversity)

Determining perspective and bias in information.

Religion 101 (Literature of the Old and New Testament)

Locating and examining primary and secondary sources in a specific discipline.

Science Reasoning (any one of a number of courses that teach the scientific method)

Differentiating among popular and scholarly sources and exploring how scientific discovery is shared with a lay audience.

Appendix C

Earned Scholarly Average (ESA) or
"How can I tell if a source is scholarly?"

A warning: This worksheet provides a way to help you think about the scholarly worth of a source, or in other words, how reliable a source is as evidence to support or disprove a thesis. Most scholars do not use a point system like this to figure out a source's ESA, but this worksheet can be a valuable tool for you to use to practice evaluating material.

Points	Journal Article	Book
	Age of Source: 3 points if the article is three years old or newer. Subtract 1 point for each year older than 3. 0 points if older than 6 years.	*Age of Source:* 3 points if the book is four years old or newer. Subtract 1 point for each year older than 4. 0 points if older than 7 years.
	Author: 1 point if the author has written on this topic before. 2 points if the author has written 3+ times on the same topic. 1 point if the author works for a college or university. Subtract 1 point if the author is a journalist.	*Author:* 1 point if the author has written on this topic before. 2 points if the author has written 3+ times on the same topic. 1 point if the author works for a college or university. Subtract 1 point if the author is a journalist.
	Type of Source: 3 points for a peer reviewed scholarly journal. 2 points for a scholarly journal. 1 point for a professional magazine. 0 points for a popular magazine (e.g. *Time, The Economist*).	*Type of Source:* 3 points for a collection of essays. 2 points for a university press or learned society as publisher. 1 point for each favorable review (up to 3).
	Bibliography: Add 1 point if the article or book has a bibliography or reference section.	
	Footnotes/References: Add 1 point if the article or book has footnotes or endnotes.	

ESA Scale:

6 points or above = Good source, provided it is relevant to your topic.
2-5 points = Worth a look and further consideration.
0-1 points = Possible background material, but keep looking.

How do I find out? Refer to:

- Ulrich's Web (via the library's web page) at Vogel Library: Library Resources: Fact Sources
- Bill Katz's *Magazines for Libraries* catalogued at Ref. 016.05 M27
- *Book Review Digest* catalogued at Index 028.1 B64d

How do I find out? Examine the article/book itself and:

- Check the biography of the author (beginning of article, back of book).
- Check the title page and the back of the title paper of a journal.
- Check to see if the publisher is a college, university, or learned society. Books published by these entities are usually scholarly. If a journal is peer reviewed, it will usually say so in the first few pages, often in a section titled "Editorial Policy."

Remember, you can limit an Internet search to refereed scholarly journals by using Academic Search Premier (EBSCOhost).

Case Study 6

Integrating Information Literacy Into a Discipline-Specific Course in the First Year: A Case Study of Sociology 101

Kathy S. Kremer & Karen Shostrom Lehmann

Information literacy played a central role in transforming a traditional introductory sociology course into a rigorous framework for active learning at Wartburg College. This case study examines the collaboration between librarian and sociologist and the implications for first-year student learning in a discipline-specific course.

Wartburg College is a liberal arts undergraduate institution located in eastern Iowa with a 2005-2006 enrollment of 1,811 students. Typical of its peer institutions, the college has a student to faculty ratio of 13:1 and an average class size of 21 students. While 70 of the 105 faculty members hold doctoral degrees and many are active scholars in their disciplines, Wartburg College emphasizes classroom instruction. Full-time faculty members have an annual teaching responsibility of seven courses.

The Wartburg College Information literacy Program

Since implementation in 2000, Wartburg College's course-integrated information literacy program has encouraged instructional collaboration between faculty members and librarians. ACRL's (2000) *Information Literacy Competency Standards for Higher Education* are infused into instruction in five first-year general education courses[1] and into academic majors through Information Literacy Across the Curriculum (ILAC) plans. To develop a comprehensive information literacy approach, college librarians placed ACRL's competency standards on a curriculum map, specifying both core objectives and those reserved for the majors. Because it is impossible to meet all information literacy outcomes in five courses, librarians selected specific outcomes based on pre-testing and those most pertinent for Wartburg's first-year students.[2] Librarians then collaborated with classroom faculty to integrate the outcomes into lessons within core courses. For example, Intermediate Composition (EN112) introduces a search strategy for information gathering that covers six steps: (a) overview sources, (b) keywords, (c) indexing and abstracting tools, (d) selection of sources, (e) evaluation, and (f) search refinement.

EN112 is a baseline course for information literacy competencies at Wartburg College because it is required of all students. The six steps noted above, each coordinated with an outcome, are emphasized by librarians in their collaborations with EN112 instructors. All outcomes were selected from among the 14 specified performance indicators deemed most appropriate to the curricular content of EN112.

Disciplinary courses, such as Introduction to Sociology (SO101), build upon this existing information literacy paradigm and select course-specific ILAC outcomes. In the case of SO101, the five ACRL standards are addressed within 22 performance indicators and 40 desired outcomes.[3]

Integrating Information Literacy Into Sociology 101

For five years, the authors (a community sociology professor and an information literacy librarian) have collaborated to incorporate research skills reflecting specific national standards for information literacy into the introductory sociology course at Wartburg College. Prior to that time, faculty designed SO101 "to equip the student with both knowledge and skills necessary to live in the world community" (Wartburg College, 2000) with a focus on workbook assignments related to topics within the discipline.

The introductory course in sociology is for majors and non-majors. For non-majors, it offers the only exposure they are likely to have to theories of social behavior, but it also provides the theoretical foundation upon which all courses in the major are based (Wagenaar, 2004). When the current community sociology professor joined the Wartburg College faculty in 2001, she redesigned SO101 to reflect the American Sociological Association's (1991) recommendation for "the development of a coherent and mature conception of sociology as a scholarly endeavor" (p. 9). The course now introduces theories, concepts, and methods that help students understand elements of society and social processes. While an elective course for other majors and the general education requirements of the college, SO101 is taught as an introductory sociology theory course. This presents a challenge for the predominantly first-year students enrolled in it.

A central component of the redesigned course is a literature review assignment. Each student selects a specific social behavior and, by completing a series of information literacy and writing activities (discussed later), prepares a 15- to 20-page review of recent scholarly literature. The result is a specifically sociological examination of the behavior. For most students, this is their first experience preparing a literature review and is a gateway to writing scholarly papers in the social sciences.

Information Literacy Content

While developing the literature review assignment for SO101, the authors found the most effective approach was working within the framework already provided by the established information literacy paradigm and using selected indicators and outcomes for the course. The authors selected seven outcomes from the ACRL standards as goals for the literature review assignment. They are:

1. *Defines or modifies the information need to achieve a manageable focus (I.1.d).* Students use "overview" sources (i.e., encyclopedic reference materials, usually including bibliographies) to write a two-page introduction to the literature review. This helps them understand and clarify the specific social phenomenon they are examining within the broader area of social behavior.

2. *Recognizes that knowledge can be organized into disciplines that influence the way information is accessed (I.2.b).* The assignment is specific to sociology; therefore, students are required to focus on sociological concepts and how the social behavior is examined and explained within the discipline.

3. *Identifies the purpose and audience of potential resources (I.2.d).* The literature review can include only scholarly sources, and 8 of the minimum 10 sources must be recent (within the

preceding seven years). Resources are used to identify sociologists' current understanding of the social behavior.

4. *Implements the search using investigative protocols appropriate to the discipline (II.2.f).* Students remain focused on discipline-specific vocabulary by using terms identified in overview sources and the online sociological thesaurus found in subscription sociology databases.

5. *Differentiates between the types of sources cited and understands the elements and correct syntax of a citation for a wide range of resources (II.5.c).* The assignment limits materials students can use to peer-reviewed journals and other scholarly sources. Conference papers, dissertations, and web sites are not permitted, so students must learn to distinguish between formats. Students become skilled at using subscription databases as they explore descriptors, abstracts, bibliographic citations, and online links.

6. *Reviews information retrieval resources used and expands to include others as needed (III.7.c).* Students focus their search for sources in Sociological Abstracts, a primary "finding" (indexing/abstracting) source for sociology. They also use the library's collection and other scholarly database products.

7. *Selects an appropriate documentation style and uses it consistently to cite sources (V.3.a).* Students read and use the *American Sociological Association Style Guide* (1997) as both their documentation and writing style guide.

Components of the Literature Review Assignment

The authors structured the literature review assignment to ensure student success. Not only does it introduce sociological concepts, but the assignment sequence also follows and reinforces the instruction of critical information literacy skills by using the same concepts and vocabulary covered by students in EN112.

Literature review guidelines. The format of the assignment is based on standards specific to the discipline of sociology. Components include an introduction, discussion, conclusion, and list of works cited. Students receive a detailed handout that clarifies the assignment and provides guidance for its preparation.

Sequenced steps and timeline. The assignment is introduced within the first two weeks of the 13-week course, and the final version of the literature review is submitted one week before the final exam. This allows time for two information literacy sessions led by a librarian and for students to access materials through interlibrary loan. As Figure 1 illustrates, students complete four separate assignments within a timeline of progressive deadlines as part of their development of the literature review. The first three assignments (i.e., introduction, references, discussion, and conclusion) are not graded, but allow the professor to review student work, make written suggestions, encourage individual information consultations with a librarian, and ascertain student progress towards completion of the assignment. The graded assignment integrates the first three, taking into account guidance provided by the professor, the librarian, and other campus support services.

Week 2	Introduction to the literature review Class session devoted to review of assignment and expectations.
Week 3	Library Day – Locating & using overview sources Reinforce search strategy for locating sources used to write introduction.
Week 4	ASSIGNMENT DUE – Term paper Introduction One-two page written introduction to the chosen social phenomenon
Week 4	Library Day – Locating scholarly materials with finding sources Reinforce process used to locate current scholarly resources including use of interlibrary loan.
Week 6	ASSIGNMENT DUE – Term paper references List of 10 or more current scholarly sources to be reviewed. Information consultation with librarian if student is having difficulty locating resources.
Week 10	ASSIGNMENT DUE – Term paper discussion and conclusion components 11- to 13-page review and summary of scholarly sources identified in previous assignment.
Week 11	Term paper conferences 15-minute individual discussion with professor to make final suggestions for improvement and to answer student questions. Information consultation or WRSL appointment suggested if student still needs guidance.
Week 13	ASSIGNMENT DUE – Term paper final version Complete assignment (all components) submitted for grade.

Figure 1. *Sample timeline for SO101 literature review assignment.*

Library sessions and exercises. Library sessions reinforce and apply the concepts taught in EN112. For example, the first session reminds students of the suggested six-step search strategy and demonstrates the use of overview sources, keyword selection, and ways to broaden or narrow a topic that are then applied to the discipline of sociology. It is also an opportunity to integrate students excused from EN112 (by transfer or AP credits) into Wartburg's information literacy approach. By using reference materials that include sociology encyclopedias, recent topical encyclopedias, and series that cover a topic comprehensively (such as ABC Clio's *Contemporary World Issues* series and *CQ Researcher Online*), students learn about their chosen topic, hone their vocabulary, become familiar with important people and dates, recognize major concepts, and take note of bibliographies in overview sources that recommend materials for further study. This exploration forms the basis of the written introduction and helps clarify the direction the student plans to take in the literature review.

The second library session focuses on finding sources, defined as the indexing/abstracting databases that lead to the required scholarly content resources. Discussion centers on specific tools, use of disciplinary thesauri, e-Books, Boolean search techniques, checking credentials of an author or journal, locating items at the college library, and obtaining materials through interlibrary loan. The outcome of this session is a list of scholarly sources that serves as the starting point for developing a working bibliography for the literature review assignment.

Information consultations. Consultations are an opportunity for students to discuss their paper one-on-one with an information literacy librarian who prepares customized assistance. These meetings are particularly helpful in developing the student's search strategy, selecting possible keywords, and locating relevant scholarly materials. In most cases, the librarian can schedule an information consultation within 24 hours of the request and will spend 15-30 minutes in personal conference with the requester. While not every student needs or takes advantage of a scheduled consultation, the opportunity is provided and is advertised at the two information literacy sessions. Consultations are considered an enhanced reference encounter and are an option available to all Wartburg College students.

Conferences can also be scheduled through the college's Writing, Reading, Speaking Laboratory (WRSL), where trained students offer individual assistance to their peers. These students provide help with grammar issues, writing strategies, generating ideas, focusing on the topic, documenting sources, and reviewing and editing suggestions. The WRSL is part of the college's academic support services.

Faculty-student conferences. The week after students hand in the full draft of their paper, they attend a 15-minute conference with the professor. The conference allows the professor an opportunity to review areas for improvement and to answer questions as students prepare the final version of the assignment.

Assessment, Outcomes, and Keys to Effectiveness

Ongoing assessment and adapting the structure of the assignment to meet student needs is central to sustaining the SO101 literature review. The authors have administered a variety of assessment surveys over the five years of this collaboration. The most recent is a "confidence check" questionnaire students complete when they turn in their first draft. The intent is to identify students unsure about their progress while there is still time to schedule information consultations or other interventions. The questionnaire asks about each step of the process: (a) the overview session, (b) modification of the chosen topic, (c) comfort level with sociology tools, (d) use of additional finding sources, (e) interlibrary loan, (f) ASA documentation, (g) assessment of sources, and (h) decisions about scholarly materials. Students rate how well they think they did in each step and respond to specific questions related to each category. They also indicate their confidence level about their sources and ability to meet the expectations of the assignment. An earlier version of the questionnaire focused on ratings and left space for comments at the end, but this elicited few additional remarks from students each term. Since the purpose of this assessment is to measure the helpfulness of the process from the students' perspective, the revised assessment has been more successful in obtaining both ratings and useful narrative responses.

At the end of each semester, the authors examine the questionnaires along with comments made on the college-administered Student Ratings of Instruction to revise problematic portions of the assignment process. The professor also attends each library session, which allows informal discussion between the collaborators following the class period. Ongoing assessment has led to changes in both the assignment and the course. Information literacy components have increased from one class session that explored a few sociological reference tools and provided a handout of resources, to the more comprehensive approach described here. One outcome of the evaluation process is ongoing purchases by librarians of new reference materials on topics of sociological interest, driven by both the need for comprehensive overview sources and the desire to meet the seven-year currency requirement in the literature review assignment. The popularity of this course, as demonstrated by increasing enrollment, has also led the library's director to increase funding for both the sociology resources budget and online research databases in the discipline.

Even more significant, EN112 was approved as a prerequisite to SO101 in 2004. The Educational Policies Committee of the college granted this approval based on evidence of the interconnected nature of the library/sociology content sequencing. This requirement reinforces concepts previously taught, while permitting SO101 to focus primarily on the seven selected information literacy outcomes. Despite adding the prerequisite, enrollment in the course continued to increase and the department added an additional section in 2004. Because of the prerequisite, students who do not take EN112 in their first semester may now be forced to postpone SO101 to their second year, although permission to take the class as a co-requisite is sometimes given. Nevertheless, the sequencing provides a scaffolded classroom experience for students regardless of their academic year.

This case study exemplifies the integration of information literacy in a discipline-specific course in the first year, an approach transferable to similar courses at other undergraduate institutions. Working within the existing information literacy paradigm reinforces previously learned skills and introduces new skills through a pedagogically sound approach. The information literacy foundation laid by Wartburg's ILAC plan, curriculum mapping, the library's mission to educate information-literate lifelong learners, and the professor's desire to increase scholarly content, provide a structure that allows the literature review assignment to evolve. The partnership also resulted in the librarian's increased understanding of the academic discipline, and the professor's increased understanding of concepts of information literacy

Results will be similar when elements, such as those described here, are developed through ongoing collaboration between professor and librarian. While the SO101 literature review is an ambitious assignment, even information literacy programs that are not as developed can successfully build ACRL standards and outcomes into their course objectives for first-year college students. Use of the literature review assignment teaches students in an introductory course a transferable process required for academic success, with standards and outcomes reinforced in future courses. By structuring research with steps, checkpoints, and consultations built into the process, student achievement is fostered and academic rigor is maintained. This is clearly of interest across disciplines.

Notes

[1] As part of the ILAC program, information literacy lessons are in five of the essential education courses required for graduation. Each lesson is integrated into classroom curricular content and covers information literacy competencies and selected outcomes:

1. EN 112: Search strategy: using overview, finding and fact sources.
2. IS 101: Information universe and evaluation of books, periodicals, and web sites.
3. IS 201: Bias and perspective in information.
4. RE 101: Introduction to primary versus secondary discipline-specific information sources.
5. Scientific reasoning (a suite of course choices): Popular vs. scholarly information, how scientific discovery is shared with a lay audience.

[2] Placement of information literacy outcomes is further delineated on a comprehensive curriculum map suggesting by whom (librarian or faculty) and when (in essential education courses or in the majors) these competencies will be taught. There are also separate documents listing outcomes for each of the five essential education courses and ILAC plans for each major. These plans and details on the use of pre- and post-testing in assessment are available on the library's information literacy web page at www.wartburg.edu/library/infolit

[3] For detailed explanation of community sociology outcomes, see Departmental ILAC Plans: Community Sociology at www.wartburg/edu/library/infolit

References

Association of College and Research Libraries (ACRL). (2000). *Information literacy competency standards for higher education.* Chicago: Author.

American Sociological Association. (1991). *Liberal learning and the sociology major.* Washington, DC: Author.

American Sociological Association. (1997). *American Sociological Association style guide.* Washington, DC: Author.

Wagenaar, T. C. (2004). Is there a core in sociology? Results from a survey. *Teaching Sociology, 32*(1), 1-18.

Wartburg College. (2000). *SO 101 syllabus, fall 2000.* Waverly, IA: Author.

Case Study 7

Reducing Library Anxiety
Through Career Explorations
at Eastern Kentucky

Linda Klein

Institutional Description

Eastern Kentucky University (EKU) is a regional, coeducational, public university with a liberal admissions policy and a full-time equivalent of approximately 14,000 students. More than 90% of the students are from Kentucky with almost 60% of the university's total enrollment coming from 20 economically struggling rural counties in southeastern Kentucky (EKU's service region). Approximately 60% of its students are first-generation college students (neither parent has earned a four-year degree), which means that many students come to EKU with little or no family tradition of postsecondary education.

First-Year Seminars and the NOVA Program

All new students enroll in mandatory first-year orientation seminars, which introduce students to college life. The seminars include a required library orientation that familiarizes students with library services and policies. A special program at EKU, called NOVA, enrolls approximately 100 first-year students in a special seminar intended to provide a more structured social and academic environment than the general orientation seminars. NOVA is one of many federal TRIO programs, which include Upward Bound, Educational Talent Search, and the McNair Scholarships. The federal government created TRIO programs to help low-income students overcome class, social, and cultural barriers to higher education. For admittance to NOVA, first-year students must be (a) first-generation college students, (b) enrolled full-time, and (c) able to demonstrate financial need as determined by the U.S. Department of Education. Based on these criteria, 54% of all EKU undergraduates would qualify for the NOVA program. Studies have shown that being first-generation and having a low-income status put these students at risk for not persisting in higher education.

Students in NOVA are expected to (a) demonstrate knowledge of EKU resources, (b) pursue a path to career discovery, (c) identify successful student behavior, and (d) formulate a plan for academic development. In support of those goals, librarians, in collaboration with NOVA administrators, designed a specialized library orientation to help NOVA students identify and use library resources and personnel to explore potential career paths, research career opportunities, and develop basic skills necessary for information literacy. Since 2003, the orientation has consisted of two library-instruction sessions tied to a career-exploration assignment. The class sessions introduce students to research in an academic library. The career-exploration assignment requires students to articulate critical statements about information resources. The collaborative effort serves NOVA's learning objectives and addresses information literacy principles related to information access and evaluation. By tabulating results of pre- and posttests, and by conducting qualitative analysis of the completed career-exploration assignments and follow-up questionnaires, we have been able to assess student learning and the impact of the program on students' attitudes toward the library and resources.

Anxieties

Library Anxiety

Researchers have studied anxiety and frustration related to the library in a variety of academic contexts. Mellon (1986) coined the term "library anxiety" when an analysis of personal writings of college students engaged in research assignments revealed that a high percentage of students described their initial response to the library in terms of fear or anxiety. This is not the only time negative feelings toward the library may arise. Kuhlthau's (1988, 1991) examination of the cognitive and affective states of students engaged in research suggests that episodes of anxiety, confusion, and doubt also can occur at other stages of the research process. She found these episodes can profoundly affect a student's ability to work through the process to completion. Jiao, Onwuegbuzie, and Lichtenstein (1996) found library anxiety typically plagues most first-year and sophomore students. Their research indicates that these students, more so than juniors, seniors, or graduate students, may experience anxiety at various times in the library, such as when conducting research, doing homework, or doing something as seemingly innocuous as returning a library book.

Preparation for Career Choices by the First-Generation College Student

Another area of concern for college students is career selection. Perry, Cabrera, and Vogt (1999) found that "career maturity," which they describe as a student's vision of his or her academic and professional goals, indirectly influences retention of students in higher education. They recommended bolstering college retention strategies through enhanced career-counseling services. They also suggested that these services should not be limited to graduating seniors but should consist of a series of interventions throughout the college career. In fact, some students may have an interest in more career-related assistance in their first year of college. For example, Davig and Spain's (2004) study of EKU first-year students found that these students wanted more hands-on activities and more emphasis on helping them choose college majors and careers in the first-year seminar.

First-generation, first-year students also may need even more attention regarding careers and choice of majors. Gibbons and Shoffner (2004) found that typical problems facing first-generation college students include less exposure to information resources about choosing a college or a major, more difficulty accessing information about planning for college and careers, and the likelihood of not having taken courses that prepare them for college-level work.

Overcoming Anxiety and Improving Attitudes by Exploring Careers

Academic librarians often work with faculty to develop instruction sessions that relate information literacy skills to a course-based research assignment. Kirk (1999) gives an overview of the development of course-integrated library instruction. Representative examples of such integrated instruction include Zhang (2001), Larkin and Pines (2005), and Kohl and Wilson (1986). Following these precedents, EKU librarians strive to tailor their library-instruction sessions to students' research assignments to make such sessions more meaningful for students. Course-integrated library instruction, reduction of library anxiety in first-year students, and career-guidance assistance for first-generation college students provided the motivation in designing the career-exploration assignment used for NOVA seminars. EKU librarians and NOVA administrators also wanted these students to have a positive learning experience that would likely have a successful outcome to bolster confidence in seeking information. We designed the NOVA library orientation to combine specialized library instruction with a hands-on research assignment on the topic of career exploration.

The assignment. We ask students to select an occupation of interest and research that career using four types of information sources. The sources include (a) a book found via the online catalog, (b) an article found in the online EBSCOhost database Academic Search Premier, (c) the online *Occupational Outlook Handbook* from the U.S. Department of Labor, and (d) one web site found via a method of the student's choosing. They then write a brief paper summarizing differences among the four information sources and complete a worksheet assigning a number value to each resource. Using two criteria, students are asked to rate the resources based on "ease of use," with ratings ranging from one (easy to use) to four (not easy to use), and "quality of information," with ratings ranging from one (highest quality) to four (lowest quality).

Instruction sessions. In two library-instruction sessions, librarians introduce the library and its services and tell students about the research assignment. Librarians demonstrate how to use the catalog, the Academic Search Premier database, and the *Occupational Outlook Handbook.* Librarians share tips for evaluating web sites and explain how to interpret results in the database and catalog. Time is allotted for hands-on searching. Librarians and NOVA instructors are in the classroom to assist as needed.

Quantitative and Qualitative Assessment and Outcomes

Pre- and Posttests: Quantitative Data

During the first two years of the collaboration, we measured attitudinal changes using pre- and posttests. The 2003 student cohort, after library instruction, indicated less uncertainty in searching for information and a greater sense of independence in searching for periodical articles. Even though many students believed, after instruction, that they would have less need to ask for help from a librarian, more than 80% of the NOVA students agreed or strongly agreed that they were comfortable asking a librarian for help and that they would use the library to meet their information needs (Marcum, 2005). Jiao et al. (1996) connect their findings that first-year and sophomore students are typically the most library-anxious to Mellon's (1988) findings that these students are also the least likely to seek library assistance in order to hide their lack of library experience. If NOVA students are more likely to seek help, this may suggest that they have experienced a reduction in library anxiety.

While the collaboration continued in the fall 2004 semester, the pre- and posttests changed significantly. The changes consisted of revising some questions to reduce ambiguity and adding some questions to collect more data. These changes made it difficult to correlate results directly from one year to the next. We learned, however, that the program continued to have an impact on students' confidence levels. In the pretest, 55% either agreed or strongly agreed that they considered themselves confident in their ability to use the library to meet their information needs; after the sessions, this number increased to 82.9%. While not implemented in 2004, further enhancements to assessment in 2005 will include the introduction of a control group receiving only the generic library orientation without the specialized library-instruction sessions or the career-exploration assignment.

Assignment Results and Questionnaires: Qualitative and Quantitative Data

Content analysis of the written assignment reveals some feelings of frustration or confusion when students discussed ease of use of the various resources. The most common reason for negative attitudes occurred when students perceived a resource's lack of relevance to their specific career questions. A few students expressed a preference for online resources rather than physical print resources. Ease of navigation proved a big factor in preferring electronic resources. Some wrote that they considered finding books in the online catalog easy, but considered navigating the physical space of the library to find the actual book daunting. While some expressed frustration when they found their search for materials to be difficult or unproductive, others who had success in their searches expressed feelings of confidence. The most common positive reactions to resources were related to quality and relevance to specific questions about a career. A small number of students related how the assignment helped them learn more about the library and researching.

Because an important motivation for the creation of this assignment was to reinforce NOVA's goals of career discovery and academic development, we also analyzed what students said they learned about their careers. Most students indicated the research had not changed their career choice. However, many expressed that they had a more realistic picture of the career's requirements, benefits, and drawbacks. A few, after learning more about their careers, mentioned that they reconsidered their original career plans.

We also assessed students' attitudes and confidence levels with a follow-up questionnaire in spring 2005, soliciting responses from 55 NOVA students who participated in the fall 2004 library program. Based on content analysis of written responses to our questionnaire, we found that nearly 7% of the respondents indicated that students still felt intimidated, lost, or overwhelmed by the library; 10% indicated that they had positive feelings about the library prior to the library instruction sessions and still did. Over 43% of the students reported changes in attitude, such as feeling more at ease in the library and in searching for information, or indicated less fear and more confidence than before. Some students also considered the library instruction and assignment useful because what they learned helped them complete other class assignments or learn about a potential career.

Future Collaboration and Additional Assessment

The evaluation of the completed career-exploration assignments revealed that many students had difficulty finding relevant articles in the online database Academic Search Premier. As a result, they felt frustrated with this portion of the assignment. We neither expected nor wanted to achieve this particular outcome, since one of the goals of the assignment was to create the opportunity for a successful learning experience so that students would feel more confident about searching for information and accessing library resources. The article databases are not necessarily appropriate for researching some careers. Therefore, to adjust for this finding, we will ask the 2005 student cohort to search the database for an article that provides information about the general job market rather than ask them to search for an article addressing their specific careers. By making this adjustment to the assignment, we hope more students will achieve success in searching and, therefore, experience less frustration. Students will continue to search for specific information about their chosen careers in a book, the *Occupational Outlook Handbook*, and the self-selected web site.

Conclusion

Because EKU has more than 2,000 incoming first-year students every year and only a few reference and instruction librarians, it is not possible for EKU librarians to give all students enrolled in general first-year orientation seminars the same in-depth attention given to NOVA students. However, this collaborative effort has helped EKU librarians and NOVA administrators and instructors learn how NOVA students feel about navigating the library, why they feel frustration when searching for information in various resources, and how they evaluate information based on ease of use and quality. What librarians have learned from assessing the attitudes and confidence levels of NOVA students toward the library and resources has resulted in an increased awareness of the needs and attitudes of all first-year students at EKU.

The partnership between EKU librarians and NOVA administrators is entering its third year, and the program continues to evolve. While the librarians and administrators initially instigated the career-exploration assignment and its related library instruction with the purpose of enhancing NOVA students' library experience and providing career exploration opportunities, our research suggests a side benefit of reducing library anxiety in this group of students. The 2005 collaboration, with the help of an assessment grant, will include a more extensive assessment of students' ability to recall what they learned in the library instruction sessions, as well as the implementation of a control group to enhance ongoing research. In addition, we plan to measure ongoing attitudes toward the library. First-year students, especially first-generation students, are vulnerable to many pressures that can prevent academic success and persistence in higher education. The partners in this collaborative effort will continue to provide this special group of at-risk students an opportunity to gain confidence and achieve success, not only as students but also as lifelong learners.

Author Note

I thank Kevin Jones for tabulating quantitative data from the pretests and posttests. Some of the information regarding the career exploration project and NOVA learning community has been previously presented at national conferences.

References

Davig, W. B., & Spain, J. W. (2004). Impact on freshman retention of orientation course content: Proposed persistence model. *Journal of College Student Retention, 5*(3), 305-323.

Gibbons, M. M., & Shoffner, M. F. (2004). Prospective first-generation college students: Meeting their needs through social-cognitive career theory. *Professional School Counseling, 8*(1), 91-97.

Jiao, Q. G., Onwuegbuzie, A. J., & Lichtenstein, A. A. (1996). Library anxiety: Characteristics of 'at-risk' college students. *Library and Information Science Research, 18*(2), 151-163.

Kirk, T. G., Jr. (1999). Course-related bibliographic instruction in the 1990s. *Reference Services Review, 27*(3), 235-241.

Kohl, D. F., & Wilson, L. A. (1986). Effectiveness of course-integrated bibliographic instruction in improving coursework. *RQ, 26*, 206-211.

Kuhlthau, C. C. (1988). Developing a model of the library search process: Cognitive and affective aspects. *RQ, 28*, 232-242.

Kuhlthau, C. C. (1991). Inside the search process: Information-seeking from the user's perspective. *Journal of the American Society for Information Science, 42*(5), 361-371.

Larkin, J. E., & Pines, H. A. (2005). Developing information literacy and research skills in Introductory psychology: A case study. *The Journal of Academic Librarianship, 31*(1), 40-45.

Marcum, B. (2005). EKU Libraries and the NOVA program: Collaborating to bring information literacy to first-year students. *The Southeastern Librarian, 53*(1), 17-25.

Mellon, C. A. (1986). Library anxiety: A grounded theory and its development. *College & Research Libraries, 47*(14), 160-165.

Mellon, C. A. (1988). Attitudes: The forgotten dimension in library instruction. *Library Journal, 113*, 137-139.

Perry, S. R., Cabrera, A. F., & Vogt, W. P. (1999). Career maturity and college student persistence. *Journal of College Student Retention, 1*(1), 41-58.

Zhang, W. (2001). Building partnerships in liberal arts education: Library team teaching. *Reference Services Review 29*(2), 141-150.

Case Study 8

Catherine Rod & Rebecca Stuhr

*Using Web-Based
Instruction Guides to Teach
Information Literacy Concepts
to First-Year Students
at Grinnell College*

W̄hat is an effective way to teach first-year students basic information literacy competencies established by the Association of College and Research Libraries (ACRL) standards? How can librarians work with classroom faculty to present those concepts at the right time, in the right manner, and with the right tools? These are questions the librarians at Grinnell College ask as we reexamine and refine our work with first-year students through Grinnell's first-year seminars. One result of this process is the development of web-based instruction guides that are used in the classroom, at the reference desk, and in individualized reference appointments.

Institutional Description

Grinnell College is a private, four-year, liberal arts college located in central Iowa. The student body of 1,450 comes from all 50 states and from 49 countries. Grinnell maintains a student/faculty ratio of 10 to 1. Close student-faculty interaction and collaboration are the hallmarks of a Grinnell education. This pattern of working closely with the classroom faculty members begins with the first-year seminar and continues throughout a student's years at the college. In recognition of its tradition of student-faculty collaboration, the Howard Hughes Medical Institute awarded Grinnell College one of 53 grants that support, among other activities, student summer research with faculty mentors. Students in their junior and senior years also have the option of working individually with classroom faculty members through a semester-long Mentored Advanced Project (MAP).

The First-Year Seminar

A unique aspect of a Grinnell College education is its open curriculum. Aside from departmental requirements for majors, Grinnell has only one general requirement. The First-Year Tutorial is a one-semester seminar for entering students that serves as an introduction to college life. One classroom faculty member meets with 12 or 13 students for two hours twice a week during the fall semester and serves as their advisor until students declare their majors at the end of their second year.

Grinnell culture emphasizes individual initiative and allows for a high degree of creativity and customization. Unlike similar programs at other colleges, the Grinnell first-year seminar has no overriding theme that all students explore. Each seminar focuses on a unique topic. Past seminar topics include "Elvis Everywhere," "The Worth of Water," "The Limits of

Introspection," "Icelandic Sagas," "Capitalism Goes to the Movies," and "Decline and Renewal in the Heartland." The topics of the seminars do not necessarily correspond to the disciplinary background of the classroom faculty member. A professor of mathematics, for example, taught the seminar on Icelandic Sagas. Although each seminar topic is different, students are exposed to most aspects of study and research at Grinnell, including academic honesty, computing, and information literacy.

The content of each seminar reflects the individual style and priorities of the classroom faculty teaching the course. Some choose to include a research assignment that ensures students will use library resources. Others choose to teach critical thinking and writing skills by having students reflect on a text without consulting secondary sources. Providing information literacy instruction under these conditions has proved challenging.

Information Literacy

Librarians have worked with the first-year seminar since its inception in the early 1970s. At first, we used the library tour as an opportunity to introduce students to the services and resources of the building while describing reference sources they might find helpful when working on seminar assignments. By the mid-1980s, we began to rethink what and how to present library instruction to the seminar students and also to limit library tours to new student orientation days.[1] We developed a three-session program based on the "research spectrum" through which we followed an idea from its nascent stages with an individual scholar, to the scholar's development of the idea, its presentation as a more fully developed concept at conferences, publication in conference proceedings, and to eventual presentation in a more refined form through the peer-review process into journals or books. Finally, we talked about how students gain access to this research through its incorporation into the knowledge base of the discipline as evidenced by tertiary sources (i.e., general and subject-specific indexes and abstracts, footnotes, and bibliographies). Although this new material excited us, the first-year students found it too theoretical to be effective. The material also lacked immediate practical application.

Just as the classroom faculty teach their own content in their own unique manner, Grinnell College librarians also approach classroom work with our own styles. We have each experimented with different ideas and methods for communicating the principles associated with information literacy. Generally, we have worked toward talking less, having more hands-on experiences, and incorporating some kind of assignment either provided by the classroom faculty or the librarian. In most, but not all cases, students complete the assignments during the class period. We have continued to work with the idea of presenting information over a series of class sessions, but this also varies for each librarian and each seminar instructor.

Information Literacy Immersion

In July 2003, three librarians, a classroom faculty member from the education department, the director of the Writing Lab, and a curricular technology specialist attended the regional information literacy institute held at Coe College in Cedar Rapids, Iowa. From the many useful ideas presented at the institute, we chose three key concepts. First, information literacy is not the sole responsibility of librarians just as writing is not the sole responsibility of English departments. Classroom faculty, librarians, information technologists, writing and reading specialists, and others share the responsibility of working together with students to teach them about information literacy. Second, not all instruction needs to take place in the classroom. This was not a new idea for us since we believe that reference interactions, research appointments, and other encounters with students are also opportunities for teaching. Third, less is more.

We should limit the number of concepts presented rather than trying to fit in a little about everything related to working in libraries or with library resources. This struck a chord with all of us who attended the institute. Reviewing our previous work with the first-year seminar, we knew we tried to address too much in the time allotted and risked overwhelming the students with more than they could possibly absorb.

Armed with our new energy and ideas, we returned to Grinnell and met with all the librarians to see how what we had learned could be incorporated into our presentations to first-year seminar sections. As a result of the immersion and ensuing discussions among colleagues, we again revised our first-year information literacy program.

New Ideas

We wanted to give the seminar faculty numerous options so we could fit our work into their syllabi in ways that best suited them and the content of their courses. For instance, we suggested the option of librarians setting office hours specifically for students in a particular seminar so that students could come to "their" librarian's office for help with research. We suggested the possibility of "reference by appointment" in addition to, or instead of, class time. Finally, we proposed coming into the classroom for a series of short sessions, each devoted to one concept. This last idea led us to consider creating individual instruction guides, each addressing a single information literacy concept.

Instruction Guides for Teaching Information Literacy to First-Year Students

As a group, we first considered everything we thought we would want first-year students to know by the end of the academic year. We then winnowed the resulting list down to the essential concepts. We ended up with nine: (a) choosing a topic for research, (b) creating search statements, (c) using the library catalog, (d) using keywords versus subject headings, (e) using Internet search engines versus periodical databases, (f) choosing a periodical database, (g) distinguishing between scholarly and popular periodicals, (h) searching the Internet effectively, and (i) evaluating resources in print and electronic formats. Once we had identified these concepts, we developed a set of guidelines. Each instruction guide would focus on a single concept, could be presented in 20 to 30 minutes, would be web-based and visually interesting, and would be possible to teach without electronic technology (i.e., the web-based guide could be used as an overhead transparency or as a handout if necessary). As we developed the guides, we also planned short assessments for each session that could be done in class with or without computers.

Instruction Guides in Practice[2]

Two librarians took the primary responsibility for developing the nine information literacy instruction guides. Each guide has text but also makes heavy use of screen captures taken from the online catalog and indexes and other illustrative images. Our intention in developing these guides was that they be used as examples, not as scripts. As noted earlier, Grinnell College has an individual-oriented culture. We did not consider it possible to write a script that would suit all seminars, and we would be uncomfortable walking into a classroom with a canned presentation. The guides are short lessons. Each one is designed to introduce students to one aspect of information literacy. We think of them as starting points and always encourage students to work directly with a librarian. At the web site, each two- to three-page instruction guide has a brief abstract and a link to the full guide. The following is an example:

Creating a Search Statement

Boolean searching allows you to expand or limit your search for information by using the terms AND, OR, and NOT. Learn how to create effective search statements using Boolean operators.

How Are the Guides Used?

We have used the guides in numerous ways, and we continue to experiment with different approaches to working with students in the first-year seminar. A librarian might use examples from one or two of them to illustrate a point or choose to distribute the half-sheet colored handouts developed from "Creating a Search Statement" and "Evaluating Resources." We refer students to these guides in our handouts and in classroom discussions, include them as links from our customized class web pages, and use them when working with students at the reference desk.

Classroom faculty show a distinct interest in using the guides. At a meeting of first-year seminar faculty, one participant asked if he could use the instruction guides in class without having a librarian present them. We encouraged him to talk with a librarian first so we could discuss the logic and purpose behind the guides. Nevertheless, we saw no reason to discourage classroom faculty from incorporating the guides into their teaching. We believe the more students use the guides, the more likely they are to absorb the concepts.

We have used the guides to initiate conversations with classroom faculty members in preparation for working with both first-year seminars and upper-level courses. The guides make it easy to talk about information literacy concepts; and instructors can choose what they would most like their students to learn, what they are comfortable teaching themselves, and what they would like the librarian to address. For example, a history professor felt comfortable addressing the difference between scholarly and popular sources but did not feel comfortable talking to her class about Boolean logic and searching databases. Learning to work with the expertise of each classroom faculty member has been a useful way to incorporate information literacy into more courses.

Are the Guides Working?

The Grinnell College librarians continue to find an effective means of assessing our work with the first-year seminars. We have used a short, half-sheet form with three to four questions where students are asked to rank the librarian's presentation on a 1 to 5 scale. We determined that these brief surveys have a limited value for a number of reasons. Librarian sessions are all different depending on the requests of the professor and the librarian's inclinations. Not all librarians use the guides, and those who do, do not use them in a uniform manner. There is no consistency, then, in what is being assessed. Finally, we find the student ratings unreliable. Most librarians receive high rankings of 4 or 5 regardless of their own or their peers' assessment of the same class.

As we developed the guides, we created a series of nine assignments that could serve as assessments. One assignment was designed for each concept and could be completed with or without a computer. For example, the assignment used with "Selecting a Topic" is quite simple. Students choose a topic, defining it broadly first, and then more narrowly in two or three different ways. The librarian brings a variety of reference books to the classroom so students can look through them for background information that will help them define their topic. Another example, the assignment for "Creating a Search Statement," is also easily done without computers. The librarian works with the entire class to create a search statement on a topic provided by the instructor or one of the students. For the assignment, the librarian can brainstorm with the students for a variety of keywords. Then, each student creates two or more search statements with at least one very specific statement and one more general statement. If there is time, students report their statements to the class. If not, they turn them in to the librarian. If there are computers in the classroom, students enter their statements in one or more databases and report the results of their searches to the class or on paper to be turned in. Observing students' success in completing the assignments gives us some idea of how well they understood the concepts presented.

Because all first-year seminars are scheduled at the same time, a librarian cannot count on teaching in a room with a computer for each student. Often, librarians are in a classroom with a single computer-projector and no hands-on capability for the students. Because we may go into the classroom for three 20- to 30-minute sessions, we do not always find it expedient to have the class move to a computer lab.[3] One significant difficulty with carrying out any kind of assessment is that we are often in the classroom for a short time and it is difficult to fit the assignment into one session. To make these assignments useful as assessment tools, we need to experiment more with using them in the classroom, especially during these short presentations.

An additional form of assessment is provided by librarian peer review of instruction sessions. Librarians who are under review for contract renewal have several of their peers observe at least three of their class sessions. This gives all librarians an opportunity to learn from each other and provides constructive feedback to the library faculty member under review. We also do this for all new library faculty members. We can, thus, see how the guides are being used and whether they appear to be effective. The librarians also meet regularly during the semester to go over first-year seminar experiences, share interesting ideas, successes, and problems. We treat our work with the first-year seminar as a work in progress, refining our plans and work as the semester progresses.

The web-based presentations have been used frequently in information literacy sessions in the first-year seminars. Librarians use them to review key concepts and to talk with classroom faculty members when preparing to meet with the faculty member's students. We expect to have more data on our first-year students' information literacy strengths and weaknesses as we study the results of the pilot survey administered during the spring of 2005. This pilot survey, called the First-Year Information Literacy in the Liberal Arts Assessment (FYILLAA), is the result of a grant from the Midwest Information Technology Center (MITC) and the collaboration of a group of Associated Colleges of the Midwest (ACM) libraries (Carleton, St. Olaf, Macalester, and Grinnell). The official survey was administered with an expanded participation list in the early weeks of fall 2005. Preliminary results from the pilot have not been analyzed in a manner that allows us to present any accurate data at the time of this writing. A very cursory look at responses suggests that most students find the process of research "very easy" or "somewhat easy." Most respondents sought assistance of some kind, from librarians or other sources "now and then" or "never." However, a clear majority of the respondents enjoyed conducting research. When we have analyzed the results of the first official round of the survey, we hope to use the findings to refine the session guides and assignments, develop additional guides for upper-level courses, and encourage faculty to incorporate information literacy into their teaching.

Notes

[1] Primarily, parents take advantage of our new student day tours. Interestingly, some students and a few classroom faculty members continue to want a tour during the time we spend with their classes. Although we have a small library and the main service points are the first thing a student will see as he or she walks into the building, there does seem to be some anxiety about locating everything, and a hesitancy to ask for directions.

[2] The guides are available at http://www.lib.grinnell.edu/research/InstructionGuides/index.html

[3] The library has a teaching space that we call the Interactive Instructional Facility (IIF). It has 11 computer stations around the periphery of the room. Each station easily seats two students. We also have moveable tables in the center of the room that can be pushed together, used separately, expanded, and collapsed. All librarians prefer to teach in this room, but it must be scheduled early.

Case Study 9

Emergence / Emergency?
The Earlham Libraries and
the First-Year Experience

Neal Baker & Thomas G. Kirk, Jr.

Institutional Description

Earlham College is a coeducational, four-year, residential, liberal arts institution in Richmond, Indiana. Founded in 1847 by the Religious Society of Friends (Quakers), the College enrolls approximately 1,200 undergraduates. About two thirds of Earlham students participate in off-campus study programs in more than 20 countries and around the United States. The 12:1 student/faculty ratio allows for collaborative research between professors and undergraduates. The Earlham Libraries consist of the main Lilly Library and the branch Wildman Science Library. The staff includes seven librarians, two professional archivists, six paraprofessional staff, and the equivalent of about 10 full-time student staff. The seven librarians, including the director and the chief cataloger, have liaison responsibilities to academic departments. In these roles, all librarians are responsible for collection development, information literacy program development, and other activities designed to make the library an effective asset in support of academic programs.

A Tradition of Library Instruction

Earlham College undergraduates have been formally educated about libraries since the early 1960s when the profession adopted the term, "course-related bibliographic instruction." Evan I. Farber was appointed library director in 1961 and championed the development of a course-integrated bibliographic instruction program based on collaborative work between librarians and classroom faculty.

When it became clear that four librarians would retire within a few years of each other between 1990 and 1995, the librarians and college administration developed a staff "succession" plan to ensure sustainability of the course-related bibliographic instruction program. This effort included hiring new people prepared to take on the instructional and liaison roles commonplace at Earlham and, by mutual agreement, librarians timed their retirements so that traditions could evolve into new programs without losing the valuable accumulated experience.

229

Capitalizing on Tradition and Change

The tradition of course-integrated bibliographic instruction at Earlham assures that classroom faculty and the administration view librarians as educators whose contributions are important to the mission of the college. Consequently, Earlham librarians have been asked for many years by their classroom faculty and administrative colleagues to serve in important roles outside the libraries. For example, Earlham librarians now teach courses, lead off-campus study programs, participate on major committees, and help administer both cocurricular and curricular programs. While these activities have served the college well and increased the value of the libraries and librarians, the challenge remains of keeping the libraries' services and collections relevant to a changing academic environment.

Recently, the libraries have capitalized on change by giving highest priority to the first-year experience of both students and faculty. The organization has recently confronted three intersecting vectors of change. First, changes in technology use and expectations catalyzed a closer alliance between the libraries and other service units and resulted in the emergence of a hybrid service team under the title of Information Services. Second, Earlham has seen the advent of radically new general education requirements. Last, the college has experienced a sudden influx of new tenure-track faculty. What might be viewed as a tripartite "emergency" actually became an opportunity for renewing the integration of information literacy in the first-year experience at Earlham.

Technological Change and the First-Year Experience

Technological change led to the merger of the Earlham Libraries, Computing Services, and Media Resources units into an Information Services organization in January 2001. In 2002, the College formalized Web Management and Services, which reports to both Information Services and Public Affairs. Coordinated by the college librarian, the organization covers the expanding set of responsibilities related to information technology: (a) library services, (b) instructional technology and media, (c) administrative computing services, (d) micro-computing services, (e) systems and network services, and (f) web services. The resulting synergy has benefited all units, allowing for the cross-pollination of technological expertise and a wider emphasis on customer service.

In January 2002, librarians approached Information Services with an idea to enhance the first-year experience. They proposed replacing the long-standing library orientation required during New Student Week with an information technology equivalent. Inspired in part by the publication of the *Information Literacy Competency Standards for Higher Education*, the coordinator of information services and college administration approved the proposal. In consultation with computing services staff, a librarian and an instructional technologist developed a content outline that would be used in 50-minute orientation sessions by instructors from all Information Services units during the 2002 New Student Week.

The required sessions introduced all first-year students to information technology resources at Earlham. In 2002 and 2003, the overview encompassed the computing labs and network infrastructure, providing hands-on experience with the campus online course registration tool, campus e-mail, and the library catalog. In 2004, the overview dropped the library catalog in favor of a brief discussion about intellectual property as it pertains to copyrighted digital material, thereby addressing other aspects of the *Information Literacy Competency Standards for Higher Education*.

The information technology orientation sessions have been successful. Assessment of students indicates that they view the sessions as extremely relevant, since they learn practical skills such as how to register their computers on the campus network and how to check their campus e-mail accounts. Classroom faculty have come to rely on students' newly learned ability to save coursework to the campus network, and college academic administrators appreciate how the sessions teach students to use the campus online course registration tool. Information services staff enjoy the public exposure and benefit from not having to answer the same basic questions repeatedly. The librarians, meanwhile, demonstrate their general technological proficiency.

Curricular Change and the First-Year Experience

Curricular revision is often a slow and almost invisible activity. Rather than working at institution-wide changes from the top down, much of the change in Earlham's curriculum is the work of individual classroom faculty experimenting with and revising their courses. To stay in touch with the incremental curricular change, librarians focus their attention on communication with individual faculty. Librarians regularly solicit syllabi or initiate conversations about course activities in an effort to help faculty identify information resources and information literacy skills needed to carry out course assignments. They also collaborate with classroom faculty to create assignments and the type and content of instruction needed to develop information literacy skills. In addition to teaching information resources, librarians provide course-integrated sessions on using software such as Microsoft Excel, Microsoft PowerPoint, and Macromedia Dreamweaver.

Despite this tradition of incremental curricular change, the faculty in 2002 approved a radical restructuring of the general education program. From the librarians' perspective, the replacement of core first-year courses titled Humanities I and II with Interpretative Practices and Earlham Seminar represented the most significant change. Humanities I and II courses shared common reading lists. Although these courses did not have any library-research assignments, the faculty agreed on the importance of introducing students to the library. To do that, the librarians created a workbook/exercise that became a required component of the course. As of fall 2004, however, the new general education requirements for first-year courses allowed individual classroom faculty members to choose readings and library instruction at their discretion. At the same time, the guidelines approved by the faculty required a research assignment and library instruction of all Earlham Seminar sections. The new requirements stipulate that all first-year students take an Earlham Seminar.

In the summer of 2004, the librarians sponsored a series of full-day workshops for classroom faculty designed to foster reflection on the appropriate content of information literacy in first-year courses. The College paid stipends to attendees. The workshops began with a model interview between a classroom faculty member and a librarian working to develop an information literacy assignment. The interview was followed by a discussion and brainstorming session in which each attendee explored assignment ideas they would like to try. Librarians then presented their observations about information literacy needs and opened the floor for faculty/librarian dialogue. After lunch, a panel of faculty members talked about both information literacy difficulties and solutions they found. The panel then held a concluding discussion about using the web in first-year course assignments.

Faculty feedback on the workshop expressed a desire for readily available documentation about suggested information literacy assignments for first-year courses. In response, the librarians distributed a list of sample assignments to all classroom faculty in 2004. In fall 2005, the librarians followed up with a one-page list of information literacy skills that could be developed in any first-year seminar. Librarians refer to these documents when communicating with individual faculty members about their course activities.

Generational Change and the First-Year Experience

Since good relationships with classroom faculty are central to librarianship at Earlham, the arrival of 11 new tenure-track faculty (about 10% of the total, full-time teaching faculty) in fall 2004 was a critical development. Just as librarians had recently focused on the first-year experience of students, they prioritized the first-year experience of their faculty colleagues. Outreach efforts began in the late spring and early summer prior to the academic year 2004-2005, when the coordinator of information services encouraged librarians to contact their new departmental liaisons via e-mail and introduce themselves and the services of the libraries. At the same time, the librarians and the College administration planned four initiatives to promote the role of the libraries vis-à-vis new faculty.

First, all new tenure-track faculty received invitations to a late summer workshop entitled "Integrating the Research Assignment Into First-Year Courses." They were paid for their attendance at the workshop. This full-day event began with a discussion of how to plan effective research assignments; and the librarians followed with a series of queries, based on their observations of student behavior, as a way to stimulate discussion of some key concepts relevant to designing library-based research. After lunch, faculty members shared their experiences or ideas about assignments based on student research activities and student-generated information resources. The purpose of the session was to exchange ideas and explore possible implementations of assignments. Throughout, the workshop exposed new faculty members to the perspectives of veteran faculty members selected by the librarians.

Second, the associate academic dean and the registrar invited the librarians to participate in a workshop that introduced the guidelines for teaching the required first-year course—Interpretative Practices, Earlham Seminar—held during the College's official new faculty orientation. The librarians outlined their course-integrated approach to information literacy and fielded questions about the services offered by the libraries. They also distributed copies of sample information literacy assignments for first-year courses.

Third, the academic dean and provost invited a librarian to make a 45-minute presentation on students, plagiarism, and intellectual property during this same new faculty orientation program. This presentation addressed why students plagiarize, what assignments prevent plagiarism, and how to detect plagiarism. It also connected plagiarism to related, ubiquitous, and problematic uses of digital intellectual property such as peer-to-peer file sharing. The talk also provided a tour of online term-paper mills.

Finally, librarians participated in a wider Information Services venture intended to establish good relations with all incoming faculty. Emulating the library liaison concept, the coordinator of information services assigned computing personnel to work with librarians as liaisons to new classroom faculty. Instead of individual liaisons, teams of people from various information technology sub-units scheduled appointments at the beginning of the academic year to offer their services to new faculty members. Thus, a librarian and a hardware repair specialist might meet with a new member of the philosophy department, while the Science Librarian and an instructional technologist might meet with a new biologist.

Assessing Change

Assessment of Earlham's bibliographic instruction/information literacy program has taken new directions in the past two years (Earlham Libraries, 2004). Earlham has been a participant in the National Survey of Student Engagement (NSSE), and the libraries have used NSSE results to examine the impact of its program. Because of the newness of the curriculum revision, there has been insufficient time for the NSSE results to reflect any changes. At this point, we can only speculate as to what the data will reveal.

In 2005, the Earlham Libraries participated in the LibQual+™ for the first time (Association of Research Libraries, 2005). LibQual+™ is a set of tools that libraries purchase to assess their users' opinions of service quality. At the time of this writing, the complete results have not been received; however, the libraries' staff are pleased with preliminary data, which indicate they have exceeded minimum expectations in all categories of the survey. The comments, which were provided by about 45% of all those who completed the survey, indicated a strong level of satisfaction with the services and collections provided. The librarians plan to follow up the survey results with a series of focus-group interviews to evaluate the impact of the information literacy program and other aspects of the libraries' program on students' perceptions of their information literacy development.

At a more targeted level, the College's curricular policy committee asked the librarians to provide data assessing the extent of the inclusion of a library experience in first-year courses during the implementation of general education reform, 2002-2005. In year one of the new general education program (2003-2004), 46% of required first-year Earlham Seminar courses contained a library-instruction component with similar figures obtained for required first-year Interpretive Practices sections. In year two (2004-2005), 65% of required first-year Earlham Seminar and 48% of Interpretive Practices courses contained library-instruction components. The overall numbers are a concern to the librarians and to the College's curricular policy committee, because students not exposed to library instruction may be less able to undertake research assignments in upper-level courses.

Conclusion

Clearly, a good deal of work has yet to be done, despite the advocacy efforts already undertaken. The development and maintenance of a strong, course-related information literacy program, given the changes in technology, styles of teaching, curriculum, and make-up of faculty, requires close working relationships across the campus community. An information literacy program for first-year students is not solely the responsibility of the librarians, although they should take a leadership role. Academic administrators, classroom faculty, instructional technologists, as well as librarians, must work in concert to make the program effective. Earlham's success in navigating the institutional changes described above can be attributed to the collaborative work of many faculty and staff under the librarians' leadership. The ability to provide that leadership is grounded in the many years of experience in a course-related program of instruction. Most important, our efforts are not to maintain the status quo, but to enhance the effective use of information resources in active learning that engages students.

References

Association of Research Libraries. (2005). *LibQual+: Charting library service quality*. Retrieved May 25, 2005, from http://www.libqual.org

Earlham Libraries. (2004). *Publications*. Retrieved May 10, 2005, from http://www.earlham.edu/~libr/library/publications.htm

Case Study 10

Librarians in the Wired Classroom: The Seton Hall University Experience

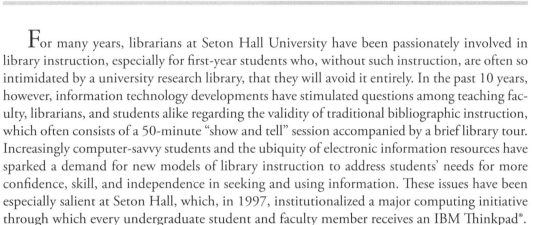

Mary McAleer Balkun, Beth Bloom, & Marta Mestrovic Deyrup

For many years, librarians at Seton Hall University have been passionately involved in library instruction, especially for first-year students who, without such instruction, are often so intimidated by a university research library, that they will avoid it entirely. In the past 10 years, however, information technology developments have stimulated questions among teaching faculty, librarians, and students alike regarding the validity of traditional bibliographic instruction, which often consists of a 50-minute "show and tell" session accompanied by a brief library tour. Increasingly computer-savvy students and the ubiquity of electronic information resources have sparked a demand for new models of library instruction to address students' needs for more confidence, skill, and independence in seeking and using information. These issues have been especially salient at Seton Hall, which, in 1997, institutionalized a major computing initiative through which every undergraduate student and faculty member receives an IBM Thinkpad®.

Traditionally, library instruction has taken place in several venues over the course of a student's years at the University: (a) in a one-credit University Life course for first-semester students; (b) as part of two required first-year writing classes with research components; and (c) in advanced, discipline-specific courses at the request of classroom faculty. In most cases, students go to the library for a one-hour instructional session. Ideally, the librarian conducting the session and the students in the class have received some information about the assignment and have been able to prepare for the lesson accordingly. However, this often did not happen for a variety of reasons, including scheduling difficulties and a lack of communication. In addition, librarians and classroom faculty have not systematically followed up the instruction with additional contact or assessment. Other than providing reference service or individual reference by appointment, the library has lacked a systematic way for students and librarians to interact or establish a working relationship. Other problems have emerged as students confused the ease of access to electronic information with an ability to research effectively. Increasingly, students do most, if not all, their research online from their residence halls and from home, further decreasing their time in the library and their contact with the librarians.

In response to this situation, and with new tools and techniques at their disposal, librarians and classroom faculty began to experiment with innovative strategies for information literacy training. One such strategy, adopted with promising results, is the "Librarians in the Wired Classroom" project. Together with classroom faculty from the English department, librarians have worked to change the traditional modes of library instruction in first-year English classes, taking advantage of the university's technology infrastructure and the commitment to use

Blackboard (i.e., an online classroom management system). A two-part plan emerged that included (a) a database designed to facilitate the scheduling of library instruction and (b) the enrollment of librarians into Blackboard course sections.

The online scheduling database, developed by the codirector of the university's Teaching, Learning, and Technology Center (TLTC), the coordinator of library instruction, and the director of First-Year Writing, streamlined the onerous task of class scheduling to such a degree that far more instructors actually scheduled library sessions for their students, and far more instructors worked with librarians to develop the sessions. In fact, use of the database resulted in a higher percentage of library sessions in College English I and II than in the past (90% of total first-year English classes in both 2003-2004 and 2004-2005 as opposed to 70% in previous years).

The writing program director asked English instructors to select dates for library instruction well in advance of the actual session. Librarians also agreed to sign up for those sessions weeks in advance, giving instructors and librarians an opportunity to discuss the goals, needs, and assignment for each session. Faculty members availed themselves of this opportunity, creating workable assignments that used resources tailored to the specific project at hand. More important, the scheduling system allowed English faculty members to codify and record assignments into the database in advance, thus, allowing both librarians and students more time to prepare for the library session. Perhaps most significant, this new arrangement allowed the writing program director to assess the extent of library instruction across course sections.

While the scheduling database used technology to improve the timing and assessment of the traditional library sessions, the "Librarians in the Wired Classroom" project, initiated in the second phase of the collaboration, proved even more innovative. The "Librarians in the Wired Classroom" project enabled librarians and classroom faculty to take full advantage of certain elements of Seton Hall's technology infrastructure. For example, the mobile computing program meant that all students had access to the same tools and programs. The university's commitment to a course-management system (i.e., Blackboard) meant that a common platform existed where the instructor, the students, and a librarian could interact and share information easily and efficiently. Finally, frequent training opportunities for classroom faculty meant that members of the English department had the technological skills to undertake such a project. Based on these factors, the writing program director decided to enroll university librarians into the Blackboard courses for all College Writing I sections for fall 2002.

The project had relatively simple aims: (a) to improve communication between the librarians, who are experts in information literacy, and students working on research projects and (b) to give students access to a librarian in the same way they now have access to their classroom instructor. Once enrolled in a Blackboard course, the librarian had a connection to every student in the class, received all e-mail communication through Blackboard, and saw the students' work on the discussion board and other areas of the course site. The enrollment of librarians into Blackboard sections increased the day-to-day interaction between librarians and students working on research and other projects. While instructors generally supported the project, it had mixed results for a number of reasons.

- First, as with many new initiatives, the plan proved far too ambitious. Each of the five librarians who agreed to participate had the responsibility for as many as 15 sections of College English I, with approximately 225 students in all. While not all students were expected to take advantage of the program, too many students and too many sections resulted in the librarians being overwhelmed with requests to which they did not have adequate time to respond.

- Classroom faculty, while willing to have the librarians enrolled in their Blackboard courses, had no actual investment in the project and often felt unsure about how to make the best possible use of this new resource.

- Finally, with a few exceptions, there was no communication between the classroom faculty and the librarians "enrolled" in their courses. Already overburdened with the standard requirements of the course, many English faculty did not have time to work on refining this project.

Nevertheless, this first iteration had some success. Librarians gave the classroom instructors access to Kuhlthau's (1996) information literacy assessment test. Initial results indicated that students eagerly engaged in library research and saw themselves as savvy researchers (mainly on the web). Those instructors who were committed to the project and who encouraged their students to contact the librarian demonstrated that, with some modifications, the project could work. For example, one goal of the Seton Hall writing program is to help students become better locaters and users of information. This is especially important for the final paper in College English I, a research essay. In end-of-course evaluations, most classroom faculty agreed that they received fewer basic research questions, and students who used the librarian as a resource produced better papers. As a result, faculty and librarians both agreed on the merits of the basic concept of the project and expressed a willingness to pursue it in another form.

The second iteration of the "Librarians in the Wired Classroom" project occurred on a much smaller scale and in advanced literature electives. These courses typically have enrollments similar to those in College English I and II (between 15 and 22 students), and the requirements include a research paper. We sought to refine the project by including more experienced students and a single librarian linked to one course each semester taught by the same faculty member, thereby providing a controlled environment for the experiment. We made several key changes to the original plan. First, the librarian actually visited the class early in the semester to introduce herself, talk about some of the available resources for projects in literature, and discuss the class research assignment. The librarian showed students how to contact her through Blackboard, and, that same evening, students received a follow-up message encouraging them to contact her as needed for projects in this class or any other. The research project had staggered deadlines (i.e., several students worked on either a presentation or paper rather than having all projects due at the same time), so requests for help had the potential to be more evenly spaced throughout the semester. The classroom faculty sent students e-mails reminding them about the librarian's availability and pointing out potential problem areas in the research process.

The issues students brought to the librarian provided insights for both the librarian and the classroom instructor into students' research methods and problems. Typical student issues included:

- "Whenever I go to the library to do research, I usually get overwhelmed. Am I wasting my time by using books of literary criticism instead of library databases?"
- "I can't find anything at the library on my topic about Kate Chopin." (The student had begun her search by typing the phrase "marriage and divorce in America in the 19th century" into the catalog.)
- "I want to write about culture shock in *The Witch of Blackbird Pond.* Can you help me? I didn't find anything in JSTOR."
- "I am writing my research paper on the book *Wicked.* I haven't found any secondary sources. I don't know what to look for in the catalog or online databases. I want to write about the nature of evil. Do you have any psychology books that explain this subject so I can understand it?"

These questions suggest the variety of ways students can become stalled at the very beginning of the research process, as well as the need for a resource person they trust. These are the kinds of questions students will rarely ask in or even outside class for fear of looking "stupid." Having their misconceptions addressed sensitively and early in the research process can mean the difference between success and failure. The librarian can be a "safe" resource because students can ask questions in the privacy of e-mail and the librarian is never in the position of giving them a grade for their work.

Over the course of several semesters, the librarian and the classroom instructor made additional refinements to the collaborative design. For example, the librarian became a more active participant in the course in which she was enrolled, posting materials in a specially designated "Information Fluency" area in Blackboard and posing her own research-related questions in the discussion board. The classroom instructor required students in one class to keep a log in order to record and assess their research process. Students also posted their logs in Blackboard, and the instructor counted them toward the final grade.

In this iteration, the collaboration had more successful results. Feedback from the instructor, the students (questions on the course evaluation specifically addressed the project), and the librarian indicate that the primary goals of the project—to help students improve their research skills, to help them become more comfortable with the research process, and ultimately to help them produce better papers—had been achieved. Students described themselves as more confident during the research process. They also established a working relationship with a university librarian that sometimes continued beyond the course. Finally, they described the research experience in positive terms overall and, ultimately, wrote more sophisticated and better researched papers.

We realized at this stage that the size of the project depended on the number of librarians available for participation. We also realized that the project was most effective when the librarian worked with two or three groups of students rather than five or six. Thus, this project is scalable, it can be sustained, and it can even be expanded. However, there are two important variables: the number of librarians available to participate and class size. A librarian can work very effectively with three or four sections of a course when each section has just 15 students; however, the larger the course enrollment, the greater the demands on the librarian. Two sections of a course that contain 25 students each are manageable, especially if the same faculty teaches both sections. Working with a regular group of five librarians who are consistently able to commit to the project (as a result of scheduling and other variables), we decided that targeting a small group of first-year students—those with very specific needs—was the logical next step.

The next iteration of the "Librarians in the Wired Classroom" project will be to return the application of the model to first-year writing courses, specifically to Business Writing (now required of all first-year business majors) and selected College English I and II classes. This model will combine lessons learned in both the first and second iterations, with instructors using the scheduling database to arrange for library instruction, but now with the librarian teamed with their classes. This will allow the librarians to review assignments and prepare in advance of the class. The model developed in the second iteration, in which a librarian and instructor "team taught" the research component of a course, proved particularly effective, as did individual, one-on-one follow-up sessions between librarians and students who are in need of further help. Thus, we will continue the team teaching and individualized follow-up.

Clearly, some of the technology tools—such as e-mail and discussion boards—offer advantages to librarians working with first-year students. These students, who are "digital natives," a phrase coined by Prensky (2001), are comfortable communicating in online forums. They use them extensively and are willing to reveal themselves in a way that may not occur in face-to-face contact. The responses of classroom faculty who participated in a survey about their involvement in the project reinforced this observation. The first-year students generally used e-mail and discussion boards much more easily and effectively than the advanced students who participated in the second iteration of the project. The first-year students expressed more candor about their problems and abilities in online discussions, and they asked more process-oriented questions about the research. The students in the advanced electives, on the other hand, simply wanted direction to good resources or to receive validation as to the adequacy of their research methods.

While we could not require all English instructors to participate in the project, we anticipate that more will volunteer as word of its success spreads. And, indeed, our assumptions already have proven true. Individual faculty also have found other ways to collaborate with the librarians. For example, one instructor who taught several Business Writing courses invited a librarian to lecture and demonstrate specialized databases.

This project also has profound implications for the university's new core curriculum, which has a strong first-year component and features a proficiencies-infusion piece. One of these proficiencies is information literacy. In faculty development workshops, classroom faculty work with librarians to create assignments that stress good research practices. The workshop leaders will encourage instructors who "infuse" information literacy into a course to use the "Librarians in the Wired Classroom" model.

Lessons Learned

The evolving model of library instruction at Seton Hall has yielded a number of important insights into the design and implementation of such practices. For example,

- The role of the librarian in this hybrid format (one that combines online and in-class instruction) should be coach as well as an instructor. Communication from the librarian is most effective when it is both positive and non-judgmental.
- Consistent classroom faculty support is essential, and participation ideally should be part of the course requirements. This can happen in two ways: (a) the classroom instructor assigns a portion of the final grade to a research journal or (b) the student submits evidence of interaction with the librarian—such as printed out e-mail correspondence or notes from a meeting in the library—with the final research paper.
- The faculty member should set aside time for the librarian in class and needs to be in contact with the librarian regularly.
- While expansion of this type of program is possible over time, it should be initiated on a relatively small scale, with a few sections of a similar course and a few fully committed librarians.
- Identifying a specific cohort of students—such as business majors or developmental English students—is an important step. A required first-year course, such as Business Writing, is a perfect example. The enrollments in this course are small (17 students), and it has very specific learning goals. The course is project oriented, and the students are highly motivated to succeed. We also hope to institute this model in our developmental English courses, where students traditionally struggle with research and writing and are even more likely to be intimidated by the library.
- Having the librarian come to the classroom serves several purposes. First, students meet the librarian in an environment where they feel comfortable. Second, when the students do reach out to the librarian, they are corresponding with someone they have met. Finally, when students go to the library, they can turn to someone they already know to help them.
- Scheduling student papers so they are being produced throughout the course, rather than having all papers due at the same time, is also advantageous. The librarian participating in the class is not overwhelmed with numerous requests at one time, especially if he or she is working with more than one class.

Both the scheduling database and the incorporation of librarians into Blackboard courses—neither of which would have been possible without the advent of very specific technologies—have potential widespread ramifications for library instruction at Seton Hall. The results suggest that the technology can be used to foster a better working relationship between instructors, librarians, and students, and more effective library instruction as part of the first-year experience.

References

Kuhlthau, C. C. (1996). *Seeking meaning: A process approach to library and information services.* Norwood, NJ: Ablex.

Prensky, M. (2001, October). Digital natives, digital immigrants. *On the Horizon, 9*(5), 1.

Case Study 11

The Development and Management of the Online Information Literacy Tutorial at the HKUST Library[1]

Sam Chu

This case study discusses the online Information Literacy Tutorial (ILT)[2] for 1,900 first-year students at the Hong Kong University of Science and Technology (HKUST), a research university emphasizing teaching and research in science, engineering, and business. Before the ILT, the orientation program for first-year students consisted of a walking tour of the library and a hands-on library class. The tour familiarized students with the facilities, collection, and services of the library; the class taught students how to search effectively for information in the library catalog and databases. To offer students an alternative way of learning, librarians created the ILT. Since then, our students have had the option of learning from the ILT on their own in addition to being able to join a tour and a class.

The librarians designed the ILT to help students develop skills in searching, locating, evaluating, and using information effectively in their lifelong learning. When created in August 2000, it consisted of six modules: (a) Explore the Library, (b) Search the Library Online Catalog I, (c) Search the Library Online Catalog II, (d) Find Periodical Articles, (e) Search the Web, and (f) Evaluate and Cite Sources. We began to design the first three modules in March 2000 and finished them in August 2000. We completed modules 4 to 6 several months later and released them in February 2001. The appendix, Designing Online Tutorials With WebCT: A Flow Chart, summarizes all the key steps we took in producing and managing the ILT.

Quality Assurance Strategies

Perhaps the best feature of our ILT is that it is highly user-oriented. We employed six quality assurance strategies in building and managing it: (a) project management, (b) best practice benchmarking, (c) user-needs assessment, (d) usability testing, (e) formative evaluation, and (f) "outsourcing" the design and technical expertise.

Project Management

Project management is the planning, scheduling, and controlling of activities to meet project objectives. As anyone can imagine, designing and managing an online tutorial for 1,900 students is a difficult task. Without proper project-management techniques, the effort, no doubt, would take more time and the results would probably be much less satisfying. The creation of the project management web site and the establishment of a timetable helped ensure the success of the ILT development.

241

The web site "Information Literacy Tutorial for New Students" ties everything related to the project together.[3] It helped us maintain clear direction and facilitated communication among the project members. By keeping this working document up-to-date, we saved considerable time since everything related to the project (i.e., proposal, style guide, students' comments) could be found on the site easily and quickly. We also tried to set realistic deadlines for various stages of the project and adhere to them.

Best Practice Benchmarking

Bogan and English (1994) suggest, "Learning by borrowing from the best and adapting their approaches to fit your own needs is the essence of benchmarking" (p. 3). We identified excellent online tutorials from other libraries worldwide and learned from them. We posted a question on BI-L[4] (a global online discussion group on library instruction that has about 3,000 members) asking for online tutorials created using WebCT (i.e., the courseware we decided to use for designing our tutorial). We examined instruction programs of award winners and major university libraries from around the world. Searching and browsing key information science journals also helped us locate excellent online tutorials. We also used search engines to mine relevant tutorials. Finally, we identified some useful tutorials through personal contact.

After trying out and comparing a number of online tutorials, we determined the characteristics we hoped to emulate when producing our own tutorial such as standardization across modules, a user-friendly visual environment, and hands-on user interactive learning. This exercise spared us the problem of re-inventing the wheel and shortened the development time tremendously. It ensured the quality of our tutorial could compare with the best tutorials available.

User Needs Assessment

The first step in designing a user-centered tutorial is to learn the needs of the target group. We assessed our users' needs for the tutorial in two ways. First, we solicited input from colleagues in the circulation and reserve departments on what should be included in module 1 (e.g., Explore the Library, which essentially covers the various library services, facilities, and collection). These colleagues manage the physical facilities and collections of the library. They have frequent contact with first-year students and understand what concerns students most regarding our services at the Circulation and Reserve counters.

We also interviewed nine second- and third-year students to find out their information needs while they were in their first year. We divided the interviews into two parts. First, we solicited feedback from the students about the services and resources of the library they consider important to know in their first month of their studies. Then, we prompted them by following a tentative outline of the three modules, asking about the omission of any important items from the proposed modules. This exercise helped the designers identify things important to students. For example, seven of the nine students pointed out the importance of Course Reserve to first-year students since all of them had to determine the location of assigned readings.

HKUST Library's Usability Study

The next step involved a usability study. Usability studies are designed to examine and improve the accessibility of a product. The product can be anything: a software program, a web site, or an online tutorial. These studies help create a user-friendly product. As Fowler (1998) said:

> Probably the best reason to test for usability is to eliminate those interminable arguments about the right way to do something. Your design team can go around in circles for years without finding the right solution to an interface problem....With human-factors input and

testing, however, you can replace opinion with data. Real data tends to make arguments evaporate and meeting schedules shrink.

In the past several years, many libraries have conducted usability studies on their online tutorials (Bender & Rosen, 2000; Bury & Oud, 2005) or library web sites (McGillis & Toms, 2001; Prown, 1999). One of the most popular and important usability methodologies is the "think aloud" method, which asks participants to verbalize their thoughts while working on a task. This methodology allows developers to observe and analyze user behavior of a product to achieve a goal (Clairmont, Dickstein, & Mills, 1998).

The initial usability test for modules 1 to 3 involved two groups of testers: (a) a think-aloud group and (b) a self-paced group. The think-aloud group had five students. We asked each student to think aloud while "test-driving" the tutorial. A project team member observed the students and noted problems that they encountered. The self-paced group consisted of 15 students who went through the three modules on their own and e-mailed us their comments.

Most of the group of 20 students consisted of undergraduates from different departments in their first three years of study. We preferred undergraduate students since they were our target group; however, we invited a few graduate students, anticipating that their more mature ideas would add another dimension and further help improve the tutorial. To minimize the gender effect, we recruited an equal number of male and female testers. The students offered a good mix of feedback and different opinions.

The usability test results from both the think-aloud group and the self-paced group revealed that our ILT had considerable room for improvement. An example of this need for further improvement is exhibited by a sentence on the final page of each module, which included icons to return to the home page and to take a quiz. Many students repeatedly clicked on the home and quiz icons as if they were hyperlinks. Once we discovered this problem, we removed these misleading cues by replacing the icons with text.

Conducting the usability test for the think-aloud group proved a time-consuming process. Each of the five testers took an average of three hours to complete the tutorial. Nevertheless, the think-aloud group gave us more critical comments than the self-paced group. Despite the time commitment, we decided to use the think-aloud method when we conducted the second usability study for modules 1 to 3.

Formative Evaluation

A formative evaluation process takes place during the creation or implementation of a product, allowing modifications to be made before the product is complete. For modules 1 to 3, we went through five stages of formative evaluation: (a) initial evaluation, (b) design evaluation, (c) content evaluation, (d) product evaluation, and (e) implementation evaluation.

At the initial evaluation stage, three reference librarians assessed the feasibility of producing the tutorial and studied the needs of the target user group. For design evaluation, three other reference librarians had to address fundamental design issues: How many modules are needed? What should be included in each of the modules? When the design team (i.e., the group of reference librarians) finished creating the first draft of the tutorial, we invited the instructional design team of the university's Center for Enhanced Learning and Teaching (CELT) to examine the content of the tutorial. Based on their evaluations, the designers made revisions and enriched the tutorial with relevant graphics.

By the time the design team completed building the entire tutorial, all the reference librarians evaluated the product by assessing the tutorial's content, design, presentation, usability, and interactivity. The product evaluation involved a usability test as described above. Two weeks before going live with the tutorial, the team conducted an implementation evaluation by having a second usability test with five new first-year students. Several librarians then looked at the tutorial again and made final revisions. We officially launched the ILT at the end of August 2000.

Outsourcing the Design and Technical Expertise

Our library did not build and run the online tutorial alone. We tapped into the expertise of the University's CELT. To save time and cost, we used their licensed courseware WebCT as a platform for our tutorial. We kept our user database on their server. Whenever we had technical questions regarding the use of WebCT, CELT's colleagues provided immediate assistance. CELT also lent us their design expertise by creating an attractive home page with a coherent tone and style and interesting graphics and animations for the tutorial.

Assessment and Outcomes

Users of ILT Decrease over Time

Figure 1 shows that the tutorial had a high rate of use initially, with 1,516 users (82% of all first-year students) in 2000-2001. Unfortunately, this figure dropped in the following years, and we reached only 65 students in year 2003-2004. When we first implemented the tutorial, we had permission from all schools to advertise it as a school requirement in our promotion leaflets and e-mails. This requirement was the driving force for most students to attempt the tutorial. However, students soon found out that no penalty existed for not completing the tutorial. Possibly, senior students tipped off new students about this and the participation rate of our ILT suffered three years in a row. The drop in year 2003-2004 was particularly profound, largely because we replaced the unenforceable requirement with the statement "highly recommended by the schools." Thus, it is quite a challenge to motivate students to use the tutorial.

In 2004-2005, the tutorial use had a minor revival because the library partnered with a semi-online English course offered by the Language Center that reached 20% of all first-year students. The course director realized the usefulness of the tutorial, and he allocated a few extra points for students who completed it. Besides, the library motivated the students by giving those who scored at least 90% on all the quizzes a chance to win one of the two HK$500 book coupons. As a result, 378 students took the tutorial.

We continually explore new channels to boost the participation rate of the ILT. Recently, we shared our library-instruction effort, the new one-credit elective course for undergraduates, Eureka! Information Skills for Lifelong Learning, with the associate vice president for academic affairs (undergraduate studies) of our university. Our efforts so impressed him that he asked

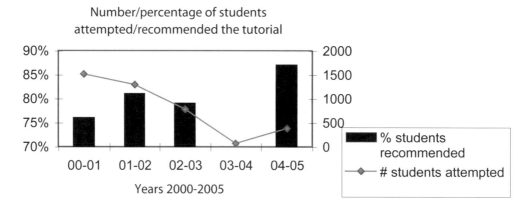

Figure 1. Number/percentage of students attempted/recommended the tutorial.

us to submit a proposal to make it a required course for all undergraduates when our ongoing program expands from three to four years in 2008. We plan to integrate ILT into this required course.

Students' Satisfaction of ILT Increases During the Same Period

While the tutorial participation declined over the years, students' satisfaction with the ILT increased. In 2000-2001, the tutorial had a moderately positive evaluation with 702 out of 922 students (76%) indicating they would recommend the tutorial to others. This percentage fluctuated for the next two years. Due to the limited sample size, we did not analyze the data for 2003-2004. In 2004-2005, the tutorial enjoyed the highest rating with 87% of the students who completed the evaluation recommending the tutorial.

How Does Our Library Upgrade the Tutorial?

Every year, we examine students' evaluation on various aspects of the tutorial including content, design, and quizzes of the modules. In 2000-2001, our tutorial had 116 content pages, 58 self-test questions, and about 60 quiz questions. The evaluation consistently showed that the number of topics and amount of material covered overwhelmed the students. We, therefore, combined two modules into one and trimmed down the content substantially. By 2004-2005, the ILT had 68 content pages, 26 self-test questions, and 37 quiz questions. Our students taught us one important principle in bibliographic instruction: "Less is more."

How Do We Know if Students Are Learning? What Do We Expect Them to Learn?

Our goal is to help students learn the materials presented in the ILT efficiently and effectively. On average, 86% of the students achieved the pass mark for the quizzes in all four years. Thus, students on the whole have met our expectations. Beyond this overall picture, we also analyzed the data on students' performance for each quiz question. We paid particular attention to questions on the two extremes—the very difficult questions and the very easy ones. For year 2001-2002, only 17% of the students selected the right answer for the most difficult question, while 92% answered the easiest question correctly. As a result, we modified content pages related to the difficult questions so these pages explained concepts and ideas more clearly. In addition, we revised the difficult questions by making them easier to understand and/or providing students with more hints. For overly easy questions, we made them more challenging or replaced them with higher-level questions.

Conclusion

A tremendous amount of time and effort are involved in building and maintaining a user-oriented online tutorial. Is it worth the effort? For our library, the answer is clearly "yes." The 4,000 students who have been trained online in the past five years have justified our original decision. The high percentage of students who indicated that they would recommend the tutorial to others demonstrates that our alternative mode of teaching has been successful. The library has been recognized as one of the earliest pioneers in applying online teaching and learning on campus. The ILT has been featured twice as a good model for online education. We have been invited to give a talk to our faculty and staff to share our experience in creating the tutorial. Yet, we realize that one library's experience may not be transferable to another. What works well on one campus may not be worth the time and effort on another. The feasibility and desirability of finding and committing sufficient resources for the development of a successful online tutorial is dependent on the particular circumstances of a library. One must carefully examine the potential costs and benefits before arriving at a decision.

For librarians who would like to take on the challenge, they will find the six quality assurance strategies discussed in this article useful. Obtaining students' feedback on the tutorial and analyzing whether or not they are learning as expected are essential. Updating the tutorial on an ongoing basis to reflect the current needs of the users is also vital for its continual success. A high-quality, user-friendly tutorial will certainly be welcomed by many students, as exemplified by this encouraging remark from one of our ILT users:

> The ILT modules help me to revise what I've learned and enhance my skill. I'm very pleased with how UST librarians made the modules and set the quizzes. It made me feel that the staff here is serious about academic studies. This gives me confidence in studying at this University, and now I feel I [am] start[ing] to love UST!!

Notes

[1]This paper was first written at the time when the author worked as the Bibliographic Instruction Librarian at the Hong Kong University of Science and Technology. I would like to thank my former colleagues Dr. Samson Soong (the university librarian), Ms. Diana Chan (head of reference), and reference librarians, Ms. Catherine Kwok and Ms. Eunice Wong, for providing valuable comments on the paper.

[2]The online tutorial can be viewed at http://library.ust.hk/serv/skills/inforliteracy.html

[3]The project-management site for the online tutorial can be viewed at http://web.hku.hk/~samchu/ILT00/onl-clas.html

[4]It is now called Information Literacy Instruction List (ILI-L).

[5] The pass mark for each of the five quizzes of the five modules was originally set at 80% for 2000-2001 and 2001-2002, and it was lowered to 70% for 2003-2004 and 2004-2005.

References

Bender, L. J., & Rosen, J. M. (2000). Working toward scalable instruction: Creating the RIO tutorial at the University of Arizona library. *Research Strategies, 16*(4), 315-325.

Bogan, C. E., & English, M. J. (1994). *Benchmarking for best practices: Winning through innovative adaptation.* New York: McGraw-Hill.

Bury, S., & Oud, J. (2005). Usability testing of an online information literacy tutorial. *Reference Services Review, 33*(1), 54-65.

Clairmont, M., Dickstein, R., & Mills, V. (1998). *Testing for usability in the design of a new information gateway.* Retrieved November 20, 2001, from http://dizzy.library.arizona.edu/library/teams/access9798/lft2paper.htm

Fowler, S. (1998). Appendix B: Usability test. In *GUI Design Handbook.* NY: McGraw Hill. Retrieved November 20, 2000, from http://www.fast-consulting.com/appb.htm

McGillis, L., & Toms, E. G. (2001). Usability of the academic library web site: Implications for design. *College & Research Libraries, 62*(4), 355-367.

Prown, S. (1999). *Detecting 'broke': Usability testing of library web sites.* Retrieved May 8, 2005, from http://www.library.yale.edu/~prowns/nebic/nebictalk.html

Appendix

**Designing Online Tutorials with WebCT:
A Flow Chart**

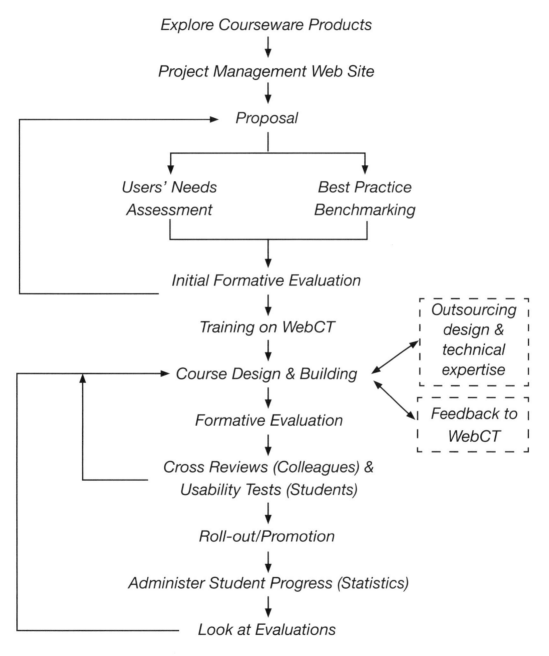

This chart was originally designed by Catherine Kwok, and was revised by Sam Chu.

Case Study 12

*Preparing Pathways
to Information Literacy:
Combining Research, Technology,
and Core College Competencies
for Select First-Year Students*

Joan Campbell, Corrine Taylor, & Pattie Orr

This case study describes Wellesley College's summer bridge program, Pathways, which provides an unusually rich environment for incoming students to gain the knowledge and skills outlined in the Association of Colleges and Research Libraries' (ACRL) *Information Literacy Competency Standards for Higher Education.* Pathways students are guided by an interdisciplinary team of classroom faculty to improve their skills in library research, quantitative analysis, writing, and computer technology. By the end of the two-and-a-half-week program, students have created electronic portfolios that showcase their proficiencies in the ACRL standards. These portfolios include analyses of various online sources and the integration of those sources in a research paper complemented by original images and graphs. This case study details how the ACRL standards are addressed in the unique, integrative structure of Pathways.

Institutional Description

Wellesley College is a highly selective, four-year, liberal arts college for women. Established in 1875, the mission of Wellesley College is to provide an excellent education for women who will make a difference in the world. The student body is composed of 2,300 undergraduates; 45% are racial or ethnic minorities, 7% are international students, and 4% are nontraditional-aged students. The college is in Wellesley, Massachusetts, about 12 miles west of Boston.

Brief History of the Program

Pathways is a credit-bearing program developed in 2002 by Wellesley faculty and staff to facilitate the transition from high school to the first year of college. The two-and-a-half-week summer bridge program is designed to improve students' understanding of the Internet as a research tool and introduce students to college-level research and writing. The admissions office identifies eligible students who may be first-generation college students, who have not taken advanced placement classes, who come from less-advantaged, rural, or inner-city high schools, and/or who have lower SAT scores than the average incoming Wellesley student. Students learn to use technology, including effective Internet search techniques, and are guided through a step-by-step research process that includes critical analysis, writing, and quantitative reasoning. The program began with a cap of 18 students and has now grown to 24.

The core of the Pathways program is Computer Science 100: Introduction to Internet Research and Resources (CS 100), designed and cotaught by the director of user services and a research and instructional services librarian. The goal of this half-unit course is for students to develop the critical-thinking and technical skills needed to find, evaluate, and use information and to provide them with the basic computer science underpinnings needed to manage and communicate information effectively. The director of the Quantitative Reasoning Program (also an assistant professor of economics) joins the team to teach a segment on working with quantitative information, including creating appropriate charts and graphs. CS 100 also includes an exploration of copyright, privacy, and security issues of digital data and electronic communications. Students use web-authoring tools to create and maintain a web-published portfolio of their Internet research, which highlights a short research paper with original charts and graphics.

A campus-wide committee, formed in 2000, studied the effectiveness of the traditional summer bridge program that Wellesley had been offering for more than a decade. The study found that to improve the effectiveness of the program, incoming students needed more exposure to the research process and development of their technology skills. Committee members agreed that CS 100, supplemented by faculty support of critical analysis and writing would address these deficits. While CS 100 has been taught during the regular school year since 1998, it became the centerpiece of the College's summer bridge program in 2002. Thus, was born Pathways, an integrated, intensive program providing information literacy training up-front to select students who otherwise would be expected to face the greatest challenges in making the transition from high school to college.

Program Overview

Integrated Structure of Pathways

Each morning, all Pathways students attend CS 100. In the afternoon, they work closely with one of three writing faculty members, putting into practice their newly acquired information and technology skills in the context of their reading, critical thinking, and writing. The morning and afternoon sessions complement each other and greatly reinforce the interrelationships of research and writing. For example, students are required to write a short research paper with a thesis related to some aspect of "the digital divide" during the program. In the morning sessions, students learn the skills needed to find, evaluate, and cite appropriate sources, while in the afternoon sessions, they work with writing faculty members on integrating their sources and organizing and presenting persuasive evidence for their theses. In the evenings, students work with tutors (juniors and seniors with strong skills in quantitative reasoning, writing, and computer technology) in the computer lab to complete assignments for CS 100 and work on their research papers. With this integrated structure and support throughout each day from instructors and peer tutors, Pathways students are guided in their development of many information literacy competencies.

Addressing the ACRL Standards

The CS 100 syllabus addresses many components of the ACRL *Information Literacy Competency Standards*. Topics include (a) learning how the Internet really works; (b) searching for, evaluating, and citing information in a subscription database and on the web; (c) constructing a basic web page; (d) receiving an introduction to the library and scholarly research; (e) learning about virtual communities, privacy, and copyright online; (f) creating original graphics and animation; (g) creating tables and charts; and (h) discussing the future of the Internet. The following sections explain in more detail how the integrated structure of the Pathways program addresses each of the five ACRL standards (listed by number in this monograph's Appendix).

The first standard focuses on determining the "nature and extent of the information need" and serves as the foundation for the goals of the entire program. In the initial days of the program, during the afternoon writing and critical analysis component, students work intensively on identifying a research topic, developing a thesis statement, and achieving a workable focus (I.1.a-d).[1] In CS 100, they perform some initial database and web exploration to gain familiarity with their topic and to learn how to identify key concepts. In their assignments, they must explain the difference between a subscription database and a web site (I.2.c), identify the purpose and audience of the newspaper and magazine articles and web sites they find (I.2.d), and differentiate between primary and secondary sources (I.2.e). In the quantitative reasoning section, students learn to construct new information with raw data from the U.S. Census Bureau (I.2.f).

In the CS 100 portion of the class, students learn to perform many of the outcomes related to the second standard, the ability to access information "effectively and efficiently." They must complete an assignment in which they show they can identify keywords and synonyms (II.2.b), construct a search statement using Boolean operators and truncation (II.2.d), and implement the search in a subscription database and on the web (II.2.e). As students find potential sources, they bring them to the afternoon session and work with their writing faculty members to determine how relevant the sources are, identify possible gaps that need to be filled (II.3.a, b), and continue to revise and refine both their searches and their thesis statements. The CS 100 instructors and the writing faculty members convene daily at lunchtime and via e-mail to confer about students' progress (e.g., who is having difficulty finding information, who is changing her topic). This information enables the librarian to e-mail students with suggestions for searching. The students read those e-mails in the evening and, with the help of the peer tutors, refine their searches. In CS 100, students learn techniques for extracting and organizing information and practice copying and pasting shortcuts using the computer (some students have had *very* little experience with computers) and organizing quotes, citation information, and URLs (II.5.a-e).

The morning and afternoon sessions complement and reinforce each other effectively in teaching the competencies of standard three, which is concerned with the ability to evaluate information and incorporate it into a student's "knowledge base." At the beginning of the program, students work on active reading and note taking with the writing faculty and apply those skills in analyzing the structure and logic of an argument and summarizing the main ideas of the information they find (III.1.a-c, 2.b). Additionally, students must compose an annotated bibliography. The writing faculty members help students recognize interrelationships among concepts and combine those concepts in potentially useful primary statements with supporting evidence (III.3.a). Both the CS 100 instructors and the writing faculty members help students determine whether the information they found satisfies their research needs and assist them in selecting information that provides evidence for their topics (III.4.a, g). The CS 100 instructors emphasize evaluating sources for reliability, validity, accuracy, authority, timeliness, and point of view or bias. Students look for possible prejudice or manipulation and examine the context within which the information was created (III.2.a, c, d). These skills, of course, are critical in analyzing web sites, and the students must complete an assignment in which they evaluate four sites that they have found in their searches.

To complete their final portfolios, students must perform many of the outcomes described in standard four. They put all their skills together to "use information effectively to accomplish a specific purpose." The writing faculty work with the students in organizing their research papers and integrating new information, including quotes and paraphrases that effectively support their arguments (IV.1.a, c). In the quantitative reasoning section, students learn about different types of data and the appropriateness of various graphs for representing these data (e.g., pie charts, bar charts, histograms, line graphs). They also learn how to manipulate data and create appropriate graphs in Excel. In CS 100, students learn to use Fireworks to make original images and convert Excel graphs to .GIF files. They also use Dreamweaver to put their papers into HTML format. They learn how to make electronic folders for organizing their projects, and how to upload their final portfolios to the Wellesley server (IV.1.d and IV.3.b, c). They also are required to describe their portfolios in a five-minute oral presentation (IV.3).

CS 100 touches on some of the economic, legal, and social issues of standard five. One class session is devoted to a discussion of privacy and security issues in the electronic environment, as well as issues of intellectual property and copyright (V.1.a, d). The Pathways students are introduced to Wellesley's Acceptable Use Policy, which includes netiquette, the confidentiality of passwords, and legal acquisition of images and music files. In fact, a motivating factor in having students learn Fireworks is for them to make their own images rather than take them from the Internet. Both the CS 100 and the writing faculty members discuss plagiarism with the students (V.2.f). Finally, students learn how to cite sources, both print and electronic, in APA style and must include four to six properly documented sources in their research papers (V.3.a).

Assessment and Outcomes

Wellesley's Pathways program demonstrates four years of success in equipping the neediest incoming students with the information literacy skills necessary for making a positive transition to college. The research librarian reports continued contact with Pathways students as they work on research papers throughout their college years:

> Because they are aware that there's so much more information than what's on Google, Pathways students are far more likely than other first-year students to ask for research help. They have learned the language of research, and they certainly know to ask 'Is this an appropriate source for my paper?' This is the crux of information literacy. (J. Campbell, personal communication, July 24, 2005)

The director of Wellesley's Writing Program, who encounters Pathways students along with other students in her first-year writing courses, says:

> Entering students frequently *think* they know how to use the library and Internet, but then, all too often, hit a wall and come to class empty-handed, saying 'There isn't anything on the whole Internet on this topic.' They give up quickly. Not so with Pathways students. Pathways students are persistent and confident and are unusually comfortable locating materials. They are not at all daunted. (W. Wood, personal communication, August 25, 2005)

The Office of the First-Year Dean reports a noticeably lower proportion of Academic Review Board cases (for low grades and/or credit deficiencies) among Pathways students. The director of user services reports:

> Compared to the general student population, a higher than average number of Pathways students has been able to secure campus jobs requiring strong computer skills—jobs such as working at the College's computer help desk or multimedia technology center. Some have been hired to use their web page creation and research skills to work for academic departments. One was selected for a prestigious and competitive Wellesley College instructional technology internship. (P. Orr, personal communication, August 30, 2005)

Pathways students, themselves, rave about the importance of the skills they attained in the program. A few quotes from student evaluations reveal some of the most valuable features of the program:

- This course helped me strengthen my computer and research skills. With each research assignment, I became more concise and exact, which allowed me to be more resourceful. I can now search databases effectively, critically analyze data, and create web pages.
- Using keywords, quotations, asterisks, and the Boolean principles, I am now able to make specific and effective searches.
- The most valuable aspect of the program is how much one learns in an amazingly short period of time. I learned more being in this two-week program than I did when I was at [another prestigious institution] one summer. I can find out whether my sources are credible or not and write a research paper.
- I think that creating a web page and learning how to write a "college" research paper . . . enabled me to hit the ground running. I adjusted with ease.

Challenges

The Pathways program does have its share of challenges. With its compressed time frame and goal of imparting a combination of requisite library, computer, and writing skills in a small-group learning environment, Pathways is staff intensive. Administrators paying for this type of staffing expect measurable results, but it is not always easy to document immediate discernable gains in GPA, for example. Those administrators and faculty members at other institutions interested in replicating Wellesley's Pathways program should consider carefully institutional, financial, and staffing resources.

Conclusion

In this case study, we have emphasized the impact of Pathways on the students' information literacy skills, but we have just as much anecdotal evidence that Pathways has had a significant impact on their overall first-year experience, especially concerning social and support networks with both peers and faculty. With these many benefits, Wellesley's Pathways program may serve as a model for other institutions wishing to develop their incoming students' information literacy skills and to ease their transition to college.

Notes

[1] These number and letters refer to the sections of the ACRL *Information Literacy Competency Standards*.

Case Study 13

A Common Grading Rubric: Evolution of Library Assignments for an Orientation Course

Janice Hovis & Diane Savoca

St. Louis Community College at Florissant Valley is one of three campuses in the St. Louis Community College system. Florissant Valley is an urban campus with about 2,000 new students each year and a total enrollment of about 8,500 students. Most of these students are first-generation and academically unprepared to attend college. The average student age is 27, 76% of students are women, 52% are African American, and 43% are White. Two thirds of the students are enrolled part-time. Meeting the disparate needs of this diverse student population is a continuing challenge.

In the 1990s, the counseling department at St. Louis Community College at Florissant Valley offered a one-credit hour student success course, Personal Growth and Development 108: Success in College. The class focused on goal-setting and study skills. In 1998, the College moved this course from the Counseling Department to the Department of Student Transition and Retention and renamed it COL 100: Academic Orientation to College. The purpose of the new course was to introduce new students to the skills, knowledge, and resources needed to be successful in college. The course coordinator recruited instructors from all areas of the College, including classroom faculty, librarians, and counselors, to teach sections of the course. The instructors teaching the course each semester met monthly to discuss teaching methods, course content, and other details of the course. This group became known as the COL 100 Teaching Team.

Information acquisition and processing are central to the course, and the Teaching Team recognized that a librarian's expertise would be critical to help them guide students into a successful college career. Therefore, the Teaching Team always included a librarian as a member even during semesters when no librarian taught a course section. The librarians on the Team took an active role in shaping course content and spearheading the development of standard library assignments for use by classroom faculty teaching the course.

The COL 100 Teaching Team also functioned as a standing focus group. To assess the effectiveness of the students' library experience in COL 100, the course coordinator used pointed questioning to encourage a dialogue between classroom faculty and librarians. The monthly discussion meetings and the focus-group sessions of the COL 100 Teaching Team resulted in frequent adjustments and expansions to the library assignment and eventually to a common grading rubric for three different library assignments.

Early Versions of the Assignment

During its monthly meetings, the COL 100 Teaching Team quickly determined that the original scavenger hunt library assignment did not work. This assignment asked students to answer a few basic questions about the library and to find answers to a list of unrelated questions. As structured, the assignment did not fulfill any specific educational objectives; it only served, in a general way, to increase student familiarity with the library. Students found it frustrating and described it on course assessments as busy work. To replace it, the librarian on the Teaching Team created the genealogy assignment. This assignment first directed each student to use specific reference books to find the meaning of his or her surname and to answer basic questions about the history of his or her ethnic group. Additional questions introduced students to the library catalog, which was a tool for finding more information on ethnic groups. At the time the librarians created this assignment, the COL 100 course still focused on personal development, and this assignment reflected this objective in its individualized nature.

We successfully used this assignment for several years until increasing enrollments required that additional librarians conduct the library-instruction sessions. Assessment of the assignment revealed a major flaw. The race, gender, and personalities of the librarians and classroom faculty could be a stumbling block. The assignment proved very successful when presented by the librarian who developed it; he used his own multi-ethnic background as a research example and a way to interest the students. Other classroom faculty and librarians, however, reported discomfort when asked to use their own ethnic backgrounds as examples, especially when the results highlighted differences, rather than commonalties, between the faculty and students. Some students also objected to the assignment, and racial issues became the focus of discussion in some class sections, diverting attention away from the intended focus of developing research skills.

Another librarian on the COL 100 Teaching Team attempted to design an alternative assignment that would keep the personal connection of the genealogy assignment but remove the focus on race and ethnicity. We called this alternative the family assignment. We asked students to choose a topic related to their families and then find resources on that topic in reference books, the library catalog, and a periodical index. We only used this assignment for two semesters because students had trouble understanding it. Although attempting to keep the subject matter flexible, the assignment lost its simplicity and focus. Time and effort that students spent choosing family-related topics were excessive compared to the amount of knowledge they gained about library research. Clearly, the assignment needed revamping.

Creating a Model Assignment

The COL 100 Teaching Team considered several factors in designing a new assignment. The assignment would have to set a foundation for future library instruction sessions in other courses without these later assignments replicating the initial assignment. It also would need to engage the students in a meaningful library experience. As a one-credit course with limited classroom time, the Teaching Team wanted to accomplish the library-related objectives in one classroom visit. Thus, the assignment had to be clear enough for the students to complete independently after one library instruction session. Another challenge was bringing the subject matter of the library assignment into context with the other COL 100 course objectives. As the focus of the course shifted from personal development to academic success, a focus on family history or genealogy seemed less appropriate. The Teaching Team developed a specific set of objectives for the assignment that included a demonstrated ability to:

- Find information in reference books
- Use the library catalog to find a book by subject
- Use a periodical index to find a magazine article
- Cite the sources of the information
- Process and apply acquired information

With these objectives in mind, the librarian collaborated with the COL 100 Teaching Team to design a new assignment, titled the Master Student or biography assignment, to guide students through the process of finding further biographical information about one of the people profiled in the textbook, *Becoming a Master Student* (Ellis, 2000). In one class session, a librarian demonstrated the use of biographical reference books, the library catalog, and a periodical index using a person's name as a subject heading. The assignment sheet included fill-in-the-blank spaces for all citation data, introducing students to the concept of full documentation of sources, without going into the complexities of citation style that they would later learn in English Composition. The students then applied their research skills by finding biographical information about another person of their choice. Most Teaching Team members required their students to complete the assignment sheet during the class session and assigned the research project as homework.

The COL 100 Teaching Team developed a rubric as a guide to grading the assignments consistently across different sections of the course. Some of the Teaching Team considered the assignment a success when their students earned 70% or better on the grading rubric. The students' completion of the assignment and engagement in the process satisfied others.

We never intended the Master Student assignment as the only possible library assignment for the COL 100 course. Instead, we hoped that it would serve as a model for the development of similar assignments by classroom faculty. For this reason, the COL 100 Teaching Team developed a sufficiently flexible grading rubric for use with other assignments based on this model (see Appendix A).

Developing New Assignments

In all sections of the COL 100 course, the Teaching Team conducted a student self-assessment early in the semester. Later class sessions focused on particular concerns of the majority of students in that section, such as time management or test anxiety. Accommodating diverse needs of the multiple sections of the course while maintaining consistency in the amount of work, difficulty, and grading of the assignment provided the next challenge for the COL 100 Teaching Team librarians.

Student self-assessments often identified career planning as an area of concern. Two members of the Teaching Team, a librarian and a career counselor, collaborated to create a new assignment on career exploration. This assignment guided the students to reference books on careers, the library catalog, and a periodical database. It also included a series of questions about their career choice that students could answer using any of the sources they found (see Appendix B). This assignment and the Master Student assignment shared a common grading rubric.

After continuous assessment proved the effectiveness of these library assignments, the COL 100 Teaching Team developed a new section of the course with a service-learning theme. Given the clear learning objectives and the common grading rubric, two members of the Teaching Team developed a service-learning library assignment with only a minimal amount of input from a librarian (see Appendix C). Members of the COL 100 Teaching Team appreciated the development of a variety of library assignments, which permits them to choose the most appropriate ones to meet the diverse needs of the students in their classes.

Assessment

Most assessment for the COL 100 course is qualitative and formative. We used several methods to collect data upon which to base subsequent course decisions, including the COL 100 Teaching Team as a standing focus group, students' performance on the library assignments, and student survey results at the end of each semester. The College uses a generic student survey for all courses, so we could not ask specific questions about the library experience on the student survey. Nevertheless, when we used the library scavenger hunt, the students wrote comments identifying the assignment as busy work. With the debut of the newer library assignments, students no longer make these negative comments.

Also, student self-assessment is built into the course, giving the Teaching Team insight into their students' experiences with the library assignments. These assessments include discovery/intentional journaling, end of chapter quizzes, and teacher-directed reflective discussions. Students' journal entries show enthusiasm about the careers they investigated and an intention to use library resources for further investigation. Enthusiasm for the other two assignments is not as high, but the intent to use library reference material is still clear.

Periodically, the course coordinator holds focus-group sessions to ask the Teaching Team pointed questions about the effectiveness and efficiency of COL 100 course experiences, including the library sessions and assignments. Teachers report satisfaction with the accuracy of the completed library assignments. They indicate that the assignment sets the foundation for other library research that takes place later in the semester. We are very pleased with the results, because this is the purpose of the library experience.

Beyond the COL 100 Teaching Team, several English professors have commented that students who have completed COL 100 are better prepared for the in-depth library research required in English composition classes. An associate professor of English notes,

> The COL 100 library assignments immediately appealed to the student's interest in successful people. They wanted to know how the 'master students' did it, so they were motivated to complete the library activities. The reference librarians were so helpful that the students immediately put aside any hesitancy about library work and enjoyed their discoveries.

We find this attitude very reassuring because student motivation and anxiety are issues we must address in COL 100. The professor continues, "These library experiences provided the perfect foundation that eliminated students' fears and made my job as an English teacher so much easier when my class visited the library and began required research." This type of feedback confirms the value of the library assignment and its continuing evolution.

Challenges for the Future

The challenges continue as we address future changes. We have a new general education sequence that includes a three-credit cornerstone course for new students who test into college-level classes. The cornerstone course is theme-based and will incorporate orientation issues. Instead of the COL 100 course, an expanded three-credit academic orientation course will be required for students who test into developmental courses. The students who are placed in COL 100 now are college-level students who are in career or technical programs. Several of these programs have or plan to have orientation courses exclusively for their students. A one-credit course on library research has been revived and revamped to incorporate the principles of information literacy.

The Internet continues to have an impact on student expectations of library research and the need for critical thinking and evaluation of sources. New technology is also changing the way library instruction is conducted, with the use of a computer classroom in the library and a newly developed online tutorial. Using continuous assessment through focus groups, reflective journals and discussions, student performance on the library assignments, and feedback from faculty, we will continue to transform the library assignments and develop new tools and strategies to introduce first-year students to college-level library research.

Reference

Ellis, D. (2000). *Becoming a master student.* Boston: Houghton Mifflin.

Appendix A:

Grading Rubric

Name: _____ Total points earned: _____ /30

Library Assignment Grade Sheet
(30 points)

1. The assignment is completed using library resources.
    5   4   3   2   1

2. Sources of information are identified completely.
    5   4   3   2   1

3. Ideas are clearly stated in complete sentences and in your own words.
    5   4   3   2   1

4. All sections of the assignment are complete and accurate.
    5   4   3   2   1

5. The assignment is turned in on time.
    5   4   3   2   1

6. The assignment has no grammatical or spelling errors.
    5   4   3   2   1

Savoca – Fall 2001

Appendix B:

Career Assignment

COL 100 Library Assignment: Careers

1. Choose a career field or occupation to research: _____

2. Find at least two different sources of information about the occupation from the reference books listed in the library study guide on Careers or in the Occupational File.

Author or editor: _____

Title: _____ Edition: _____

Entry (or Occupation File folder): _____

Place published (city): _____

Publisher: _____

Year published: _____ Pages: _____

Location (call number): _____

Author or editor: _____

Title: _____ Edition: _____

Entry (or Occupation File folder): _____

Place published (city): _____

Publisher: _____

Year published: _____ Pages: _____

Location (call number): _____

3. Using the sources you listed above, answer these questions about the career or occupation.

a) Write a brief description of the work performed by a person in this career.

b) What kind of education or training is necessary to enter this career?

c) What is the average entry-level salary?

d) What is the outlook? (Is the job market expanding or will jobs be hard to find?)

e) What are the working conditions?

f) What professional organization could you contact for more information?

4. Use the SLCC Library Catalog to find a book or video about the career.

Author: _____

Title: _____ Publisher: _____

Date: _____

Location (campus and call number): _____

5. Use a periodical index such as EBSCOhost MasterFile or Readers' Guide to Periodical Literature to find a magazine article about the career field or occupation.

Author: _____

Title of the article: _____

Magazine title: _____

Volume and issue (if given): _____

Date: _____ Pages: _____

Is this article available in the library? _____

Appendix C:

Service-Learning Assignment

Name: _____ Due Date: _____

1. Choose an issue to research: _____

2. With the advice of a librarian, look at one or two reference books and find the following information:

a) Write one or two sentences that define or describe your issue (e.g., poverty, abuse, homelessness, addiction, pollution). _____

_____

_____

_____

_____

b) List some state statistics about your issue.

_____

_____

c) What book(s) did you use to find this information?

Author or editor: _____

Title: _____ Edition: _____

Place published (city): _____

Publisher: _____

Year published: _____ Pages: _____

Location (call number): _____

Author or editor: _____

Title: _____ Edition: _____

Place published (city): _____

Publisher: _____

Year published: _____ Pages: _____

Location (call number): _____

3. Use the SLCC Library Catalog to find a book or video about the issue.

Author: _____

Title: _____

Publisher: _____ Date: _____

Location (campus and call number): _____

4. Using EBSCOhost MasterFile or another periodical index, find an article about the issue.

Author: _____

Title of the article: _____

Magazine title: _____

Volume and issue (if given): _____

Date _____ Pages: _____

Is this article available in the library? _____

5. Check reference books, a periodical index, or an online search engine (use Google) to see what local information is available about this issue.

List at least two St. Louis statistics about your issue.

6. What local agencies work with this issue? (Start with United Way)

7. Look up one of the above agencies on the Internet and find out the following information about the agency you identified.

When was this agency founded?

What is the agency's mission or purpose?

List the agency
    Name: _____
    Address: _____
              _____
    Phone: _____
    E-mail: _____
    Contact person: _____

Appendix A

*Information Literacy
Competency Standards
for Higher Education*

The Association of College and Research Libraries
A division of the American Library Association

Information Literacy Defined

Information literacy is a set of abilities requiring individuals to "recognize when information is needed and have the ability to locate, evaluate, and use effectively the needed information."[1] Information literacy also is increasingly important in the contemporary environment of rapid technological change and proliferating information resources. Because of the escalating complexity of this environment, individuals are faced with diverse, abundant information choices—in their academic studies, in the workplace, and in their personal lives. Information is available through libraries, community resources, special interest organizations, media, and the Internet—and increasingly, information comes to individuals in unfiltered formats, raising questions about its authenticity, validity, and reliability. In addition, information is available through multiple media, including graphical, aural, and textual, and these pose new challenges for individuals in evaluating and understanding it. The uncertain quality and expanding quantity of information pose large challenges for society. The sheer abundance of information will not in itself create a more informed citizenry without a complementary cluster of abilities necessary to use information effectively.

Information literacy forms the basis for lifelong learning. It is common to all disciplines, to all learning environments, and to all levels of education. It enables learners to master content and extend their investigations, become more self-directed, and assume greater control over their own learning. An information literate individual is able to:

- Determine the extent of information needed
- Access the needed information effectively and efficiently
- Evaluate information and its sources critically
- Incorporate selected information into one's knowledge base
- Use information effectively to accomplish a specific purpose
- Understand the economic, legal, and social issues surrounding the use of information, and access and use information ethically and legally

Information Literacy and Information Technology

Information literacy is related to information technology skills, but has broader implications for the individual, the educational system, and for society. Information technology skills enable an individual to use computers, software applications, databases, and other technologies to achieve a wide variety of academic, work-related, and personal goals. Information literate individuals necessarily develop some technology skills.

Information literacy, while showing significant overlap with information technology skills, is a distinct and broader area of competence. Increasingly, information technology skills are interwoven with, and support, information literacy. A 1999 report from the National Research Council promotes the concept of "fluency" with information technology and delineates several distinctions useful in understanding relationships among information literacy, computer literacy, and broader technological competence. The report notes that "computer literacy" is concerned with rote learning of specific hardware and software applications, while "fluency with technology" focuses on understanding the underlying concepts of technology and applying problem-solving and critical thinking to using technology. The report also discusses differences between information technology fluency and information literacy as it is understood in K-12 and higher education. Among these are information literacy's focus on content, communication, analysis, information searching, and evaluation; whereas information technology "fluency" focuses on a deep understanding of technology and graduated, increasingly skilled use of it.[2]

"Fluency" with information technology may require more intellectual abilities than the rote learning of software and hardware associated with "computer literacy," but the focus is still on the technology itself. Information literacy, on the other hand, is an intellectual framework for understanding, finding, evaluating, and using information—activities which may be accomplished in part by fluency with information technology, in part by sound investigative methods, but most important, through critical discernment and reasoning. Information literacy initiates, sustains, and extends lifelong learning through abilities which may use technologies but are ultimately independent of them.

Information Literacy and Higher Education

Developing lifelong learners is central to the mission of higher education institutions. By ensuring that individuals have the intellectual abilities of reasoning and critical thinking, and by helping them construct a framework for learning how to learn, colleges and universities provide the foundation for continued growth throughout their careers, as well as in their roles as informed citizens and members of communities. Information literacy is a key component of, and contributor to, lifelong learning. Information literacy competency extends learning beyond formal classroom settings and provides practice with self-directed investigations as individuals move into internships, first professional positions, and increasing responsibilities in all arenas of life. Because information literacy augments students' competency with evaluating, managing, and using information, it is now considered by several regional and discipline-based accreditation associations as a key outcome for college students.[3]

For students not on traditional campuses, information resources are often available through networks and other channels, and distributed learning technologies permit teaching and learning to occur when the teacher and the student are not in the same place at the same time. The challenge for those promoting information literacy in distance education courses is to develop a comparable range of experiences in learning about information resources as are offered on traditional campuses. Information literacy competencies for distance learning students should be comparable to those for "on campus" students.

Incorporating information literacy across curricula, in all programs and services, and throughout the administrative life of the university, requires the collaborative efforts of faculty, librarians, and administrators. Through lectures and by leading discussions, faculty establish the context for learning. Faculty also inspire students to explore the unknown, offer guidance on how best to fulfill information needs, and monitor students' progress. Academic librarians coordinate the evaluation and selection of intellectual resources for programs and services; organize and maintain collections and many points of access to information; and provide instruction to students and faculty who seek information. Administrators create opportunities for collaboration and staff development among faculty, librarians, and other professionals who initiate information literacy programs, lead in planning and budgeting for those programs, and provide ongoing resources to sustain them.

Information Literacy and Pedagogy

The Boyer Commission Report, *Reinventing Undergraduate Education*, recommends strategies that require the student to engage actively in "framing of a significant question or set of questions, the research or creative exploration to find answers, and the communications skills to convey the results..."[4] Courses structured in such a way create student-centered learning environments where inquiry is the norm, problem solving becomes the focus, and thinking critically is part of the process. Such learning environments require information literacy competencies.

Gaining skills in information literacy multiplies the opportunities for students' self-directed learning, as they become engaged in using a wide variety of information sources to expand their knowledge, ask informed questions, and sharpen their critical thinking for still further self-directed learning. Achieving competency in information literacy requires an understanding that this cluster of abilities is not extraneous to the curriculum but is woven into the curriculum's content, structure, and sequence. This curricular integration also affords many possibilities for furthering the influence and impact of such student-centered teaching methods as problem-based learning, evidence-based learning, and inquiry learning. Guided by faculty and others in problem-based approaches, students reason about course content at a deeper level than is possible through the exclusive use of lectures and textbooks. To take fullest advantage of problem-based learning, students must often use thinking skills requiring them to become skilled users of information sources in many locations and formats, thereby increasing their responsibility for their own learning.

To obtain the information they seek for their investigations, individuals have many options. One is to utilize an information retrieval system, such as may be found in a library or in databases accessible by computer from any location. Another option is to select an appropriate investigative method for observing phenomena directly. For example, physicians, archaeologists, and astronomers frequently depend upon physical examination to detect the presence of particular phenomena. In addition, mathematicians, chemists, and physicists often utilize technologies such as statistical software or simulators to create artificial conditions in which to observe and analyze the interaction of phenomena. As students progress through their undergraduate years and graduate programs, they need to have repeated opportunities for seeking, evaluating, and managing information gathered from multiple sources and discipline-specific research methods.

Use of the Standards

Information Literacy Competency Standards for Higher Education provides a framework for assessing the information literate individual. It also extends the work of the American Association of School Librarians Task Force on Information Literacy Standards, thereby providing higher education an opportunity to articulate its information literacy competencies with those of K-12 so that a continuum of expectations develops for students at all levels. The competencies presented here outline the process by which faculty, librarians, and others pinpoint specific indicators that identify a student as information literate.

Students also will find the competencies useful, because they provide students with a framework for gaining control over how they interact with information in their environment. It will help to sensitize them to the need to develop a metacognitive approach to learning, making them conscious of the explicit actions required for gathering, analyzing, and using information. All students are expected to demonstrate all of the competencies described in this document, but not everyone will demonstrate them to the same level of proficiency or at the same speed.

Furthermore, some disciplines may place greater emphasis on the mastery of competencies at certain points in the process, and therefore certain competencies would receive greater weight than others in any rubric for measurement. Many of the competencies are likely to be performed recursively, in that the reflective and evaluative aspects included within each standard will require the student to return to an earlier point in the process, revise the information-seeking approach, and repeat the same steps.

To implement the standards fully, an institution should first review its mission and educational goals to determine how information literacy would improve learning and enhance the institution's effectiveness. To facilitate acceptance of the concept, faculty and staff development is also crucial.

Information Literacy and Assessment

In the following competencies, there are five standards and twenty-two performance indicators. The standards focus upon the needs of students in higher education at all levels. The standards also list a range of outcomes for assessing student progress toward information literacy. These outcomes serve as guidelines for faculty, librarians, and others in developing local methods for measuring student learning in the context of an institution's unique mission. In addition to assessing all students' basic information literacy skills, faculty and librarians should also work together to develop assessment instruments and strategies in the context of particular disciplines, as information literacy manifests itself in the specific understanding of the knowledge creation, scholarly activity, and publication processes found in those disciplines.

In implementing these standards, institutions need to recognize that different levels of thinking skills are associated with various learning outcomes—and therefore different instruments or methods are essential to assess those outcomes. For example, both "higher order" and "lower order" thinking skills, based on Bloom's Taxonomy of Educational Objectives, are evident throughout the outcomes detailed in this document. It is strongly suggested that assessment methods appropriate to the thinking skills associated with each outcome be identified as an integral part of the institution's implementation plan.

For example, the following outcomes illustrate "higher order" and "lower order" thinking skills:

"Lower Order" thinking skill:
Outcome 2.2.a. Identifies keywords, synonyms, and related terms for the information needed.

"Higher Order" thinking skill:
Outcome 3.3.b. Extends initial synthesis, when possible, to a higher level of abstraction to construct new hypotheses that may required additional information.

Faculty, librarians, and others will find that discussing assessment methods collaboratively is a very productive exercise in planning a systematic, comprehensive information literacy program. This assessment program should reach all students, pinpoint areas for further program development, and consolidate learning goals already achieved. It also should make explicit to the institution's constituencies how information literacy contributes to producing educated students and citizens.

Notes

[1]American Library Association. *Presidential Committee on Information Literacy. Final Report.* (Chicago: American Library Association, 1989.) http://www.ala.org/ala/acrl/acrlpubs/whitepapers/presidential.htm

[2]National Research Council. Commission on Physical Sciences, Mathematics, and Applications. Committee on Information Technology Literacy, Computer Science and Telecommunications Board. *Being Fluent with Information Technology.* Publication. (Washington, D.C.: National Academy Press, 1999) http://www.nap.edu/books/030906399X/html/

[3]Several key accrediting agencies concerned with information literacy are: The Middle States Commission on Higher Education (MSCHE), the Western Association of Schools and College (WASC), and the Southern Association of Colleges and Schools (SACS).

[4]Boyer Commission on Educating Undergraduates in the Research University. *Reinventing Undergraduate Education: A Blueprint for America's Research Universities.* http://naples.cc.sunysb.edu/Pres/boyer.nsf/

Standards, Performance Indicators, and Outcomes

Standard One: The information literate student determines the nature and extent of the information needed.

Performance Indicators:

1. The information literate student defines and articulates the need for information.

Outcomes include:

a. Confers with instructors and participates in class discussions, peer workgroups, and electronic discussions to identify a research topic, or other information need
b. Develops a thesis statement and formulates questions based on the information need
c. Explores general information sources to increase familiarity with the topic
d. Defines or modifies the information need to achieve a manageable focus
e. Identifies key concepts and terms that describe the information need
f. Recognizes that existing information can be combined with original thought, experimentation, and/or analysis to produce new information

2. The information literate student identifies a variety of types and formats of potential sources for information.

Outcomes include:

a. Knows how information is formally and informally produced, organized, and disseminated
b. Recognizes that knowledge can be organized into disciplines that influence the way information is accessed
c. Identifies the value and differences of potential resources in a variety of formats (e.g., multimedia, database, website, data set, audio/visual, book)
d. Identifies the purpose and audience of potential resources (e.g., popular vs. scholarly, current vs. historical)
e. Differentiates between primary and secondary sources, recognizing how their use and importance vary with each discipline
f. Realizes that information may need to be constructed with raw data from primary sources

3. The information literate student considers the costs and benefits of acquiring the needed information.

Outcomes include:

a. Determines the availability of needed information and makes decisions on broadening the information seeking process beyond local resources (e.g., interlibrary loan; using resources at other locations; obtaining images, videos, text, or sound)
b. Considers the feasibility of acquiring a new language or skill (e.g., foreign or discipline-based) in order to gather needed information and to understand its context
c. Defines a realistic overall plan and timeline to acquire the needed information

4. The information literate student reevaluates the nature and extent of the information need.

Outcomes include:

a. Reviews the initial information need to clarify, revise, or refine the question
b. Describes criteria used to make information decisions and choices

Standard Two: The information literate student accesses needed information effectively and efficiently.

Performance Indicators:

1. The information literate student selects the most appropriate investigative methods or information retrieval systems for accessing the needed information.

Outcomes include:

a. Identifies appropriate investigative methods (e.g., laboratory experiment, simulation, fieldwork)
b. Investigates benefits and applicability of various investigative methods
c. Investigates the scope, content, and organization of information retrieval systems
d. Selects efficient and effective approaches for accessing the information needed from the investigative method or information retrieval system

2. The information literate student constructs and implements effectively designed search strategies.

Outcomes include:

a. Develops a research plan appropriate to the investigative method
b. Identifies keywords, synonyms and related terms for the information needed
c. Selects controlled vocabulary specific to the discipline or information retrieval source
d. Constructs a search strategy using appropriate commands for the information retrieval system selected (e.g., Boolean operators, truncation, and proximity for search engines; internal organizers such as indexes for books)
e. Implements the search strategy in various information retrieval systems using different user interfaces and search engines, with different command languages, protocols, and search parameters
f. Implements the search using investigative protocols appropriate to the discipline

3. The information literate student retrieves information online or in person using a variety of methods.

Outcomes include:

a. Uses various search systems to retrieve information in a variety of formats
b. Uses various classification schemes and other systems (e.g., call number systems or indexes) to locate information resources within the library or to identify specific sites for physical exploration
c. Uses specialized online or in person services available at the institution to retrieve information needed (e.g., interlibrary loan/document delivery, professional associations, institutional research offices, community resources, experts and practitioners)
d. Uses surveys, letters, interviews, and other forms of inquiry to retrieve primary information

4. The information literate student refines the search strategy if necessary.

Outcomes include:

a. Assesses the quantity, quality, and relevance of the search results to determine whether alternative information retrieval systems or investigative methods should be utilized
b. Identifies gaps in the information retrieved and determines if the search strategy should be revised
c. Repeats the search using the revised strategy as necessary

5. The information literate student extracts, records, and manages the information and its sources.

Outcomes include:

a. Selects among various technologies the most appropriate one for the task of extracting the needed information (e.g., copy/paste software functions, photocopier, scanner, audio/visual equipment, or exploratory instruments)
b. Creates a system for organizing the information
c. Differentiates between the types of sources cited and understands the elements and correct syntax of a citation for a wide range of resources
d. Records all pertinent citation information for future reference
e. Uses various technologies to manage the information selected and organized

Standard Three: The information literate student evaluates information and its sources critically and incorporates selected information into his or her knowledge base and value system.

Performance Indicators:

1. The information literate student summarizes the main ideas to be extracted from the information gathered.

Outcomes include:

a. Reads the text and selects main ideas
b. Restates textual concepts in his/her own words and selects data accurately
c. Identifies verbatim material that can be then appropriately quoted

2. The information literate student articulates and applies initial criteria for evaluating both the information and its sources.

Outcomes include:

a. Examines and compares information from various sources in order to evaluate reliability, validity, accuracy, authority, timeliness, and point of view or bias
b. Analyzes the structure and logic of supporting arguments or methods
c. Recognizes prejudice, deception, or manipulation
d. Recognizes the cultural, physical, or other context within which the information was created and understands the impact of context on interpreting the information

3. The information literate student synthesizes main ideas to construct new concepts.

Outcomes include:

a. Recognizes interrelationships among concepts and combines them into potentially useful primary statements with supporting evidence
b. Extends initial synthesis, when possible, at a higher level of abstraction to construct new hypotheses that may require additional information
c. Utilizes computer and other technologies (e.g. spreadsheets, databases, multimedia, and audio or visual equipment) for studying the interaction of ideas and other phenomena

4. The information literate student compares new knowledge with prior knowledge to determine the value added, contradictions, or other unique characteristics of the information.

Outcomes include:

a. Determines whether information satisfies the research or other information need
b. Uses consciously selected criteria to determine whether the information contradicts or verifies information used from other sources
c. Draws conclusions based upon information gathered
d. Tests theories with discipline-appropriate techniques (e.g., simulators, experiments)
e. Determines probable accuracy by questioning the source of the data, the limitations of the information gathering tools or strategies, and the reasonableness of the conclusions
f. Integrates new information with previous information or knowledge
g. Selects information that provides evidence for the topic

5. The information literate student determines whether the new knowledge has an impact on the individual's value system and takes steps to reconcile differences.

Outcomes include:

a. Investigates differing viewpoints encountered in the literature
b. Determines whether to incorporate or reject viewpoints encountered

6. The information literate student validates understanding and interpretation of the information through discourse with other individuals, subject-area experts, and/or practitioners.

Outcomes include:

a. Participates in classroom and other discussions
b. Participates in class-sponsored electronic communication forums designed to encourage discourse on the topic (e.g., e-mail, bulletin boards, chat rooms)
c. Seeks expert opinion through a variety of mechanisms (e.g., interviews, e-mail, listservs)

7. The information literate student determines whether the initial query should be revised.

Outcomes include:

a. Determines if original information need has been satisfied or if additional information is needed
b. Reviews search strategy and incorporates additional concepts as necessary
c. Reviews information retrieval sources used and expands to include others as needed

Standard Four: The information literate student, individually or as a member of a group, uses information effectively to accomplish a specific purpose.

Performance Indicators:

1. The information literate student applies new and prior information to the planning and creation of a particular product or performance.

Outcomes include:

a. Organizes the content in a manner that supports the purposes and format of the product or performance (e.g. outlines, drafts, storyboards)
b. Articulates knowledge and skills transferred from prior experiences to planning and creating the product or performance
c. Integrates the new and prior information, including quotations and paraphrasings, in a manner that supports the purposes of the product or performance
d. Manipulates digital text, images, and data, as needed, transferring them from their original locations and formats to a new context

2. The information literate student revises the development process for the product or performance.

Outcomes include:

a. Maintains a journal or log of activities related to the information seeking, evaluating, and communicating process
b. Reflects on past successes, failures, and alternative strategies

3 . The information literate student communicates the product or performance effectively to others.

Outcomes include:

a. Chooses a communication medium and format that best supports the purposes of the product or performance and the intended audience
b. Uses a range of information technology applications in creating the product or performance
c. Incorporates principles of design and communication
d. Communicates clearly and with a style that supports the purposes of the intended audience

Standard Five: The information literate student understands many of the economic, legal, and social issues surrounding the use of information and accesses and uses information ethically and legally.

Performance Indicators:

1. The information literate student understands many of the ethical, legal and socio-economic issues surrounding information and information technology.

Outcomes include:

a. Identifies and discusses issues related to privacy and security in both the print and electronic environments
b. Identifies and discusses issues related to free vs. fee-based access to information
c. Identifies and discusses issues related to censorship and freedom of speech
d. Demonstrates an understanding of intellectual property, copyright, and fair use of copyrighted material

2. The information literate student follows laws, regulations, institutional policies, and etiquette related to the access and use of information resources.

Outcomes include:

a. Participates in electronic discussions following accepted practices (e.g. "Netiquette")
b. Uses approved passwords and other forms of ID for access to information resources
c. Complies with institutional policies on access to information resources
d. Preserves the integrity of information resources, equipment, systems and facilities
e. Legally obtains, stores, and disseminates text, data, images, or sounds
f. Demonstrates an understanding of what constitutes plagiarism and does not represent work attributable to others as his/her own
g. Demonstrates an understanding of institutional policies related to human subjects research

3. The information literate student acknowledges the use of information sources in communicating the product or performance.

Outcomes include:

a. Selects an appropriate documentation style and uses it consistently to cite sources
b. Posts permission granted notices, as needed, for copyrighted material

Appendix B

Objectives for Information Literacy Instruction: A Model Statement for Academic Librarians

The Association of College and Research Libraries

A division of the American Library Association

Approved by the ACRL Board January 2001

Introduction

Chronology

In 1997 the Instruction Section of ACRL created a Task Force to review the 1987 *Model Statement of Objectives for Academic Bibliographic Instruction*. The 1997 Task Force made twelve recommendations, ranging from the "title should more clearly indicate the document's content" to the "statement should be more concise." The Instruction Section subsequently created a Task Force for Revision of the Model Statement of Objectives[1] and charged it to follow those recommendations. The Task Force began its work at ALA Annual in 1998.

Concurrently, an ACRL task force was working on information literacy standards for higher education institutions. That task force's document, *Information Literacy Competency Standards for Higher Education* (herein referred to as the Competency Standards) were approved in January 2000 and are available at: http://www.ala.org/acrl/ilcomstan.html

The following Objectives for Information Literacy Instruction: A Model Statement for Academic Librarians updates and replaces the older Model Statement. The Objectives will herein be referred to as the IS Objectives for clarity and to indicate that they were written by a Task Force of the Instruction Section (IS), formerly the Bibliographic Instruction Section of ACRL.

Relationship Between the Competency Standards and the IS Objectives: Terminology and Design

The Competency Standards are designed to be used in discussions with administrators and academic departments; they suggest institutional goals or performance outcomes. The IS Objectives provide terminal objectives, those that "break down the overall objectives [the Competency

---

Editor's Note. The Objectives for Information Literacy Instruction have been abbreviated due to space considerations. The Responsibility Tags for Competency Standards' Outcomes have been incorporated here rather than being listed in a separate appendix.

Standards' 'Outcomes'] into specific discrete measurable results."[2] According to *The Cyclopedic Education Dictionary*, outcomes are "the results or the expected results of an educational plan or program." The same source defines an objective as, "In education, a specific purpose or goal to be reached/learned by the student."[3] These definitions indicate the relationship between the Competency Standards and the IS Objectives. Thus the instructing librarian may use this document for guidance in developing enabling objectives[4] for an individual teaching session, or for a course, or when collaborating with a course instructor to incorporate information literacy instruction into a specific course.

This document uses the generic term "librarian" because of different situations regarding faculty status for librarians. "Course instructor" refers to an individual other than a librarian who has instructional responsibility for a class or workshop, e.g., faculty, adjunct faculty, instructor, lecturer, Web-course developer, information technology staff person.

The numbering system used in the IS Objectives is tied to the numbers used in the print version of the Competency Standards. That is, Standard One, Performance Indicator 1, Outcome c, is numbered 1.1.c, and followed by objectives written for that Outcome. (The Web version of the Competency Standards uses a slightly different numbering system, i.e., Outcome c is Outcome 3.)

Using the IS Objectives

The Competency Standards are the basis for the IS Objectives and it is recommended that the two documents be used together. The IS Objectives flesh out and make more specific the Standards, Performance Indicators, and Outcomes of the Competency Standards. The IS Objectives may be used in a variety of instructional formats. For example, one or two objectives may be employed in a 50-minute "one-shot" class and a related assignment. A librarian working with an instructor to develop a course that infuses information literacy instruction into its content may select several objectives. An information technology staff person may collaborate with a librarian to incorporate some of the objectives into campus IT workshops. Many or all of the objectives may be adopted in a comprehensive program of instruction for information literacy or in a Web-based tutorial. Thus the IS Objectives may be used in part or whole. They expand upon the Competency Standards. The IS Objectives may be used effectively by beginning instructors as well as by experienced teachers, by librarians and other classroom instructors. They are applicable to just one or to numerous instructional sessions with the same individuals. The IS Objectives serve as a detailed supplementary aid to librarians who wish to break the Competency Standards down into smaller instructional components. They are designed to help academic librarians identify and target particular information literacy instructional outcomes. As such, they offer a variety of possible objectives from which to choose.

Librarians may want to refer to both the Competency Standards and the IS Objectives when discussing library and information literacy instruction with faculty and administrators or when planning, delivering, evaluating, and revising instructional programs and proposals. Regardless of the stage of the information literacy planning or implementation, librarians should apply such elements of the IS Objectives as are appropriate to the local setting and circumstances.

The IS Objectives provide suggestions for generating ideas about teaching concepts and skills to students, or for ways to talk about information literacy instruction with course instructors. The document provides a support structure on which librarians can build in creative and individual ways.

Responsibility for Information Literacy Instruction

Information literacy encompasses more than good information-seeking behavior. It incorporates the abilities to recognize when information is needed and then to phrase questions designed to gather the needed information. It includes evaluating and then using information appropriately and ethically once it is retrieved from any media, including electronic, human or print sources. The responsibility for helping people become information literate is best shared across a campus, as is clearly indicated in the Competency Standards. Ideally, administrators support information literacy goals for their institutions. Course instructors help their students achieve information literacy in their chosen fields, and librarians and other campus professionals collaborate with course instructors in this effort.

Levels of collaboration between librarians and academic departments differ among institutions as well as within any one institution. One college may determine that one of the Competency Standards' components indicates a clear need for collaboration while another institution may view the same component as primarily a responsibility of the library's instruction program. The tags suggest possible collaborative situations. They serve as reminders of the need for librarians to share in campus-wide collaborative efforts to develop and achieve information literacy goals.

IS Objectives Not Written for All Competency Standards

Objectives were written only for Performance Indicators in the Competency Standards that could best be addressed by the librarian or by the librarian and course instructor collaboratively. Performance Indicators such as, "The information literate student applies new and prior information to the planning and creation of a particular product or performance," refer to components of learning and instruction in ways not usually addressed by librarians. It is for this reason that Standard Four is not addressed in the IS Objectives, nor are some of the Performance Indicators in Standards One, Two, Three, and Five. Librarians could, of course, help course instructors develop objectives in these areas.

The IS Objectives and Evaluating Information

Although not all the objectives deal explicitly with the evaluation of information, the need for evaluation and critical thinking is implicit in all stages of research. An objective for Competency Standard 3, Performance Indicator 4, provides an example: "Selects information that provides evidence for the topic." A subordinate objective states that the individual describes "why not all information sources are appropriate for all purposes." Implicit in this objective is the need for the user to evaluate the information source; appropriateness is a judgment made using criteria set by the user or the course instructor.

The objective in the example above also relates closely to the objective for Competency Standard 1, Performance Indicator 1, Outcome 5: "The individual identifies and uses appropriate general or subject-specific sources to discover terminology related to an information need." Thus, subject specificity is an evaluation criterion when selecting a source. As stated above, evaluation is implicit in nearly all the IS Objectives.

Many of the outcomes from the Competency Standards that deal explicitly with evaluation are primarily the teaching responsibility of the course instructor in collaboration with the librarian. For example, the course instructor can address the quality of the content of an information source once it is retrieved; the librarian helps people learn how to interpret information in the sources that can be used for evaluating information during the research process. As reliance on Internet sources increases, the librarian's objectivity and expertise in evaluating information and information sources become invaluable.

Summary

The Competency Standards stress that information literacy "forms the basis for lifelong learning. ... It enables users to master content and extend their investigations, become more self-directed, ... assume greater control over their learning... [and] develop a metacognitive approach to learning, making them conscious of the explicit actions required for gathering, analyzing, and using information." Succinctly stated, this is the purpose of information literacy instruction. The IS Objectives can be used as a guide for the efforts of librarians who promote the Competency Standards at their institutions.

Endnotes

[1]Revision of the Model Statement of Objectives Task Force, 1998 - 2001: Marsha Forys, Main Library, University of Iowa Libraries: Francesca Lane Rasmus, Mortvedt Library, Pacific Lutheran University: Carla List, Chair; Feinberg Library, Plattsburgh State University of New York; Judith Pask, Undergraduate Library, Purdue University; Patrick Ragains, Business and Government Information Center, University Library, University of Nevada; Nancy Reinhold, Woodruff Library, Emory University; Robin R. Satterwhite, Tutt Library, Colorado College; Terry S. Taylor, Richardson Library, DePaul University; Marjorie M. Warmkessel, Ganser Library, Millersville University; Esther Grassian, Editorial Consultant; UCLA College Library

[2]Arp, Lori. "Model Statement of Objectives for Academic Bibliographic Instruction: Draft Revision." *C&RL News* 5 (May 1987): 257.

[3]Spafford, Carol Sullivan; Pesce, Augustus J. Itzo; and Grosser, George S. *The Cyclopedic Education Dictionary*. Albany, NY: Delmar, 1998.

[4]"Enabling (behavioral) objectives define the specific knowledge or skills necessary to achieve the terminal objectives. They are associated with the behavior of the person who has to master the material." Arp, "Model Statement," 257.

Objectives for Information Literacy Instruction: A Model Statement for Academic Librarians

Competency Standard One: The information literate student determines the extent of the information needed.

Performance Indicator 1: The information literate student defines and articulates the need for information.

Outcomes include:

1.1.c. Explores general information sources to increase familiarity with the topic (L)[1]

- Describes the difference between general and subject-specific information sources.
- Demonstrates when it is appropriate to use a general and subject-specific information source (e.g., to provide an overview, to give ideas on terminology).

1.1.d. Defines or modifies the information need to achieve a manageable focus (L/C)

- Identifies an initial question that might be too broad or narrow, as well as one that is probably manageable.

- Explains his/her reasoning regarding the manageability of a topic with reference to available information sources.
- Narrows a broad topic and broadens a narrow one by modifying the scope or direction of the question.
- Demonstrates an understanding of how the desired end product (i.e., the required depth of investigation and analysis) will play a role in determining the need for information.
- Uses background information sources effectively to gain an initial understanding of the topic.
- Consults with the course instructor and librarians to develop a manageable focus for the topic.

1.1.e. Identifies key concepts and terms that describe the information need (L/C)

- Lists terms that may be useful for locating information on a topic.
- Identifies and uses appropriate general or subject-specific sources to discover terminology related to an information need.
- Decides when a research topic has multiple facets or may need to be put into a broader context.
- Identifies more specific concepts that comprise a research topic.

Competency Standard One

Performance Indicator 2: The information literate student identifies a variety of types and formats of potential sources for information.

Outcomes include:

1.2.a. Knows how information is formally and informally produced, organized, and disseminated (L/C)

- Describes the publication cycle appropriate to the discipline of a research topic.
- Defines the "invisible college" (e.g., personal contacts, listservs specific to a discipline or subject) and describes its value.

1.2.b. Recognizes that knowledge can be organized into disciplines that influence the way information is accessed (L/C)

- Names the three major disciplines of knowledge (humanities, social sciences, sciences) and some subject fields that comprise each discipline.
- Finds sources that provide relevant subject field- and discipline-related terminology.
- Uses relevant subject- and discipline-related terminology in the information research process.
- Describes how the publication cycle in a particular discipline or subject field affects the researcher's access to information.

1.2.c. Identifies the value and differences of potential resources in a variety of formats (e.g., multimedia, database, website, data set, audio/visual, book) (L/C)

- Identifies various formats in which information is available.
- Demonstrates how the format in which information appears may affect its usefulness for a particular information need.

1.2.d. Identifies the purpose and audience of potential resources (e.g., popular vs. scholarly, current vs. historical) (L/C)

- Distinguishes characteristics of information provided for different audiences.
- Identifies the intent or purpose of an information source (this may require use of additional sources in order to develop an appropriate context).

1.2.e. Differentiates between primary and secondary sources, recognizing how their use and importance vary with each discipline (L/C)

- Describes how various fields of study define primary and secondary sources differently.
- Identifies characteristics of information that make an item a primary or secondary source in a given field.

Competency Standard One

Performance Indicator 3: The information literate student considers the costs and benefits of acquiring the needed information.

Outcomes include:

1.3.a. Determines the availability of needed information and makes decisions on broadening the information seeking process beyond local resources (e.g., interlibrary loan; using resources at other locations; obtaining images, videos, text, or sound) (L/C)

- Determines if material is available immediately.
- Uses available services appropriately to obtain desired materials or alternative sources.

1.3.c. Defines a realistic overall plan and timeline to acquire the needed information (L/C)

- Searches for and gathers information based on an informal, flexible plan.
- Demonstrates a general knowledge of how to obtain information that is not available immediately.
- Acts appropriately to obtain information within the time frame required.

Competency Standard One

Performance Indicator 4: The information literate student reevaluates the nature and extent of the information need.

Outcomes include:

1.4.a. Reviews the initial information need to clarify, revise, or refine the question (L/C)

- Identifies a research topic that may require revision, based on the amount of information found (or not found).
- Identifies a topic that may need to be modified, based on the content of information found.
- Decides when it is and is not necessary to abandon a topic depending on the success (or failure) of an initial search for information.

1.4.b. Describes criteria used to make information decisions and choices (L/C)

- Demonstrates how the intended audience influences information choices.
- Demonstrates how the desired end product influences information choices (e.g., that visual aids or audio/visual material may be needed for an oral presentation).
- Lists various criteria, such as currency, which influence information choices. (See also 2.4. and 3.2.)

Competency Standard Two: The information literate student accesses needed information effectively and efficiently.

Performance Indicator 1: The information literate student selects the most appropriate investigative methods or information retrieval systems for accessing the needed information.

Outcomes include:

2.1.c. Investigates the scope, content, and organization of information retrieval systems (L/C)

- Describes the structure and components of the system or tool being used, regardless of format (e.g., index, thesaurus, type of information retrieved by the system).
- Identifies the source of help within a given information retrieval system and uses it effectively.
- Identifies what types of information are contained in a particular system (e.g., all branch libraries are included in the catalog; not all databases are full text; catalogs, periodical databases, and Web sites may be included in a gateway).
- Distinguishes among indexes, online databases, and collections of online databases, as well as gateways to different databases and collections.
- Selects appropriate tools (e.g., indexes, online databases) for research on a particular topic.
- Identifies the differences between freely available Internet search tools and subscription or fee-based databases.
- Identifies and uses search language and protocols (e.g., Boolean, adjacency) appropriate to the retrieval system.
- Determines the period of time covered by a particular source.
- Identifies the types of sources that are indexed in a particular database or index (e.g., an index that covers newspapers or popular periodicals versus a more specialized index to find scholarly literature).
- Demonstrates when it is appropriate to use a single tool (e.g., using only a periodical index when only periodical articles are required).
- Distinguishes between full-text and bibliographic databases.

2.1.d. Selects efficient and effective approaches for accessing the information needed from the investigative method or information retrieval system (L)

- Selects appropriate information sources (i.e., primary, secondary or tertiary sources) and determines their relevance for the current information need.
- Determines appropriate means for recording or saving the desired information (e.g., printing, saving to disc, photocopying, taking notes).
- Analyzes and interprets the information collected using a growing awareness of key terms and concepts to decide whether to search for additional information or to identify more accurately when the information need has been met.

Competency Standard Two

Performance Indicator 2: The information literate student constructs and implements effectively designed search strategies.

Outcomes include:

2.2.a. Develops a research plan appropriate to the investigative method (L/C)

- Describes a general process for searching for information.
- Describes when different types of information (e.g., primary/secondary, background/specific) may be suitable for different purposes.
- Gathers and evaluates information and appropriately modifies the research plan as new insights are gained.

2.2.b. Identifies keywords, synonyms and related terms for the information needed (L)

- Identifies keywords or phrases that represent a topic in general sources (e.g., library catalog, periodical index, online source) and in subject-specific sources.
- Demonstrates an understanding that different terminology may be used in general sources and subject-specific sources.
- Identifies alternate terminology, including synonyms, broader or narrower words and phrases that describe a topic.
- Identifies keywords that describe an information source (e.g., book, journal article, magazine article, Web site).

2.2.c. Selects controlled vocabulary specific to the discipline or information retrieval source (L)

- Uses background sources (e.g., encyclopedias, handbooks, dictionaries, thesauri, textbooks) to identify discipline-specific terminology that describes a given topic.
- Explains what controlled vocabulary is and why it is used.
- Identifies search terms likely to be useful for a research topic in relevant controlled vocabulary lists.
- Identifies when and where controlled vocabulary is used in a bibliographic record, and then successfully searches for additional information using that vocabulary.

2.2.d. Constructs a search strategy using appropriate commands for the information retrieval system selected (e.g., Boolean operators, truncation, and proximity for search engines; internal organizers such as indexes for books) (L)

- Demonstrates when it is appropriate to search a particular field (e.g., title, author, subject).
- Demonstrates an understanding of the concept of Boolean logic and constructs a search statement using Boolean operators.
- Demonstrates an understanding of the concept of proximity searching and constructs a search statement using proximity operators.
- Demonstrates an understanding of the concept of nesting and constructs a search using nested words or phrases.
- Demonstrates and understanding of the concept of browsing and uses an index that allows it.
- Demonstrates an understanding of the concept of keyword searching and uses it appropriately and effectively.
- Demonstrates an understanding of the concept of truncation and uses it appropriately and effectively.

2.2.e. Implements the search strategy in various information retrieval systems using different user interfaces and search engines, with different command languages, protocols, and search parameters (L)

- Uses help screens and other user aids to understand the particular search structures and commands of an information retrieval system.
- Demonstrates an awareness of the fact that there may be separate interfaces for basic and advanced searching in retrieval systems.
- Narrows or broadens questions and search terms to retrieve the appropriate quantity of information, using search techniques such as Boolean logic, limiting, and field searching.
- Identifies and selects keywords and phrases to use when searching each source, recognizing that different sources may use different terminology for similar concepts.
- Formulates and executes search strategies to match information needs with available resources.
- Describes differences in searching for bibliographic records, abstracts, or full text in information sources.

2.2.f. Implements the search using investigative protocols appropriate to the discipline (L)

- Locates major print bibliographic and reference sources appropriate to the discipline of a research topic.
- Locates and uses a specialized dictionary, encyclopedia, bibliography, or other common reference tool in print format for a given topic.
- Demonstrates an understanding of the fact that items may be grouped together by subject in order to facilitate browsing.
- Uses effectively the organizational structure of a typical book (e.g., indexes, tables of contents, user's instructions, legends, cross-references) in order to locate pertinent information in it.

Competency Standard Two

Performance Indicator 3: The information literate student retrieves information online or in person using a variety of methods.

Outcomes include:

2.3.a. Uses various search systems to retrieve information in a variety of formats (L)

- Describes some materials that are not available online or in digitized formats and must be accessed in print or other formats (e.g., microform, video, audio).
- Identifies research sources, regardless of format, that are appropriate to a particular discipline or research need.
- Recognizes the format of an information source (e.g., book, chapter in a book, periodical article) from its citation. (See also 2.3.b.)
- Uses different research sources (e.g., catalogs and indexes) to find different types of information (e.g., books and periodical articles).
- Describes search functionality common to most databases regardless of differences in the search interface (e.g., Boolean logic capability, field structure, keyword searching, relevancy ranking).
- Uses effectively the organizational structure and access points of print research sources (e.g., indexes, bibliographies) to retrieve pertinent information from those sources.

2.3.b. Uses various classification schemes and other systems (e.g., call number systems or indexes) to locate information resources within the library or to identify specific sites for physical exploration (L)

- Uses call number systems effectively (e.g., demonstrates how a call number assists in locating the corresponding item in the library).
- Explains the difference between the library catalog and a periodical index.
- Describes the different scopes of coverage found in different periodical indexes.
- Distinguishes among citations to identify various types of materials (e.g., books, periodical articles, essays in anthologies). (See also 2.3.a.)

2.3.c. Uses specialized online or in person services available at the institution to retrieve information needed (e.g., interlibrary loan/document delivery, professional associations, institutional research offices, community resources, experts and practitioners) (L/C)

- Retrieves a document in print or electronic form.
- Describes various retrieval methods for information not available locally.
- Identifies the appropriate service point or resource for the particular information need.
- Initiates an interlibrary loan request by filling out and submitting a form either online or in person.
- Uses the Web site of an institution, library, organization or community to locate information about specific services.

Competency Standard Two

Performance Indicator 4: The information literate student refines the search strategy if necessary.

Outcomes include:

2.4.a. Assesses the quantity, quality, and relevance of the search results to determine whether alternative information retrieval systems or investigative methods should be utilized (L/C)

- Determines if the quantity of citations retrieved is adequate, too extensive, or insufficient for the information need.
- Evaluates the quality of the information retrieved using criteria such as authorship, point of view/bias, date written, citations, etc.
- Assesses the relevance of information found by examining elements of the citation such as title, abstract, subject headings, source, and date of publication.
- Determines the relevance of an item to the information need in terms of its depth of coverage, language, and time frame.

Competency Standard Two

Performance Indicator 5: The information literate student extracts, records, and manages the information and its sources.

Outcomes include:

2.5.c. Differentiates between the types of sources cited and understands the elements and correct syntax of a citation for a wide range of sources (L/C)

- Identifies different types of information sources cited in a research tool.
- Determines whether or not a cited item is available locally and, if so, can locate it.
- Demonstrates an understanding that different disciplines may use different citation styles.

Competency Standard Three: The information literate student evaluates information and its sources critically and incorporates selected information into his or her knowledge base and value system.

Performance Indicator 2: The information literate student articulates and applies initial criteria for evaluating both the information and its sources.

Outcomes include:

3.2.a. Examines and compares information from various sources in order to evaluate reliability, validity, accuracy, authority, timeliness, and point of view or bias (L/C)

- Locates and examines critical reviews of information sources using available resources and technologies.
- Investigates an author's qualifications and reputation through reviews or biographical sources.
- Investigates validity and accuracy by consulting sources identified through bibliographic references.
- Investigates qualifications and reputation of the publisher or issuing agency by consulting other information resources. (See also 3.4.e.)
- Determines when the information was published (or knows where to look for a source's publication date).
- Recognizes the importance of timeliness or date of publication to the value of the source.
- Determines if the information retrieved is sufficiently current for the information need.
- Demonstrates an understanding that other sources may provide additional information to either confirm or question point of view or bias.

3.2.c. Recognizes prejudice, deception, or manipulation (L/C)

- Demonstrates an understanding that information in any format reflects an author's, sponsor's, and/or publisher's point of view.
- Demonstrates an understanding that some information and information sources may present a one-sided view and may express opinions rather than facts.
- Demonstrates an understanding that some information and sources may be designed to trigger emotions, conjure stereotypes, or promote support for a particular viewpoint or group.
- Applies evaluative criteria to information and its source (e.g., author's expertise, currency, accuracy, point of view, type of publication or information, sponsorship).
- Searches for independent verification or corroboration of the accuracy and completeness of the data or representation of facts presented in an information source.

3.2.d. Recognizes the cultural, physical, or other context within which the information was created and understands the impact of context on interpreting the information (L/C)

- Describes how the age of a source or the qualities characteristic of the time in which it was created may impact its value.
- Describes how the purpose for which information was created affects its usefulness.
- Describes how cultural, geographic, or temporal contexts may unintentionally bias information.

Competency Standard Three

Performance Indicator 4: The information literate student compares new knowledge with prior knowledge to determine the value added, contradictions, or other unique characteristics of the information.

Outcomes include:

3.4.e. Determines probable accuracy by questioning the source of the data, the limitations of the information gathering tools or strategies, and the reasonableness of the conclusions (L/C)

- Describes how the reputation of the publisher affects the quality of the information source. (See also 3.2.a.).
- Determines when a single search strategy may not fit a topic precisely enough to retrieve sufficient relevant information.
- Determines when some topics may be too recent to be covered by some standard tools (e.g., a periodicals index) and when information on the topic retrieved by less authoritative tools (e.g., a Web search engine) may not be reliable.
- Compares new information with own knowledge and other sources considered authoritative to determine if conclusions are reasonable.

3.4.g. Selects information that provides evidence for the topic (L/C)

- Describes why not all information sources are appropriate for all purposes (e.g., ERIC is not appropriate for all topics, such as business topics; the Web may not be appropriate for a local history topic).
- Distinguishes among various information sources in terms of established evaluation criteria (e.g., content, authority, currency).
- Applies established evaluation criteria to decide which information sources are most appropriate.

Competency Standard Three

Performance Indicator 7: The information literate student determines whether the initial query should be revised.

Outcomes include:

3.7.b. Reviews search strategy and incorporates additional concepts as necessary (L/C)

- Demonstrates how searches may be limited or expanded by modifying search terminology or logic.

3.7.c. Reviews information retrieval sources used and expands to include others as needed (L/C)

- Examines footnotes and bibliographies from retrieved items to locate additional sources.
- Follows, retrieves and evaluates relevant online links to additional sources.
- Incorporates new knowledge as elements of revised search strategy to gather additional information.

Competency Standard Four: The information literate student, individually or as a member of a group, uses information effectively to accomplish a specific purpose.

Objectives were not written for this Standard because its Performance Indicators and Outcomes are best addressed by the course instructor, rather than by librarians. (See the Introduction and the Competency Standards document.)

Competency Standard Five: The information literate student understands many of the economic, legal and social issues surrounding the use of information and accesses and uses information ethically and legally.

Performance Indicator 1: The information literate student understands many of the ethical, legal and socio-economic issues surrounding information and information technology.

Outcomes include:

5.1.b. Identifies and discusses issues related to free vs. fee-based access to information (L/C)

- Demonstrates an understanding that not all information on the Web is free, i.e., some Web-based databases require users to pay a fee or to subscribe in order to retrieve full text or other content.
- Demonstrates awareness that the library pays for access to databases, information tools, full-text resources, etc., and may use the Web to deliver them to its clientele.
- Describes how the terms of subscriptions or licenses may limit their use to a particular clientele or location.
- Describes the differences between the results of a search using a general Web search engine (e.g., Yahoo, Google) and a library-provided tool (e.g., Web-based article index, full-text electronic journal, Web-based library catalog).

Competency Standard Five

Performance Indicator 3: The information literate student acknowledges the use of information sources in communicating the product or performance.

Outcomes include:

5.3.a. Selects an appropriate documentation style and uses it consistently to cite sources (L/C)

- Describes how to use a documentation style to record bibliographic information from an item retrieved through research.
- Identifies citation elements for information sources in different formats (e.g., book, article, television program, Web page, interview).
- Demonstrates an understanding that there are different documentation styles, published or accepted by various groups.[2]
- Demonstrates an understanding that the appropriate documentation style may vary by discipline (e.g., MLA for English, University of Chicago for history, APA for psychology, CBE for biology)

- Describes when the format of the source cited may dictate a certain citation style.
- Uses correctly and consistently the citation style appropriate to a specific discipline.
- Locates information about documentation styles either in print or electronically, e.g., through the library's Web site.
- Recognizes that consistency of citation format is important, especially if a course instructor has not required a particular style.

Endnotes

[1]To emphasize the shared nature of information literacy instruction, the components of the Competency Standards are marked with the tags L and L/C as examples of who might take the lead for a given component. "C" is the abbreviation used to indicate the "course instructor." (See the definition of this term above.) The tags applied to the Competency Standards thus are defined as: L = primarily librarians' responsibility; L/C = responsibility shared by librarians and the course instructor through guidance, consultation or collaboration. The course content is always the responsibility of the course instructor.

The tags are examples of ways to approach the shared responsibilities for information literacy instruction. Again, local preferences may vary. The examples do not include computer center staff, teaching center staff, or the many other campus professionals who may also have a role. Librarians may use the tags as they see fit at their institutions.

[2]Examples of published style manuals are: Gibaldi, Joseph. *MLA Handbook for Writers of Research Papers*. 5th ed. New York: Modern Language Association, 1999. *Publication Manual of the American Psychological Association*. 4th ed. Washington, DC: A.P.A., 1994. The Chicago Manual of Style. 14th ed. Chicago: University of Chicago Press, 1993. Council of Biology Editors, Style Manual Committee. *Scientific Style and Format: The CBE Manual for Authors, Editors, and Publishers*. 6th ed. Cambridge, England: Cambridge University Press, 1994.

Contributors

About the Contributors

Cheryl Albrecht received her master's degree in library science from the University of Wisconsin. She has held various professional positions including the coordinator of the Greater Cincinnati Library Consortium and the director of the Library at the College of Mount St. Joseph. She is currently associate dean for public services at the University of Cincinnati. While at Cincinnati, she has actively supported various first-year efforts including coauthoring a grant for the development of an Information Commons and for the creation of a First-Year Experience Librarian position.

After receiving her master's degree in library and information studies from the University of Wisconsin in 1989, **Alison Armstrong** began her career at the University of Nevada, Las Vegas (UNLV) as an instruction librarian. While at UNLV, she had the opportunity to lead the instruction program and cochair the Teaching, Learning Reference Team. In 1997, she joined the University of Cincinnati as the Head of Training and Educational Services for University Libraries. During that time, Armstrong coauthored a grant for the development of an Information Commons and for the creation of a First-Year Experience Librarian position. Since 2004, she has been the Coordinator of Information Literacy at the American University in Cairo where all first-year students are required to take an information literacy course.

Susan Avery is the undergraduate library instruction coordinator and an assistant professor of library administration at the University of Illinois at Urbana, Champaign. In this position, she is responsible for the integration of library instruction into courses fulfilling the Composition I requirement for first-year students. Prior to her current position, she served for seven years as an instruction and research librarian and library instruction coordinator at Millikin University. She has written and presented papers on the critical role of faculty/librarian collaboration. Other research interests include the use of metaphor in education, at large, and library instruction, more specifically. She received her master of information and library studies degree from the University of Michigan.

Neal Baker is the information technology and reference librarian at Earlham College, where he also teaches courses in film studies. He is a field bibliographer for the Modern Language Association (i.e., film studies and science fiction/fantasy) and reviews books for *Choice*. His articles on various topics in science fiction and fantasy have appeared in such scholarly periodicals as *Contemporary French Civilization*, *Extrapolation*, and *Journal of the Fantastic in the Arts*.

Mary McAleer Balkun is Associate Professor of English and chairperson of the English Department at Seton Hall University. She served as Director of First-Year Writing from 1996 to 2000. She teaches courses in early and 19th-century American literature, women's literature, and composition. She has published articles on Phillis Wheatley, Sarah Kemble Knight, Walt Whitman, and William Faulkner. Her book, *The American Counterfeit: Authenticity and Identity in American Literature and Culture* was published by University of Alabama Press in 2006.

Jean Beccone is a reference/instruction librarian for Macalester College. Before beginning at Macalester in 1988, she worked in public libraries in the Twin Cities and at the Legislative Reference Library in St. Paul.

Beth Bloom, MA, MLS, is librarian II/associate professor at Seton Hall University. She is coordinator of information literacy instruction and specializes in the areas of music, art, women's studies, and health sciences. She has published articles on information literacy, breast cancer, and music collections in the Federal Depository system.

Colleen Boff, an associate professor at Bowling Green State University (BGSU) Libraries, works with regional high schools, incoming first-year students, BGSU pre-service teachers, as well as masters of education students. She is actively involved with several state and national library initiatives related to integrating information literacy into the preK-16 curriculum.

Christine Bombaro is a collection and research services librarian at Dickinson College. She also earned her BA in history and secondary teaching certification from Dickinson College. She received her master's degree in library science from Drexel University, where her research focused on providing effective library service to patrons whose native language is not English. Her professional accomplishments include archiving the personal papers of Arthur M. Schlesinger, Jr. for the John F. Kennedy Memorial Library in Boston. Prior to joining Dickinson College, Bombaro was a software trainer for the Pennsylvania State Supreme Court.

Polly D. Boruff-Jones is an associate librarian at Indiana University-Purdue University Indianapolis (IUPUI) University Library where she is team leader for the Professional Programs Team, electronic resources coordinator, and liaison to the IU Kelley School of Business. Her work and research interests include promoting effective use of information resources, adapting public services to 21st century student needs, assessing information literacy initiatives, and nonprofit management. Boruff-Jones and Amy E. Mark have collaborated on several presentations and co-authored an article that correlates the National Survey of Student Engagement to information literacy efforts.

Ellysa Stern Cahoy is the information literacy librarian at Pennsylvania State University responsible for outreach and programs targeting first-year and new students. A former children's and school librarian, her research interests include strengthening the instructional bridge between K-12 and academic libraries. Cahoy's article in the March/April 2002 issue of *Knowledge Quest*, "Will Your Students Be Ready for College? Connecting the K-12 and College Standards for Information Literacy," explores this issue. Cahoy has also published research on library services for users at a distance and library orientation.

Joan Campbell is now collections librarian at Bowdoin College in Maine. Prior to that, she was research and instructional service librarian at Wellesley College where she cotaught Computer Science 100: Introduction to Internet Research and Resources, and coauthored the paper "Information Literacy is Important, but Can I Get College Credit for it?" for *Educause* in 2001. She served on the ACRL Instruction Section's Teaching Methods Committee for many years, sharing her passion for teaching undergraduate students the importance of information literacy. Inspired to become a librarian while working at a small public library in Alaska, she has twice traveled the globe as assistant librarian for the Institute for Shipboard Education's Semester at Sea program.

Sam Chu obtained his PhD in education from The University of Hong Kong and a master of library science and a bachelor of commerce degree from the University of British Columbia. He served as the bibliographic instruction librarian at the Hong Kong University of Science and Technology Library for 10 years, where he managed an instruction program that offered more than 150 classes and reached about 4,000 students and staff every year. He also taught a credit course Eureka! Information Skills for Lifelong Learning for undergraduates. Chu has written a number of conference papers and has presented papers in various local and international conferences. He currently serves as assistant professor and program director for bachelor studies in information management at The University of Hong Kong.

Previously the director of first-year writing programs at Millikin University, **Nancy C. DeJoy** is associate professor of writing, rhetoric, and American cultures at Michigan State University. DeJoy is the author of articles about service-learning and composition studies, faculty development, feminism and composition, and alternative composition pedagogies. Her book, *Process This: Undergraduate Writing in Composition Studies* (Utah State University Press, 2004), focuses on putting participation and contribution at the center of writing studies.

Marta Mestrovic Deyrup, M.Phil., MLS, is librarian II/associate professor and co-director of the Women's Studies Program at Seton Hall University. She is catalog coordinator and liaison to the Department of English. She frequently writes and presents on information literacy and scholarly communication. Deyrup holds a Ph.D. in Slavic languages and literatures from Columbia University.

Teresa (Terri) Fishel is library director for Macalester College. Prior to becoming director in 1998, she served as head of reference from 1985-1997. In addition to her MA in library science, she has an MA in American studies. Her publications include: "Areas of Cooperation Between the Library and Computing" (coauthor) in *Building Partnerships* (Library Solutions Press, 1995) and "Teaching the Internet: An Undergraduate Liberal Arts College Experience" (coauthor) in *The Internet Library: Case Studies of Library Internet Management and Use* (Mecklermedia, 1994).

Robert Fitzpatrick received his library degree from Simmons College in 1981. A member of the Beta Phi Mu international library honor society, he has served as a librarian at several colleges in the northeastern US including nearly 20 years as library instruction coordinator at Plymouth (N.H.) State University (PSU). His extensive assessment activities have varied from library-specific to institution-wide. He has served as the president of the New Hampshire Library Association, the president of the academic section of American Library Association's (ALA) New England Library Association, and was for many years an officer and active member of the New England Bibliographic Instruction Committee. In 2001, Fitzpatrick became the first librarian at PSU to receive its Distinguished Teaching Award. More recently, he served as chair and editor of PSU's 2003 decennial self-study in preparation for the New England Association of Schools and Colleges re-accreditation visit. Based on the program developed by the Policy Center on the First Year of College, Fitzpatrick spearheaded PSU's Foundations of Excellence® assessment initiative. As director of PSU's Robert Frost Faculty Center for Learning and Teaching Excellence, Fitzpatrick promoted activities fostering engaging teaching pedagogies. He is a member of the review board for *Innovative Higher Education* and has spoken frequently at regional and national conferences on the subject of library instruction and assessment. He currently serves as PSU's Dean of the Academic Experience.

John N. Gardner is founder and executive director of the Policy Center on the First Year of College, funded by a grant from Lumina Foundation for Education and located in Brevard, N.C. Gardner is also the senior fellow of the National Resource Center for The First-Year Experience and Students in Transition, and distinguished professor emeritus of library and information science at the University of South Carolina. He served as Executive Director of both the first-year seminar course at USC, University 101, and the National Resource Center. For almost three decades, Gardner's special area of expertise in higher education was the creation of programs to enhance the learning, success, retention, and graduation of students in transition, especially first-year students. His current work moves beyond these "programmatic" approaches to a holistic framework for improving the first college year through his and the Policy Center's signature work, Foundations of Excellence® in the First College Year. Gardner has authored/co-authored numerous articles and books, including *The Senior Year Experience* with Gretchen Van der Veer (Jossey-Bass, 1997), *Challenging and Supporting the First-Year Student* with M. Lee Upcraft and Betsy O. Barefoot (Jossey-Bass, 2005) and *Achieving and Sustaining Institutional Excellence for the First Year of College* with Betsy O. Barefoot and Associates (Jossey-Bass, 2005).

Kathryn Graves received her BA from the University of Minnesota and MLS from the College of Library and Information Science at the University of South Carolina. Since 1988, she has worked at the University of Kansas Libraries and currently works as the Social Sciences Council coordinator and liaison to the School of Social Welfare.

Judy Griffith is the current chair of the Department of English and Modern Languages at Wartburg College in Waverly, Iowa. She teaches introductory and advanced composition, literature, and inquiry studies courses as well as the methods courses for preservice English and language teachers. Her work with information literacy is informed by her years as a high school teacher, her graduate work in curriculum and assessment, and her productive collaboration with Wartburg's staff of information literacy librarians. She has helped design and direct many courses and programs that integrate information literary and has given a number of presentations at national conferences about instruction in teacher education.

Alan E. Guskin is distinguished university professor in Antioch University's doctoral program in leadership and change. Currently president emeritus, Guskin served as president and then chancellor of Antioch University from 1985-1997. His distinguished career in higher education includes leadership positions as chancellor, University of Wisconsin-Parkside (1975-1985); acting president, Clark University in Worcester, Massachusetts (1973-1974); and provost, Clark University (1971-1973). He has held faculty positions at the University of Michigan, Clark University, and University of Wisconsin-Parkside. Guskin has written frequently on the role of leadership, power, conflict, and change in educational organizations, especially universities. Guskin received his doctorate in social psychology from the University of Michigan, interrupting his graduate study to serve as a Peace Corps volunteer in Thailand. He served as a senior administrator in the creation of the domestic peace corps, VISTA.

After serving more than 30 years as an academic librarian, **Larry L. Hardesty** retired in 2006. His positions included dean of the library (2004-2006) at the University of Nebraska at Kearney (UNK), college librarian (1995-2004) at Austin College, director of library services (1983-1994) at Eckerd College, and head of the reference department (1975-1983) at DePauw University. He recently came out of retirement to serve as interim university librarian at Winona State University. Hardesty has served in several positions in the Association of College of Research Libraries (ACRL), including president (1999-2000), member of the board of directors, chair of the college libraries section (1995-1996), member of the *College & Research Libraries* Editorial Board (1990-1996), and chair of the Charlotte ACRL national conference (2003). His publications include *Faculty and the Library: The Undergraduate Experience* (Ablex, 1991) and *Books, Bytes and Bridges* (ALA, 2000) and numerous articles on library instruction, collection development, computer center and library relationships, and faculty and administrators attitudes towards the academic library. He currently serves on the editorial boards of *portal* and *Library Issues*. In 2001, Hardesty received the ACRL Academic Research Librarian of the Year. He received his MALA from the University of Wisconsin-Madison and his PhD in library and information science from Indiana University. He continues to serve as the founding director of the College Library Directors' Mentor program and has matched more than 200 first-year college library directors with mentors during the 15 year history of the program. He also serves as the liaison between ACRL and the National Resource Center for The First-Year Experience and Students in Transition.

Beth Hillemann is a reference/instruction librarian for Macalester College. In addition to her MA in library science, she has an MA in History. Before beginning at Macalester in 1993, she worked as a reference librarian at the University of Wisconsin-Whitewater. With Barbara Bren and Victoria Topp, Hillemann has coauthored, *Effectiveness of Hands-On Instruction of Electronic Resources* (Research Strategies, 1998).

Janice Hovis is reference librarian and assistant professor at St. Louis Community College at Florissant Valley. She holds a master of arts in library science from the University of Missouri and is currently pursuing a master of arts in teaching at Webster University. In addition to reference and instruction, Janice is responsible for the Florissant Valley campus archives and participated at the Western Archives Institute in 2004. Recent copresentations include "Navigating Liaison Land: Successful Approaches for Creating and Strengthening Library/Faculty Relationships" at the MOBIUS Conference 2006 and "The Online Study Abroad Course: Innovations in International Learning & Travel for Educators" at Hawaii International Conference on Education. Hovis is also past-president of the Greater St. Louis Library Club.

Barbara D. Jackson, associate dean of University College and professor of anthropology in the School of Liberal Arts has provided leadership for the comprehensive development of academic support programs for entering students at Indiana University-Purdue University Indianapolis (IUPUI), including first-year seminars, learning communities, structured learning assistance, and critical inquiry. She has primary responsibility for faculty development and involvement in University College first-year initiatives.

Kristin Johnson (formerly Trefts) is virtual reference coordinator at the Colorado State Library, Networking & Resource Sharing Unit. She currently oversees the AskColorado.org project. Prior to this position, she was an information literacy/instruction librarian at California State University, Chico. She has also worked at the University of Alaska, Fairbanks, and Palo Alto Community College in San Antonio, Texas. Her research interests include academic integrity, plagiarism, information literacy and the first-year experience (FYE) connection. She has extensive, hands-on experience with first-year seminars, having taught several sections of Chico's UNIV101 (formerly UNIV001C) course as well as providing information literacy training and curriculum resources to instructors of the course. She is co-author with Colleen Boff of several publications, including "The Library and First Year Experience Courses: A Nationwide Study" (*Reference Services Review*, 2002).

Thomas G. Kirk, Jr. is library director and coordinator of information services at Earlham College. He is a graduate of Earlham College (BA, biology) and Indiana University (MA, library science) and has served as director of the libraries at the University of Wisconsin, Parkside and Berea College. He was the science librarian at Earlham from 1965-1979. His professional career includes serving as president of the Association of College and Research Libraries (ACRL) from 1993-1994 and leadership roles in ACRL and library consortia. Kirk is the recipient of the ACRL Academic/Research Librarian of the Year (2004); the Miriam Dudley Bibliographic Instruction Librarian award (1984); and the Kentucky Library Association Academic Librarian of the Year (1991).

Linda Klein, formerly first-year initiatives librarian at Eastern Kentucky University, is currently a youth services librarian at Anchorage Municipal Libraries, Alaska. She earned her MLIS at University of Washington Information School and her BA in English Literature at Arizona State University. She serves as a field bibliographer for the MLA International Bibliography. She has presented on library programs for first-generation college students at the Kentucky Conference on the Scholarship of Teaching and Learning, the Lilly Conference on College Teaching, the Annual Conference on The First-Year Experience, and the National Conference of the Association of College & Research Libraries.

Presently serving as the director of Purdue University's Student Access, Transition and Success Programs department, **Andrew (Drew) Karl Koch** has been professionally involved with student access and success-enhancing efforts for nearly 15 years. He has extensive experience with learning communities, summer bridge programs, first-year seminars, precollege outreach programs, orientation programming, efforts for first-year honors students, supplemental instruction, diversity initiatives, and a host of other efforts designed to enhance the first college year. In addition to his work experiences, Koch is the author of several publications, including *The Freshman Year Experience in American Higher Education: An Annotated Bibliography* (2nd edition) and *The First-Year Experience in American Higher Education: An Annotated Bibliography* (3rd edition), both published by the National Resource Center for The First-Year Experience and Students in Transition in 1995 and 2001, respectively. He is presently working with several colleagues on a revision of that publication. Koch holds a BA degree in history and German from the University of Richmond, an MA degree in history from the University of Richmond, and an MA in higher education administration from the University of South Carolina. In addition to his professional responsibilities, he is presently completing the requirements for a PhD in American Studies at Purdue University, where he is writing a dissertation on the manner in which the first year of college is portrayed in popular publications and film.

Kathy S. Kremer joined the Department of Sociology at Aquinas College in January 2007. Her previous academic positions were at Wartburg College from 2001-2006 and the North Central Regional Center for Rural Development at Iowa State University. Kremer holds a BS and MS from Minnesota State University-Mankato, a PhD in rural sociology from Iowa State University, and worked in community organizations and community development from

1982-1997. Her current research focuses on rural communities, social change, and gender. She has served as chair of the Minnesota Housing Partnership, chair of the Community Interest Group of the Rural Sociological Society, and chair of College-University Relations for the American Association of University Women-Iowa.

George D. Kuh is Chancellor's Professor of Higher Education at Indiana University, Bloomington where he directs the Center for Postsecondary Research, home to the National Survey of Student Engagement (NSSE). A past president of the Association for the Study of Higher Education, Kuh has written extensively about student engagement, assessment, institutional improvement, and college and university cultures and has consulted with more than 150 educational institutions and agencies in the US and abroad. He has received awards from various professional groups including the National Center on Public Policy in Higher Education and the Council for Adult and Experiential Learning. Kuh has also received Indiana University's prestigious Tracy Sonneborn Award for a distinguished career of teaching and research. His most recent book is *Student Success in College: Creating Conditions That Matter* (Jossey-Bass, 2005).

Karen Shostrom Lehmann is an information literacy librarian at Wartburg College's Vogel Library. She coordinates delivery of instruction to individuals (e.g., reference services, consultations) within the context of a comprehensive, integrated library program selected as 1 of 10 recognized by ACRL for "Best Practices in Information Literacy." Lehmann has presented at ALA's RUSA Reference Research Forum and AAHE's Assessment Conference and was invited to join a team representing Wartburg at the inaugural CIC Transformation of the College Library Workshop. She holds a BA from Luther College and an MA in library science from the University of Iowa.

Debbie Malone graduated from Ursinus College with a degree in English Literature and received her MLS from Drexel University. She has worked as a library assistant at Hahnemann Medical College and as the technical services librarian at Ursinus College. For the past five years, she has been the library director at DeSales University. Malone has served in various positions with the Pennsylvania Library Association, and has edited ACRL's *Chapter Topics* newsletter for the past five years. In 2003, she was the cocompiler of "First Year Student Library Instruction Programs: CLIP Note 33."

Amy E. Mark is the coordinator of library instruction and associate professor at the University of Mississippi. She has a BA in English from Kalamazoo College, an MA in library and information studies from the University of Wisconsin-Madison, and is currently enrolled in PhD program in leadership in higher education at the University of Mississippi. Mark has co-authored and presented several research projects on information literacy assessment with Polly Boruff-Jones and has published articles on student learning, prison librarianship, and assessment with rubrics.

William A. Orme received his MLS degree from Indiana University in 1981. He is currently an associate librarian at Indiana University-Purdue University Indianapolis (IUPUI), where he serves as instructional coordinator. Previously, he was head of public services at Columbia College, Chicago. Orme has been actively involved in information literacy issues through the American Library Association where he most recently served on the Information Literacy Best Practices Project Team. In 2002, Orme was the IUPUI nominee for the Outstanding First-Year Student Advocate award, sponsored by the National Resource Center for The First-Year Experience and Students in Transition.

Pattie Orr is the director of user services at Wellesley College, where she oversees the HelpDesk, ResNet, computing documentation, and all aspects of user support and education. Orr also serves as the Digital Millennium Copyright Act agent for Wellesley and spends much of her time on policy issues. For the past 10 years, she has also taught introductory computer science and information literacy courses at Wellesley. A 2000 Frye Fellow, Orr is involved in many professional associations, including EDUCAUSE, CLAC, and NERCOMP. She has served in many leadership roles, including the NERCOMP board of trustees and the Coalition for Networked Information (CNI) New England Task Force, and presently serves as chair for the EDUCAUSE Member Information Services Committee. Orr provides IT management consulting for colleges in on-site meetings, workshops, and working groups. Her areas of expertise include user-support reorganization, library/IT integration, and IT policy creation and incident response.

Leticia Oseguera is an assistant professor in the Department of Education at the University of California, Irvine (UCI). Oseguera received her PhD in higher education and organizational change from UCLA in 2004. Prior to UCI, she served as the interim director of follow-up surveys for the Higher Education Research Institute at UCLA. Her research focuses on the stratification of American higher education, the civic role of higher education, college transitions, and baccalaureate degree attainment for underrepresented groups. Oseguera's work has been published in the *Review of Higher Education*, the *Journal of College Student Retention*, and the *Journal of Hispanic Higher Education*. Currently, Oseguera is working on a project funded by the Mott Foundation, examining promising after-school programs for low-income youth.

Cindy Pierard is currently the department head of reference and research services at the New Mexico State University Library, responsible for managing reference services, collection development, instruction, and government documents and maps. She earned her undergraduate degree in international studies from Earlham College and her MLS from Indiana University.

Ilene F. Rockman served as the manager of the Information Competence Initiative for the Office of the Chancellor of the 23 campuses of the California State University (CSU) until her death in fall 2005. Throughout her career, she taught information literacy credit courses at two- and four-year institutions for first-year students, developed summer information literacy workshops for faculty members, and was a frequent author and speaker on these topics. Rockman was the recipient of the 2005 Miriam Dudley Instruction Award from the ACRL Instruction Section and the 2003 ACRL Distinguished Education and Behavioral Sciences Librarian of the Year Award. She was a past member of the Executive Committee of the ACRL Institute for Information Literacy and the Association of College and Research Libraries/American Association of School Libraries Interdivisional Task Force on Information Literacy. She was the editor-in-chief of *Reference Services Review*, a member of the editorial boards of the *Journal of Academic Librarianship* and *Library Hi Tech*, and the editor and contributing author of *Integrating Information Literacy into the Higher Education Curriculum: Practical Models for Transformation* (Jossey-Bass, 2004).

Catherine Rod is associate librarian and college archivist at Grinnell College. A graduate of Augustana College in Illinois, she obtained her library degree from the University of Iowa, and her master's in history from Iowa State University. Her work with first-year students has spanned almost three decades and has included services to a variety of institutions ranging from large research universities to small liberal arts colleges.

Diane Savoca is a seasoned educator who started as a high school teacher before moving into higher education 20 years ago. Currently, Savoca is the coordinator of student transition at St. Louis Community College at Florissant Valley and a principal partner of Communicate Plus, a company of professional educators in St. Louis. In March 2005, she represented the community college perspective on the National Resource Center's teleconference "Facilitating Transfer Student Success: Creating Effective Partnerships." She is a reviewer for three of the top-selling college success textbooks and a frequent presenter at student success national conferences across the country. She is a keynote speaker and a consultant at public and private schools as well as colleges in Missouri, Illinois, and Texas. Savoca is a contributor to the monograph *Appreciative Inquiry in the Community Colleges: Early Stories of Success* (League for Innovation, 2004).

Randall Schroeder is the information literacy librarian at the Wartburg College library. A 1982 Wartburg graduate, he earned his MA degree in library and information science at the University of Iowa in 1988. He is coordinator of Wartburg's nationally recognized "Information Literacy Across the Curriculum" (ILAC) program. His information literacy lessons have been published in such books as *Designs for Active Learning: A Sourcebook of Classroom Strategies for Information Education* (ACRL, 1998). He is also a regular book reviewer for *Library Journal*, specializing in German and baseball history. He is known around Waverly, Iowa as the "Voice of the Knights" for his work as P.A. announcer for Wartburg home football, basketball, and baseball games.

Loanne Snavely is head of instructional programs/Gateway Library at Penn State University Libraries where she leads the libraries' initiatives for first-year students and first-level information and instructional needs, including online and face-to-face learning, library technology classrooms, integration of library resources into course-management systems and portals, teaching effectively with technology, and basic information services for undergraduates. She has been a reference and instruction librarian at institutions large and small, private and public, for more than 20 years. Snavely completed a master of librarianship degree at Emory University and a masters in art at Rochester Institute of Technology. Her research focus has been teaching and learning in the library. She has authored and coauthored a number of publications including *Designs for Active Learning* (ACRL, 1998), "The Information Literacy Debate" (*Journal of Academic Librarianship*, 1997) and "The Learning Library" (*Research Strategies*, 2000). She has been chair of the ACRL Instruction Section and the Institute for Information Literacy's Executive Committee and was the recipient of the Miriam Dudley Instruction Librarian Award.

John C. Stachacz is currently the director of library services at Indiana University Kokomo. He held several positions, including department chair during his 23 years of service at Dickinson College and was present at the inception of the first-year seminars in 1981. Stachacz has published articles on bibliographic instruction in the sciences, serials cataloging, and mentoring library school students. He is a prolific book reviewer for *Choice* magazine and reviews works on library facilities for the *Journal of Academic Librarianship*. He is also past president of the consortiums, Associated College Libraries of Central Pennsylvania and the Delaware Valley Chapter of the Association of College and Research Libraries.

Rebecca Stuhr graduated from St. Olaf College with a BA in English and from the University of California, Berkeley, with her MLIS. She is currently the collection development and preservation librarian at Grinnell College. She has been active in preservation as a founding member of the Iowa Conservation and Preservation Consortium and in her state library organization, as chair of the Library Technical Resources Round Table, and as secretary/treasurer and vice president/president elect of the Iowa branch of the Association of College and Research Libraries. Stuhr has published two books: *Autobiographies by Americans of Color, 1980-1994: An Annotated Bibliography* (Whitston Publishing, 1997) and *Autobiographies by Americans of Color, 1995-2000: An Annotated Bibliography* (Whitston Publishing, 2003).

Randy L. Swing's work at the Policy Center on the First-Year of College includes developing, with colleagues, the Foundations of Excellence® project, an aspirational and measurement model for the first college year. He coauthored *Achieving and Sustaining Excellence in the First College Year* (Jossey-Bass, 2005), contributed chapters to *Challenging and Supporting the First-Year Student* (Jossey-Bass, 2005), and edited *Proving and Improving – Vol I & II* (National Resource Center for The First-Year Experience and Students in Transition, 2001, 2004). His work at the Policy Center focuses on assessment of the first college year and institutional change. Swing is a frequent speaker at national and international conferences. For two decades prior to 1999, he held various leadership positions at Appalachian State University in assessment, advising, Upward Bound, and first-year seminar. He holds a PhD in higher education from the University of Georgia.

Corrine Taylor is director of the quantitative reasoning program and assistant professor of economics at Wellesley College. She joined the faculty in 1998 after receiving her PhD in economics from the University of Wisconsin Madison. Taylor is a 1988 graduate of the College of William and Mary, where she was elected to Phi Beta Kappa. At Wellesley, Taylor has taught courses in quantitative reasoning, social science data analysis, statistical analysis of education issues, microeconomics, public economics, and the economics of education. Her research focuses on the economics of education, in particular, elementary and secondary school finance. She has presented her research at conferences of the American Economic Association, the National Tax Association, and the American Education Finance Association (AEFA) and was awarded the AEFA's Jean Flanigan Outstanding Dissertation Award for her work on K-12 school finance Since 2002, Taylor has taught critical analysis and basic quantitative analysis as components of the College's summer bridge program "Pathways" which she helped develop. She has been invited to speak on quantitative reasoning (QR) issues at the annual meetings of the Association of American Colleges & Universities and the National Numeracy Network, and she has hosted the annual meeting of the North East Consortium on Quantitative Literacy. Additionally, Taylor has led workshops, given invited lectures, and served as a consultant at other colleges and universities that are developing new QR initiatives.

Carol Videon graduated from Drexel University with a master's degree in library science. She has been a reference librarian at Delaware County Community College (Media, Pennsylvania) since 1991, where she facilitates approximately 60 information literacy sessions per year. Videon serves on the committee to draft a comprehensive information literacy plan, which includes several models for delivery (i.e., online, collaborative, teach-the-teacher, one-shot) of instruction. She compiled a 2003 monograph entitled *First-Year Student Library Instruction Programs* with Debbie Malone published by the Association of College and Research Libraries.